kare kano

his and her circumstances

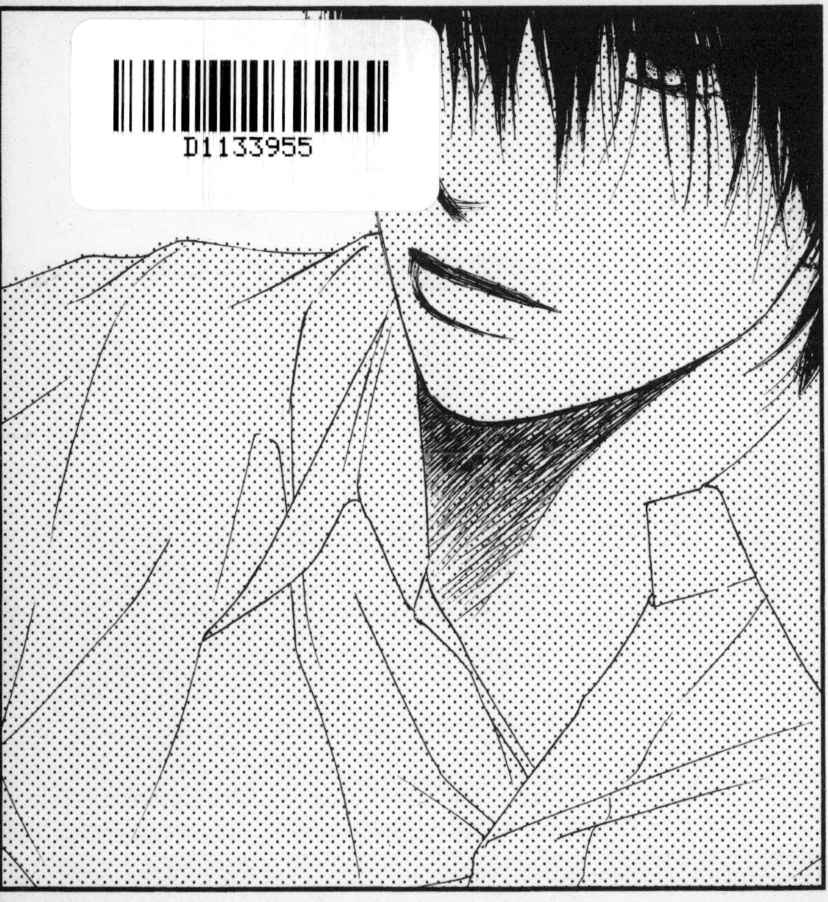

Kare Kano Vol. 18
Created by Masami Tsuda

Translation - Michelle Kobayashi
Copy Editor - Peter Ahlstrom
Retouch and Lettering - Bowen Park
Production Artist - Jose Macasocol, Jr.
Cover Design - Gary Shum

Editor - Carol Fox
Digital Imaging Manager - Chris Buford
Production Managers - Jennifer Miller and Mutsumi Miyazaki
Managing Editor - Lindsey Johnston
VP of Production - Ron Klamert
Publisher and E.I.C. - Mike Kiley
President and C.O.O. - John Parker
C.E.O. - Stuart Levy

A  Manga

TOKYOPOP Inc.
5900 Wilshire Blvd. Suite 2000
Los Angeles, CA 90036

E-mail: info@TOKYOPOP.com
Come visit us online at www.TOKYOPOP.com

ISBN: 1-59532-592-1

First TOKYOPOP printing: December 2005
10 9 8 7 6 5 4 3 2
Printed in the USA

kare kano

his and her circumstances

volume eighteen

by Masami Tsuda

HAMBURG // LONDON // LOS ANGELES // TOKYO

KARE KANO: THE STORY SO FAR

Yukino Miyazawa seemed like the perfect student: kind, athletic and smart. But in actuality, she was the self-professed "queen of vanity"--her only goal was to win the praise and admiration of others, and her sacred duty was to look and act perfect during school hours. Only at home would she let down her guard and let her true self show.

But when Yukino entered high school, she met her match: Soichiro Arima, a handsome, popular, ultra-intelligent guy. At first when he stole the top seat in class from her, Yukino saw him as a bitter rival. But over time, she learned that she and Soichiro had more in common than she had ever imagined. As their love blossomed, the two made a vow to finally stop pretending to be perfect and simply be true to themselves.

Still, they had plenty of obstacles. Jealous classmates tried to break them up, and so did teachers when their grades began to suffer as a result of the relationship. Yet somehow Yukino and Soichiro's love managed to persevere. But their greatest challenge was yet to come.

For although Soichiro's life seemed perfect, he'd endured a very traumatic childhood...and the ghosts were coming back to haunt him. His father left him early, and his mother was so abusive that his uncle adopted him and raised him as his own. But when Soichiro started to get nationwide attention for his high school achievements, his birth mother resurfaced, hoping to cash in. Soichiro met with her a few times to learn more about the family that abandoned him...until he realized she had nothing for him but more abuse and lies. With that (and a little help from his friends), he severed contact.

Soichiro had been keeping the family drama secret from Yukino, afraid it would destroy everything they'd worked for in their relationship. But she finally broke down his walls and made him tell her everything. Now their relationship is stronger than ever. Which is good, because Yukino thinks that she might be pregnant...

And now Soichiro's delinquent dad has returned to Japan, after years of touring the world as a jazz musician. Soichiro has very mixed feelings about the man who abandoned him, but is enjoying his father's company somewhat in spite of himself. If nothing else, it's another opportunity to learn about his family's checkered past...

kare kano
volume eighteen

TABLE OF CONTENTS

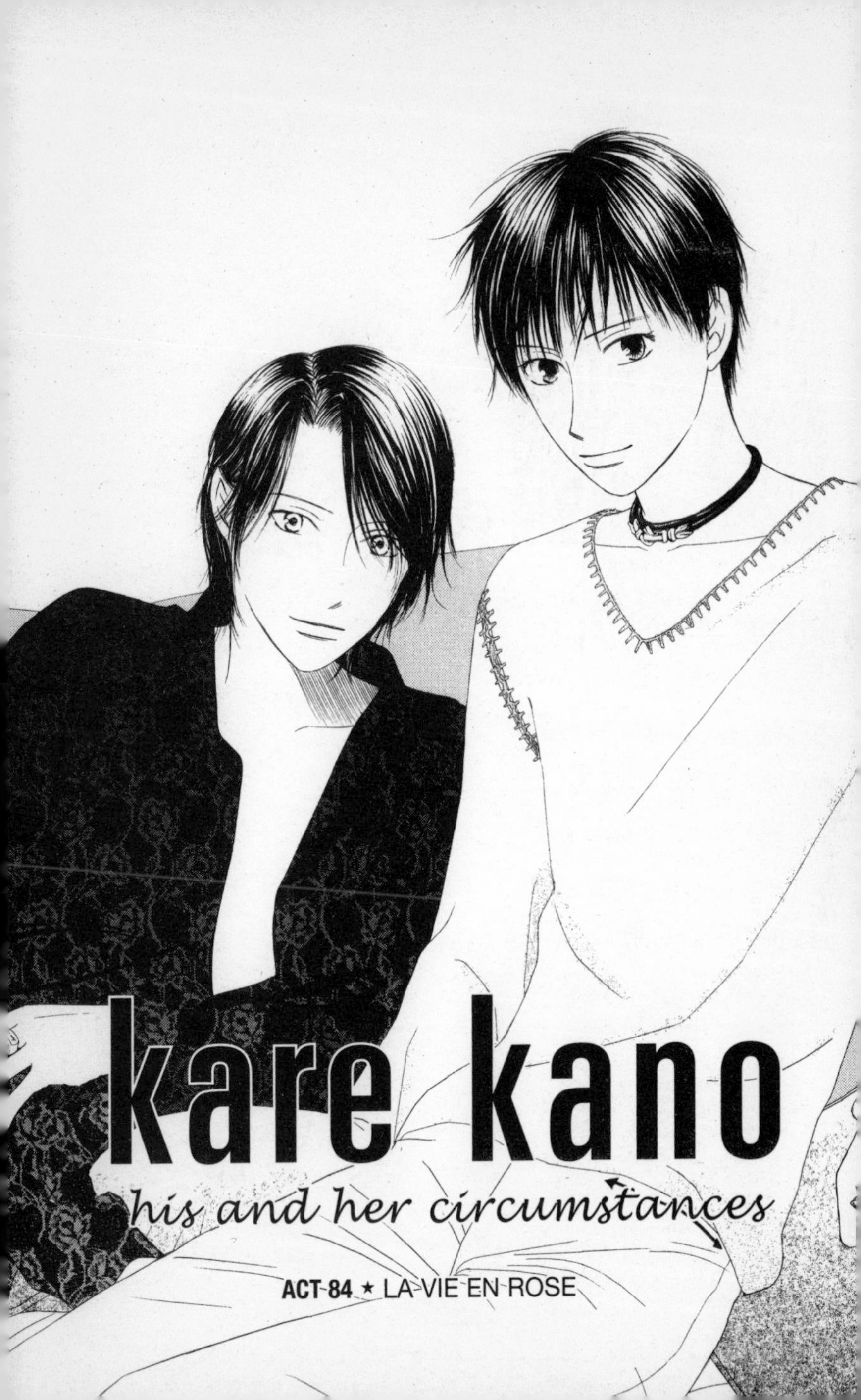
kare kano
his and her circumstances
ACT 84 ★ LA VIE EN ROSE

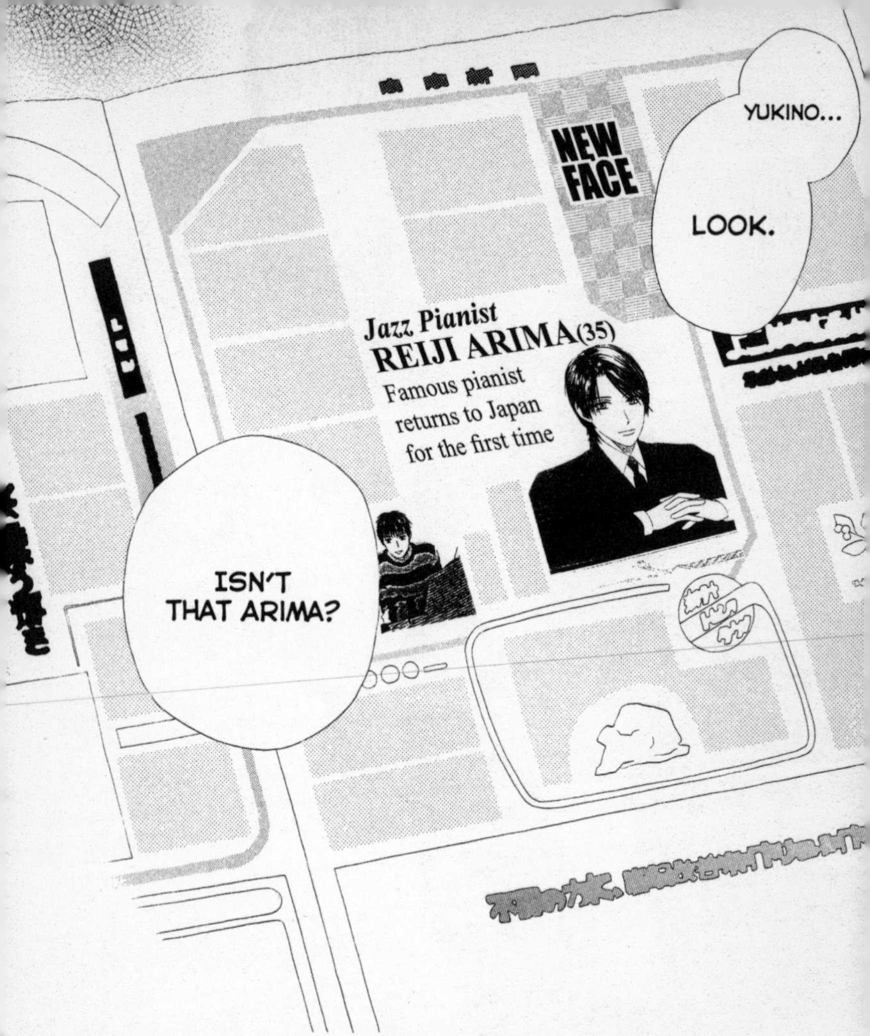
YUKINO...
LOOK.
NEW FACE
Jazz Pianist
REIJI ARIMA(35)
Famous pianist returns to Japan for the first time
ISN'T THAT ARIMA?

Popular things to do for fun:

Accounting Drills

This seems to be all the rage among adults!

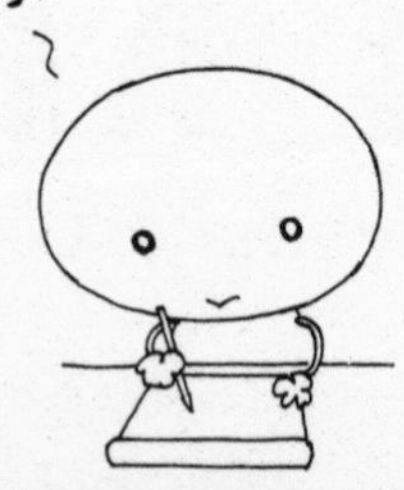

No, it's more like, because of my work, I feel like I'm only using the part of my brain that deals with language. So using a different part—the math part—is pretty fun.

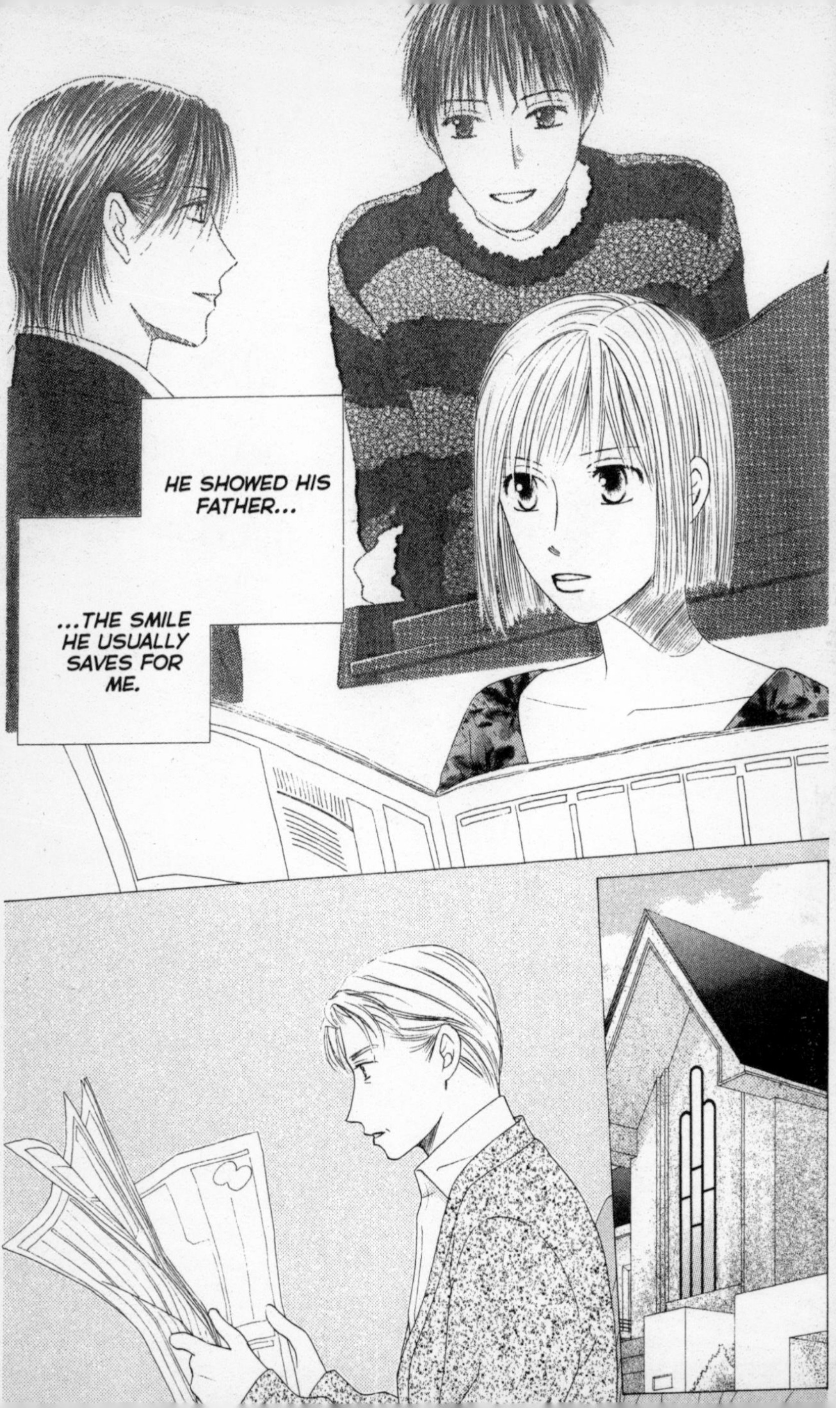
HE SHOWED HIS FATHER...
...THE SMILE HE USUALLY SAVES FOR ME.

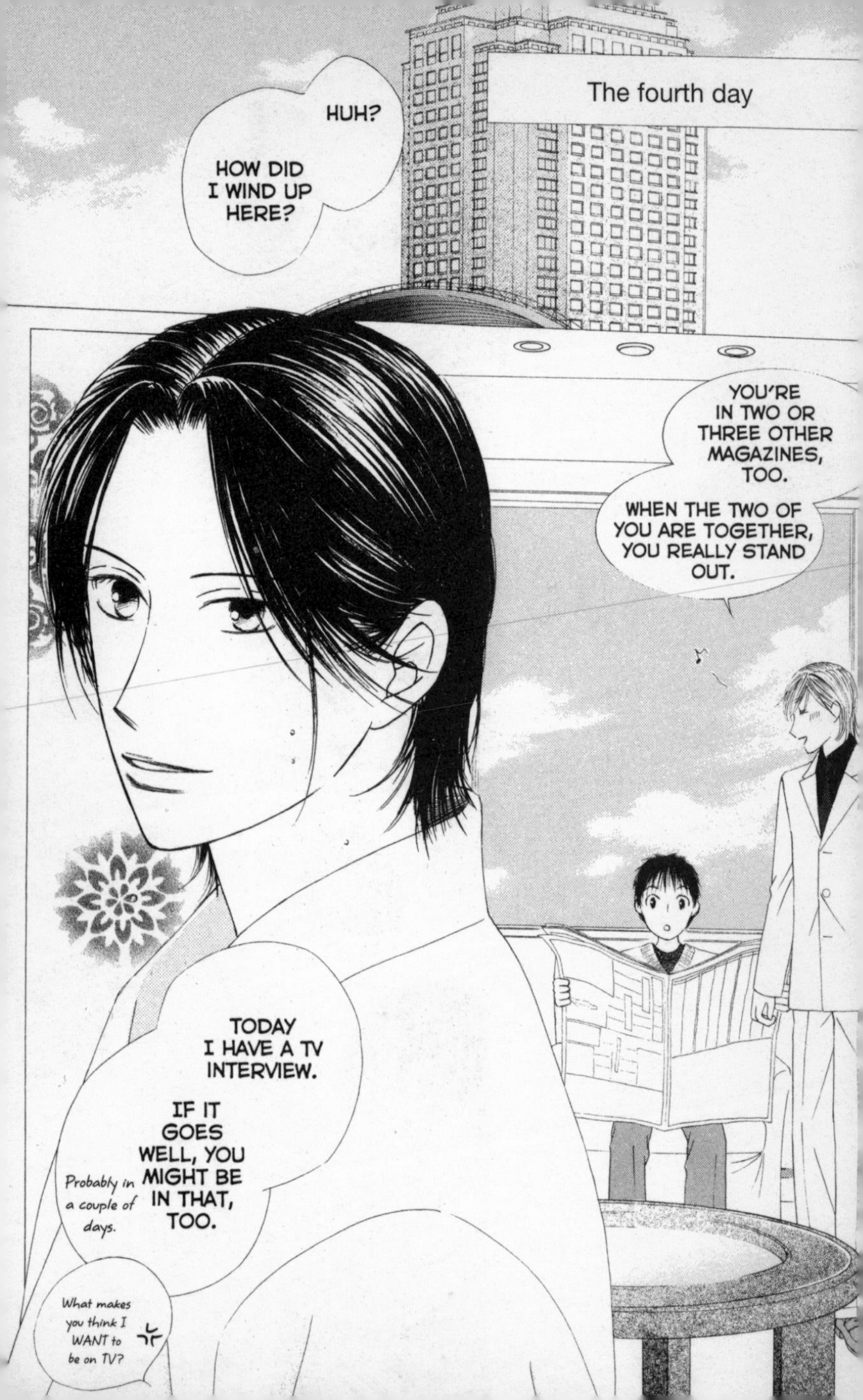
The fourth day
HUH?
HOW DID I WIND UP HERE?
YOU'RE IN TWO OR THREE OTHER MAGAZINES, TOO.
WHEN THE TWO OF YOU ARE TOGETHER, YOU REALLY STAND OUT.
TODAY I HAVE A TV INTERVIEW.
IF IT GOES WELL, YOU MIGHT BE IN THAT, TOO.
Probably in a couple of days.
What makes you think I WANT to be on TV?

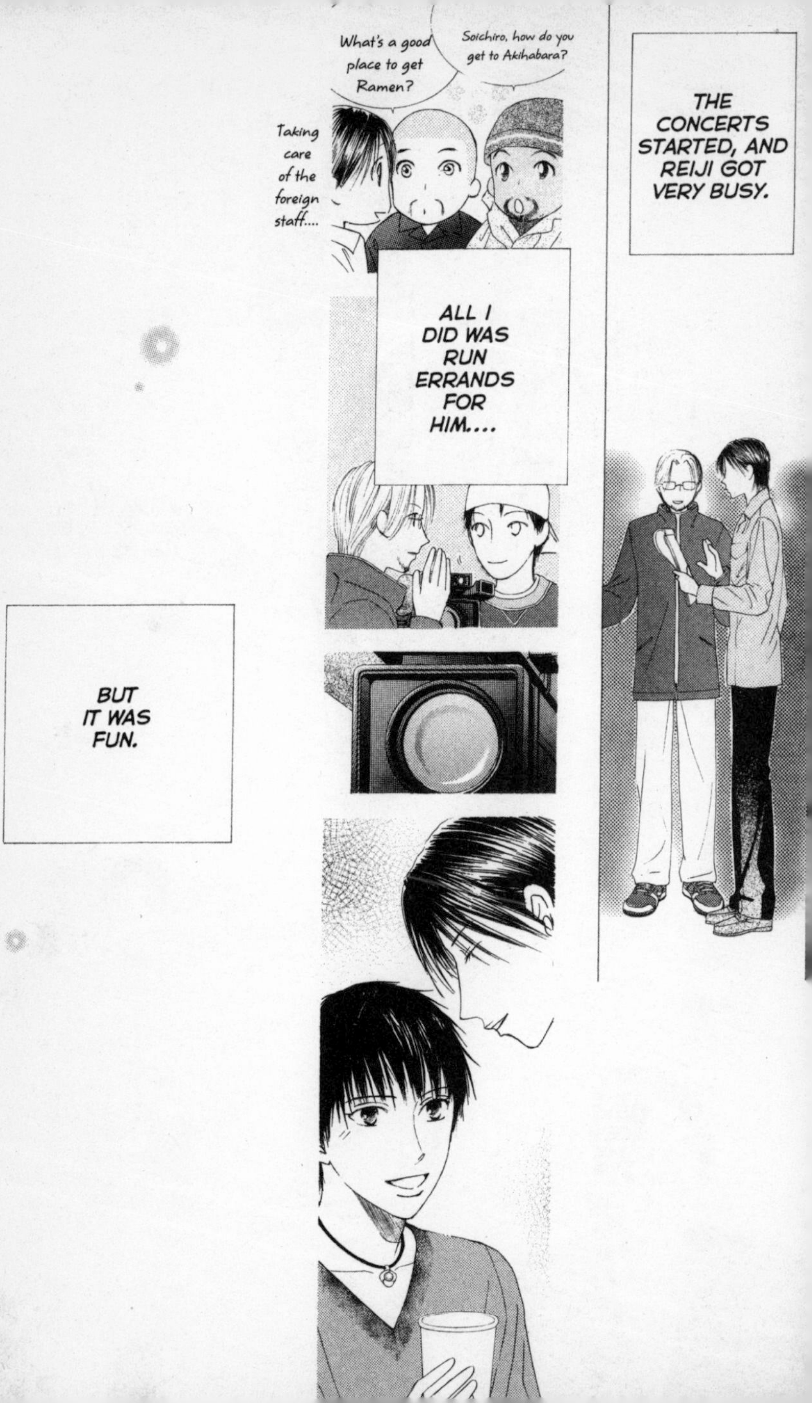
THE CONCERTS STARTED, AND REIJI GOT VERY BUSY.
Soichiro, how do you get to Akihabara?
What's a good place to get Ramen?
Taking care of the foreign staff....
ALL I DID WAS RUN ERRANDS FOR HIM....
BUT IT WAS FUN.

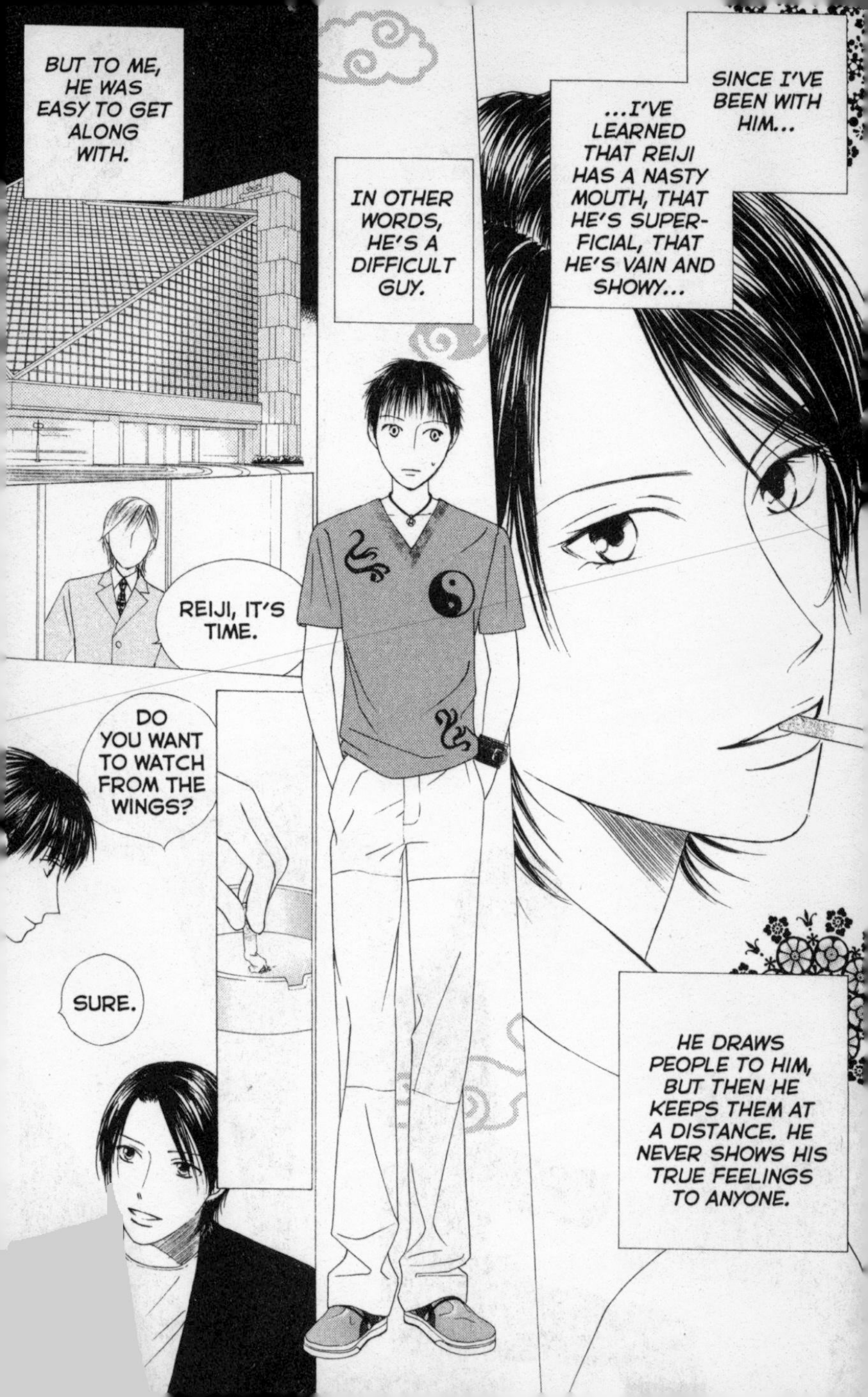
SINCE I'VE BEEN WITH HIM...
...I'VE LEARNED THAT REIJI HAS A NASTY MOUTH, THAT HE'S SUPER-FICIAL, THAT HE'S VAIN AND SHOWY...
HE DRAWS PEOPLE TO HIM, BUT THEN HE KEEPS THEM AT A DISTANCE. HE NEVER SHOWS HIS TRUE FEELINGS TO ANYONE.
IN OTHER WORDS, HE'S A DIFFICULT GUY.
BUT TO ME, HE WAS EASY TO GET ALONG WITH.
REIJI, IT'S TIME.
DO YOU WANT TO WATCH FROM THE WINGS?
SURE.

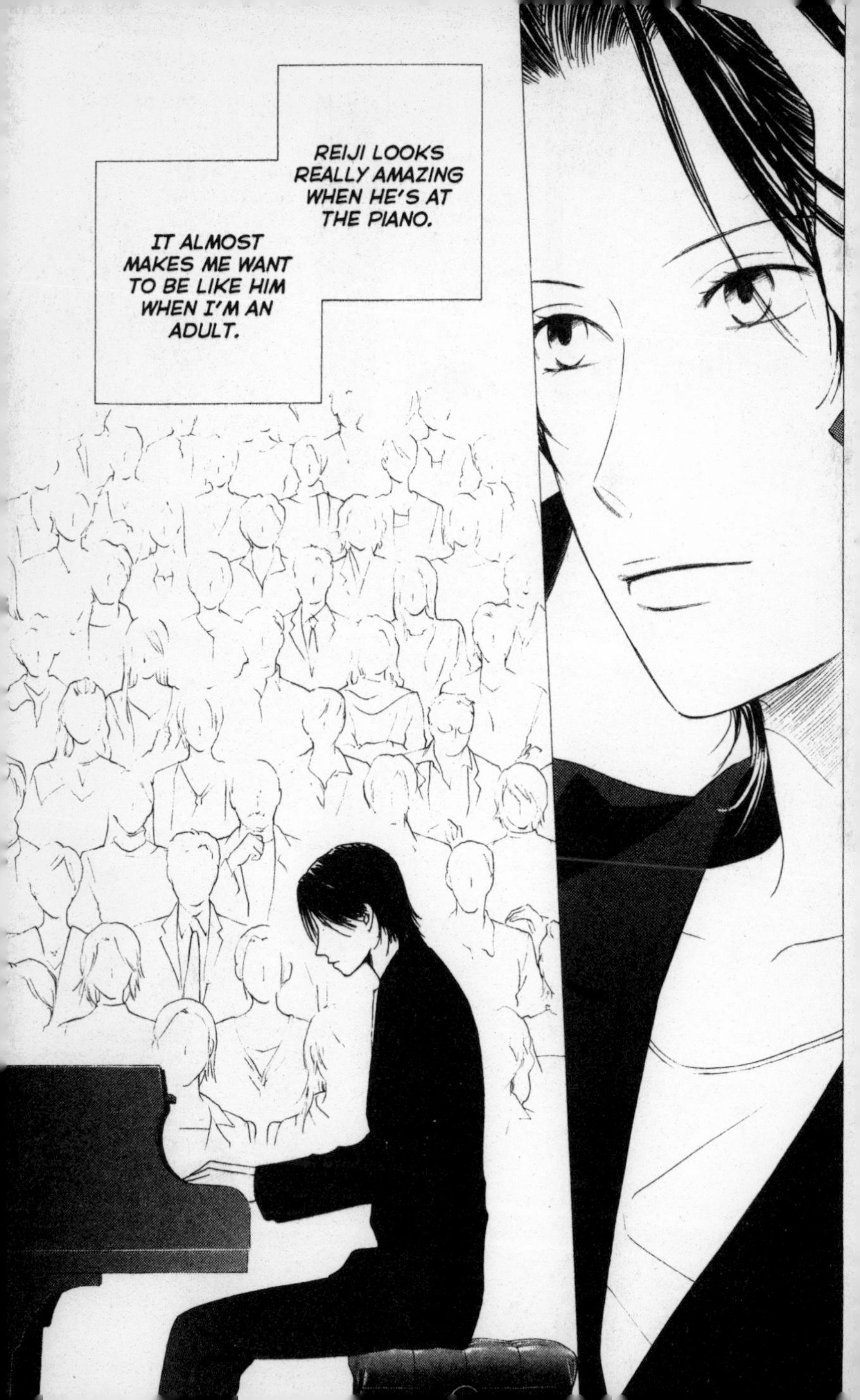
REIJI LOOKS REALLY AMAZING WHEN HE'S AT THE PIANO.
IT ALMOST MAKES ME WANT TO BE LIKE HIM WHEN I'M AN ADULT.

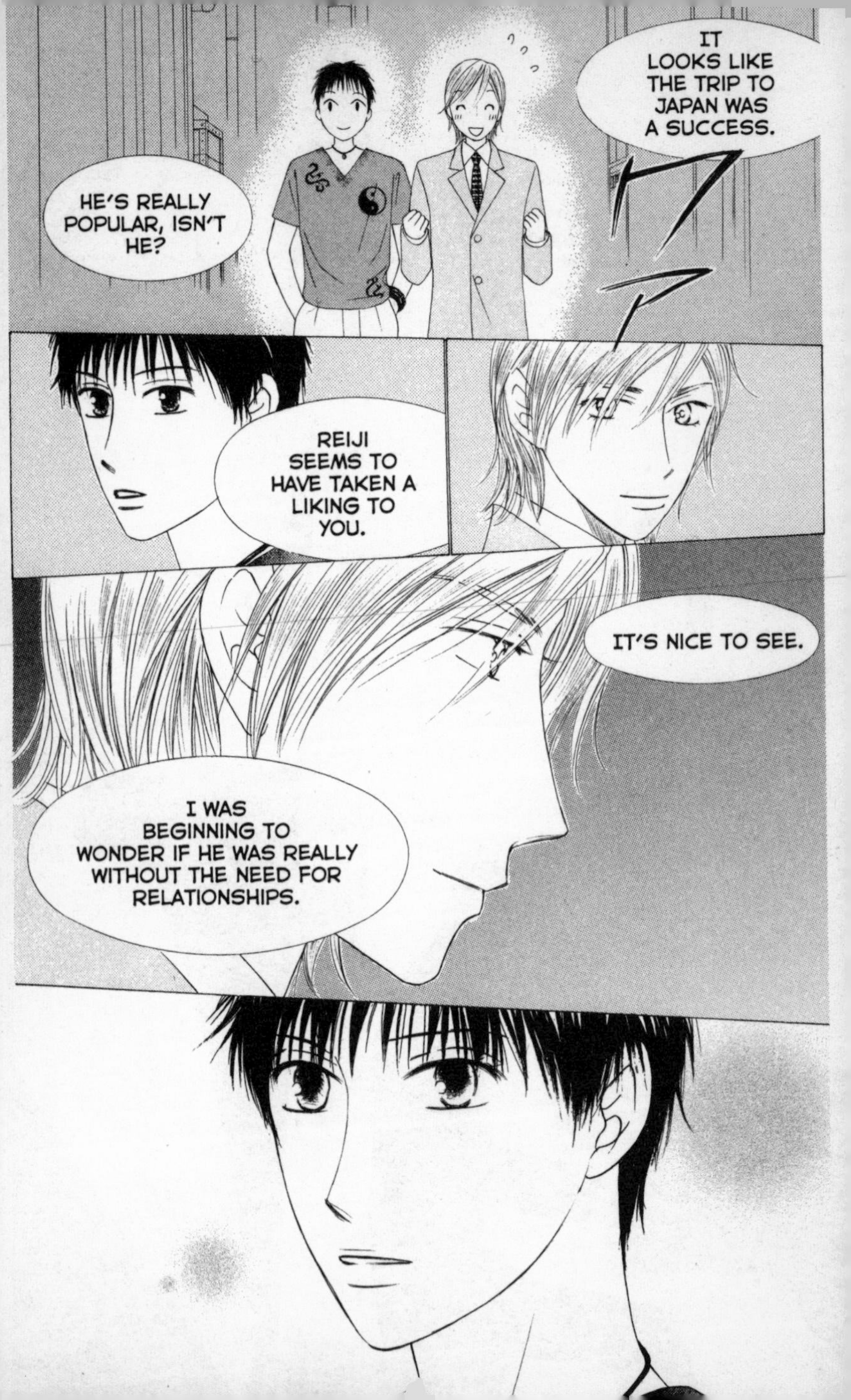
IT LOOKS LIKE THE TRIP TO JAPAN WAS A SUCCESS.
HE'S REALLY POPULAR, ISN'T HE?
REIJI SEEMS TO HAVE TAKEN A LIKING TO YOU.
IT'S NICE TO SEE.
I WAS BEGINNING TO WONDER IF HE WAS REALLY WITHOUT THE NEED FOR RELATIONSHIPS.

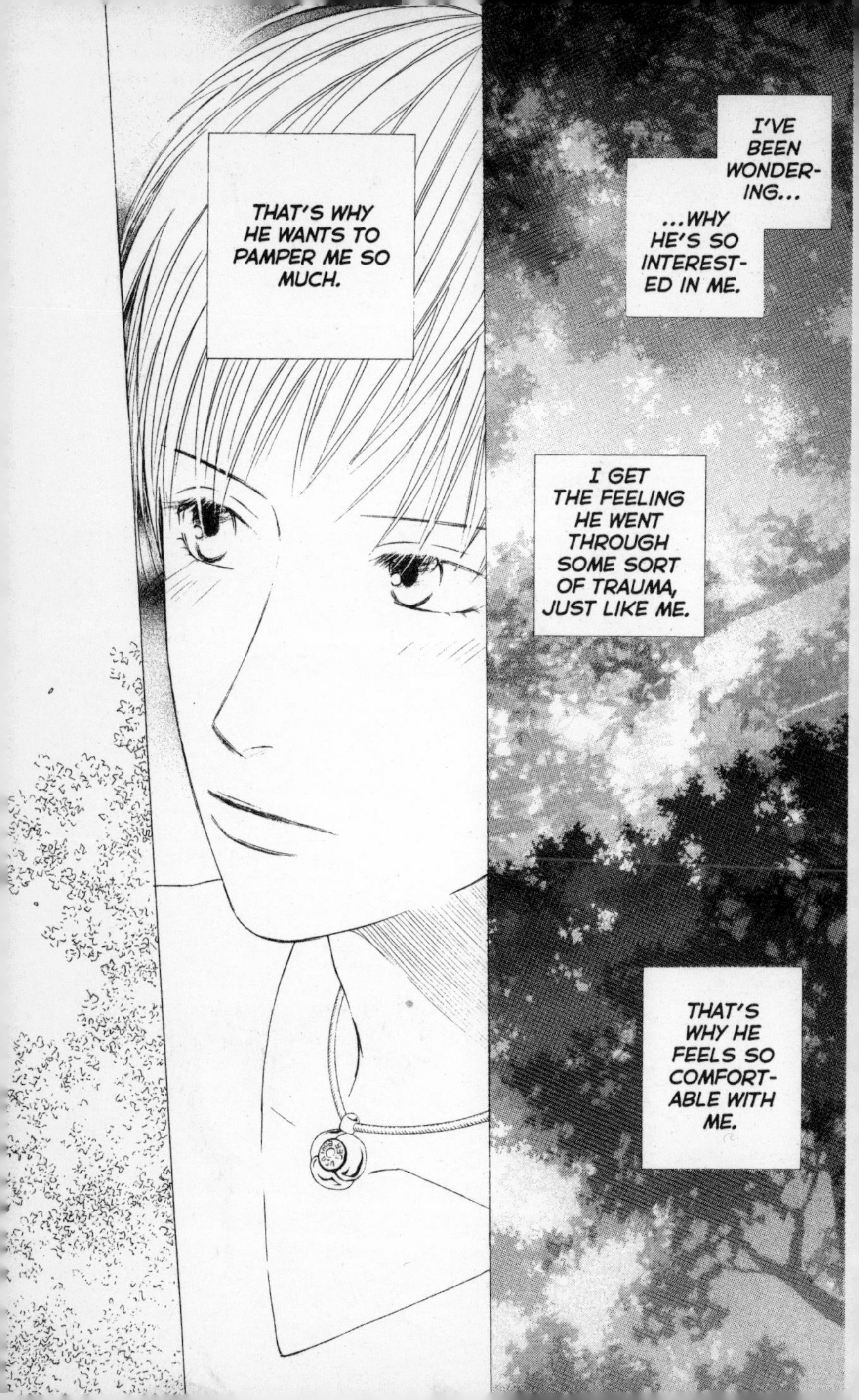
I'VE BEEN WONDERING...
...WHY HE'S SO INTERESTED IN ME.
I GET THE FEELING HE WENT THROUGH SOME SORT OF TRAUMA, JUST LIKE ME.
THAT'S WHY HE FEELS SO COMFORTABLE WITH ME.
THAT'S WHY HE WANTS TO PAMPER ME SO MUCH.

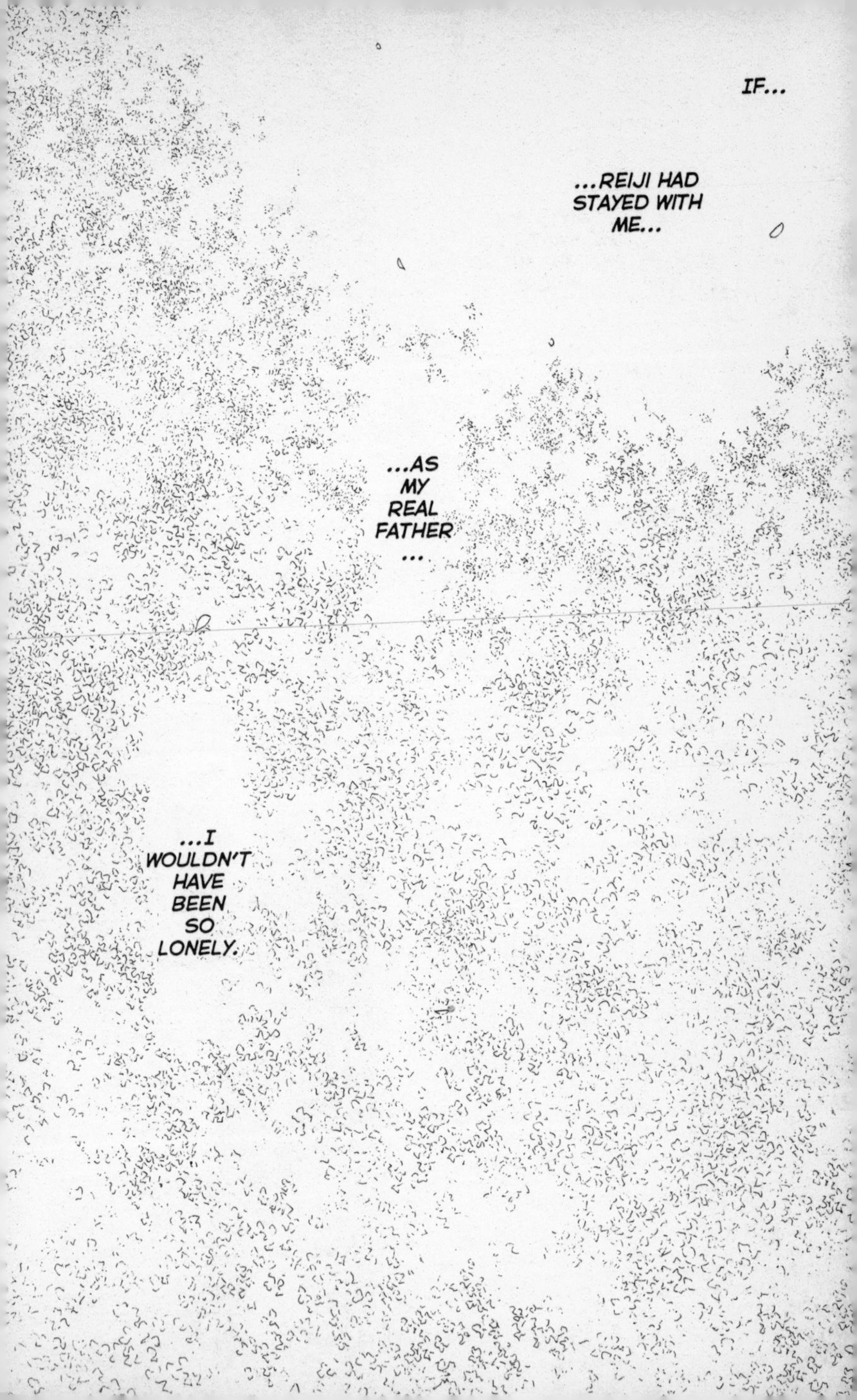
IF...
...REIJI HAD STAYED WITH ME...
...AS MY REAL FATHER...
...I WOULDN'T HAVE BEEN SO LONELY.

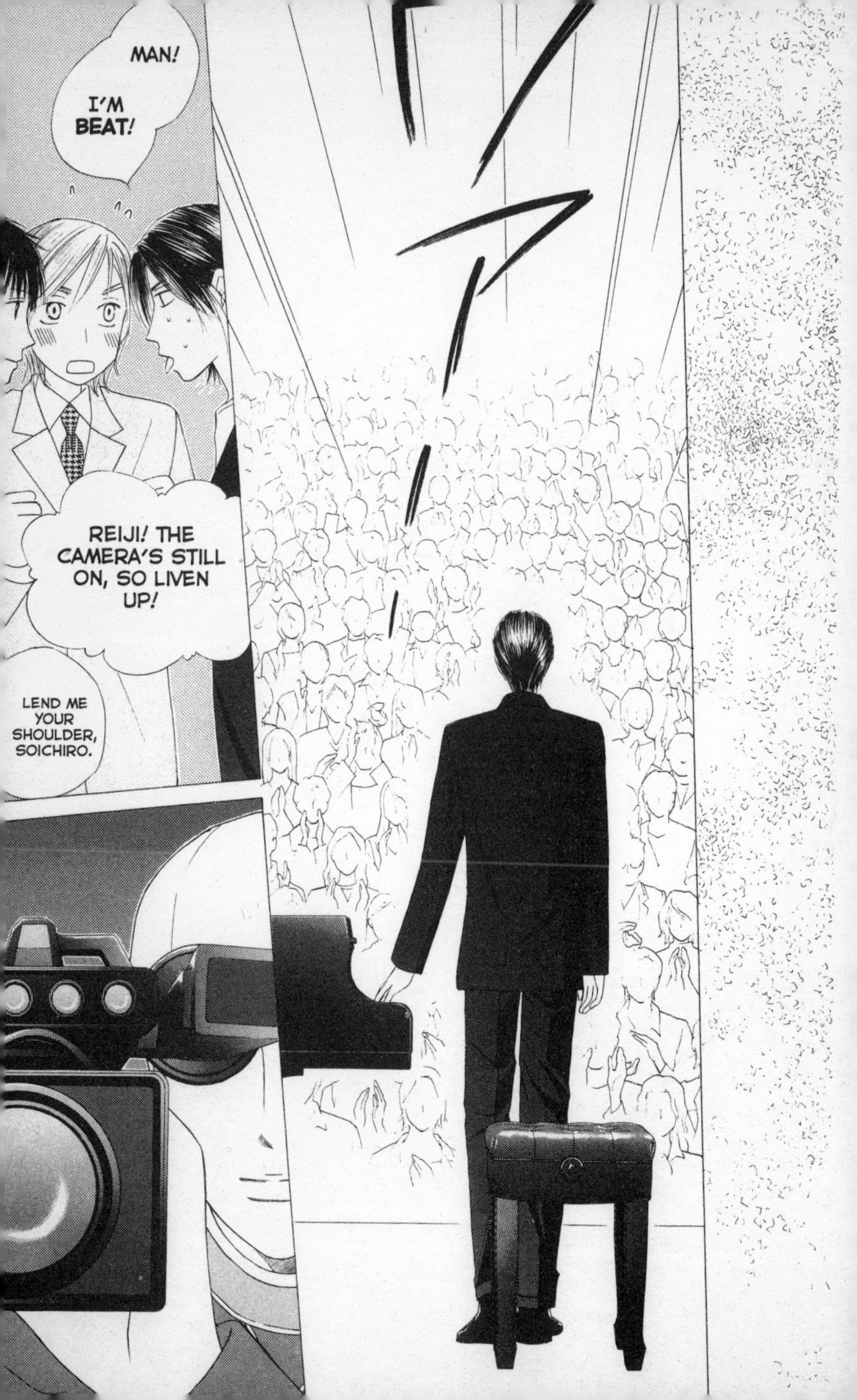
MAN! I'M BEAT!
REIJI! THE CAMERA'S STILL ON, SO LIVEN UP!
LEND ME YOUR SHOULDER, SOICHIRO.

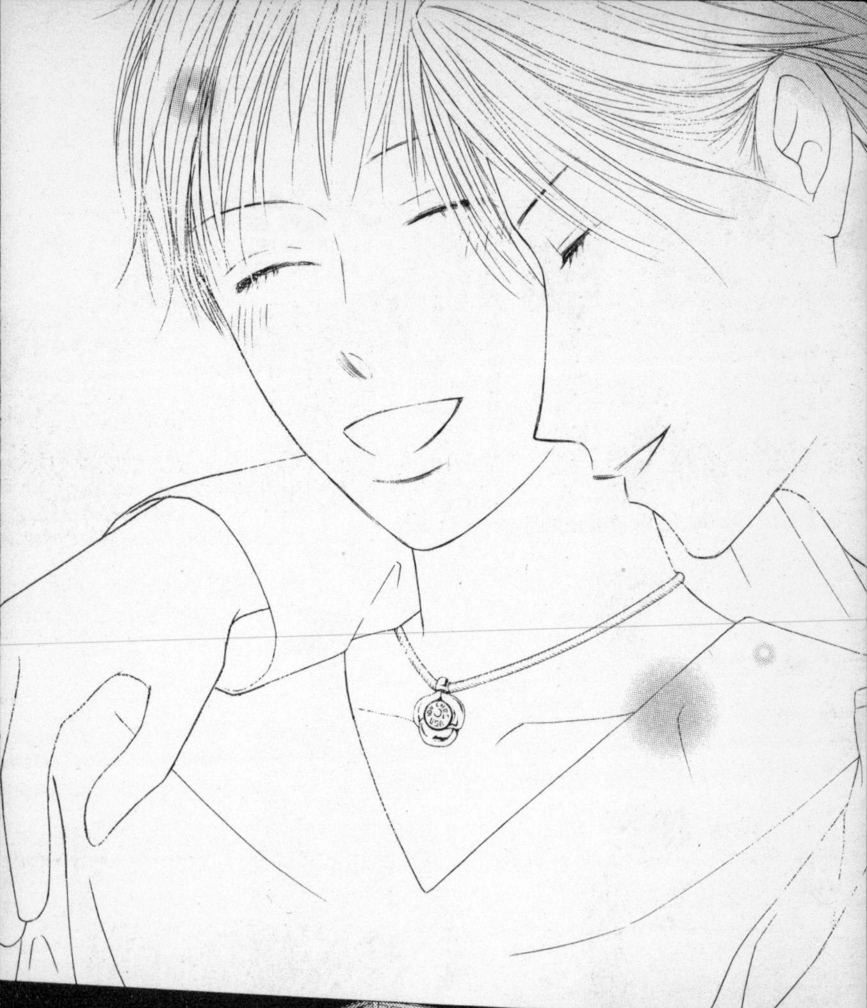

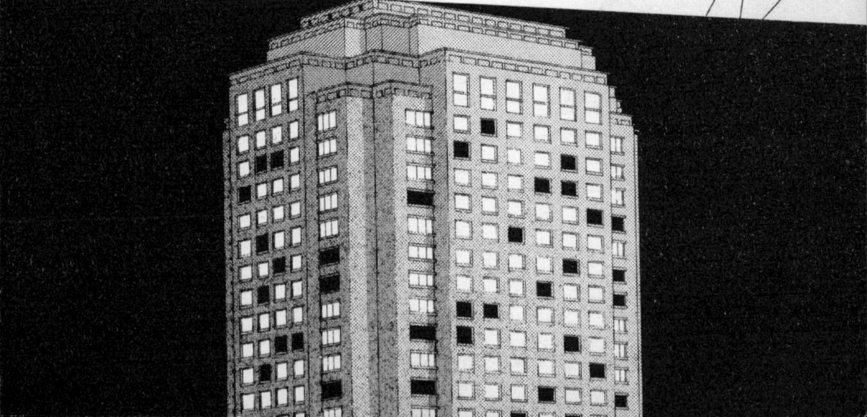

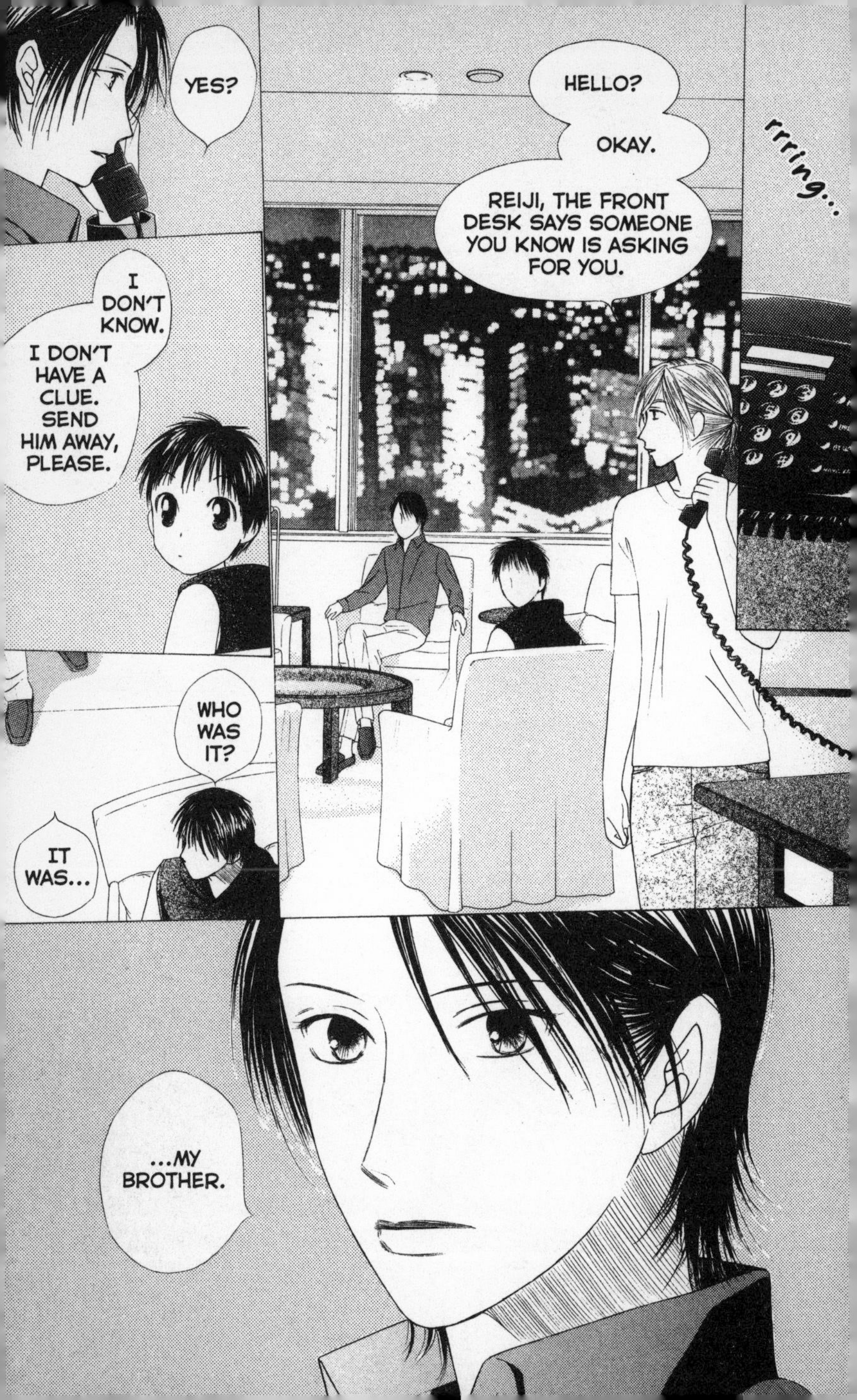
rrring...
HELLO?
OKAY.
REIJI, THE FRONT DESK SAYS SOMEONE YOU KNOW IS ASKING FOR YOU.
YES?
I DON'T KNOW. I DON'T HAVE A CLUE. SEND HIM AWAY, PLEASE.
WHO WAS IT?
IT WAS...
...MY BROTHER.

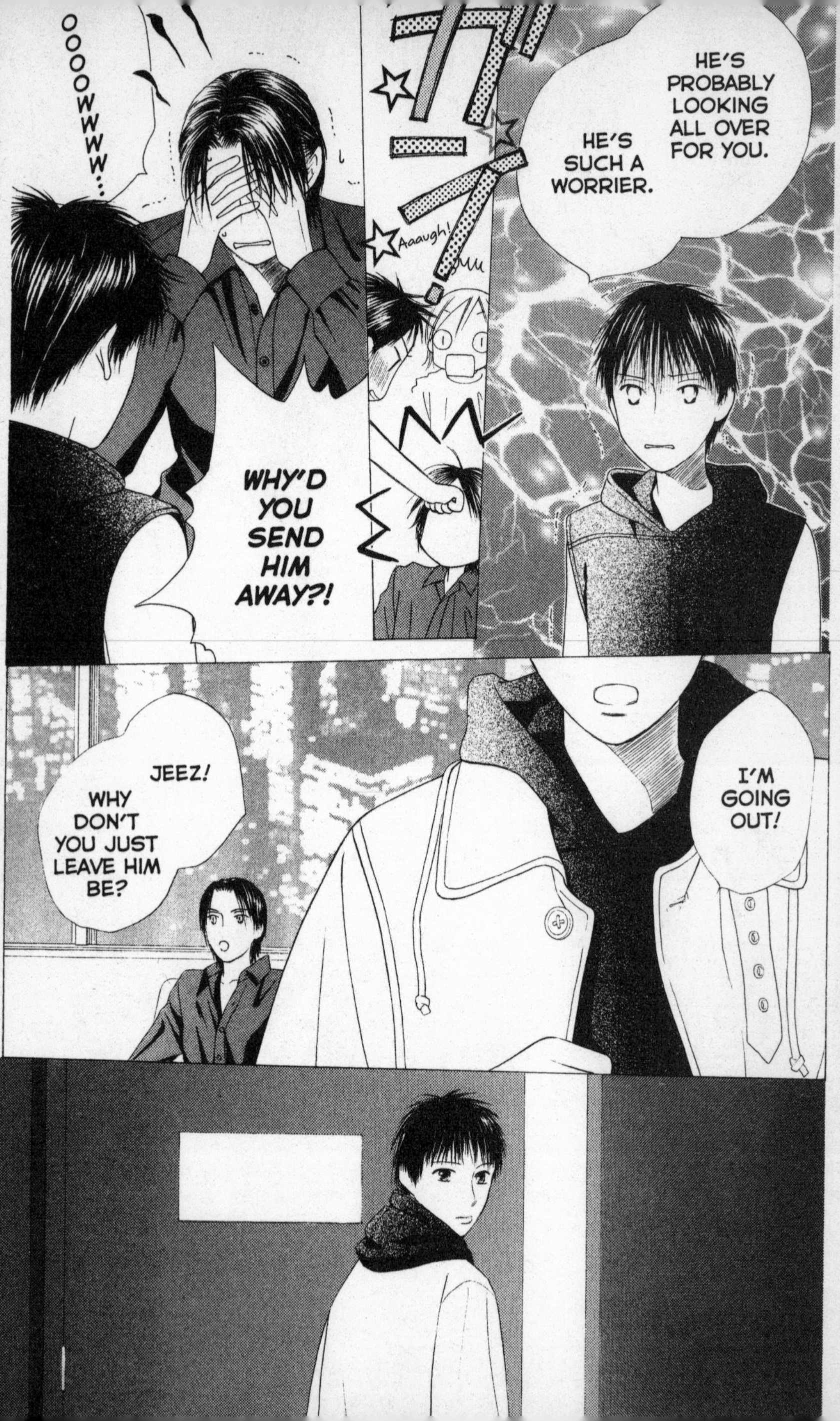

HE'S PROBABLY LOOKING ALL OVER FOR YOU.
HE'S SUCH A WORRIER.
Aaaugh!
WHY'D YOU SEND HIM AWAY?!
OOOOWWWWW...
I'M GOING OUT!
JEEZ!
WHY DON'T YOU JUST LEAVE HIM BE?

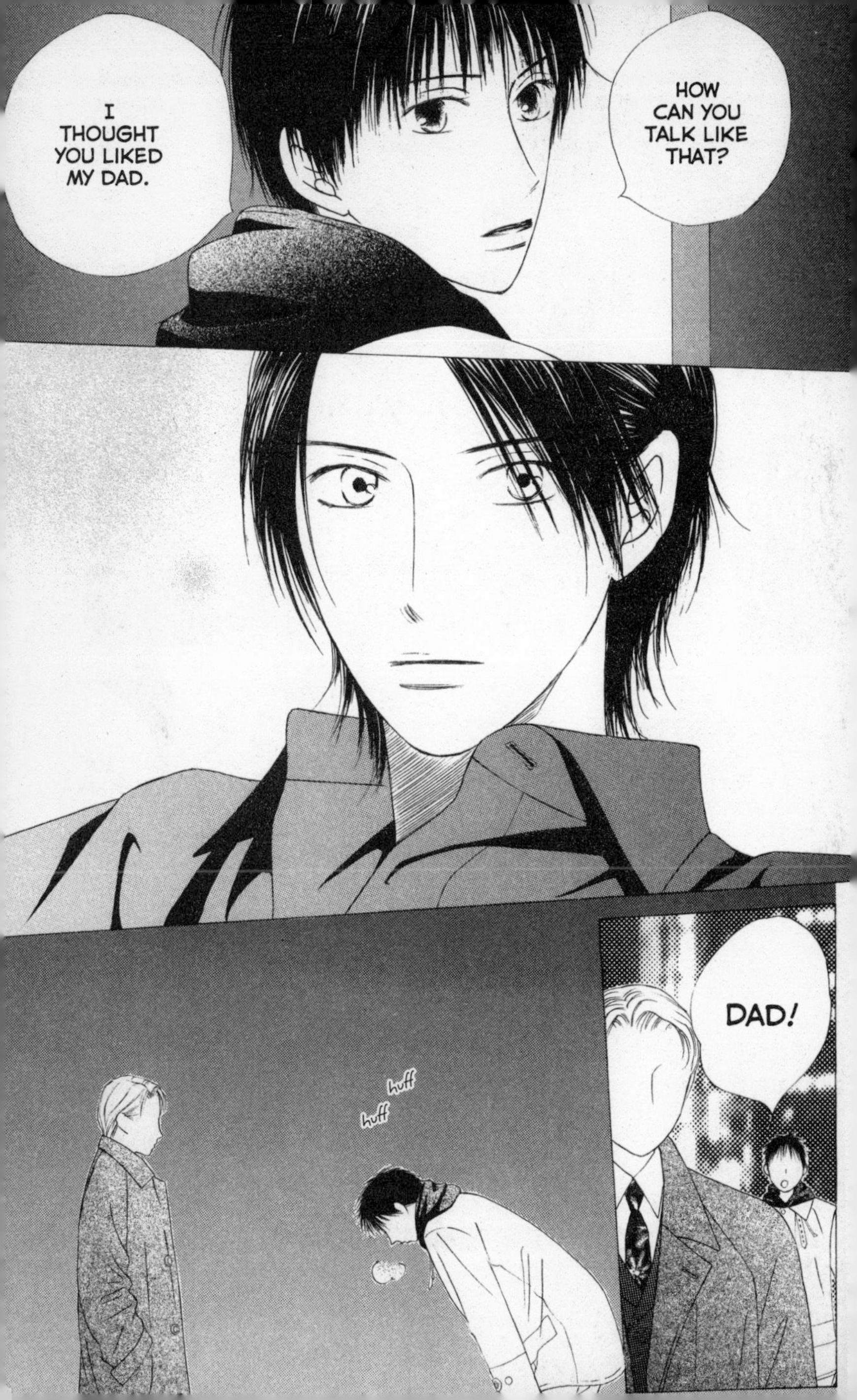
HOW CAN YOU TALK LIKE THAT?
I THOUGHT YOU LIKED MY DAD.
DAD!
huff
huff

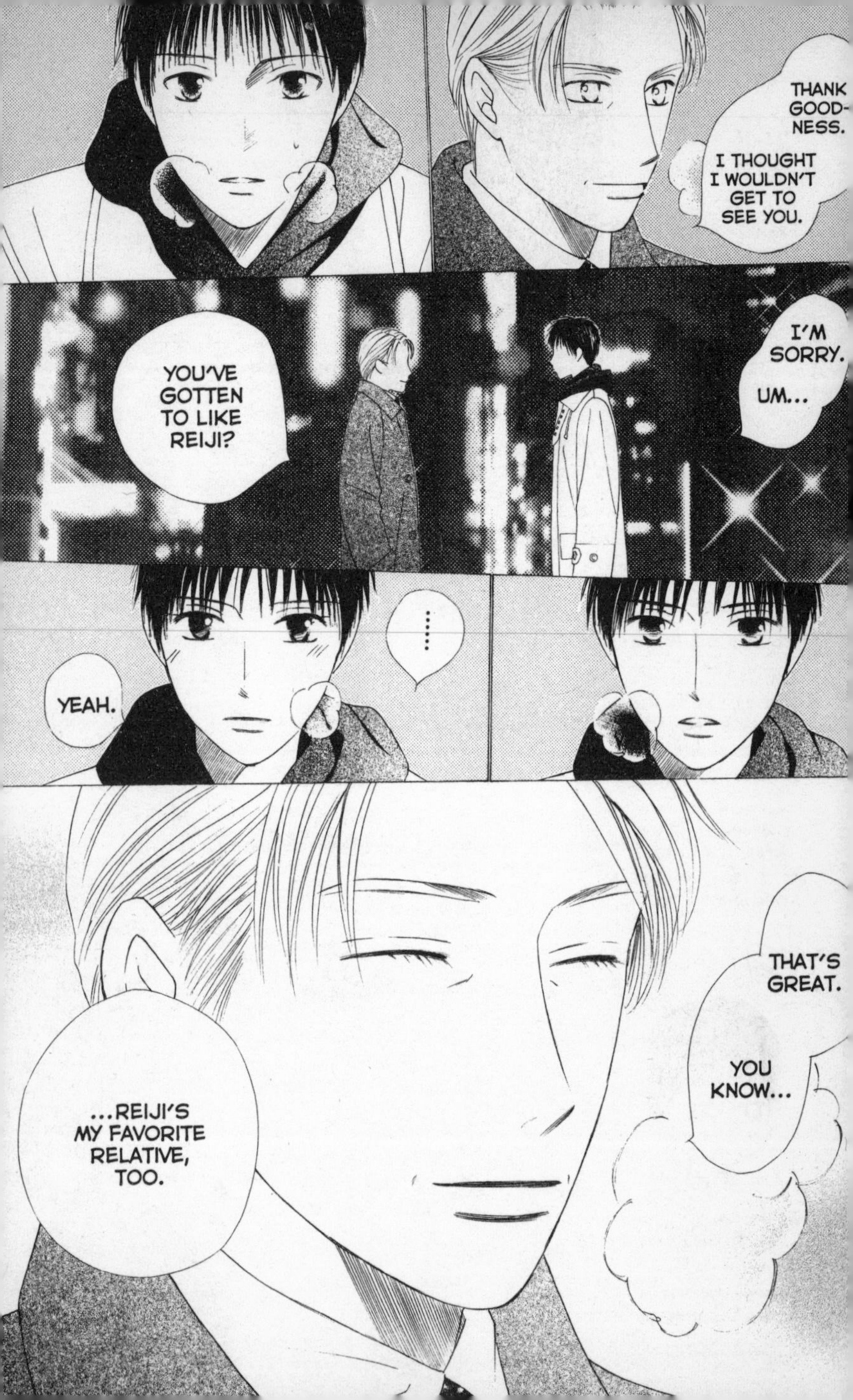
THANK GOODNESS.
I THOUGHT I WOULDN'T GET TO SEE YOU.
I'M SORRY.
UM...
YOU'VE GOTTEN TO LIKE REIJI?
......
YEAH.
THAT'S GREAT.
YOU KNOW...
...REIJI'S MY FAVORITE RELATIVE, TOO.

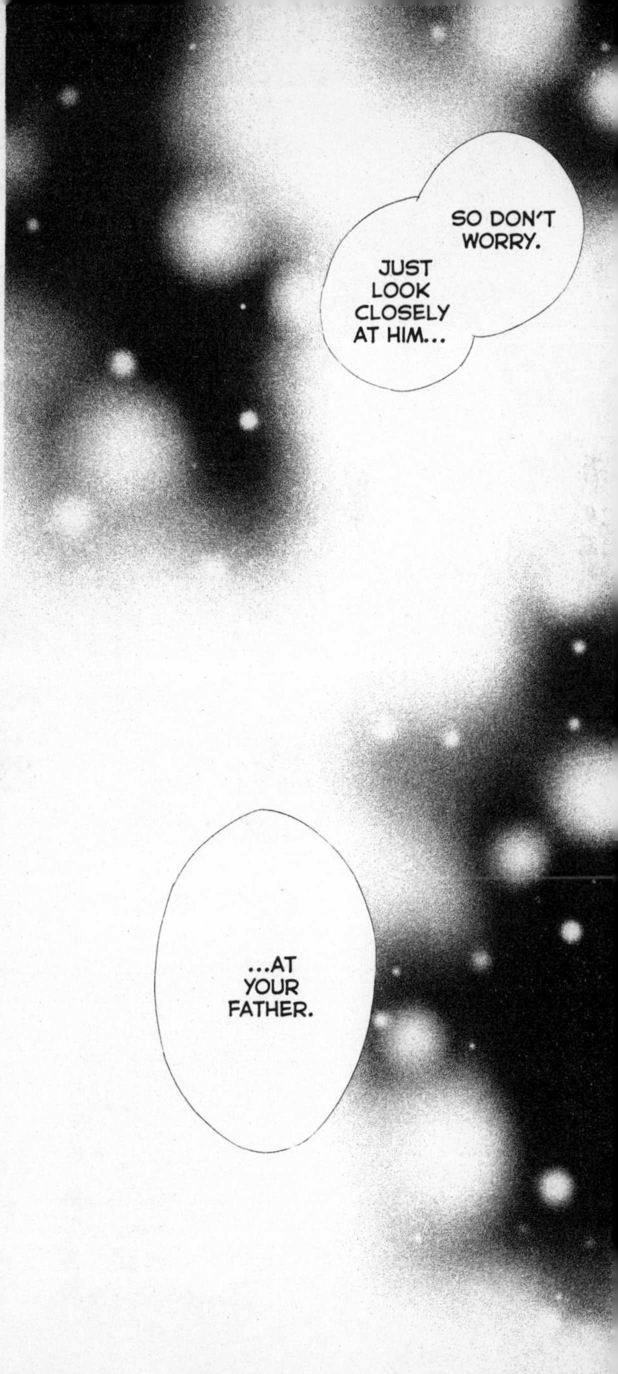
SO DON'T WORRY.
JUST LOOK CLOSELY AT HIM...
...AT YOUR FATHER.

1

Hello. This is my 22nd comic, *Kare Kano* Volume 18.

* * *

There's something I've wanted to do for a long time, but couldn't find the courage.

And I finally did it in the previous volume.

That is...I cut Arima's hair!

I'm so happy. Now it's a lot easier for me to put him in different clothes.

I was worried about the reaction the readers would have, but it seems positive, which is a big relief.

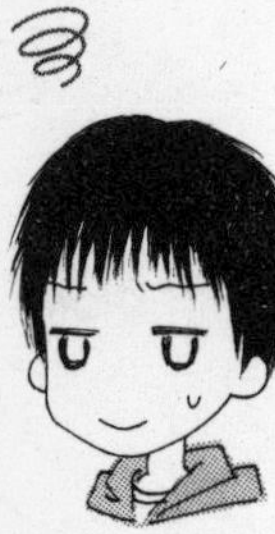

Now he can be casual, formal, or even sweet and innocent.

There're so many clothes I want to put on him!

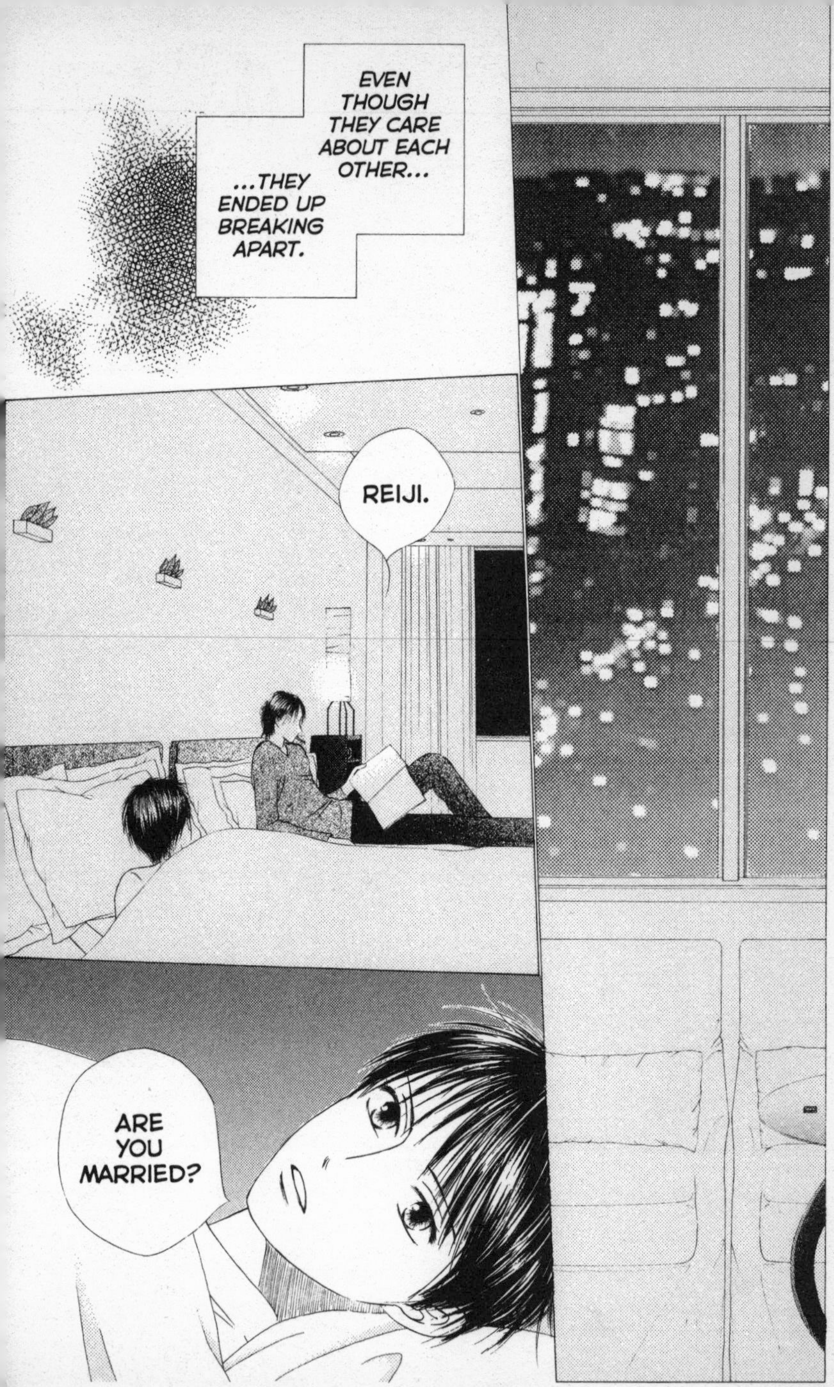
EVEN THOUGH THEY CARE ABOUT EACH OTHER...
...THEY ENDED UP BREAKING APART.
REIJI.
ARE YOU MARRIED?

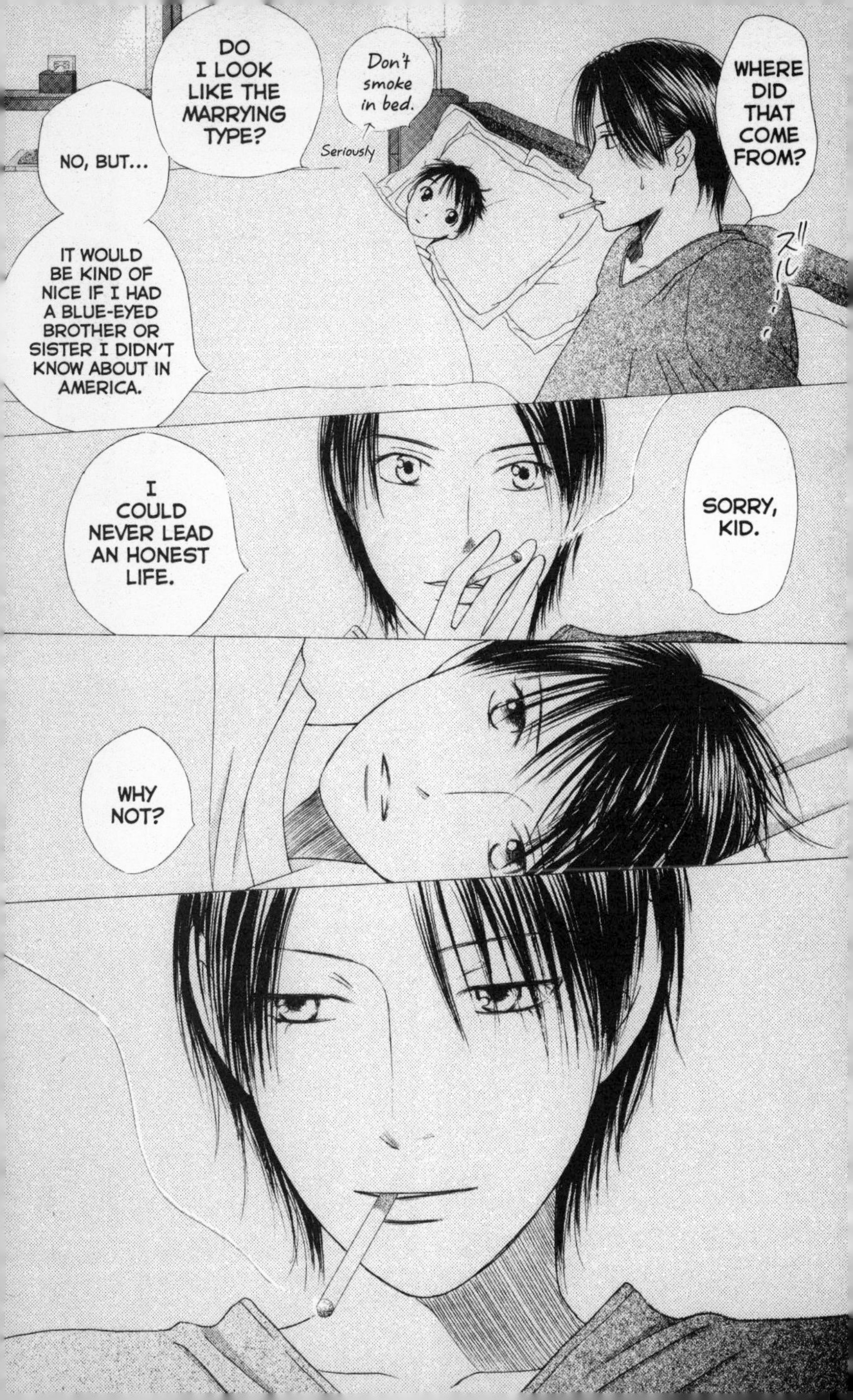
WHERE DID THAT COME FROM?
ズル!!
Don't smoke in bed.
Seriously
DO I LOOK LIKE THE MARRYING TYPE?
NO, BUT...
IT WOULD BE KIND OF NICE IF I HAD A BLUE-EYED BROTHER OR SISTER I DIDN'T KNOW ABOUT IN AMERICA.
SORRY, KID.
I COULD NEVER LEAD AN HONEST LIFE.
WHY NOT?

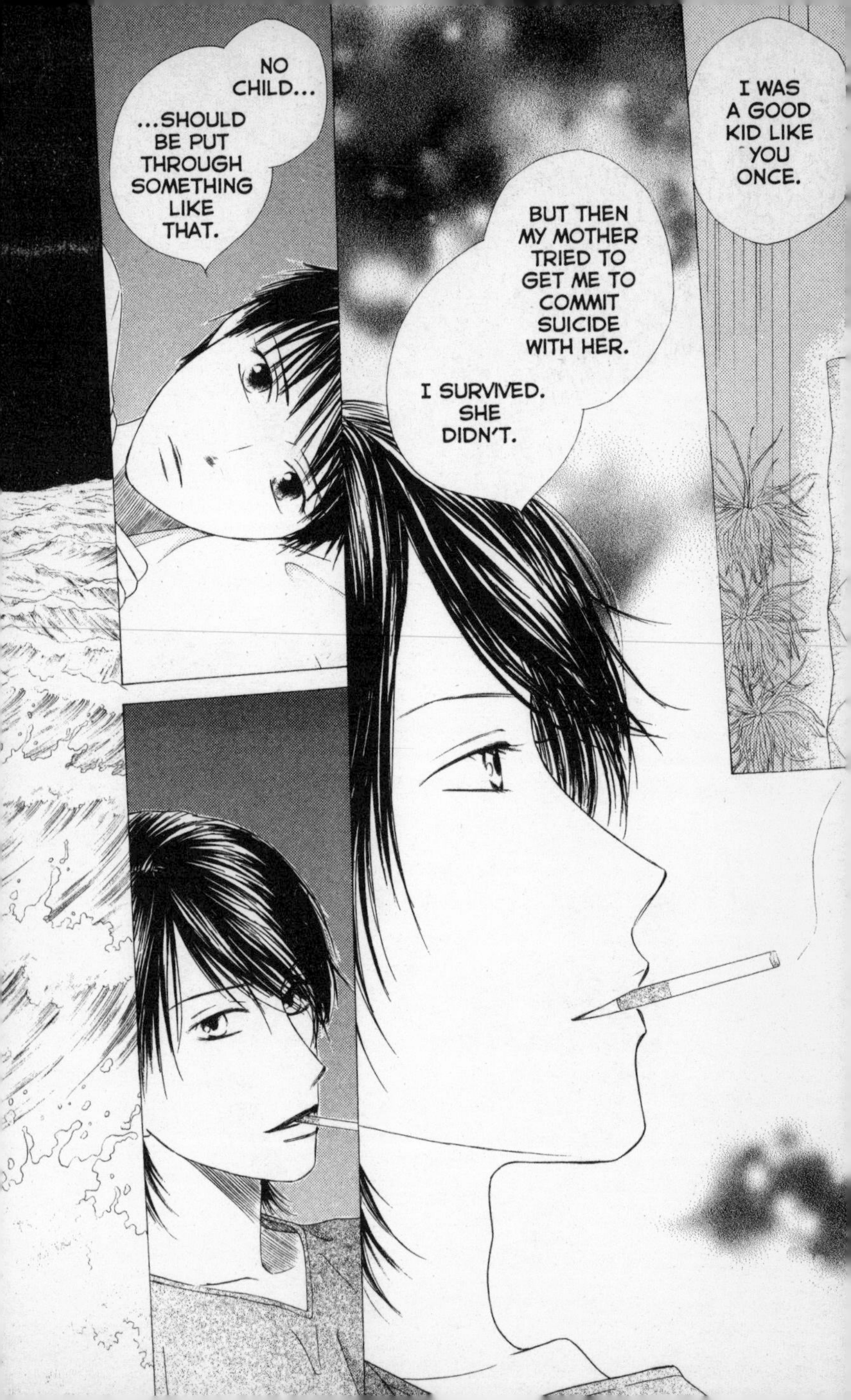
I WAS A GOOD KID LIKE YOU ONCE.
BUT THEN MY MOTHER TRIED TO GET ME TO COMMIT SUICIDE WITH HER.
I SURVIVED. SHE DIDN'T.
NO CHILD...
...SHOULD BE PUT THROUGH SOMETHING LIKE THAT.

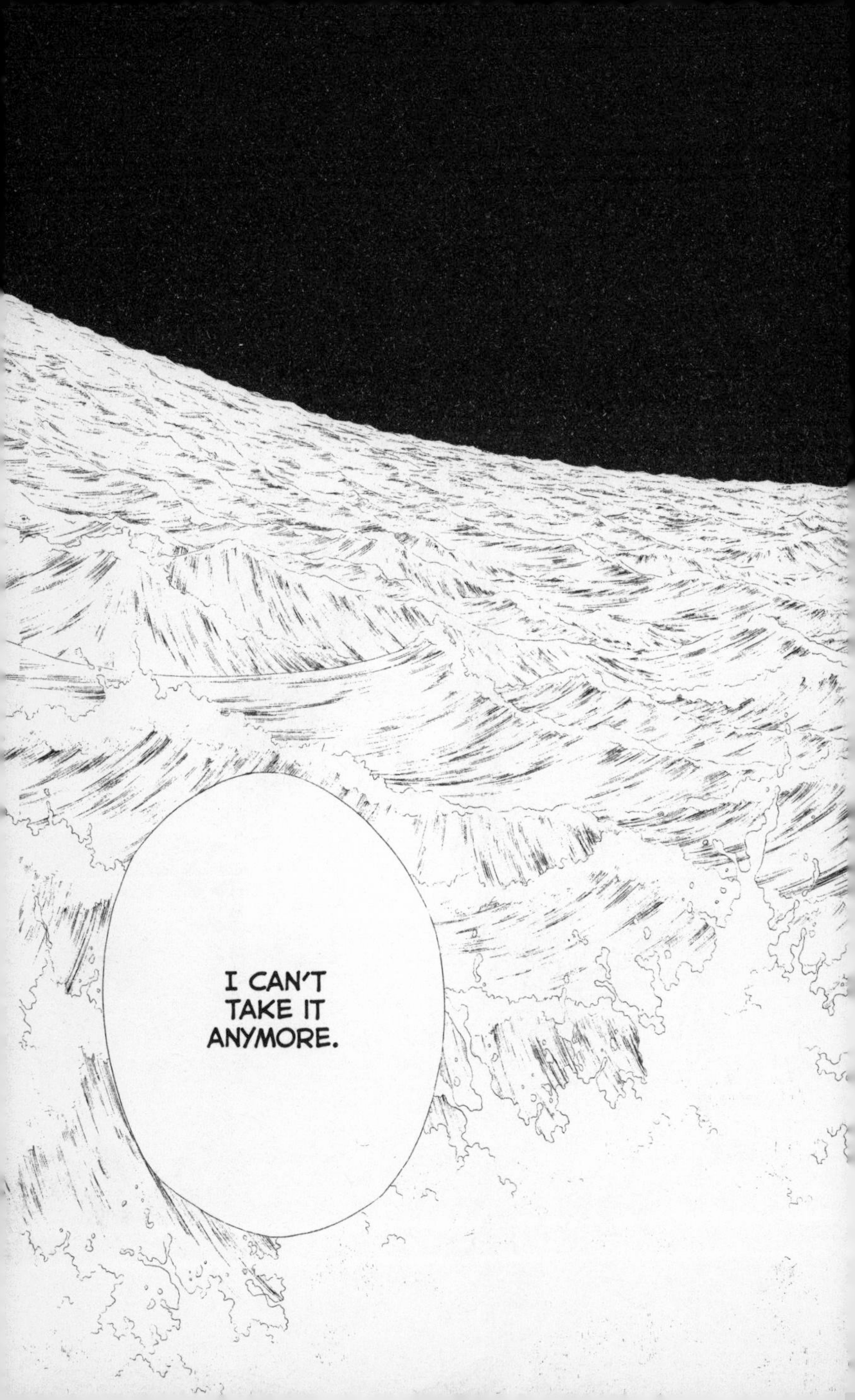
I CAN'T
TAKE IT
ANYMORE.

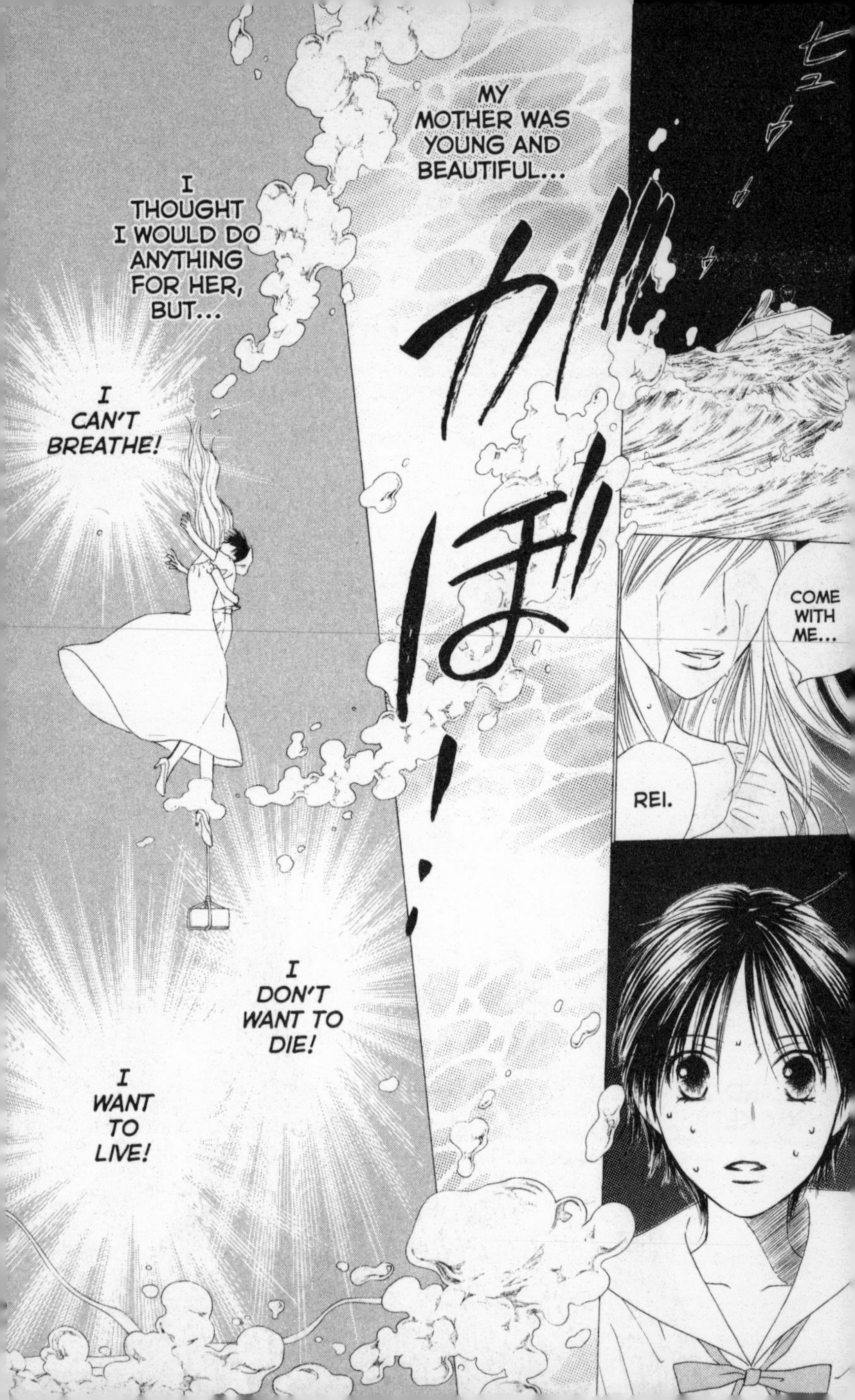
COME WITH ME...
REI.
MY MOTHER WAS YOUNG AND BEAUTIFUL...
I THOUGHT I WOULD DO ANYTHING FOR HER, BUT...
I CAN'T BREATHE!
I DON'T WANT TO DIE!
I WANT TO LIVE!

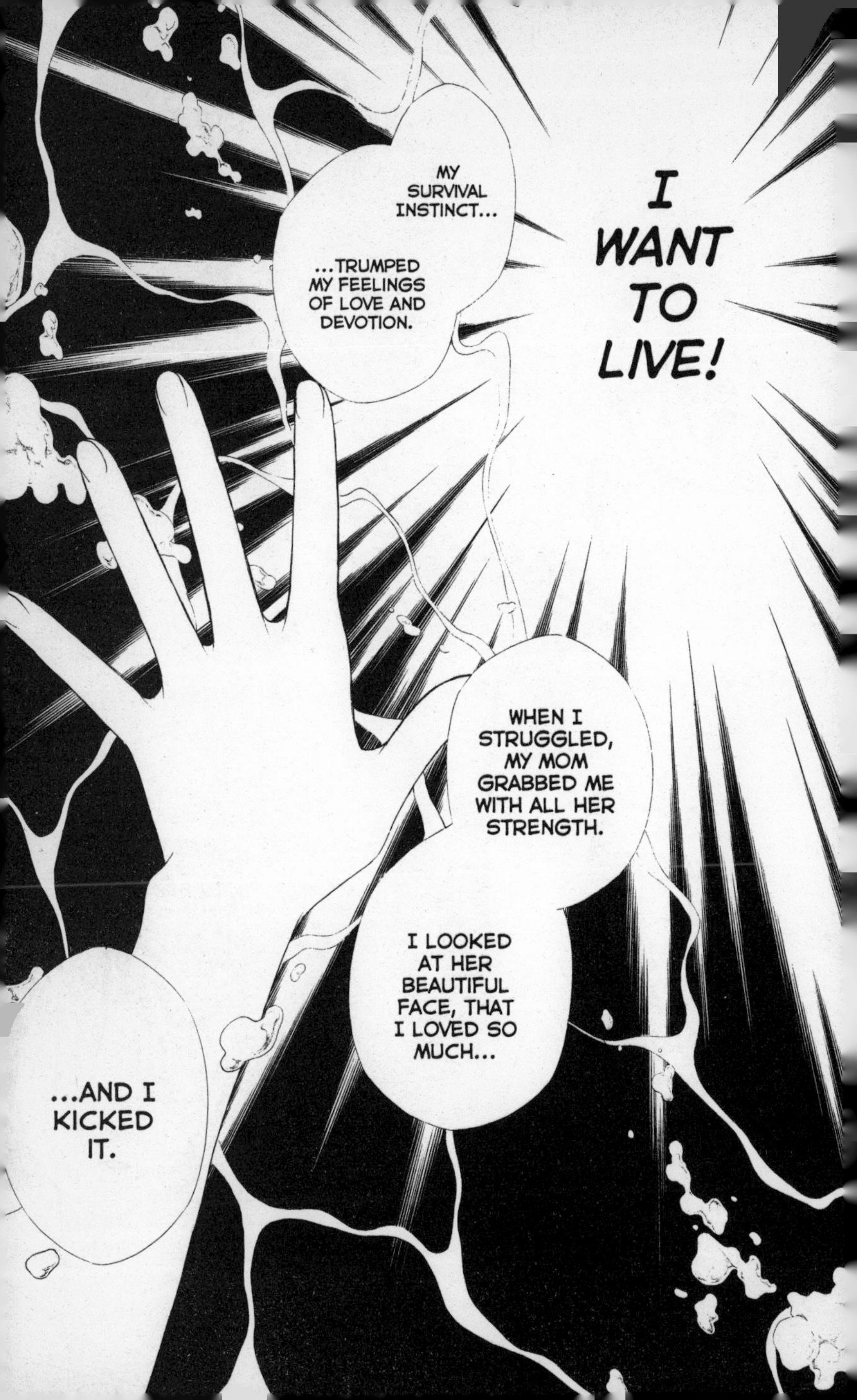
I WANT TO LIVE!
MY SURVIVAL INSTINCT...
...TRUMPED MY FEELINGS OF LOVE AND DEVOTION.
WHEN I STRUGGLED, MY MOM GRABBED ME WITH ALL HER STRENGTH.
I LOOKED AT HER BEAUTIFUL FACE, THAT I LOVED SO MUCH...
...AND I KICKED IT.

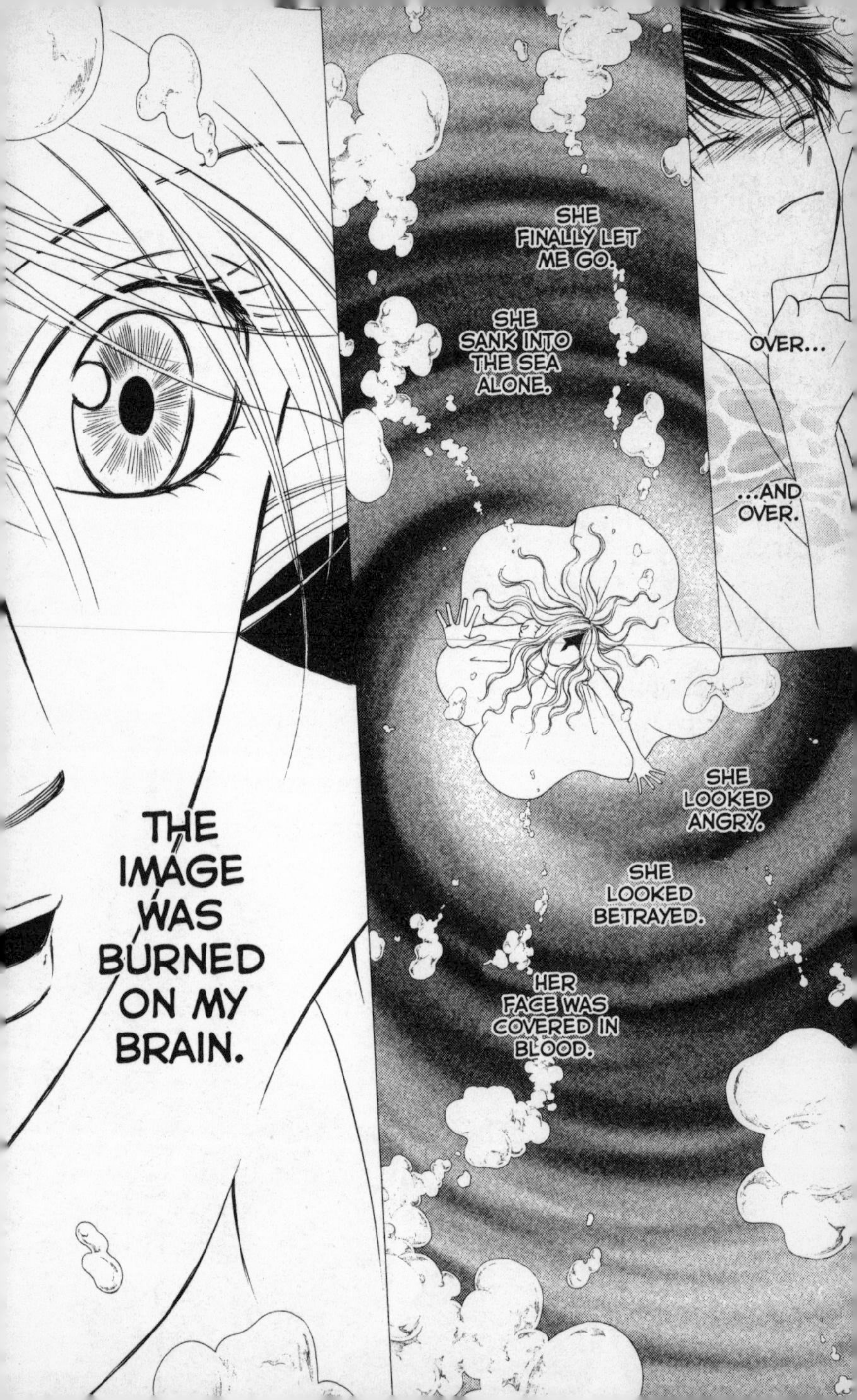
OVER...
...AND OVER.
SHE FINALLY LET ME GO.
SHE SANK INTO THE SEA ALONE.
SHE LOOKED ANGRY.
SHE LOOKED BETRAYED.
HER FACE WAS COVERED IN BLOOD.
THE IMAGE WAS BURNED ON MY BRAIN.

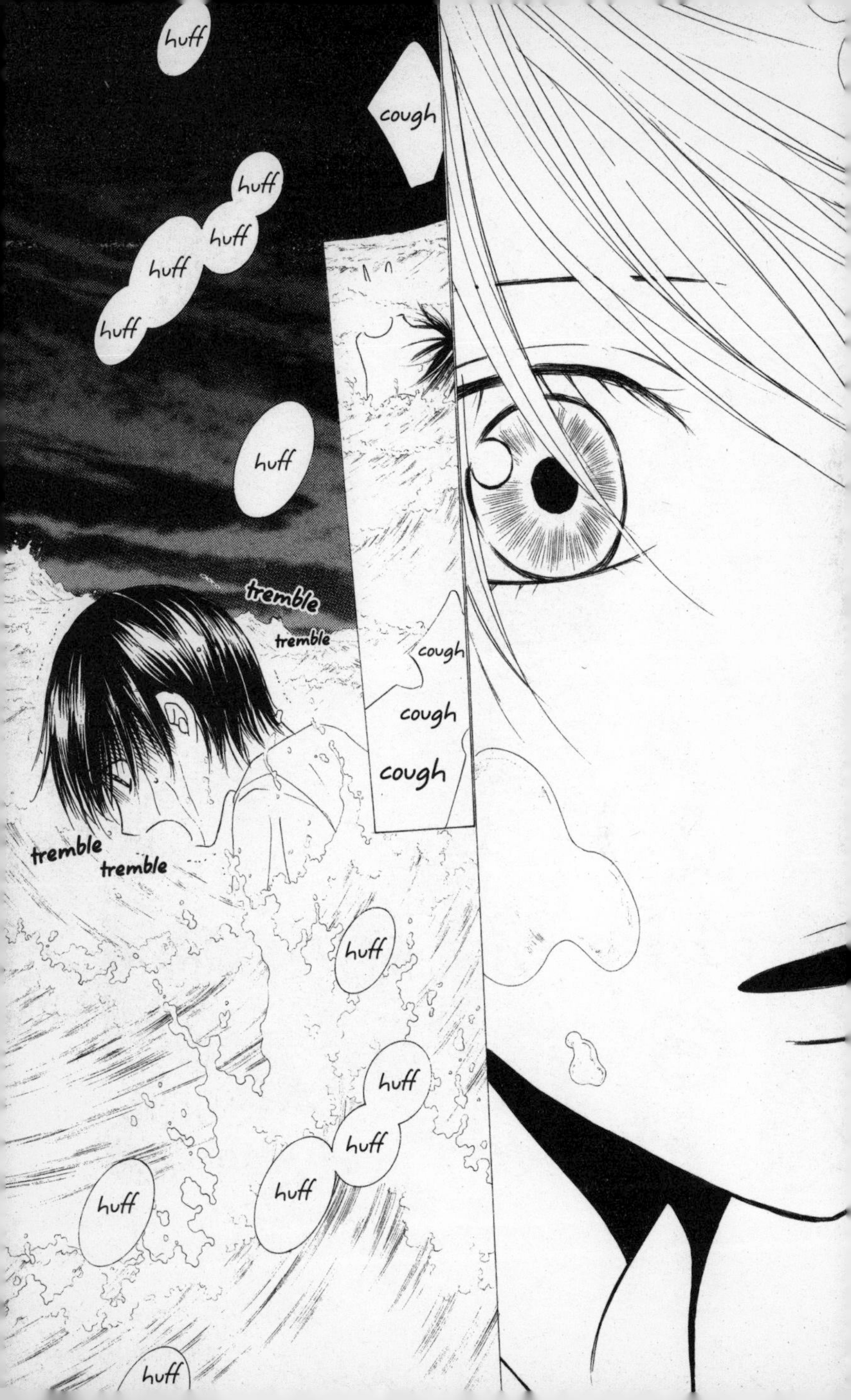
cough
huff
huff
huff
huff
huff
huff
tremble
tremble
cough
cough
cough
tremble
tremble
huff
huff
huff
huff
huff
huff

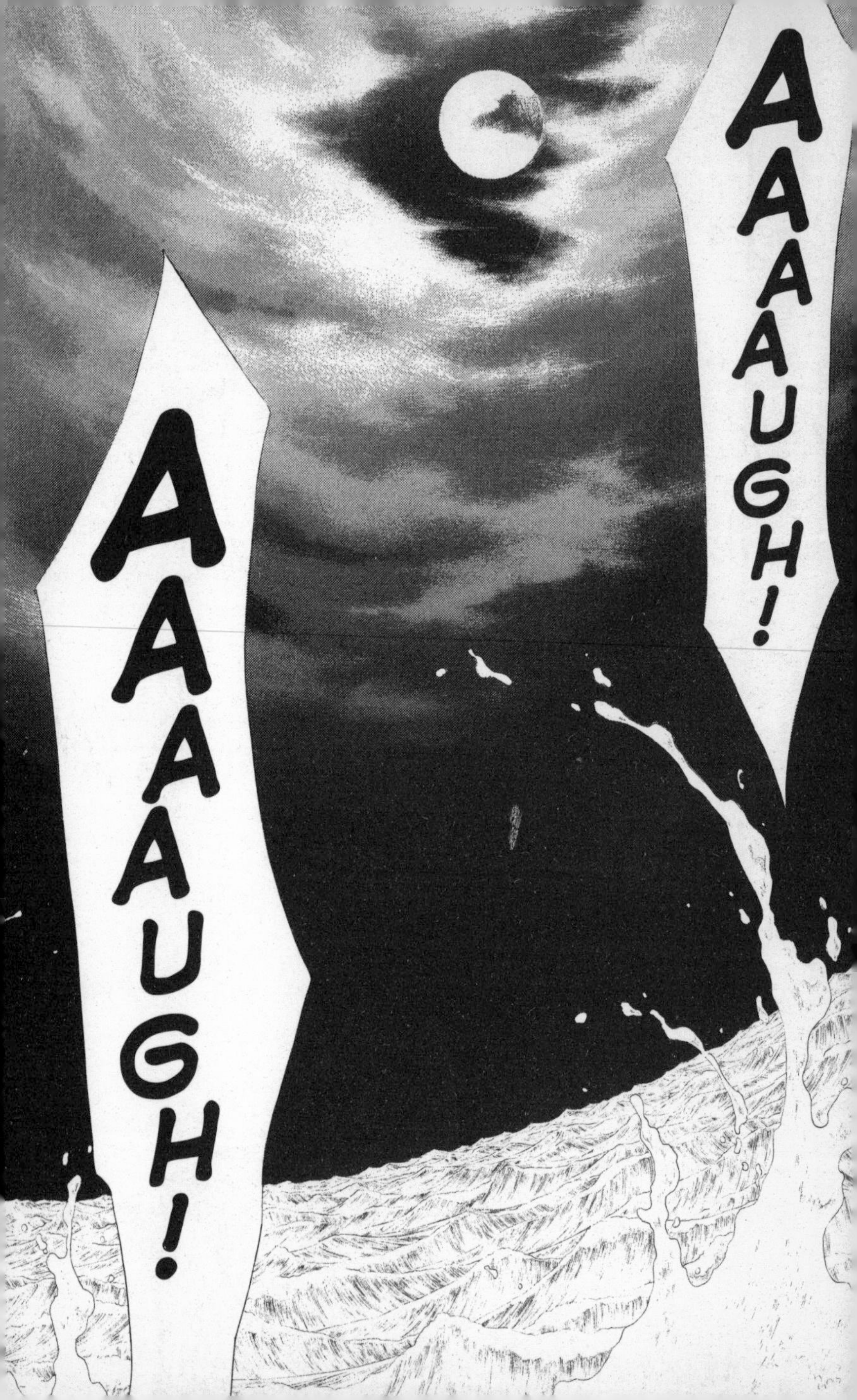
AAAAUGH!
AAAAUGH!

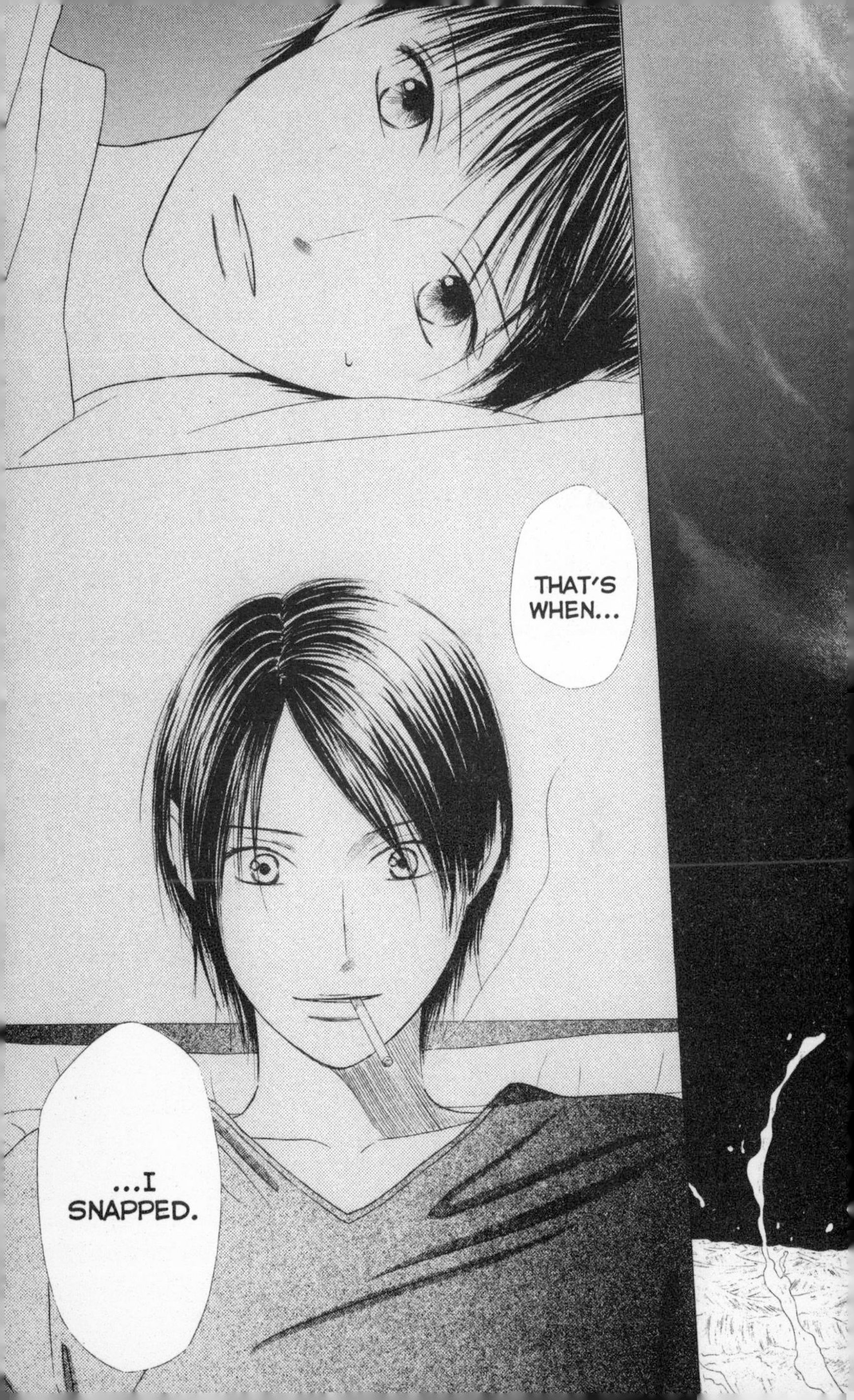
THAT'S WHEN...
...I SNAPPED.

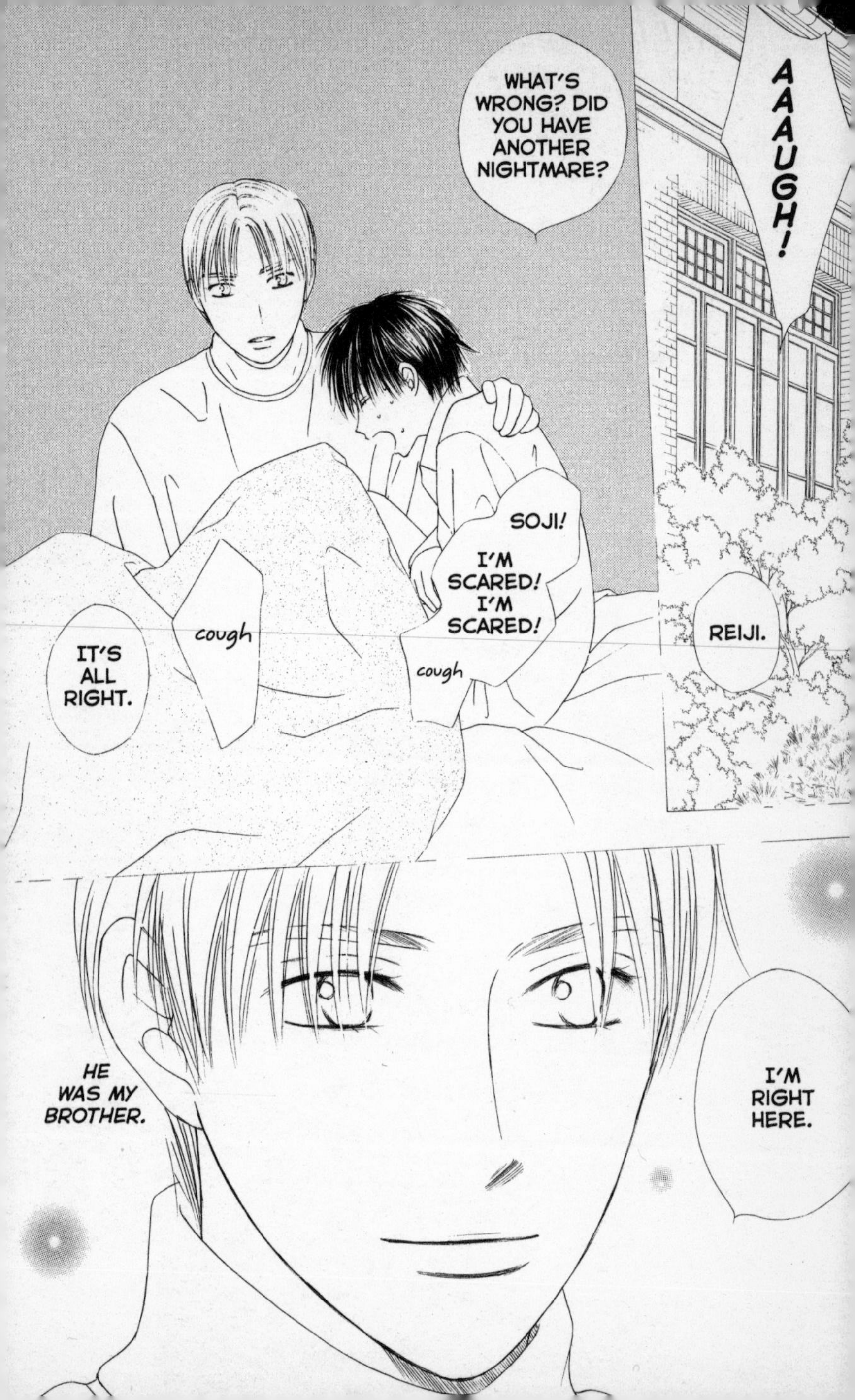
AAAUGH!
REIJI.
WHAT'S WRONG? DID YOU HAVE ANOTHER NIGHTMARE?
SOJI!
I'M SCARED! I'M SCARED!
cough
cough
IT'S ALL RIGHT.
I'M RIGHT HERE.
HE WAS MY BROTHER.

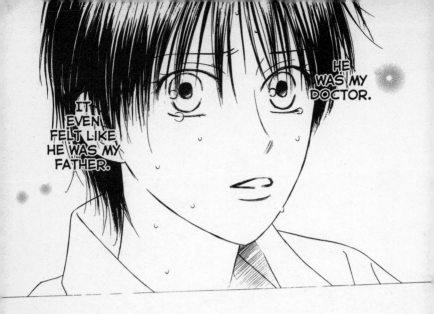

HE WAS MY DOCTOR.
IT EVEN FELT LIKE HE WAS MY FATHER.

THAT WAS SOJI.

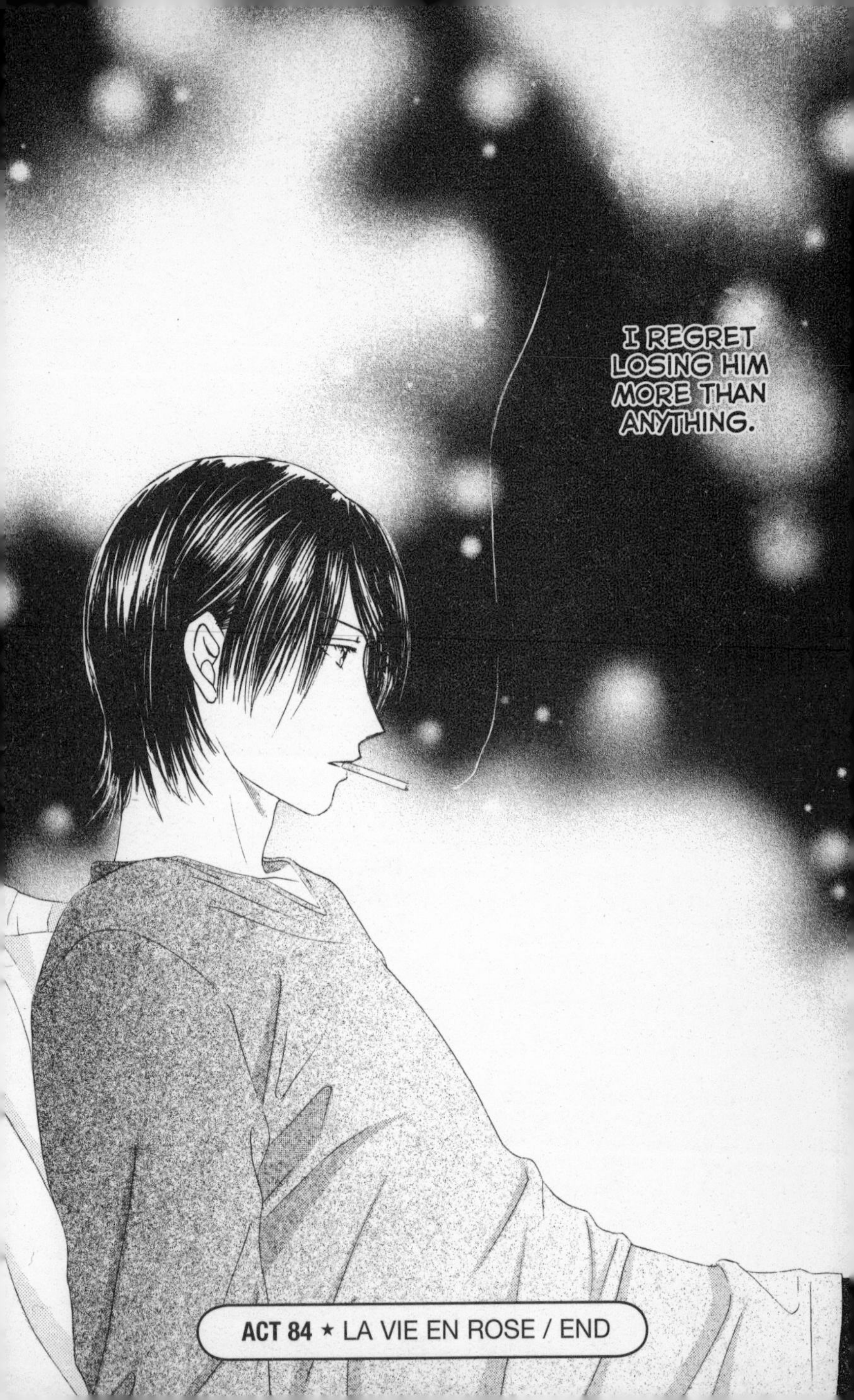
I REGRET LOSING HIM MORE THAN ANYTHING.
ACT 84 ★ LA VIE EN ROSE / END

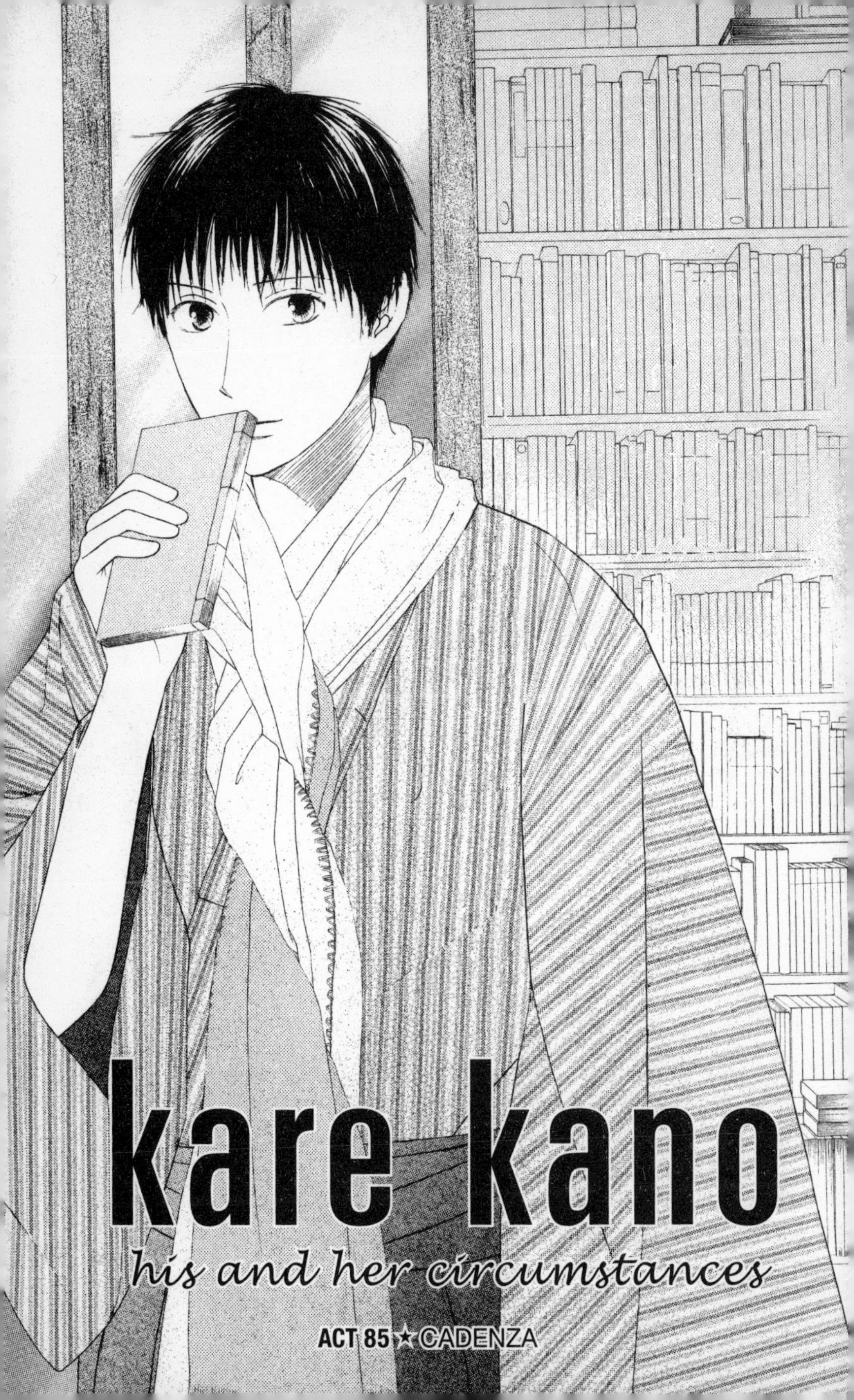
kare kano
his and her circumstances
ACT 85★CADENZA

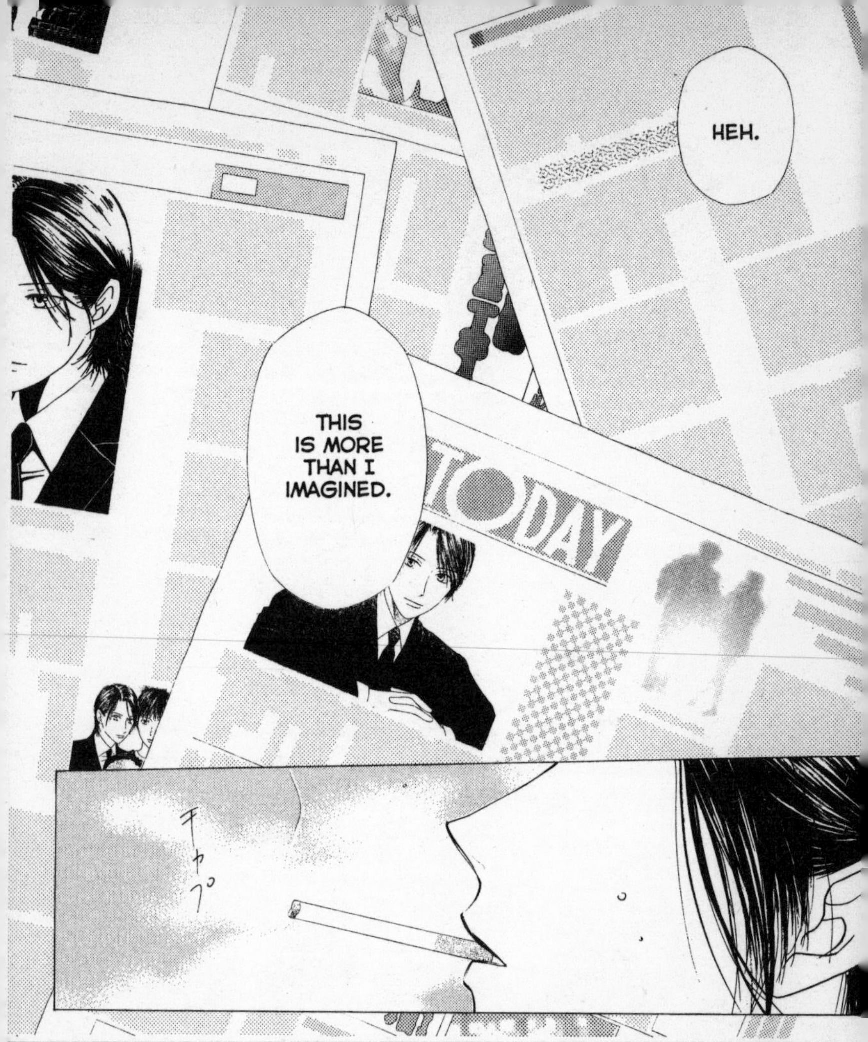
HEH.
THIS IS MORE THAN I IMAGINED.
TODAY
チャプ

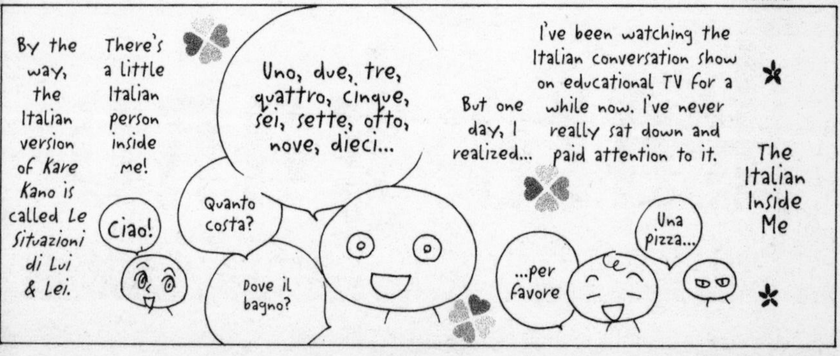
The Italian Inside Me
I've been watching the Italian conversation show on educational TV for a while now. I've never really sat down and paid attention to it.
But one day, I realized...
Uno, due, tre, quattro, cinque, sei, sette, otto, nove, dieci...
Una pizza...
...per favore
Quanto costa?
Dove il bagno?
Ciao!
There's a little Italian person inside me!
By the way, the Italian version of Kare Kano is called Le Situazioni di Lui & Lei.

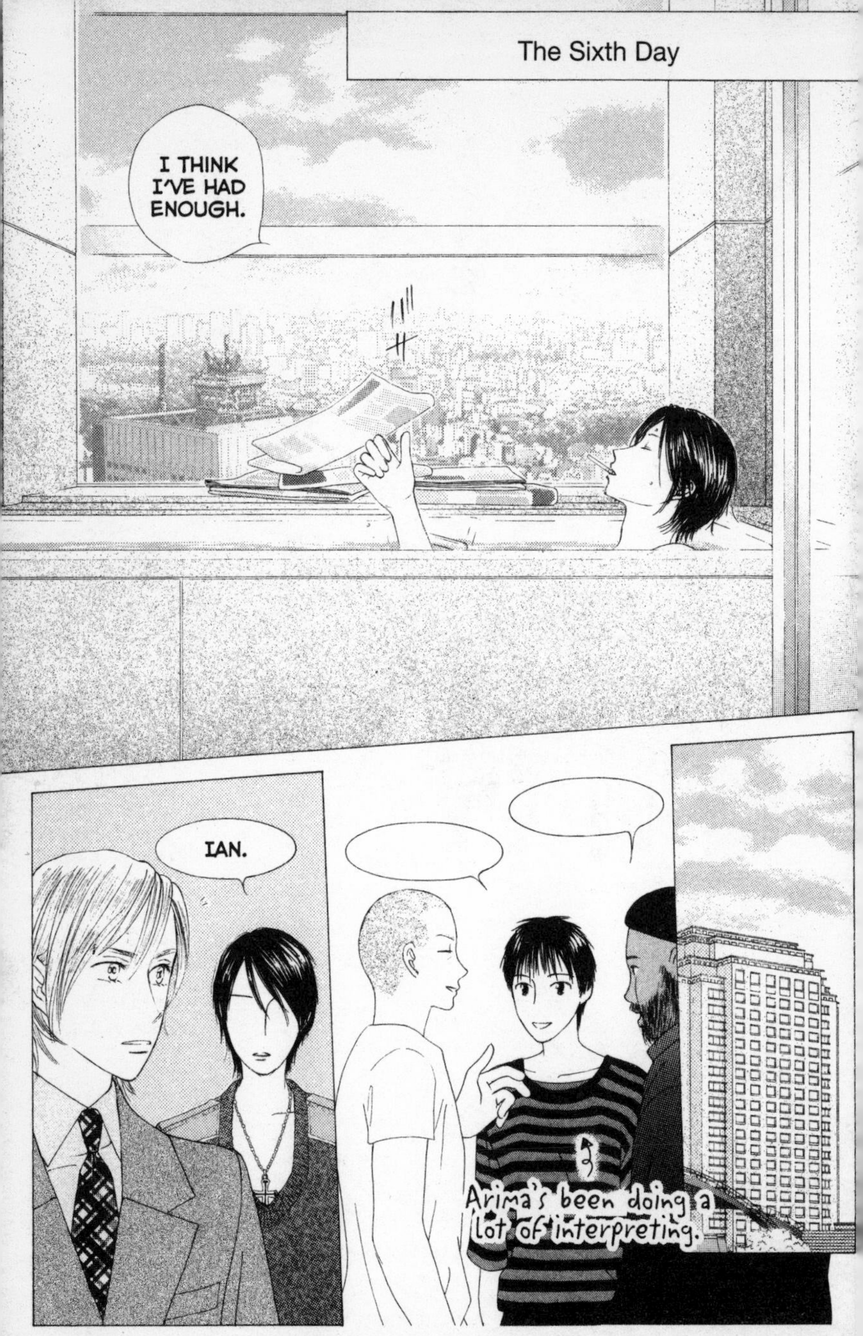
The Sixth Day
I THINK I'VE HAD ENOUGH.
Arima's been doing a lot of interpreting.
IAN.

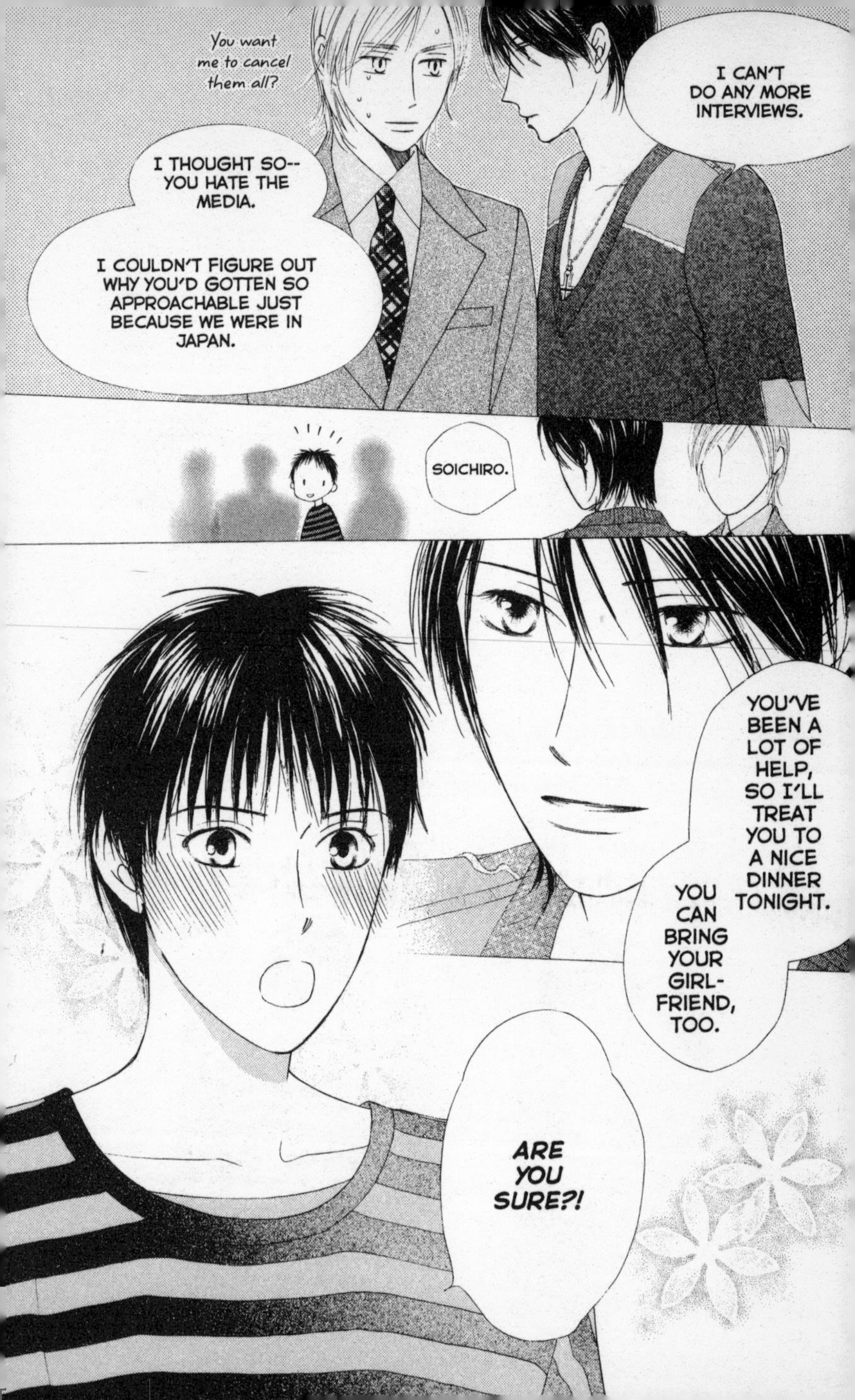
I CAN'T DO ANY MORE INTERVIEWS.
You want me to cancel them all?
I THOUGHT SO-- YOU HATE THE MEDIA.
I COULDN'T FIGURE OUT WHY YOU'D GOTTEN SO APPROACHABLE JUST BECAUSE WE WERE IN JAPAN.
SOICHIRO.
YOU'VE BEEN A LOT OF HELP, SO I'LL TREAT YOU TO A NICE DINNER TONIGHT.
YOU CAN BRING YOUR GIRL-FRIEND, TOO.
ARE YOU SURE?!

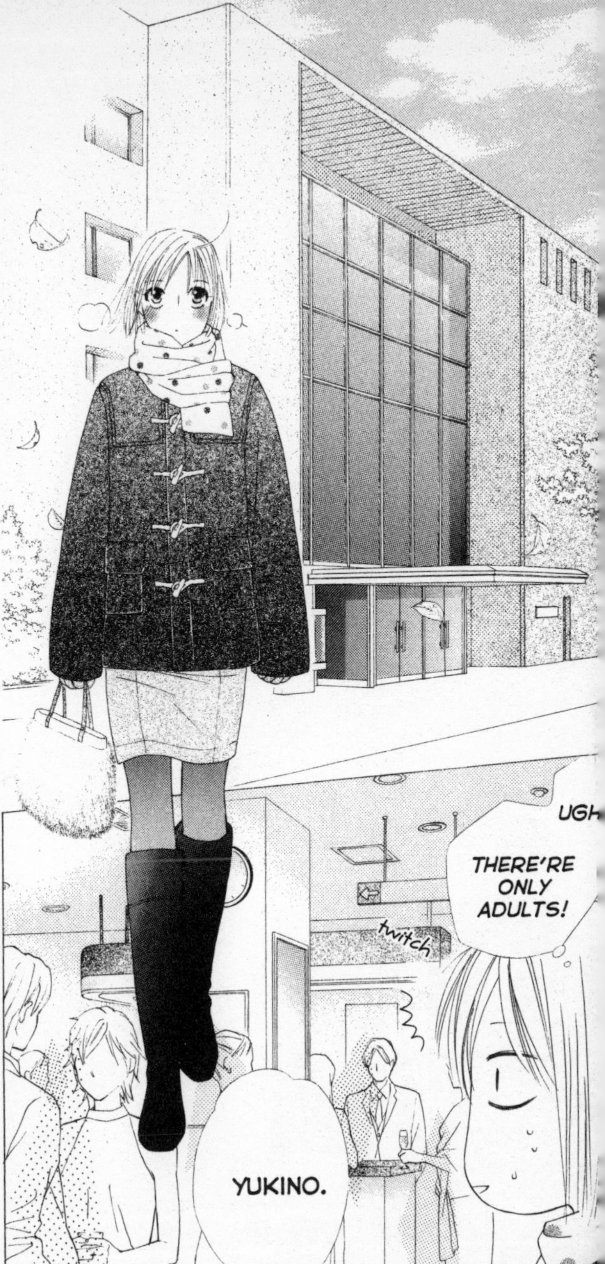
UGH
THERE'RE ONLY ADULTS!
twitch
YUKINO.

2

Organic cotton pajamas

I've been feeling like I need some new pajamas, and I happened to find this great store.

Everything's made of this airy, soft, warm cloth. They're perfect for winter. ♡

Good for lounging around the house, too.

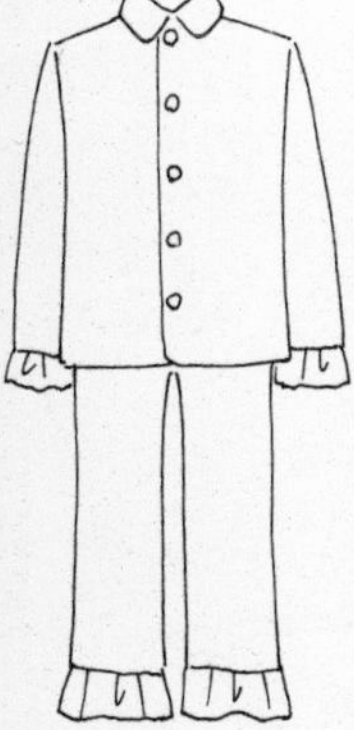

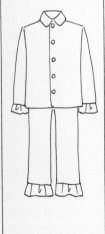

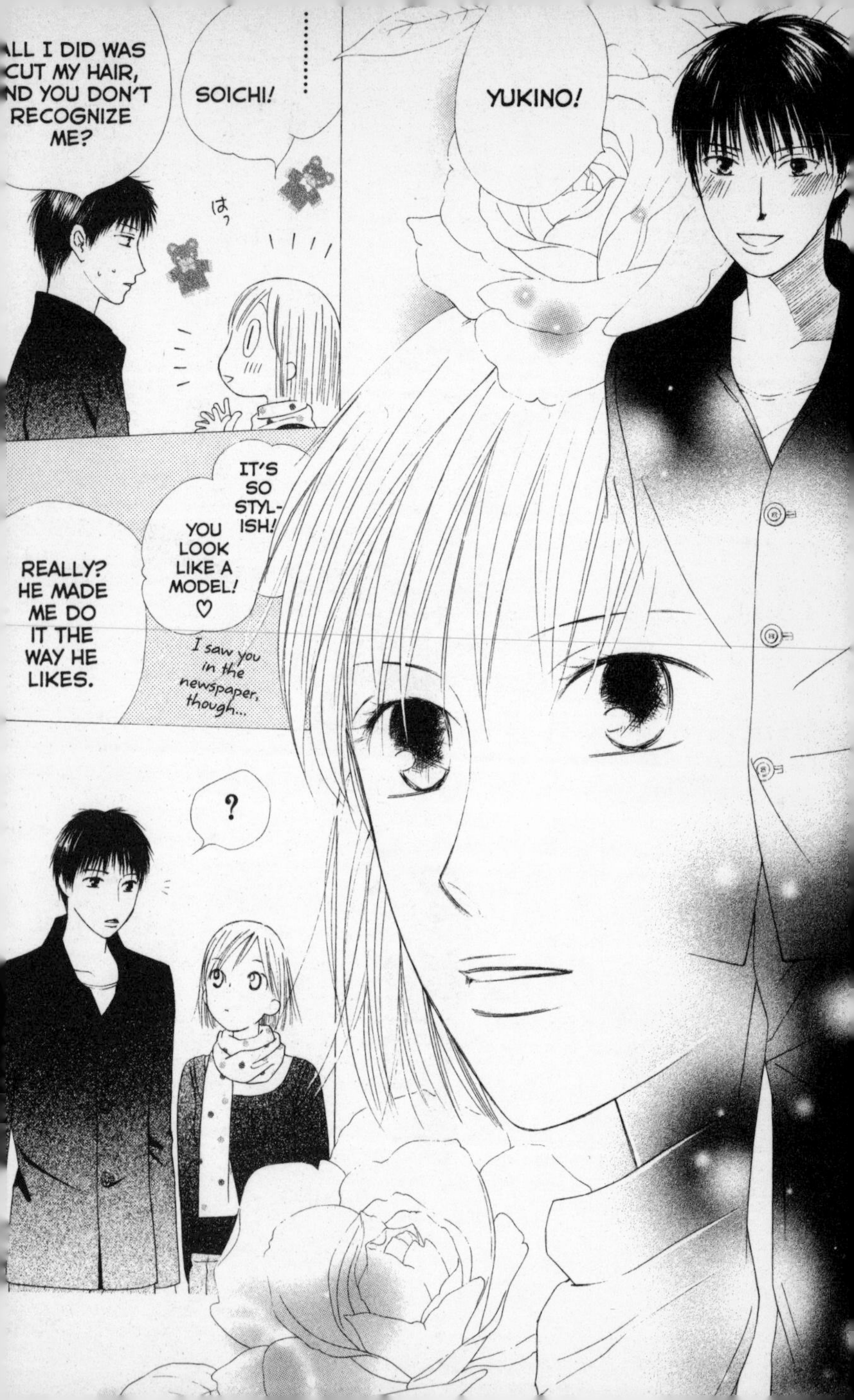

YUKINO!
......
SOICHI!
LL I DID WAS CUT MY HAIR, ND YOU DON'T RECOGNIZE ME?
はっ
IT'S SO STYL-ISH!
YOU LOOK LIKE A MODEL! ♡
REALLY? HE MADE ME DO IT THE WAY HE LIKES.
I saw you in the newspaper, though...
?

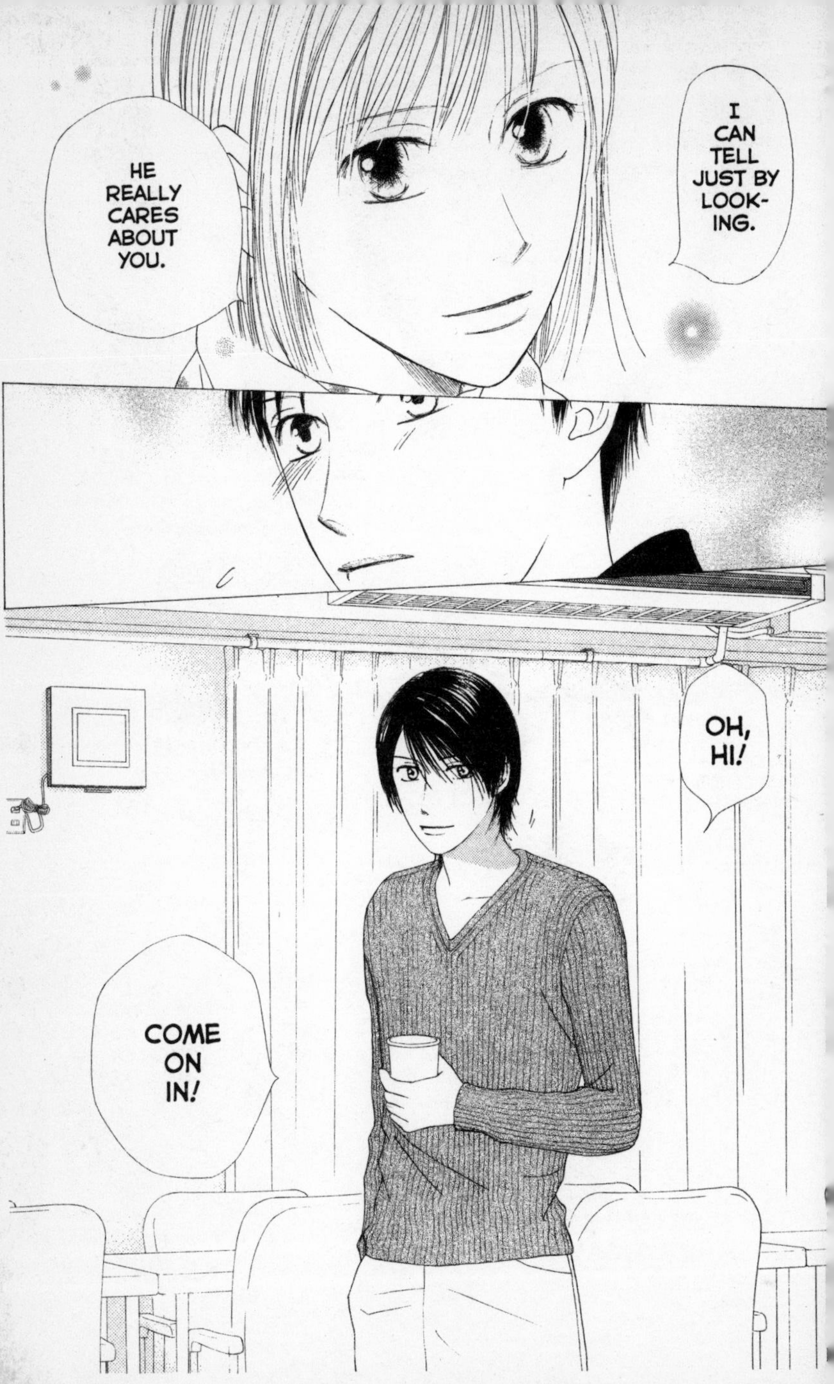
I CAN TELL JUST BY LOOK-ING.
HE REALLY CARES ABOUT YOU.
OH, HI!
COME ON IN!

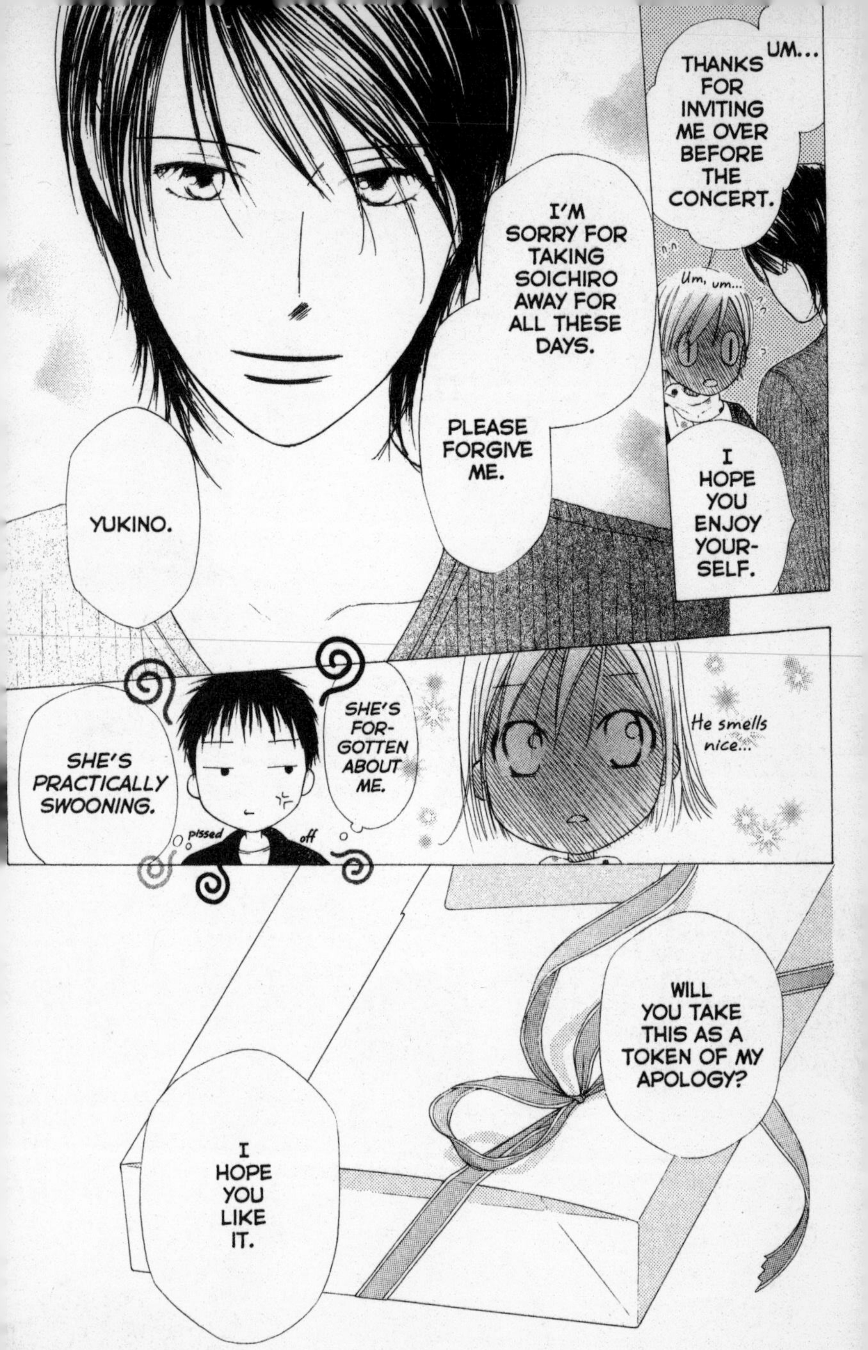
UM...
THANKS FOR INVITING ME OVER BEFORE THE CONCERT.
Um, um...
I HOPE YOU ENJOY YOUR-SELF.
I'M SORRY FOR TAKING SOICHIRO AWAY FOR ALL THESE DAYS.
PLEASE FORGIVE ME.
YUKINO.
He smells nice...
SHE'S FOR-GOTTEN ABOUT ME.
pissed off
SHE'S PRACTICALLY SWOONING.
WILL YOU TAKE THIS AS A TOKEN OF MY APOLOGY?
I HOPE YOU LIKE IT.

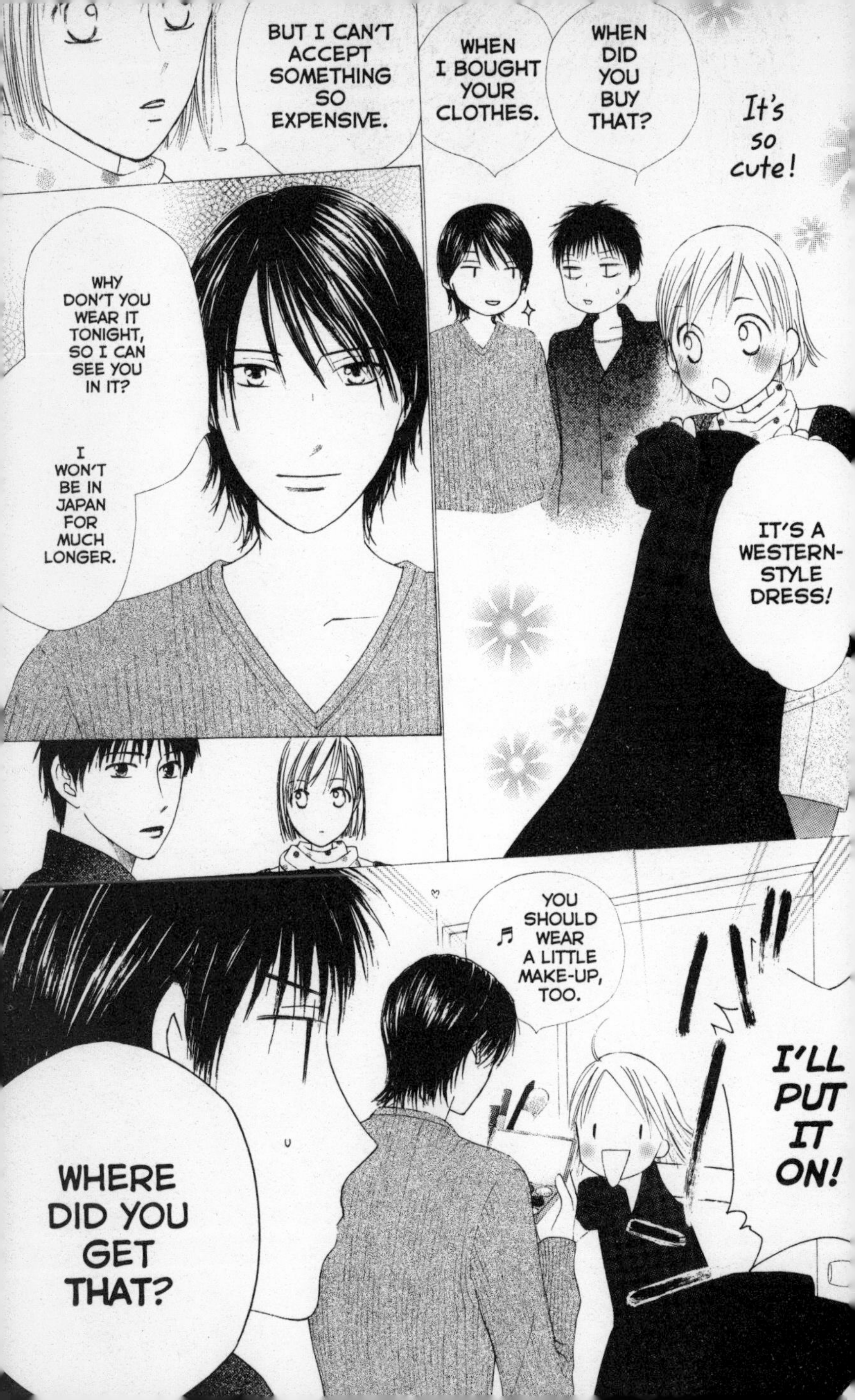
WHEN DID YOU BUY THAT?
WHEN I BOUGHT YOUR CLOTHES.
It's so cute!
IT'S A WESTERN-STYLE DRESS!
BUT I CAN'T ACCEPT SOMETHING SO EXPENSIVE.
WHY DON'T YOU WEAR IT TONIGHT, SO I CAN SEE YOU IN IT?
I WON'T BE IN JAPAN FOR MUCH LONGER.
I'LL PUT IT ON!
YOU SHOULD WEAR A LITTLE MAKE-UP, TOO. ♬
WHERE DID YOU GET THAT?

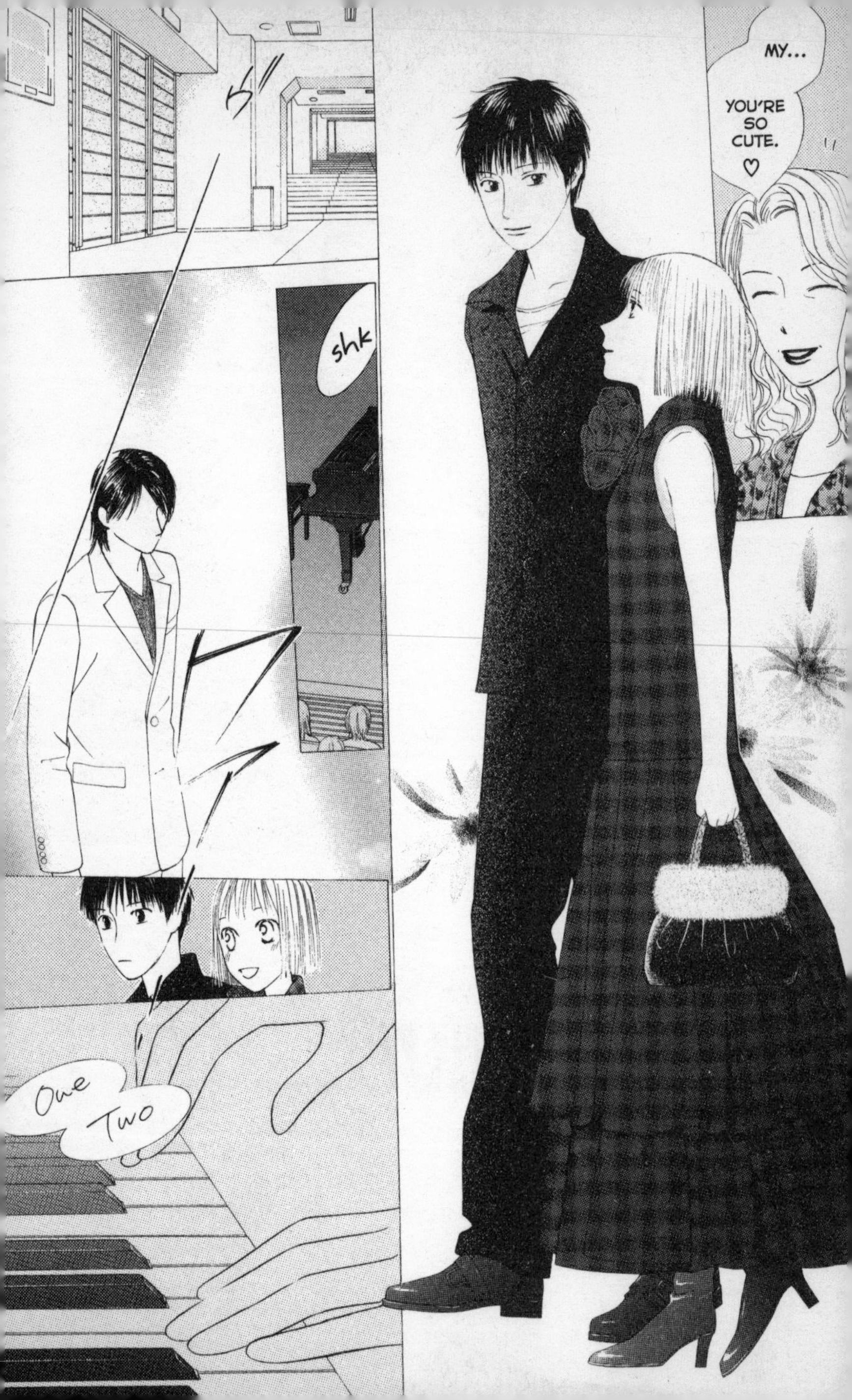
MY...
YOU'RE SO CUTE. ♡
shk
One Two

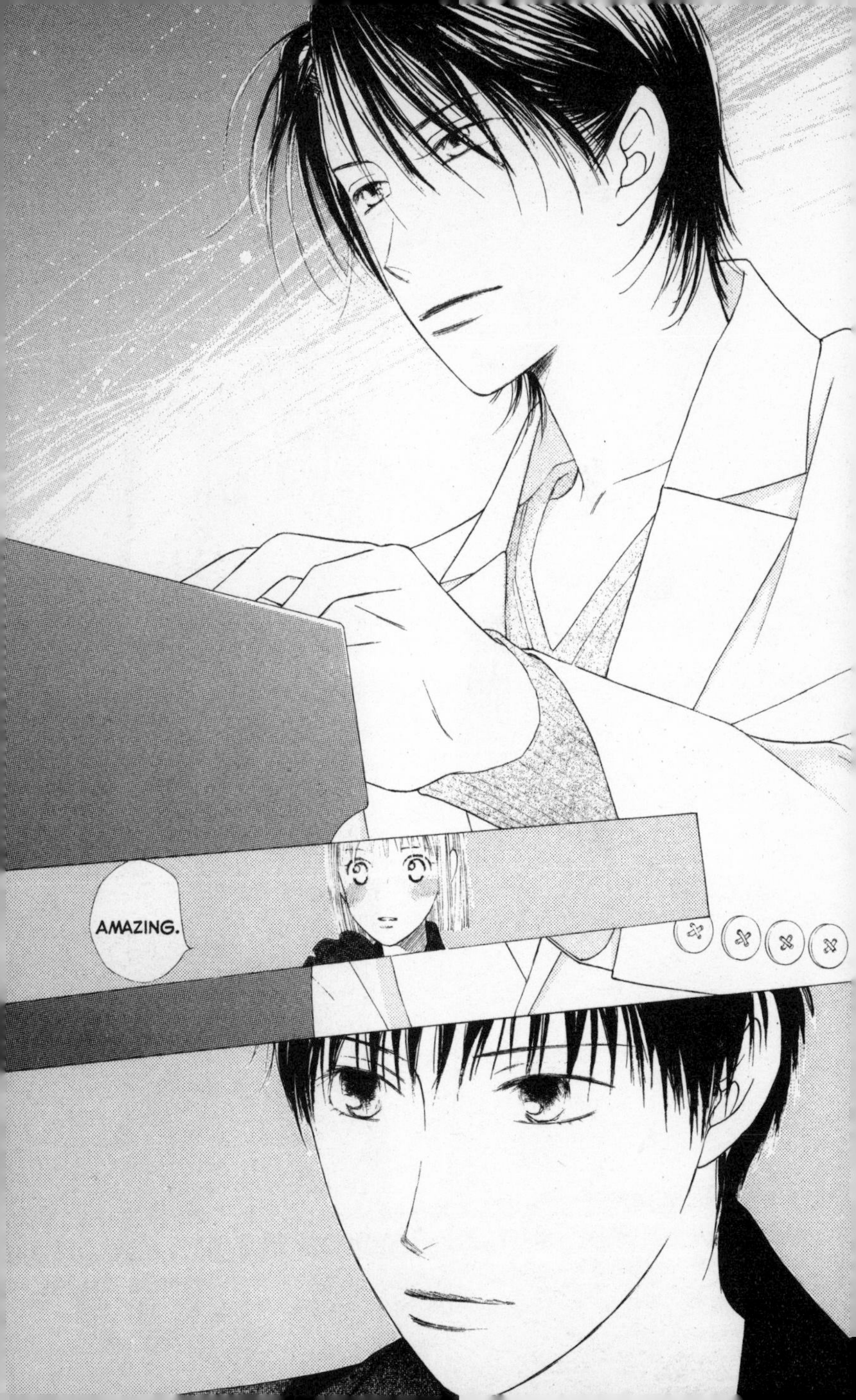
AMAZING.

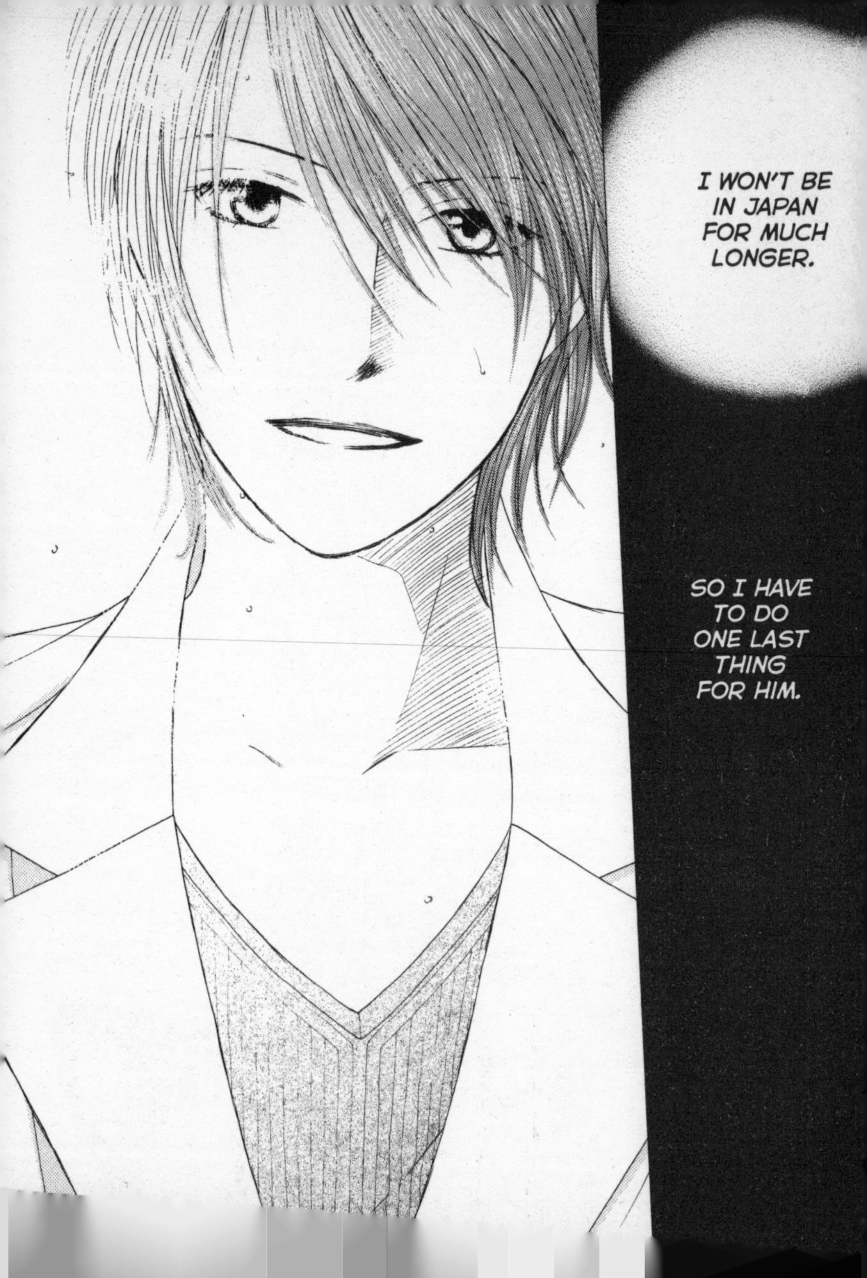
I WON'T BE IN JAPAN FOR MUCH LONGER.
SO I HAVE TO DO ONE LAST THING FOR HIM.

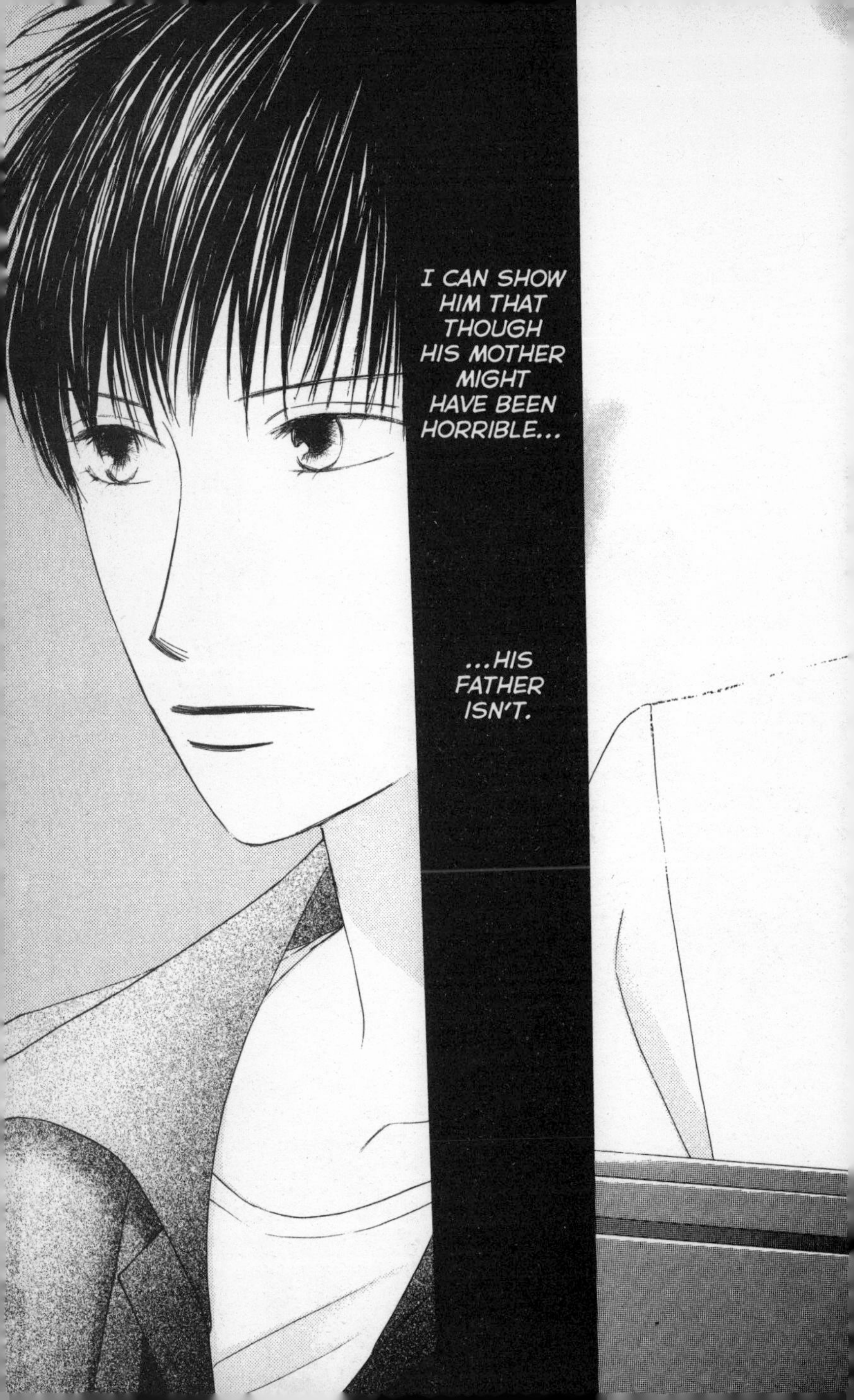
I CAN SHOW HIM THAT THOUGH HIS MOTHER MIGHT HAVE BEEN HORRIBLE...
...HIS FATHER ISN'T.

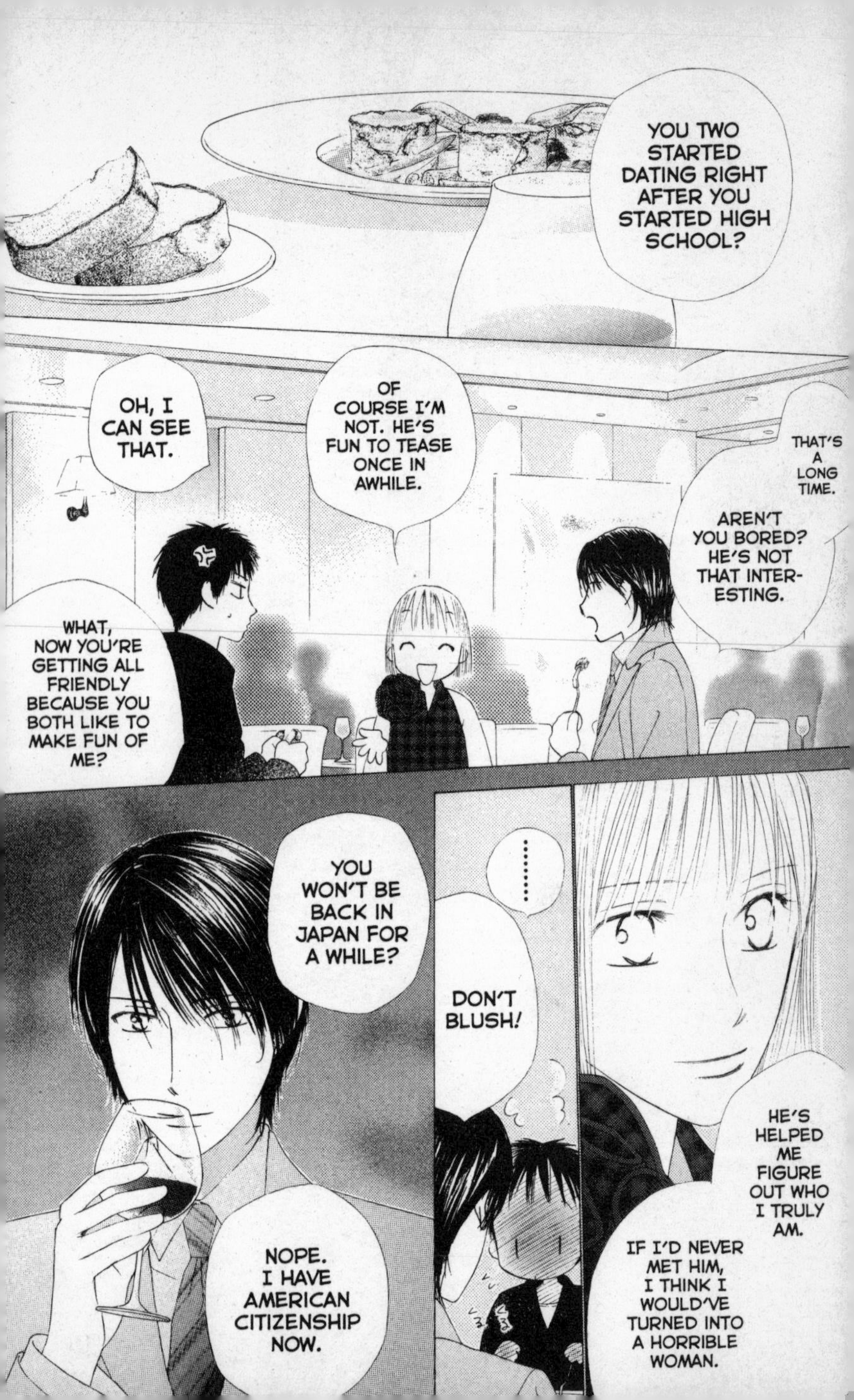
YOU TWO STARTED DATING RIGHT AFTER YOU STARTED HIGH SCHOOL?
THAT'S A LONG TIME.
AREN'T YOU BORED? HE'S NOT THAT INTER-ESTING.
OF COURSE I'M NOT. HE'S FUN TO TEASE ONCE IN AWHILE.
OH, I CAN SEE THAT.
WHAT, NOW YOU'RE GETTING ALL FRIENDLY BECAUSE YOU BOTH LIKE TO MAKE FUN OF ME?
HE'S HELPED ME FIGURE OUT WHO I TRULY AM.
IF I'D NEVER MET HIM, I THINK I WOULD'VE TURNED INTO A HORRIBLE WOMAN.
......
DON'T BLUSH!
YOU WON'T BE BACK IN JAPAN FOR A WHILE?
NOPE. I HAVE AMERICAN CITIZENSHIP NOW.

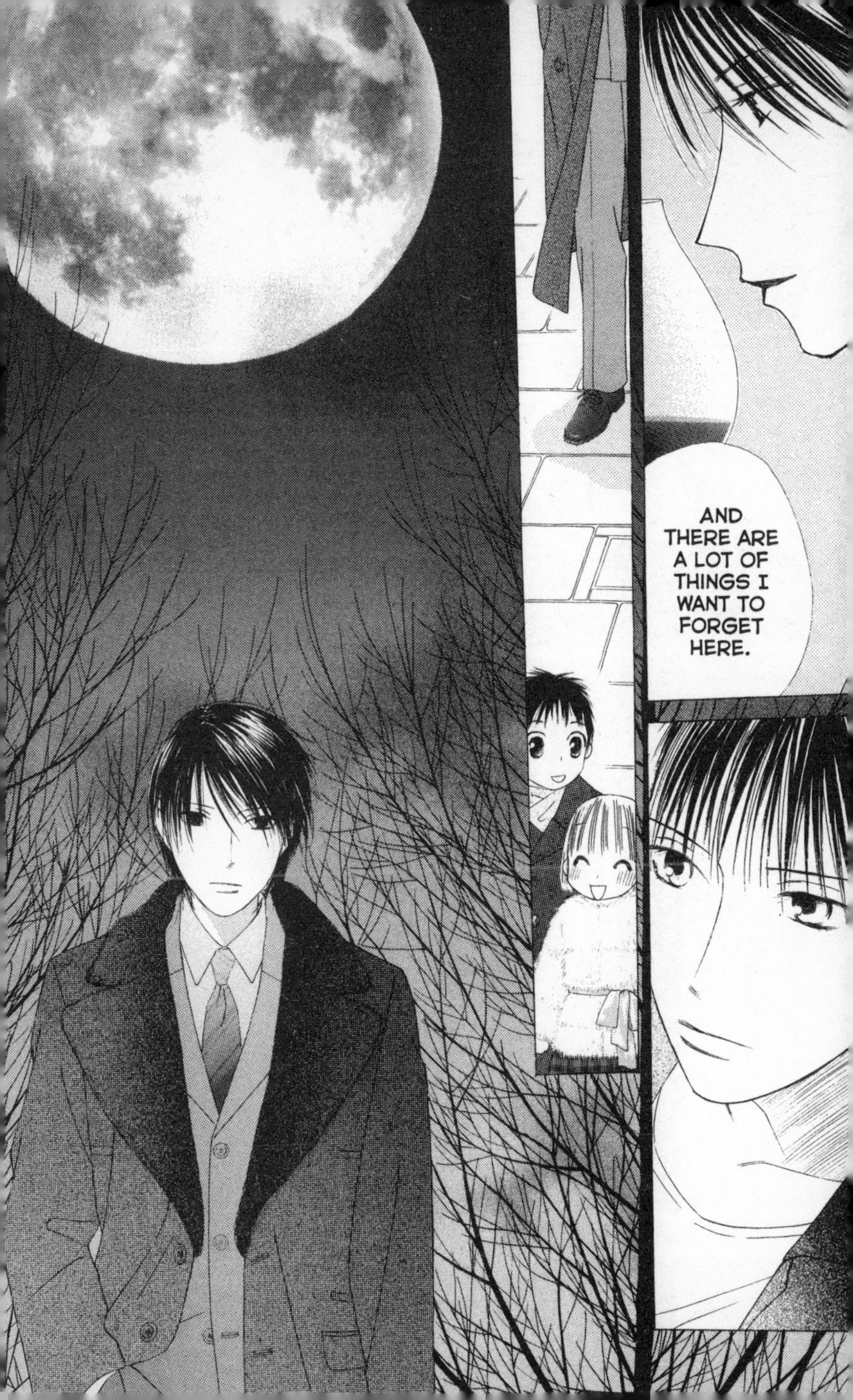
AND THERE ARE A LOT OF THINGS I WANT TO FORGET HERE.

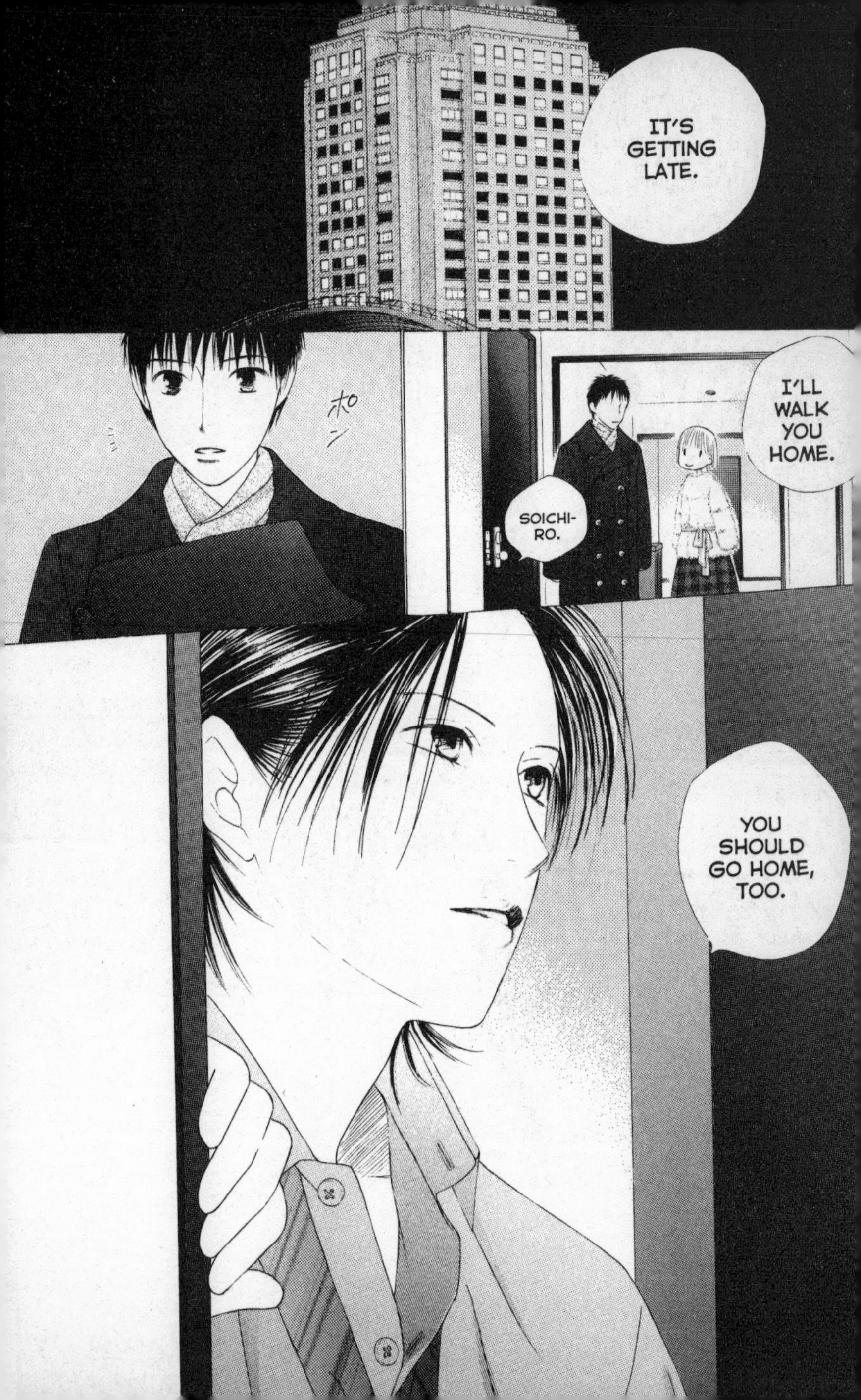
IT'S GETTING LATE.
I'LL WALK YOU HOME.
SOICHI-RO.
ポン
YOU SHOULD GO HOME, TOO.

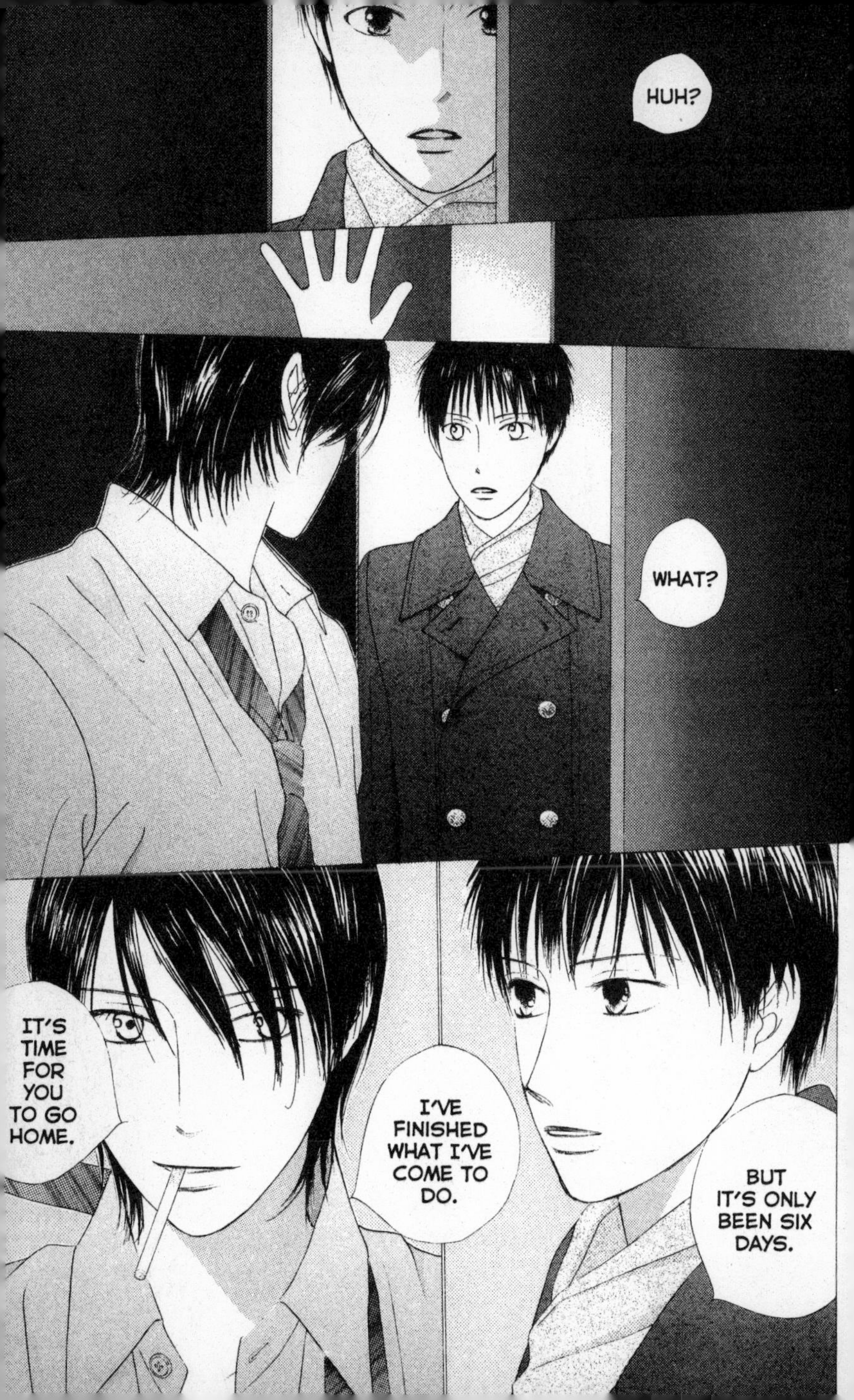
HUH?
WHAT?
BUT IT'S ONLY BEEN SIX DAYS.
I'VE FINISHED WHAT I'VE COME TO DO.
IT'S TIME FOR YOU TO GO HOME.

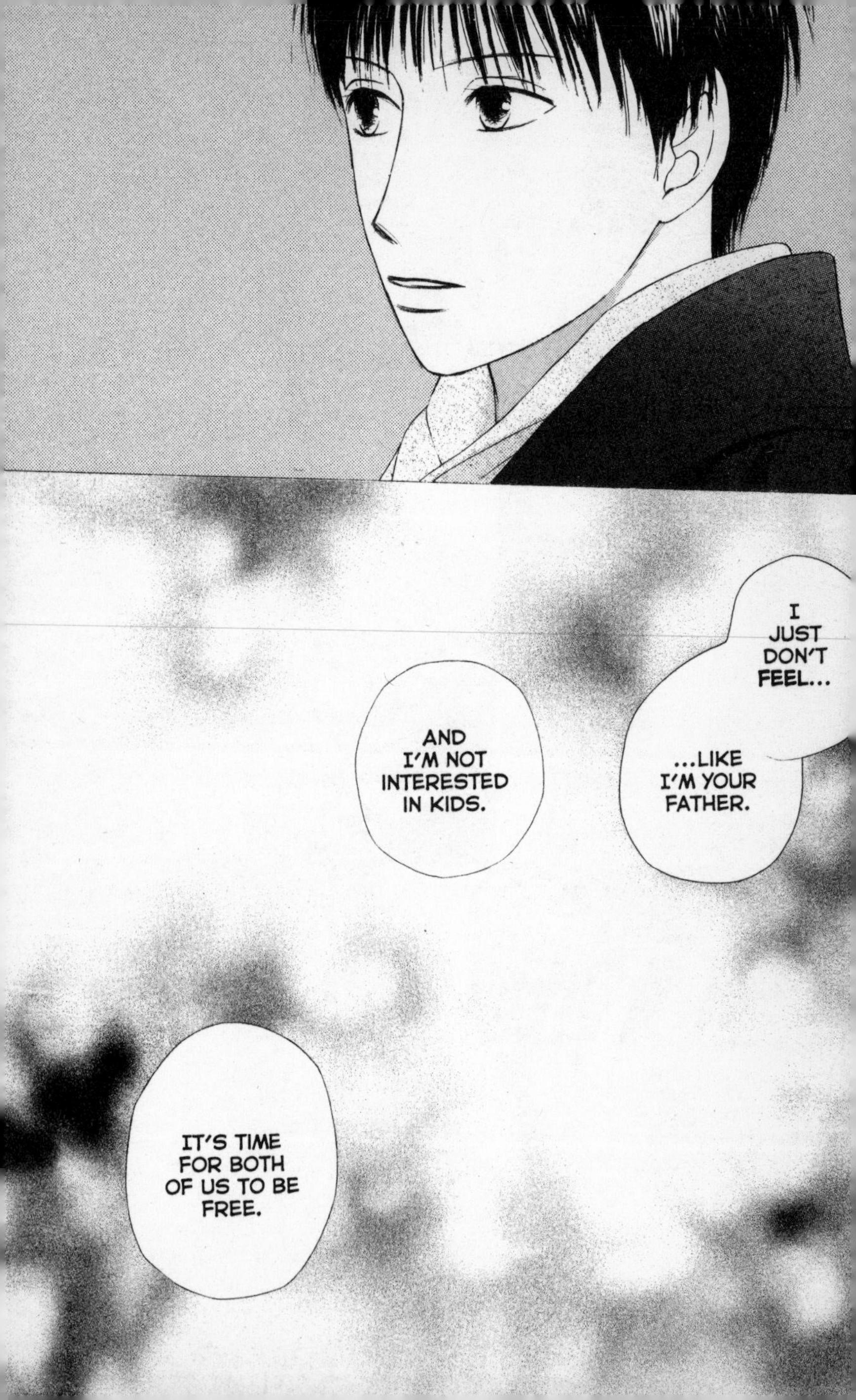
I JUST DON'T FEEL...
...LIKE I'M YOUR FATHER.
AND I'M NOT INTERESTED IN KIDS.
IT'S TIME FOR BOTH OF US TO BE FREE.

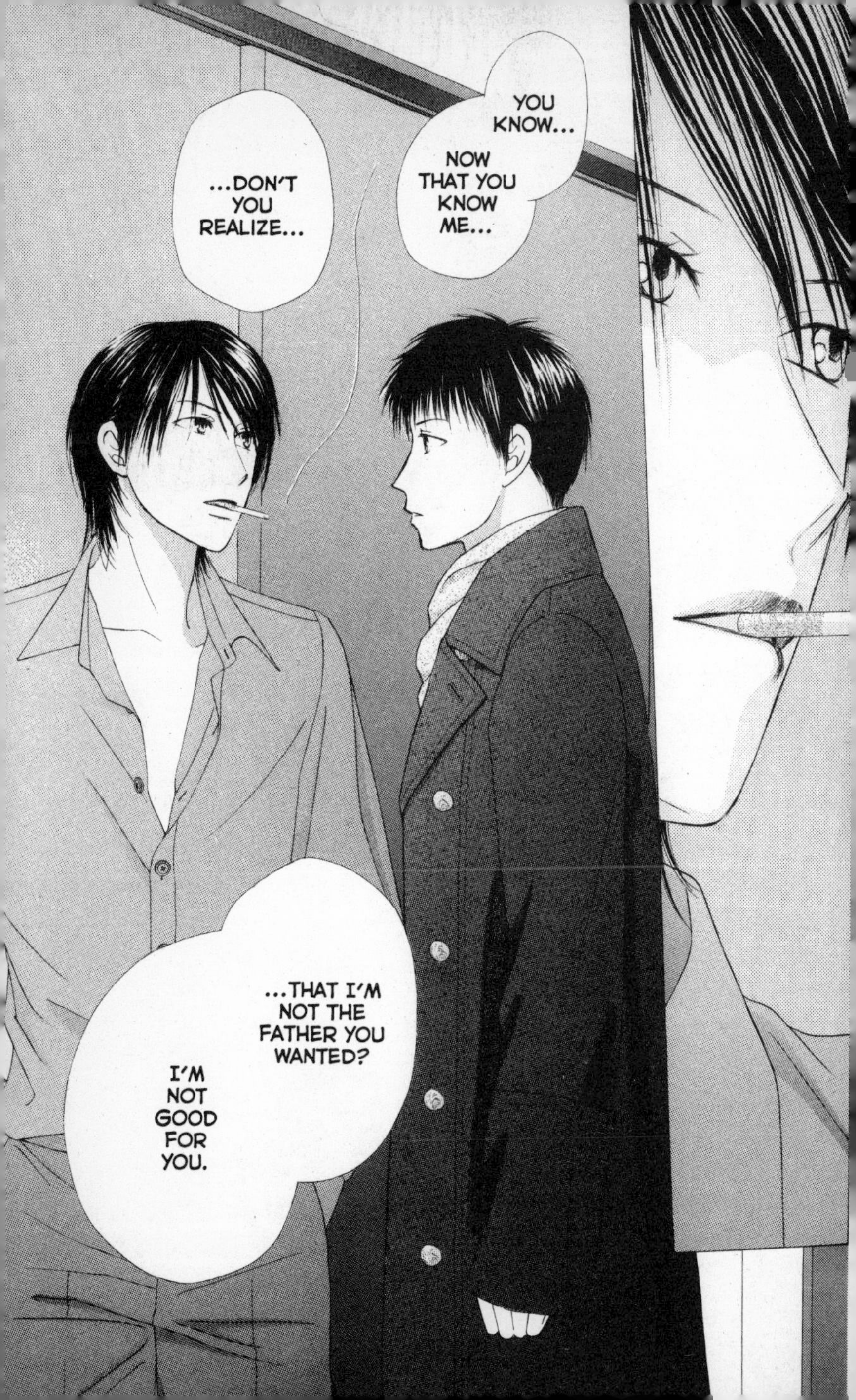
YOU KNOW...
NOW THAT YOU KNOW ME...
...DON'T YOU REALIZE...
...THAT I'M NOT THE FATHER YOU WANTED?
I'M NOT GOOD FOR YOU.

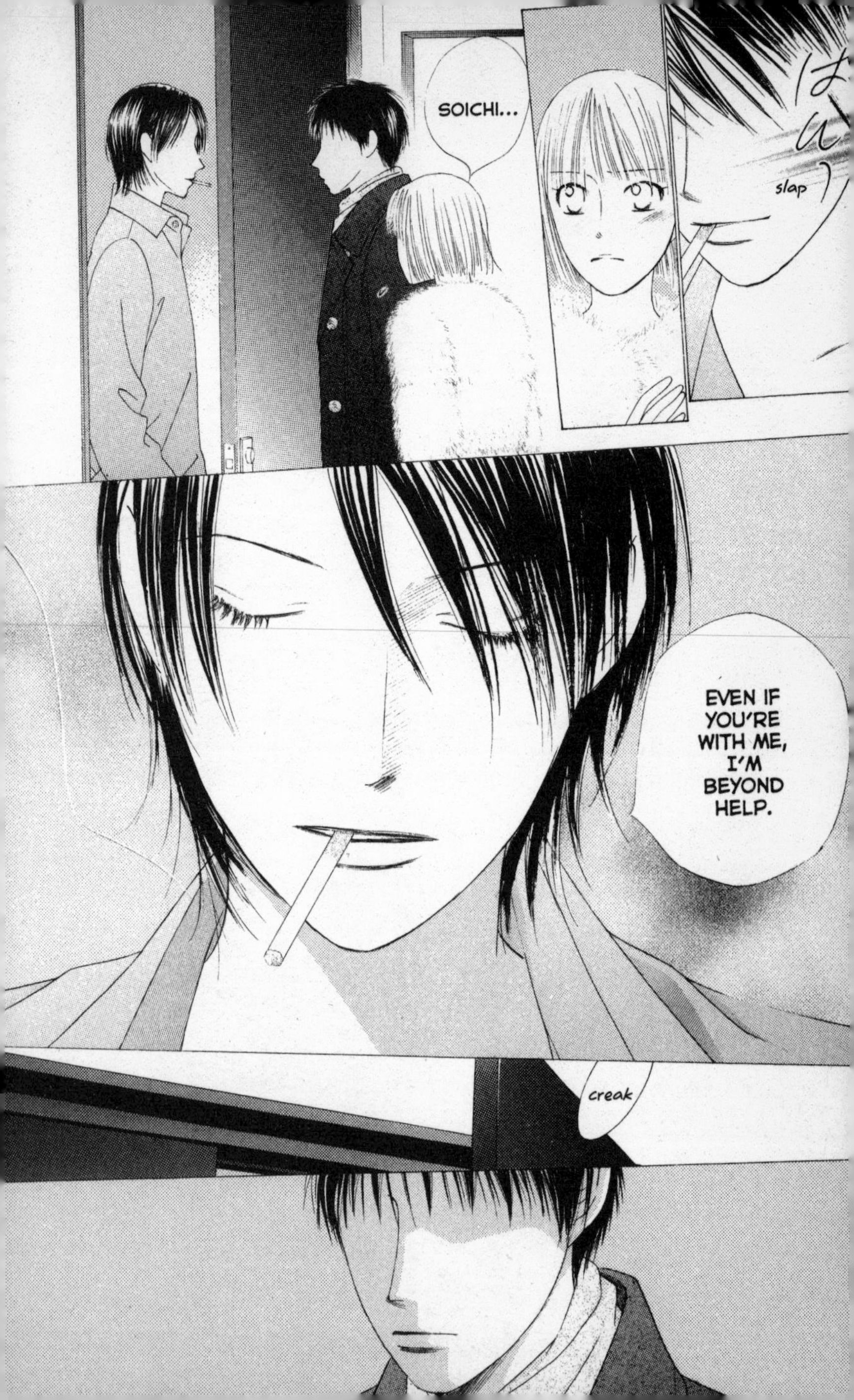
slap
SOICHI...
EVEN IF YOU'RE WITH ME, I'M BEYOND HELP.
creak

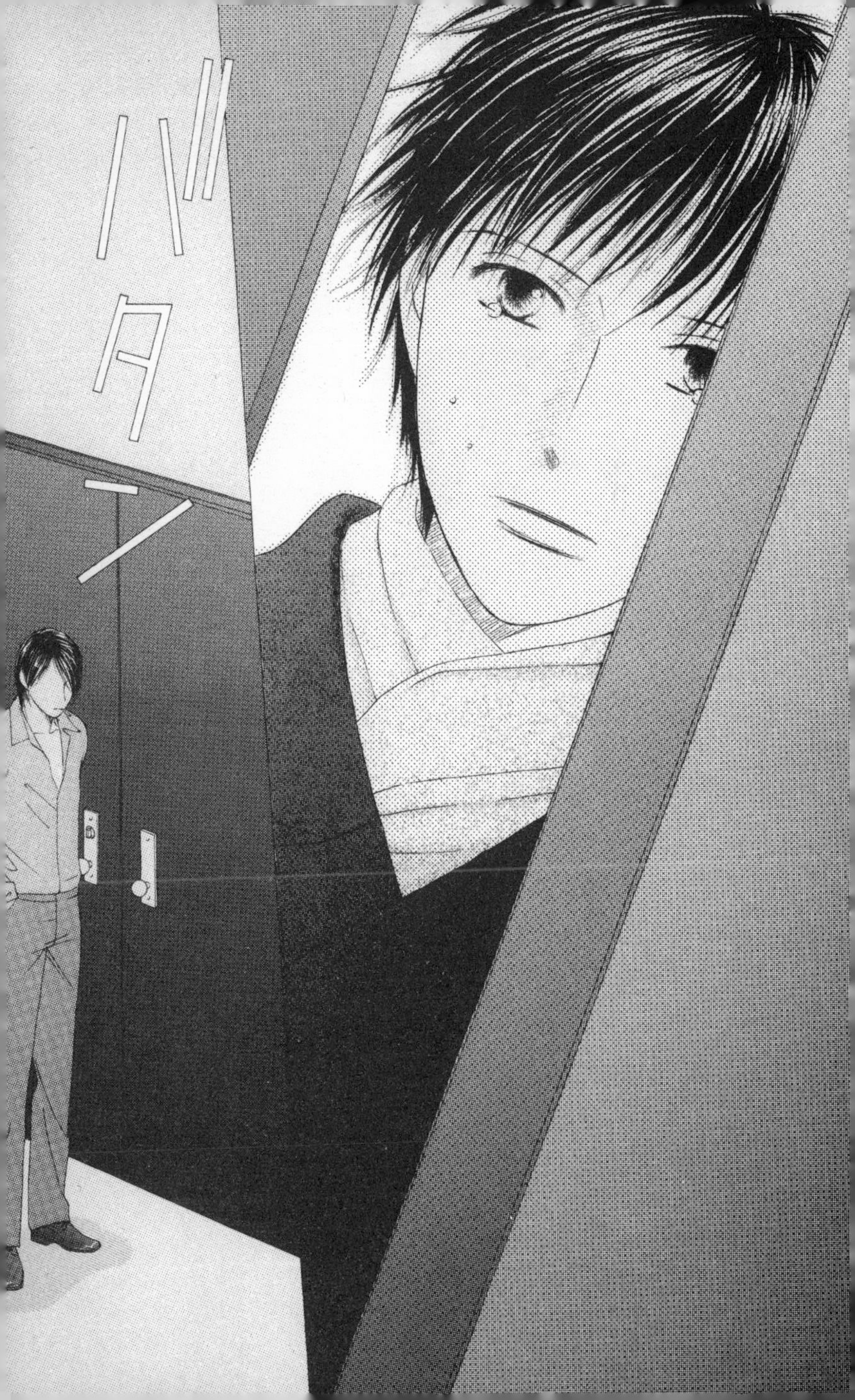
バタン

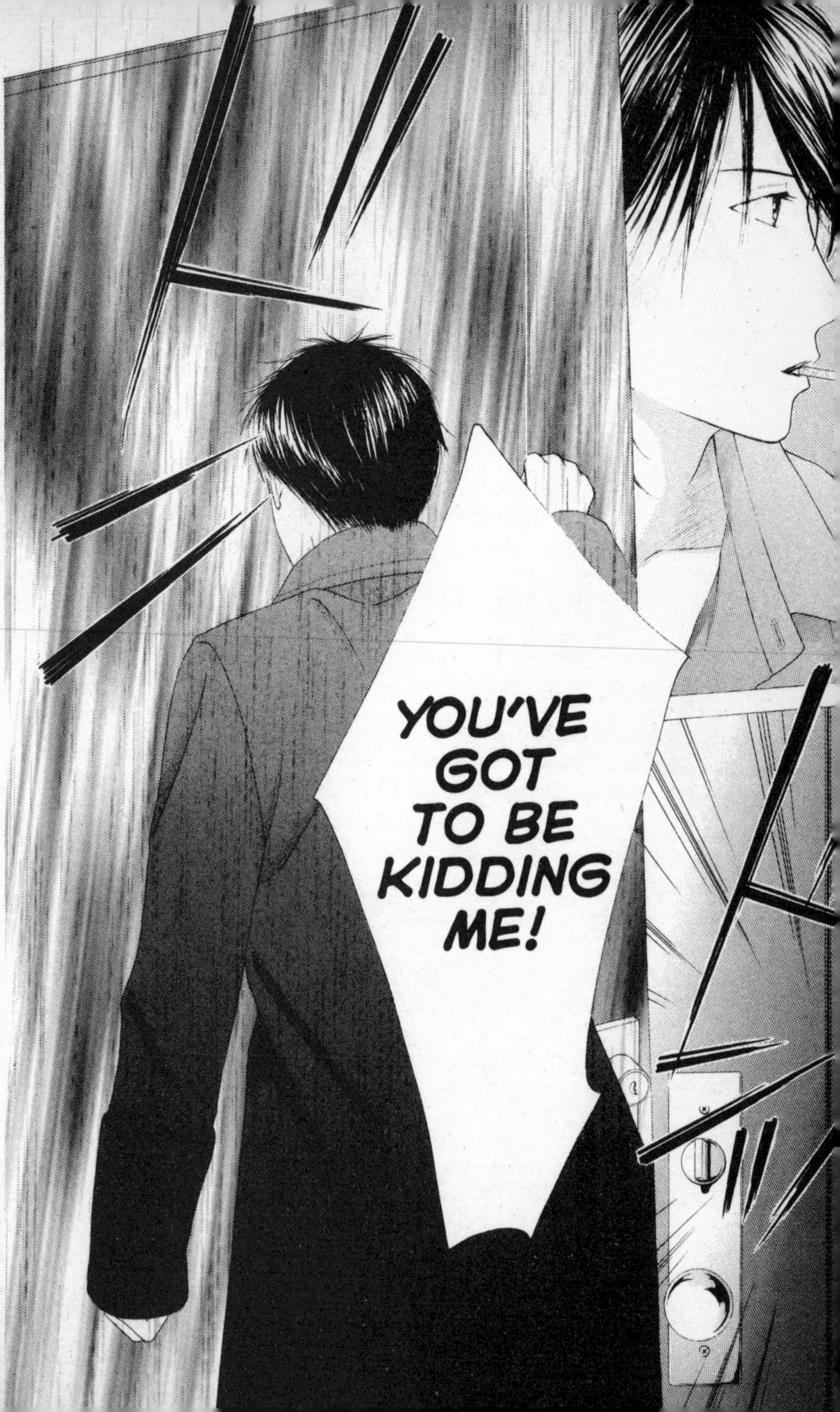
YOU'VE GOT TO BE KIDDING ME!

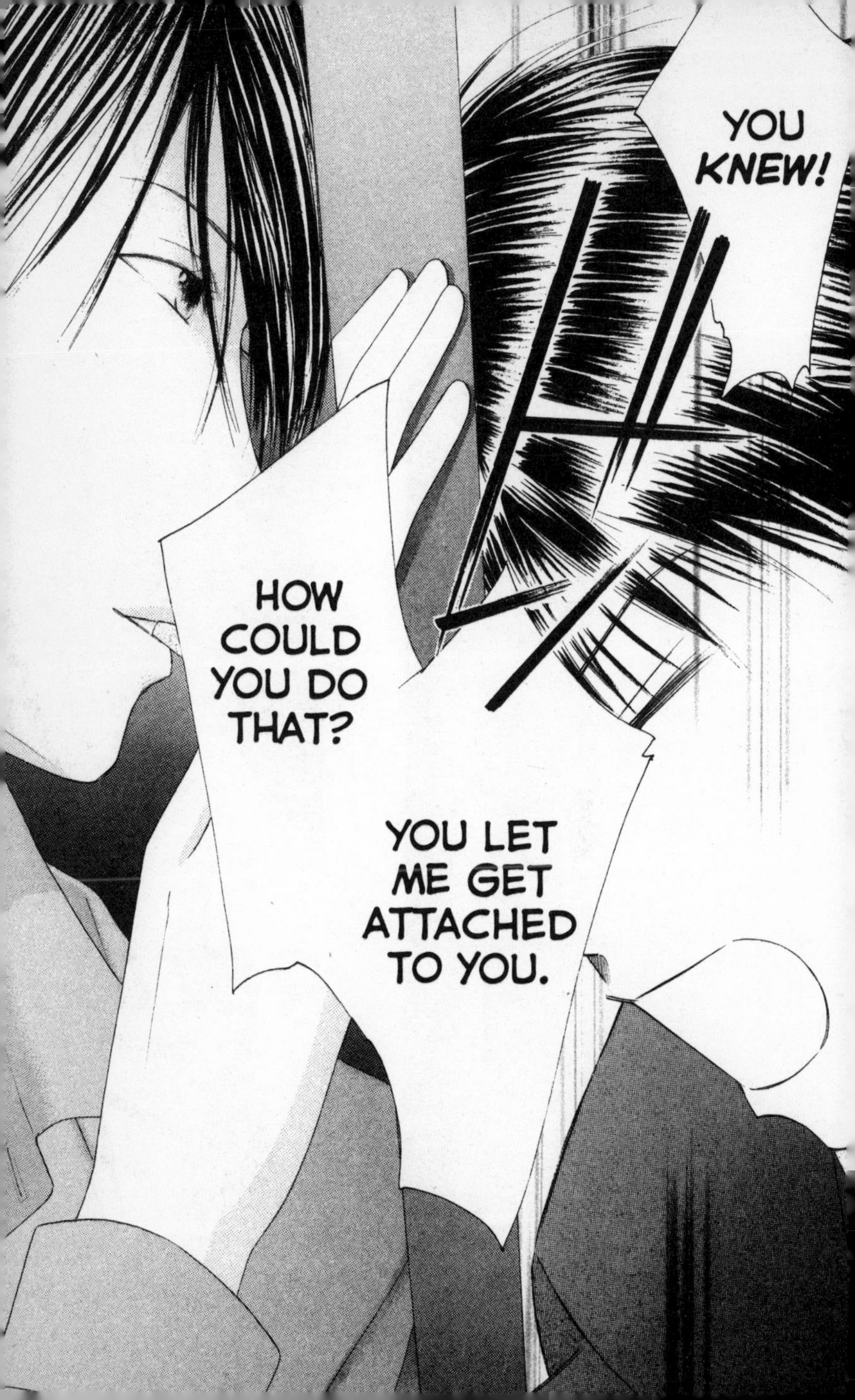
YOU KNEW!
HOW COULD YOU DO THAT?
YOU LET ME GET ATTACHED TO YOU.

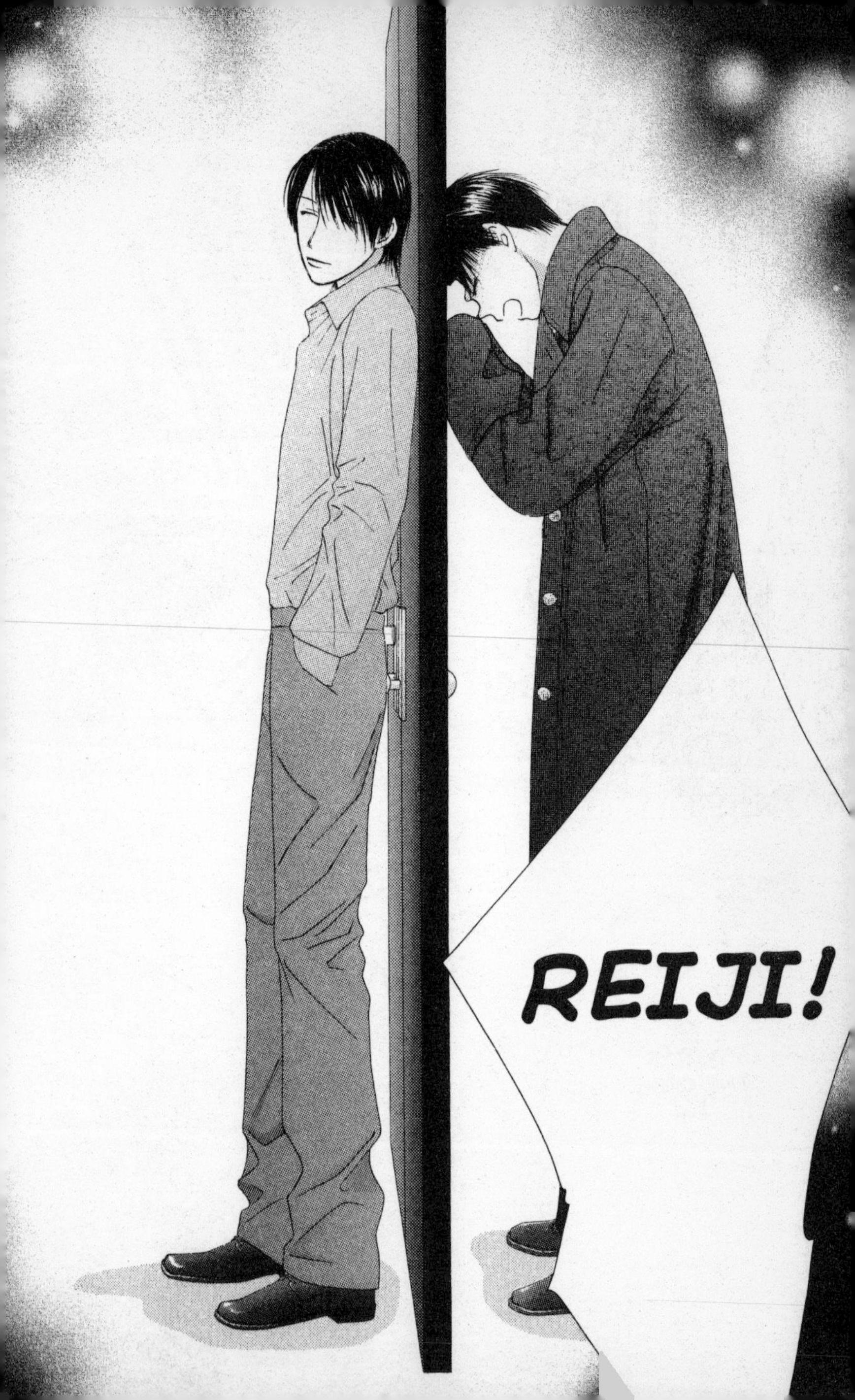
REIJI!

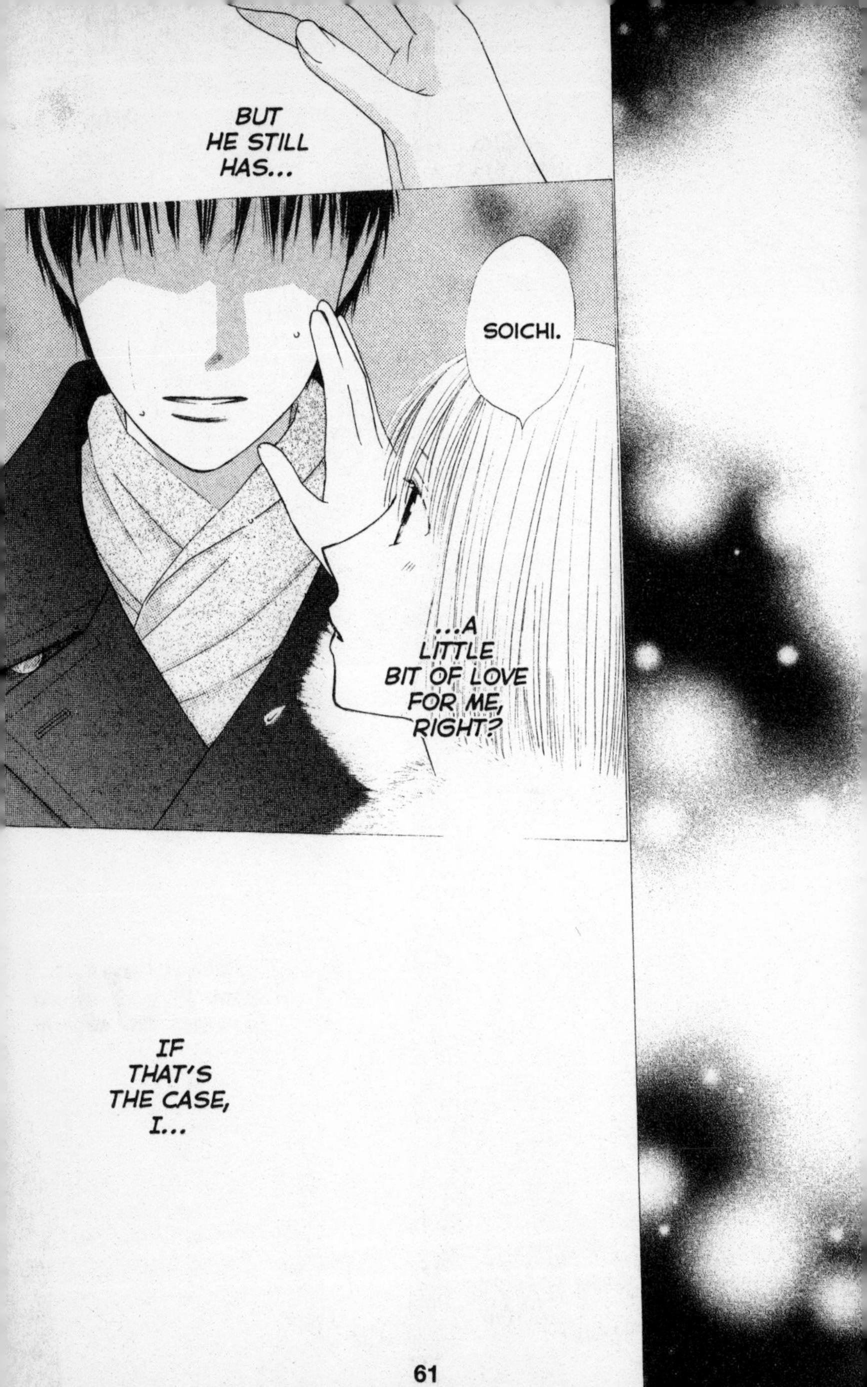
BUT HE STILL HAS...
SOICHI.
...A LITTLE BIT OF LOVE FOR ME, RIGHT?
IF THAT'S THE CASE, I...

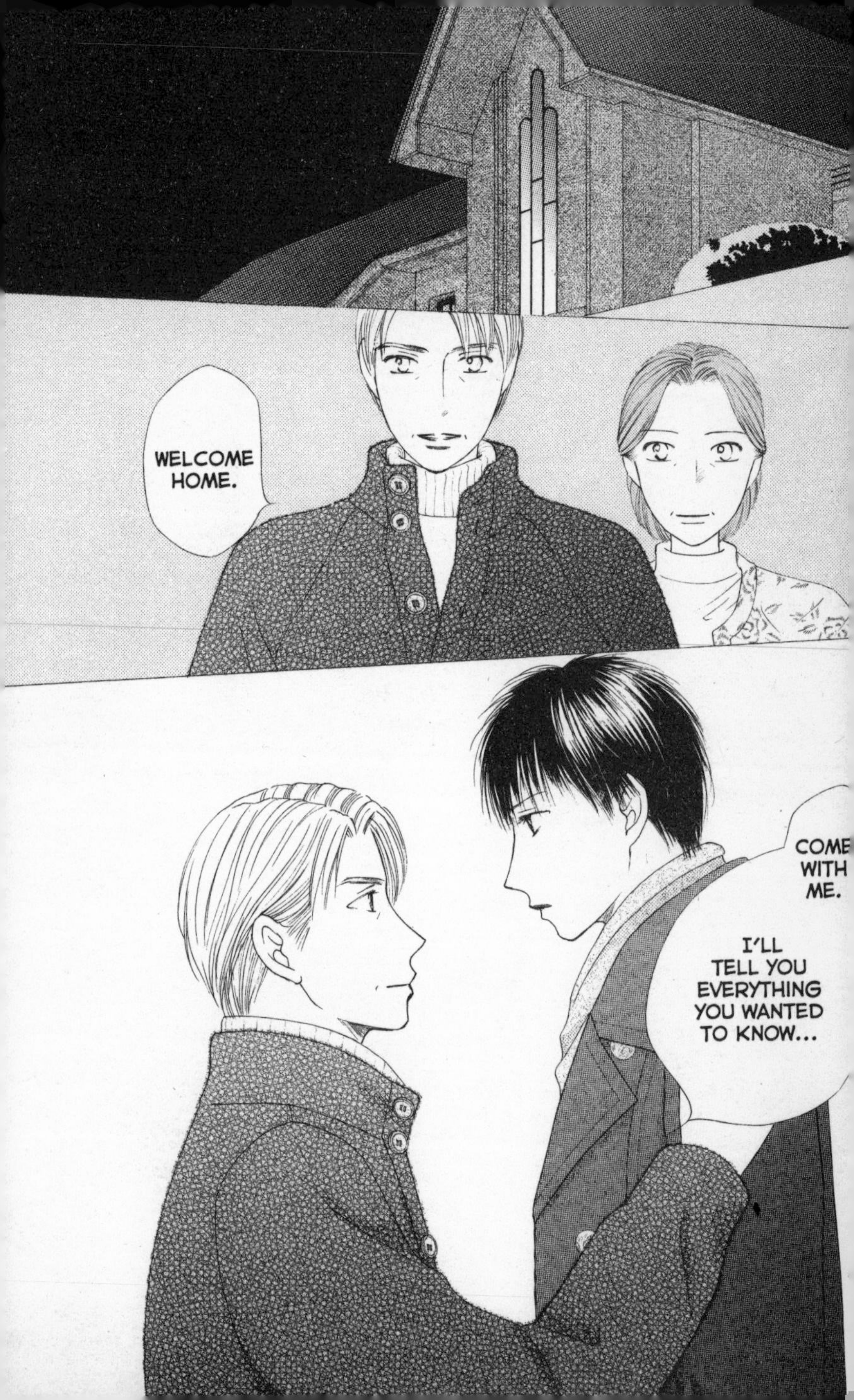
WELCOME HOME.
COME WITH ME.
I'LL TELL YOU EVERYTHING YOU WANTED TO KNOW...

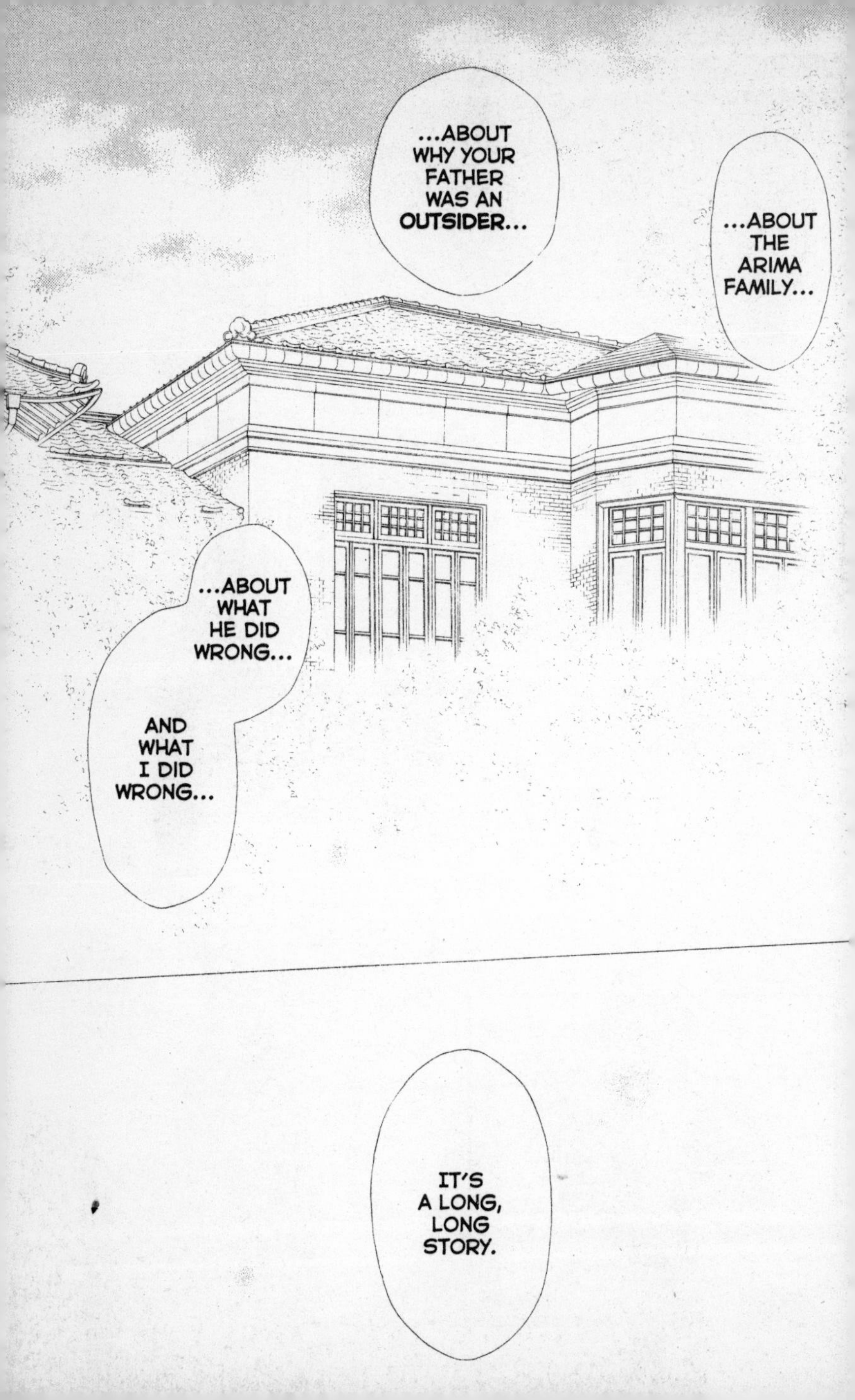
...ABOUT THE ARIMA FAMILY...
...ABOUT WHY YOUR FATHER WAS AN OUTSIDER...
...ABOUT WHAT HE DID WRONG...
AND WHAT I DID WRONG...
IT'S A LONG, LONG STORY.

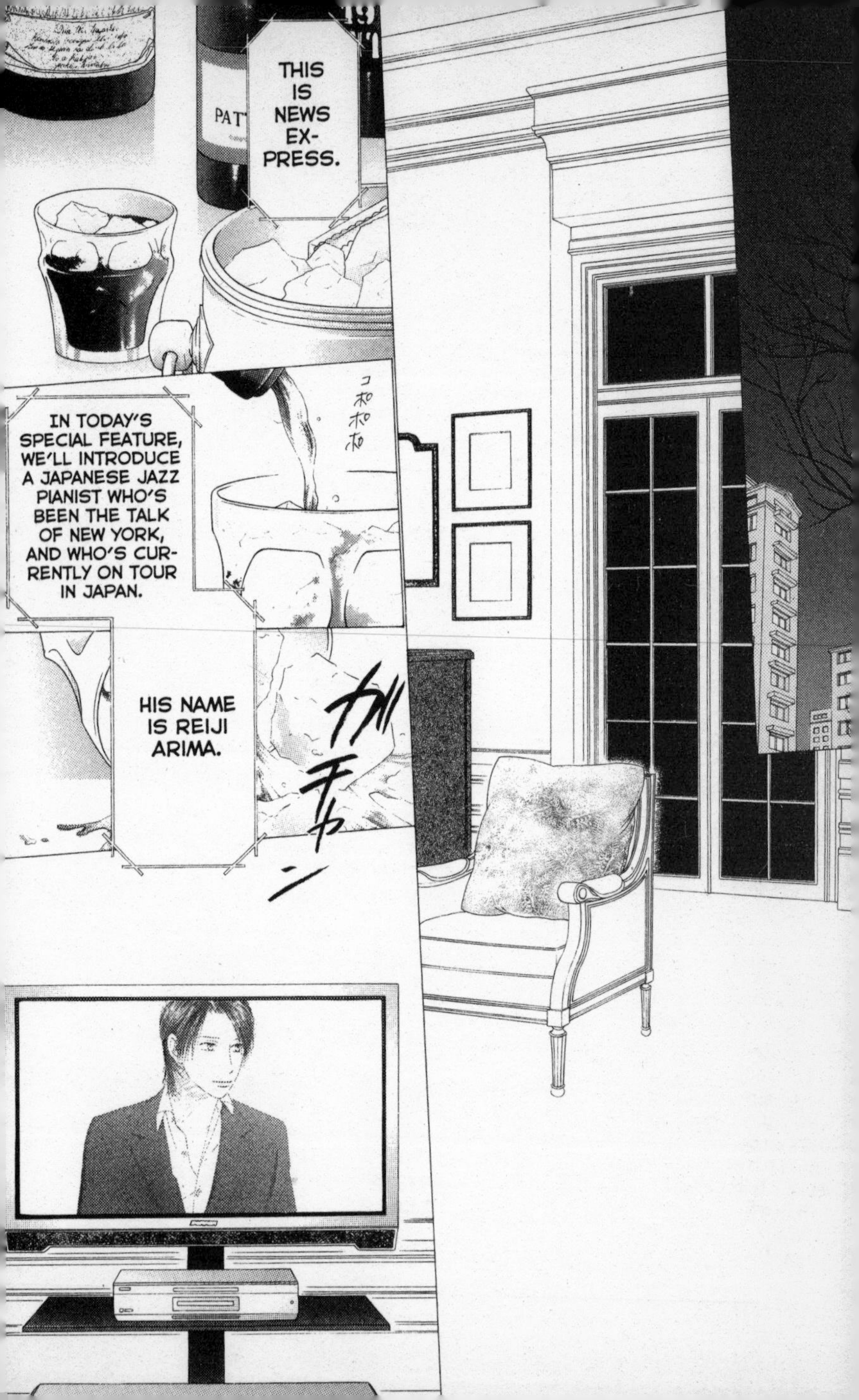

THIS IS NEWS EX-PRESS.
PATT
コポポポ
IN TODAY'S SPECIAL FEATURE, WE'LL INTRODUCE A JAPANESE JAZZ PIANIST WHO'S BEEN THE TALK OF NEW YORK, AND WHO'S CUR-RENTLY ON TOUR IN JAPAN.
ガチャン
HIS NAME IS REIJI ARIMA.

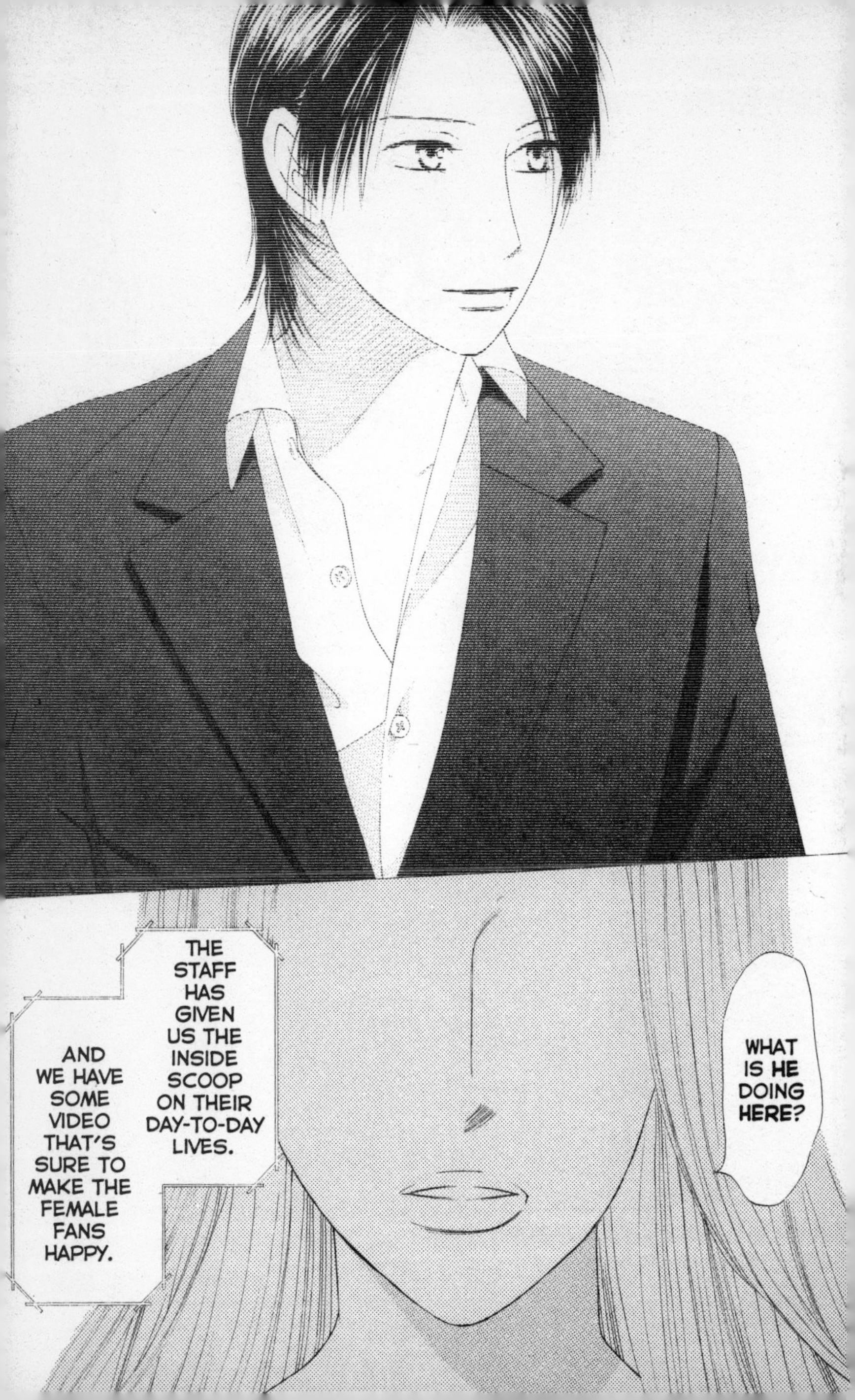
WHAT IS HE DOING HERE?
THE STAFF HAS GIVEN US THE INSIDE SCOOP ON THEIR DAY-TO-DAY LIVES.
AND WE HAVE SOME VIDEO THAT'S SURE TO MAKE THE FEMALE FANS HAPPY.

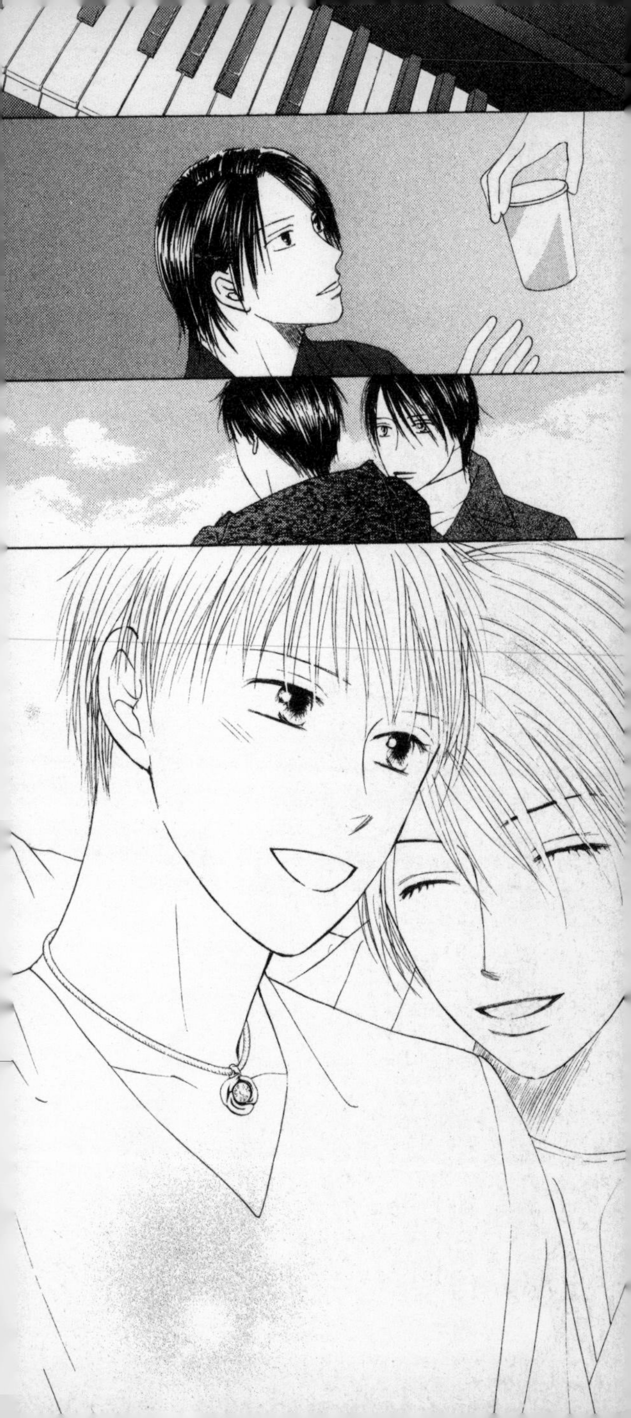

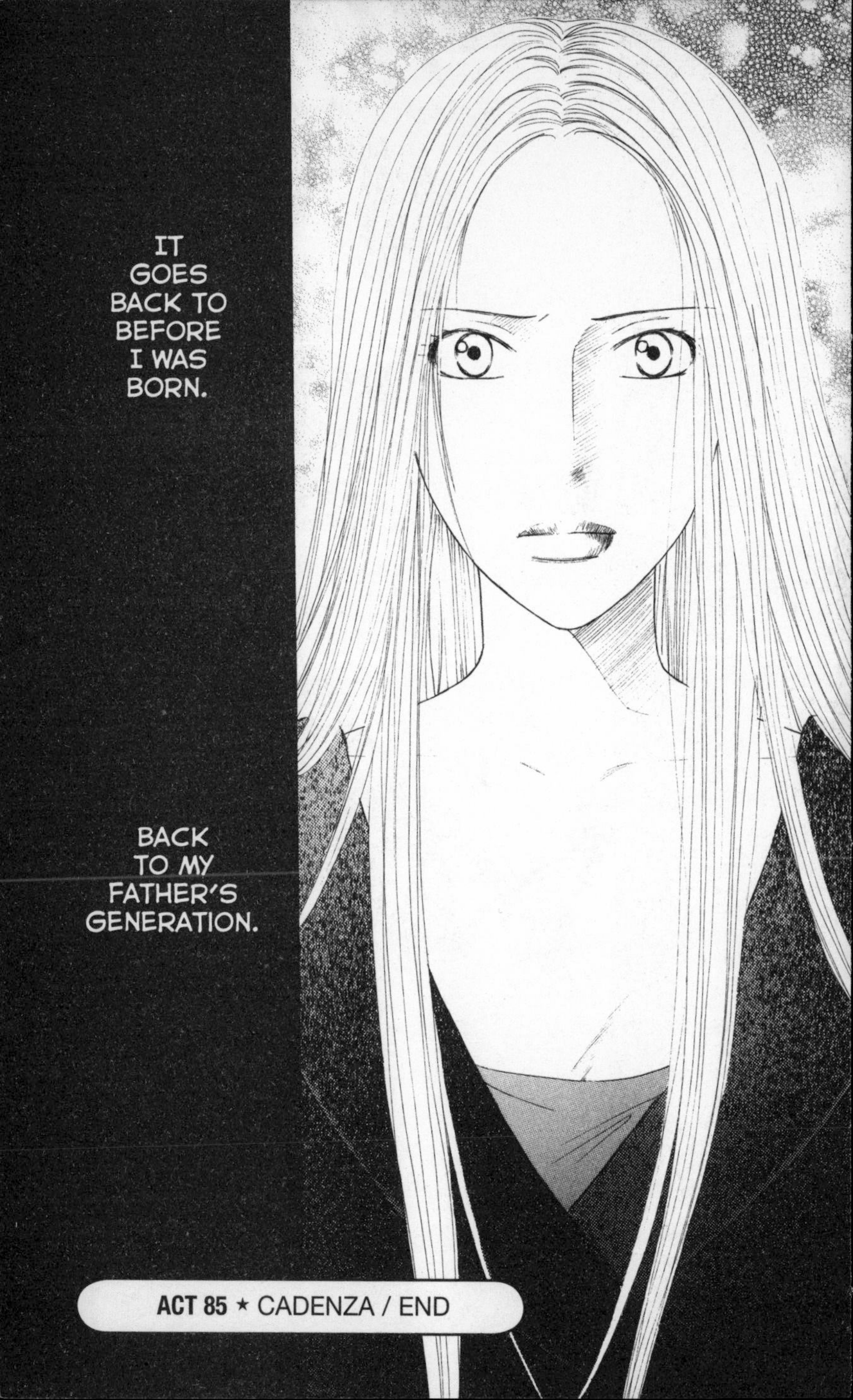
IT GOES BACK TO BEFORE I WAS BORN.
BACK TO MY FATHER'S GENERATION.
ACT 85 ★ CADENZA / END

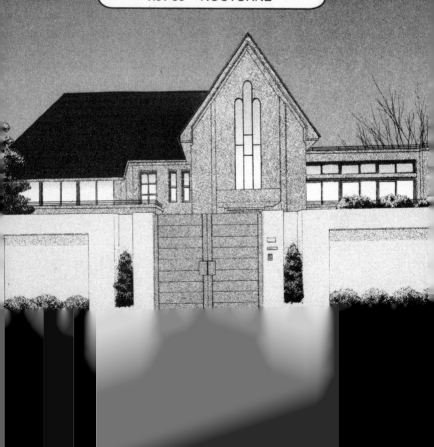

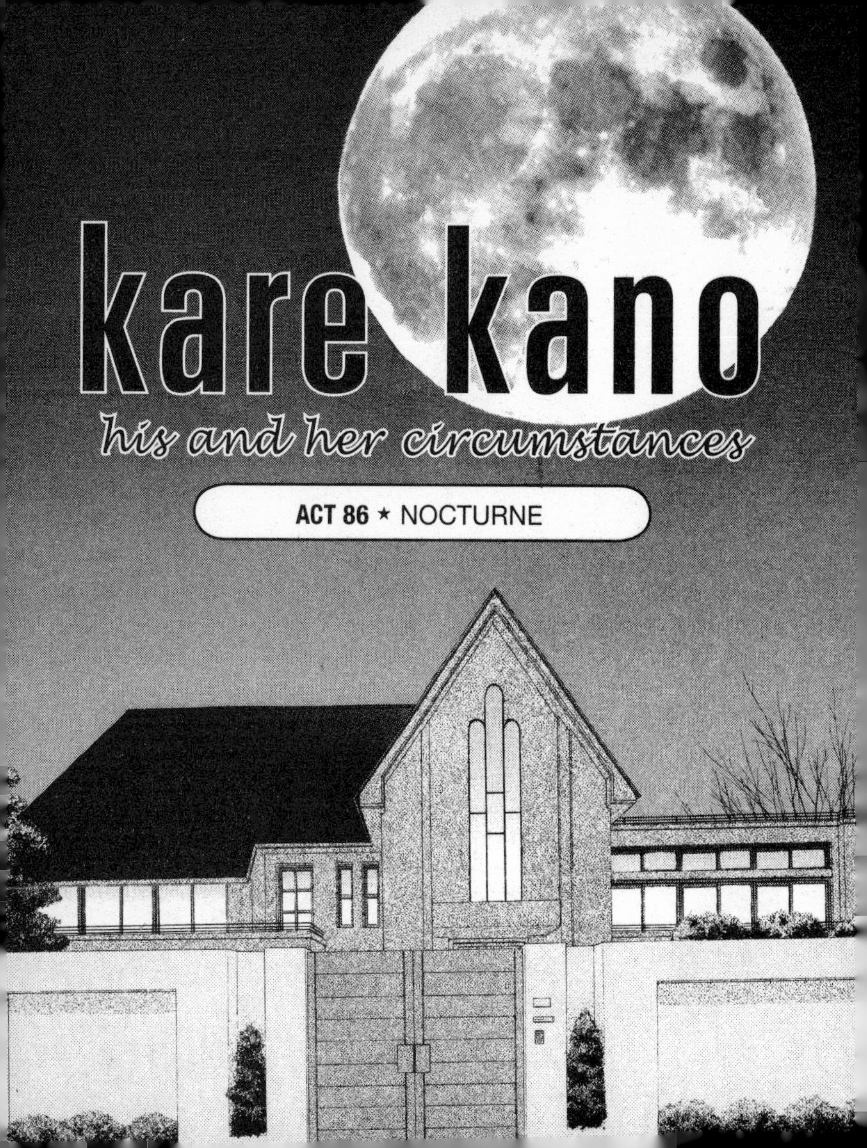
kare kano
his and her circumstances
ACT 86 ★ NOCTURNE

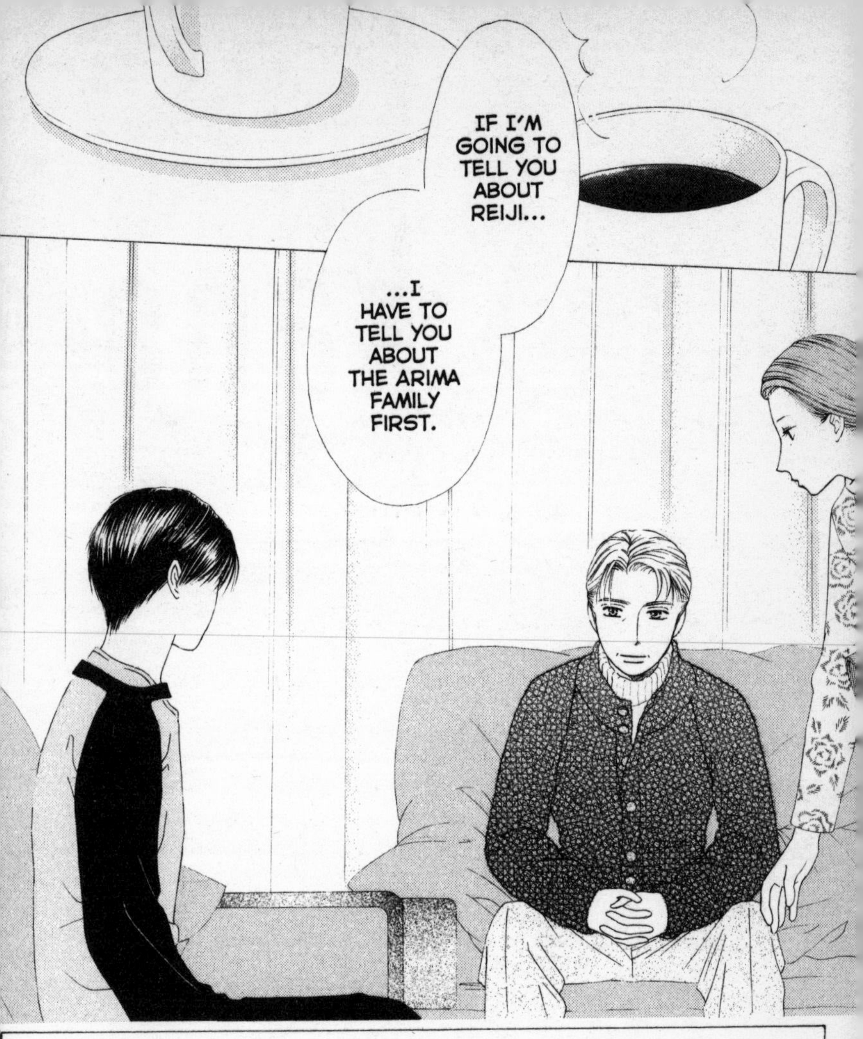
IF I'M GOING TO TELL YOU ABOUT REIJI...
...I HAVE TO TELL YOU ABOUT THE ARIMA FAMILY FIRST.

* I'm losing my taste for sweets. *

I don't even want a single piece of chocolate. I can't eat cake anymore.

It's not such a bad thing. It's like I've been released from the burden of one of my worldly desires.

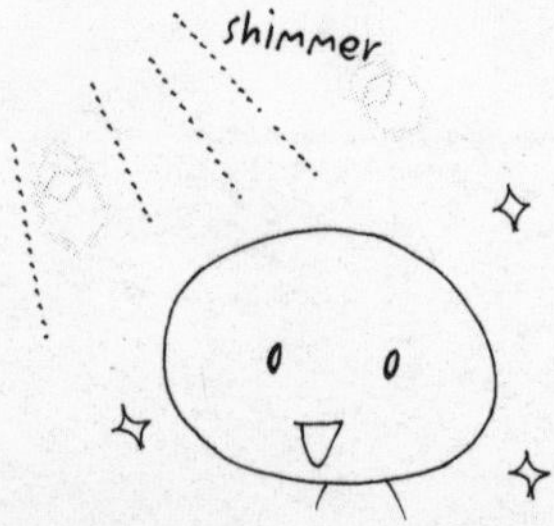
shimmer

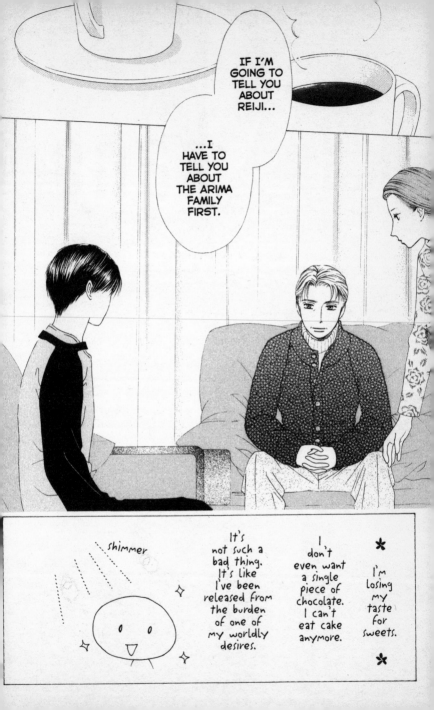

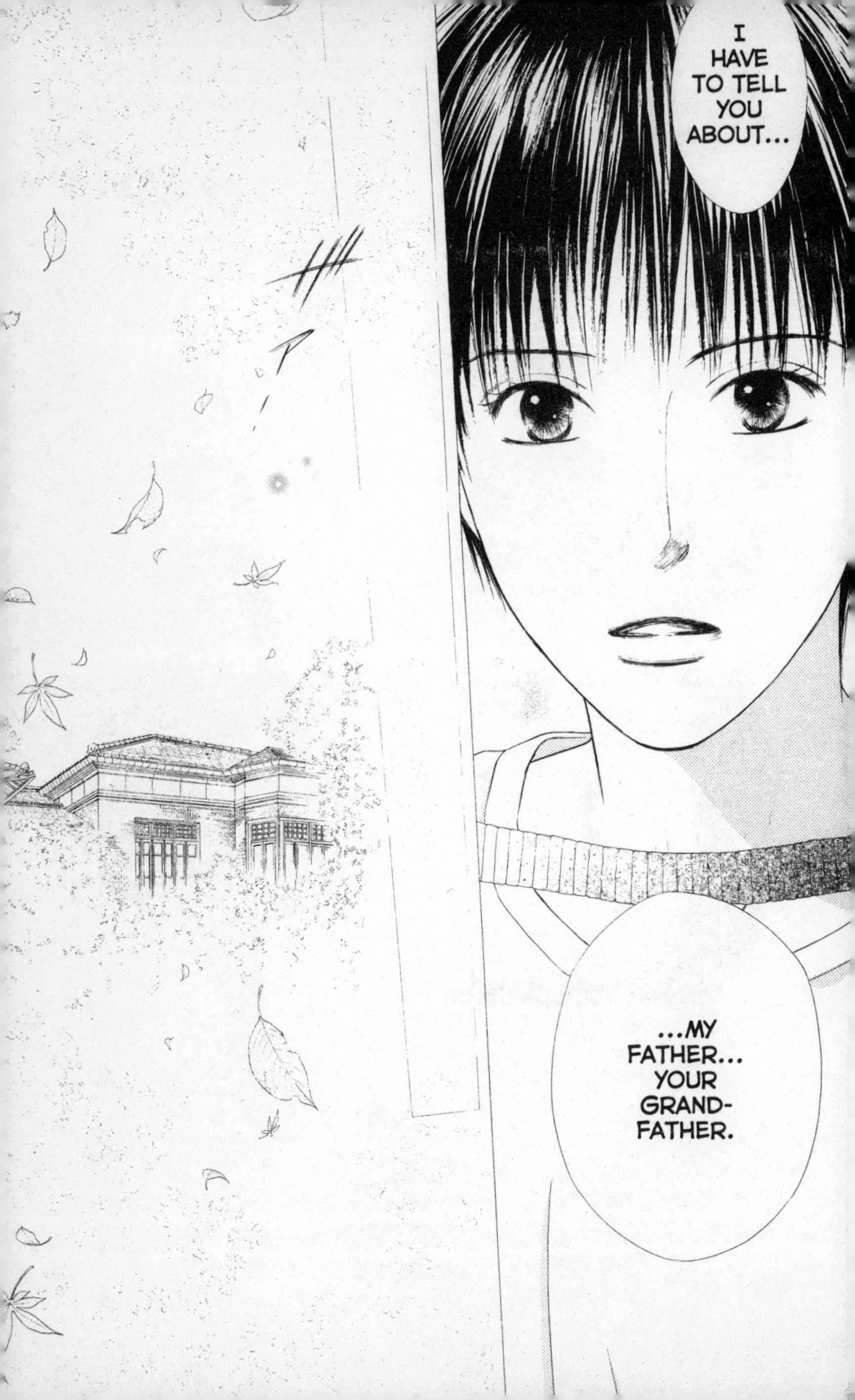
I HAVE TO TELL YOU ABOUT...
...MY FATHER... YOUR GRAND-FATHER.

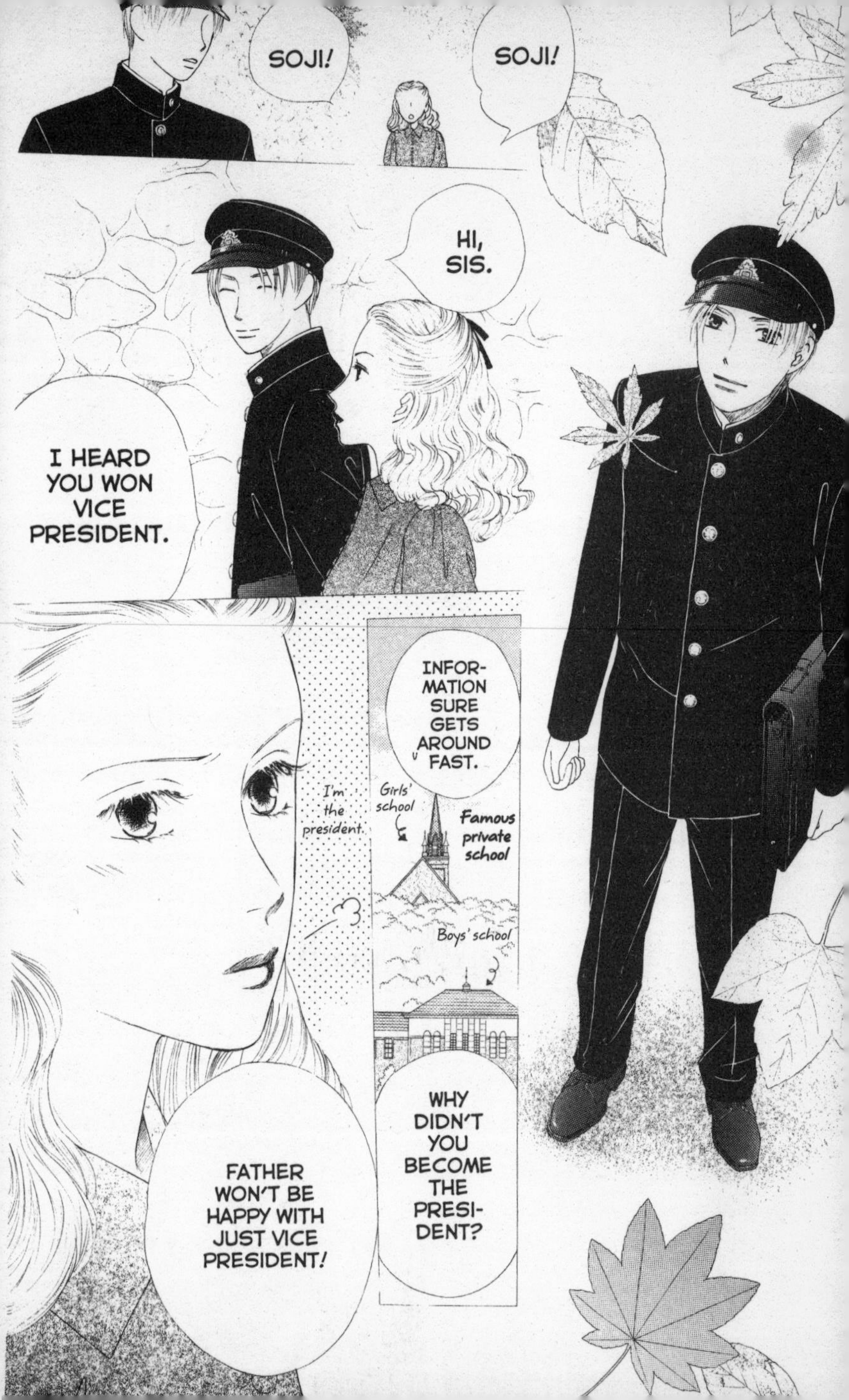
SOJI!
SOJI!
HI, SIS.
I HEARD YOU WON VICE PRESIDENT.
INFORMATION SURE GETS AROUND FAST.
Girls' school
Famous private school
Boys' school
WHY DIDN'T YOU BECOME THE PRESIDENT?
I'm the president.
FATHER WON'T BE HAPPY WITH JUST VICE PRESIDENT!

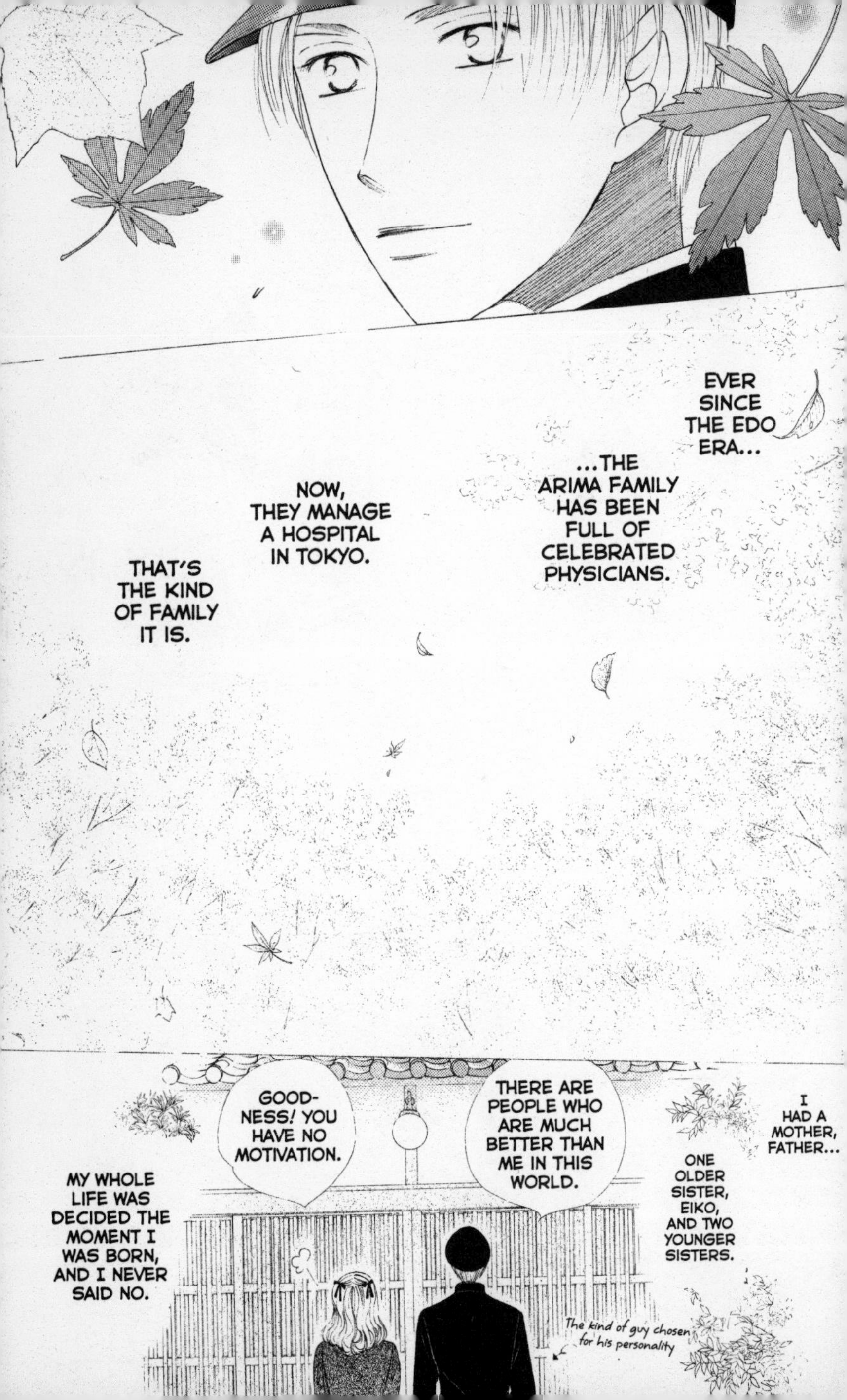
EVER SINCE THE EDO ERA...
...THE ARIMA FAMILY HAS BEEN FULL OF CELEBRATED PHYSICIANS.
NOW, THEY MANAGE A HOSPITAL IN TOKYO.
THAT'S THE KIND OF FAMILY IT IS.
I HAD A MOTHER, FATHER...
ONE OLDER SISTER, EIKO, AND TWO YOUNGER SISTERS.
THERE ARE PEOPLE WHO ARE MUCH BETTER THAN ME IN THIS WORLD.
GOOD-NESS! YOU HAVE NO MOTIVATION.
The kind of guy chosen for his personality
MY WHOLE LIFE WAS DECIDED THE MOMENT I WAS BORN, AND I NEVER SAID NO.

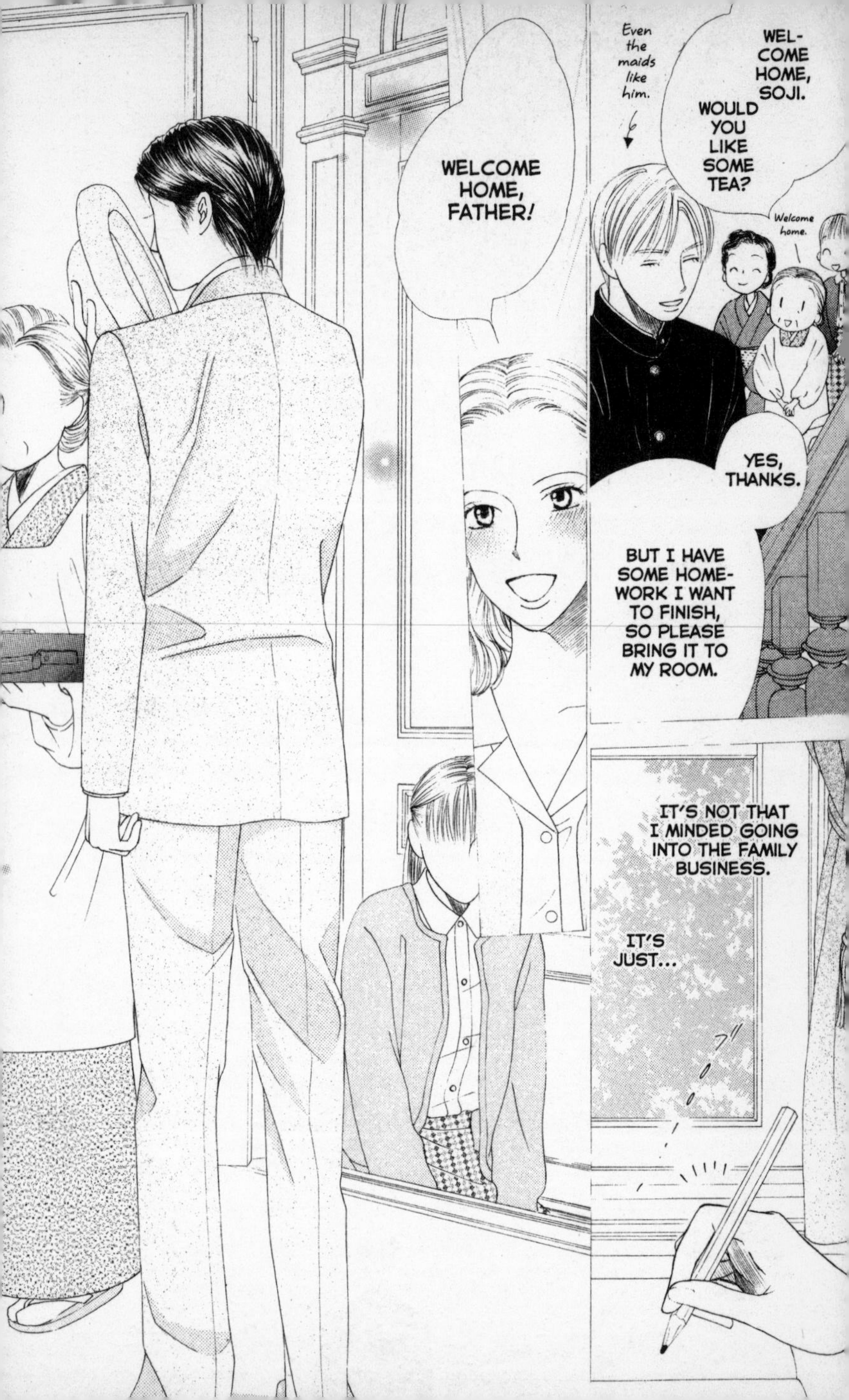
WEL-COME HOME, SOJI. WOULD YOU LIKE SOME TEA?
Even the maids like him.
Welcome home.
YES, THANKS.
BUT I HAVE SOME HOME-WORK I WANT TO FINISH, SO PLEASE BRING IT TO MY ROOM.
IT'S NOT THAT I MINDED GOING INTO THE FAMILY BUSINESS.
IT'S JUST...
WELCOME HOME, FATHER!

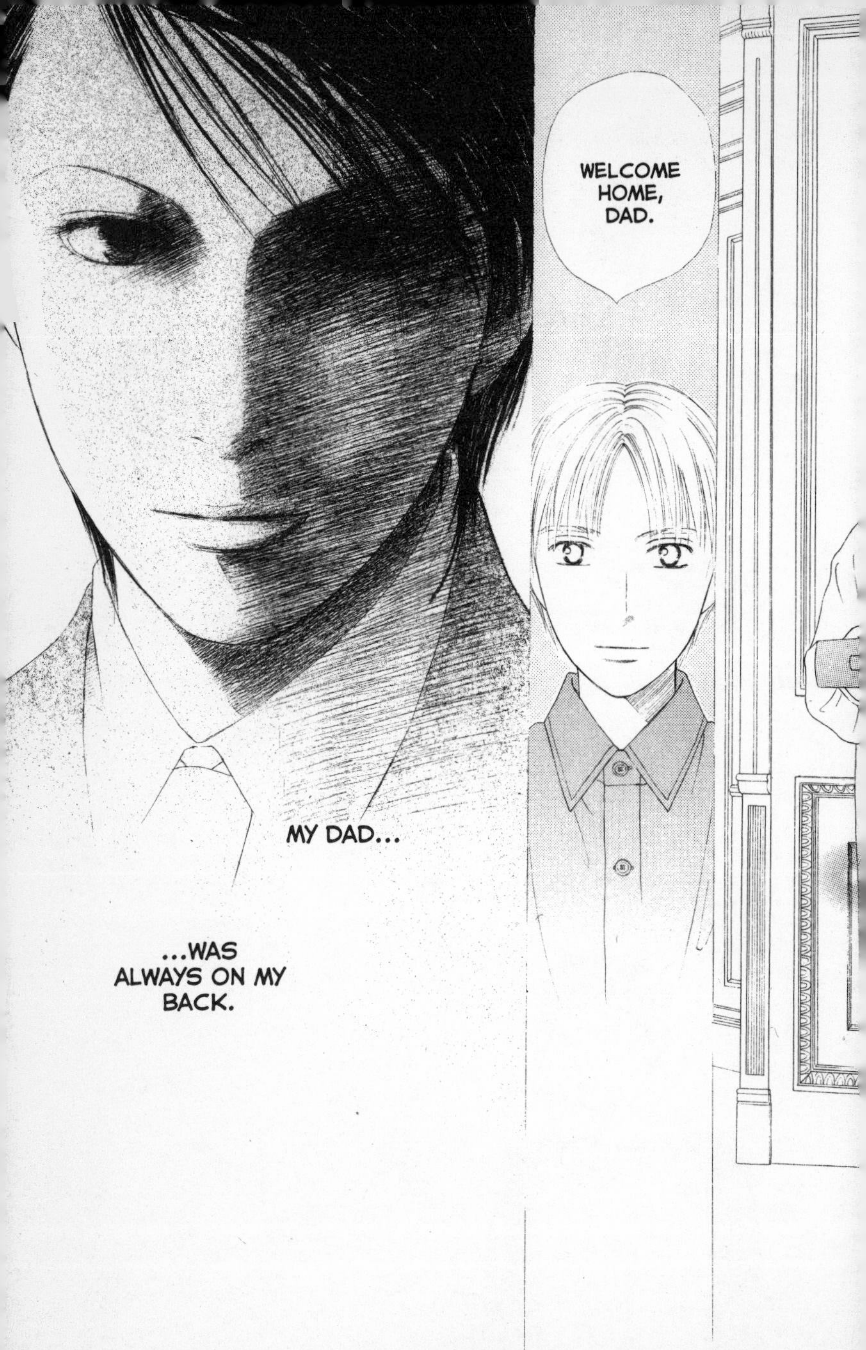
WELCOME HOME, DAD.
MY DAD...
...WAS ALWAYS ON MY BACK.

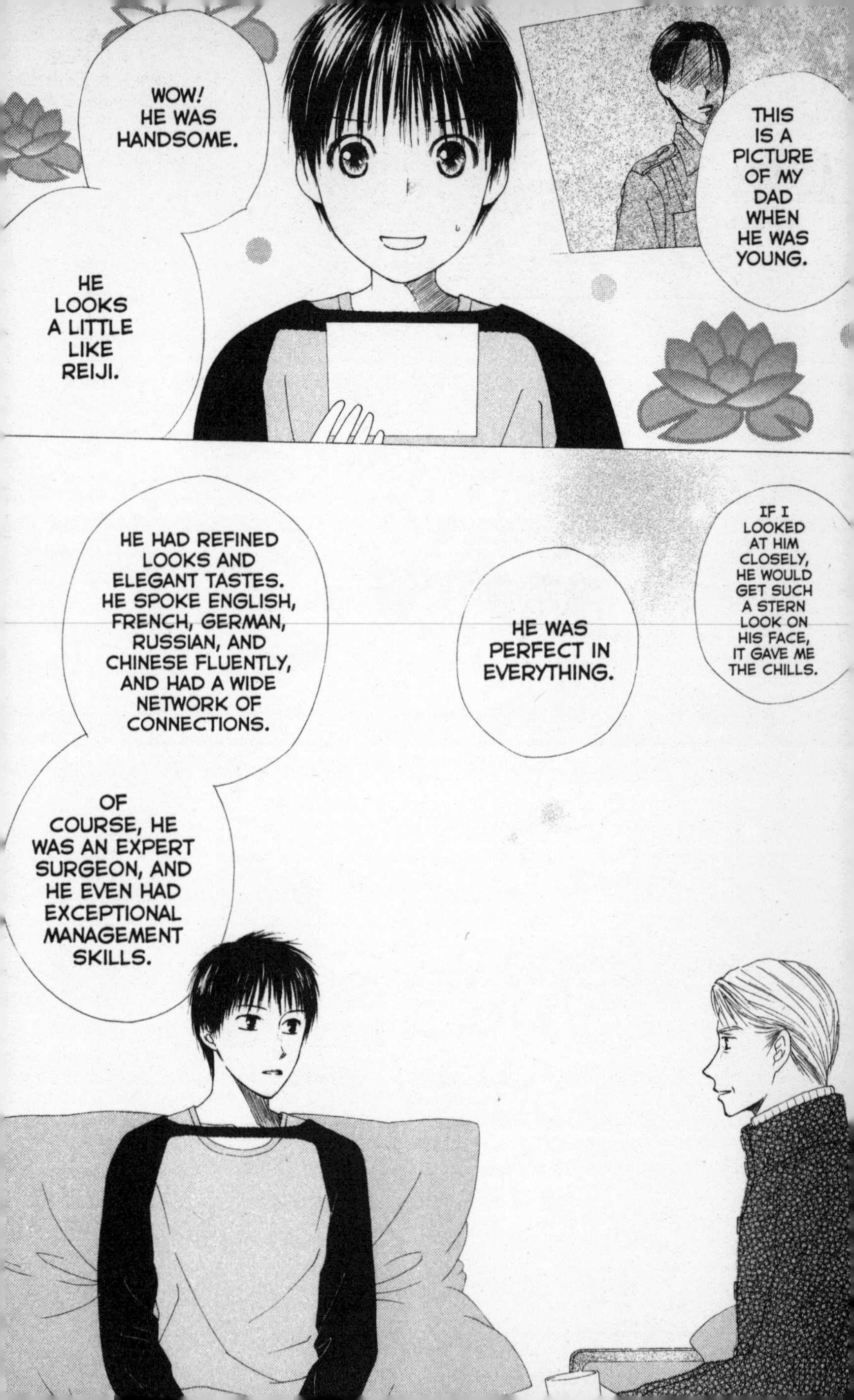
THIS IS A PICTURE OF MY DAD WHEN HE WAS YOUNG.
WOW! HE WAS HANDSOME.
HE LOOKS A LITTLE LIKE REIJI.
IF I LOOKED AT HIM CLOSELY, HE WOULD GET SUCH A STERN LOOK ON HIS FACE, IT GAVE ME THE CHILLS.
HE WAS PERFECT IN EVERYTHING.
HE HAD REFINED LOOKS AND ELEGANT TASTES. HE SPOKE ENGLISH, FRENCH, GERMAN, RUSSIAN, AND CHINESE FLUENTLY, AND HAD A WIDE NETWORK OF CONNECTIONS.
OF COURSE, HE WAS AN EXPERT SURGEON, AND HE EVEN HAD EXCEPTIONAL MANAGEMENT SKILLS.

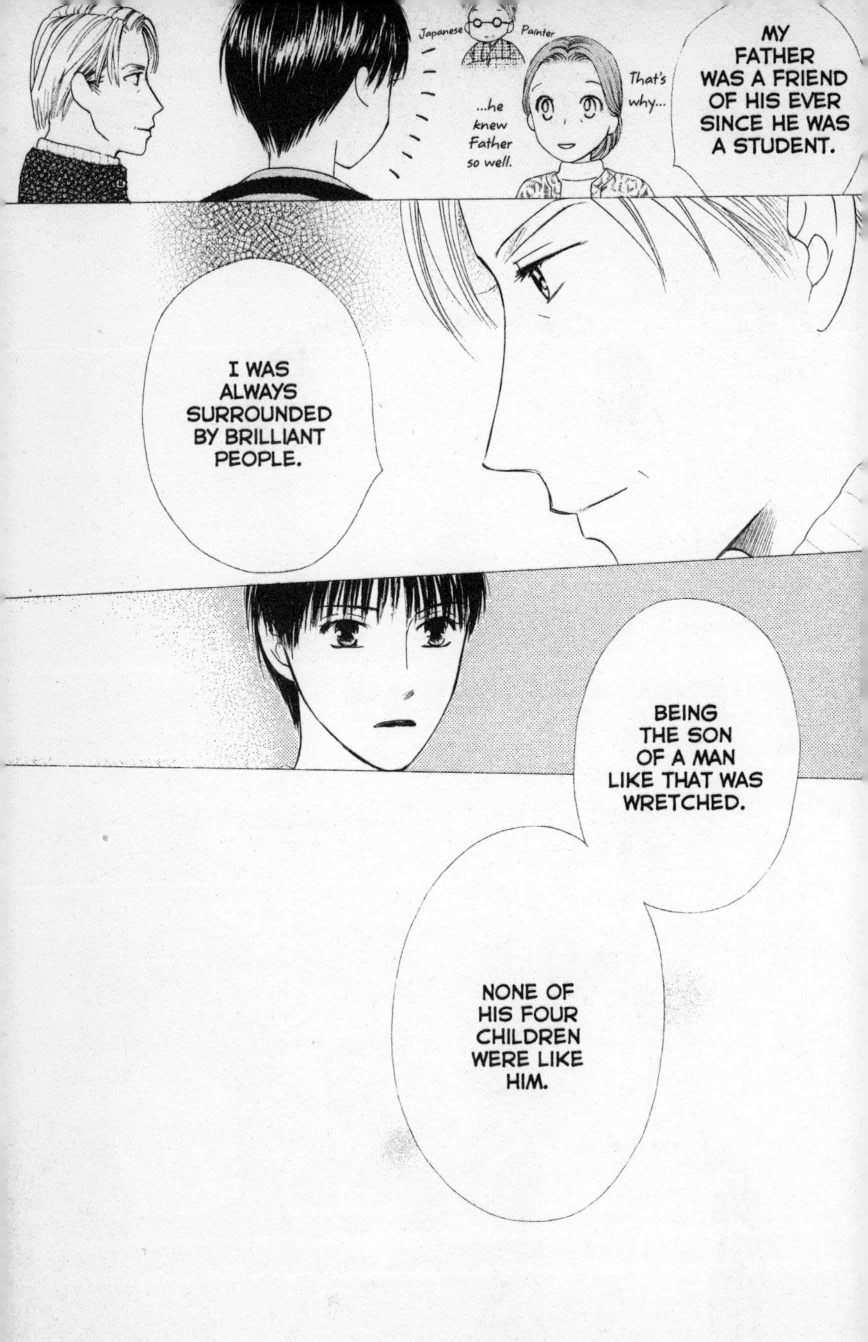
MY FATHER WAS A FRIEND OF HIS EVER SINCE HE WAS A STUDENT.
That's why...
...he knew Father so well.
Japanese
Painter
I WAS ALWAYS SURROUNDED BY BRILLIANT PEOPLE.
BEING THE SON OF A MAN LIKE THAT WAS WRETCHED.
NONE OF HIS FOUR CHILDREN WERE LIKE HIM.

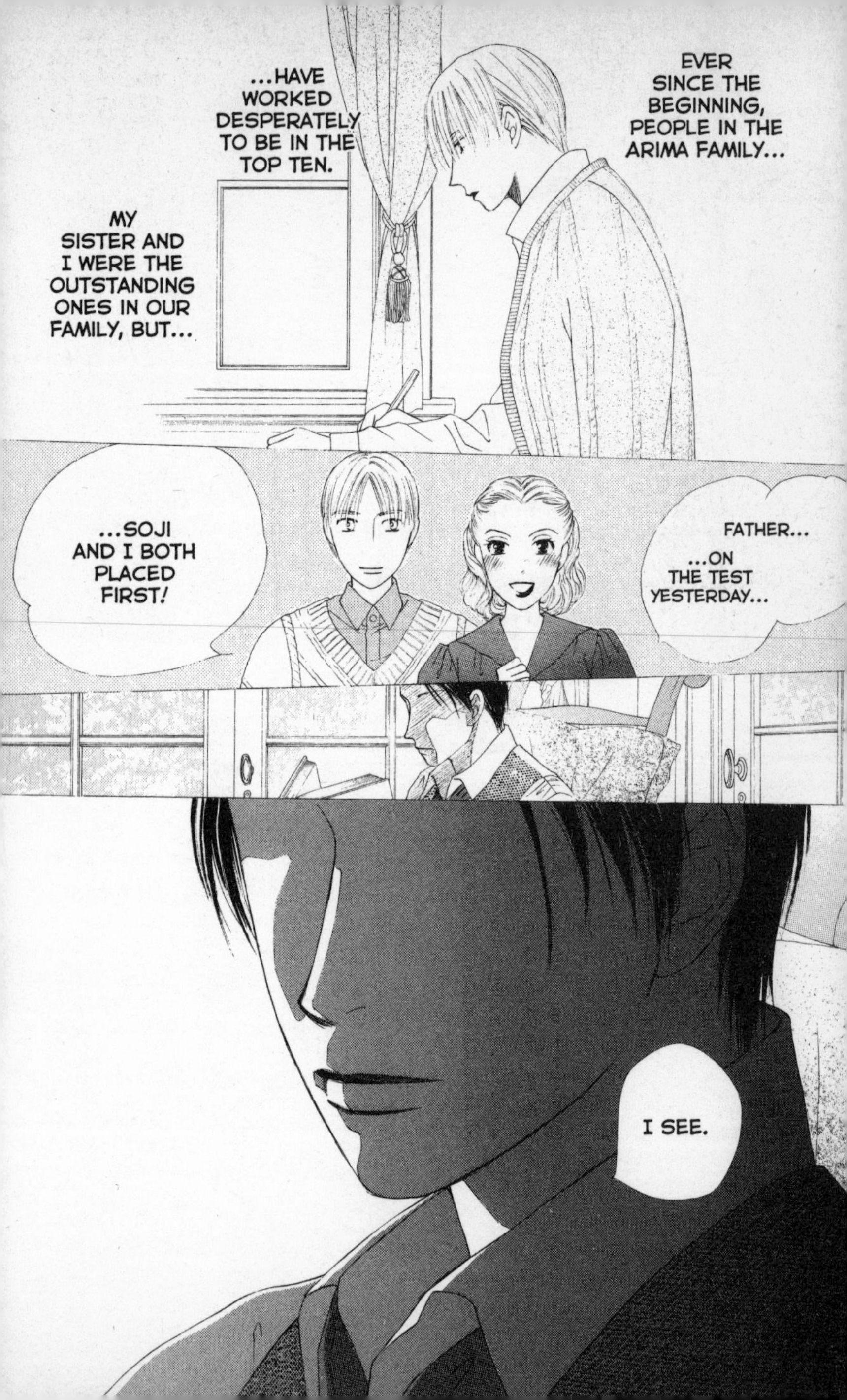
EVER SINCE THE BEGINNING, PEOPLE IN THE ARIMA FAMILY...
...HAVE WORKED DESPERATELY TO BE IN THE TOP TEN.
MY SISTER AND I WERE THE OUTSTANDING ONES IN OUR FAMILY, BUT...
FATHER...
...ON THE TEST YESTERDAY...
...SOJI AND I BOTH PLACED FIRST!
I SEE.

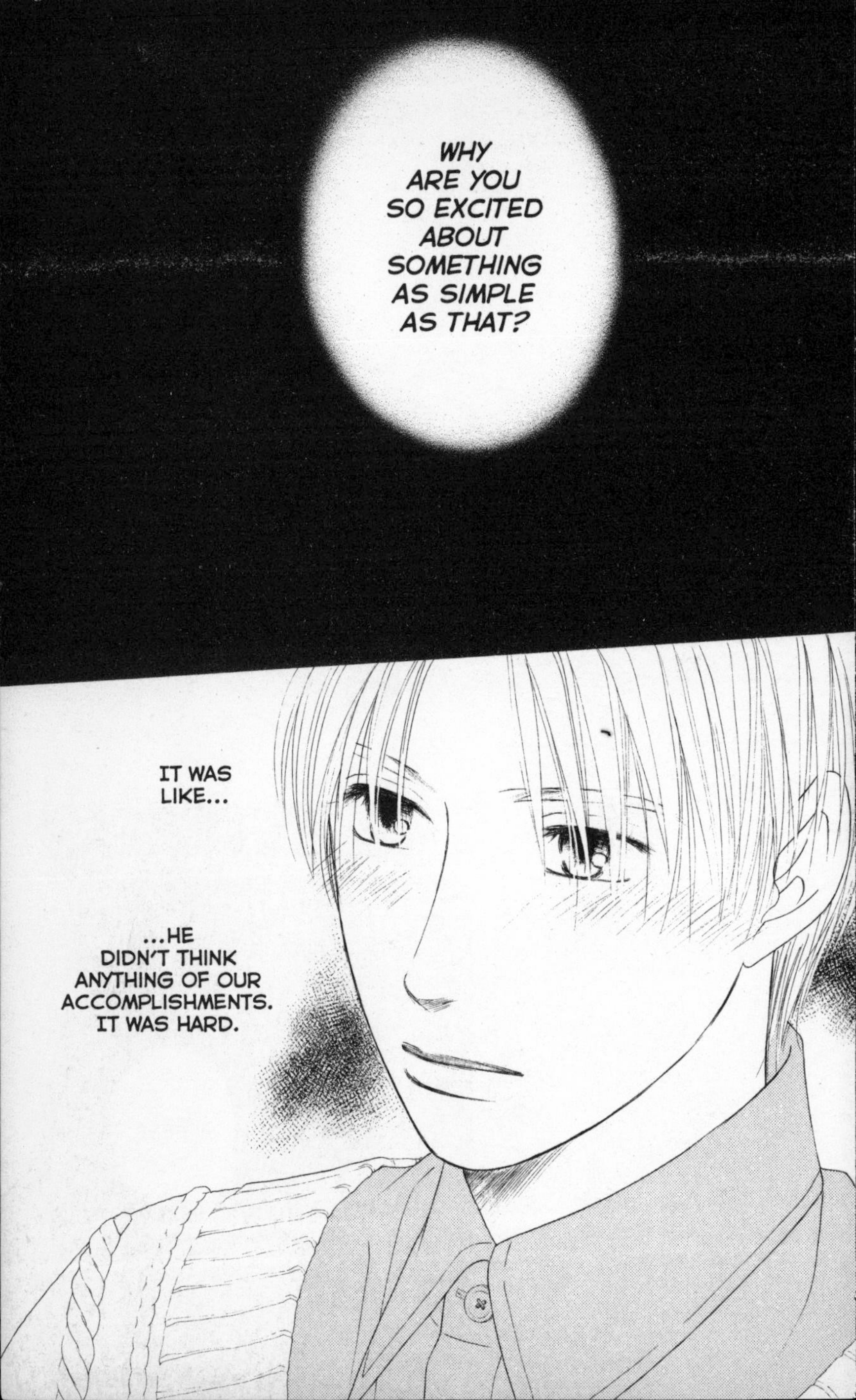
WHY ARE YOU SO EXCITED ABOUT SOMETHING AS SIMPLE AS THAT?
IT WAS LIKE...
...HE DIDN'T THINK ANYTHING OF OUR ACCOMPLISHMENTS. IT WAS HARD.

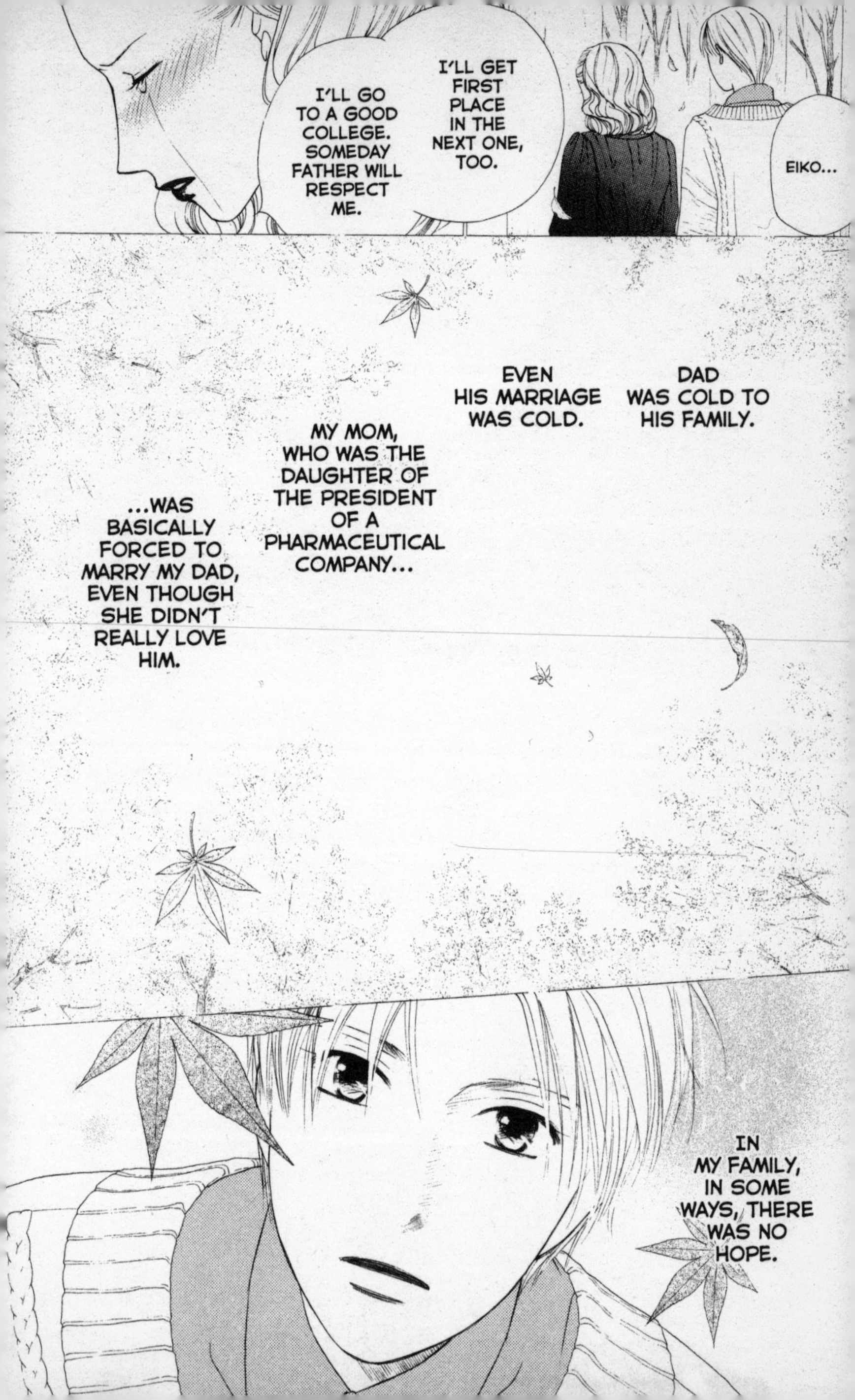
EIKO...
I'LL GET FIRST PLACE IN THE NEXT ONE, TOO.
I'LL GO TO A GOOD COLLEGE. SOMEDAY FATHER WILL RESPECT ME.
DAD WAS COLD TO HIS FAMILY.
EVEN HIS MARRIAGE WAS COLD.
MY MOM, WHO WAS THE DAUGHTER OF THE PRESIDENT OF A PHARMACEUTICAL COMPANY...
...WAS BASICALLY FORCED TO MARRY MY DAD, EVEN THOUGH SHE DIDN'T REALLY LOVE HIM.
IN MY FAMILY, IN SOME WAYS, THERE WAS NO HOPE.

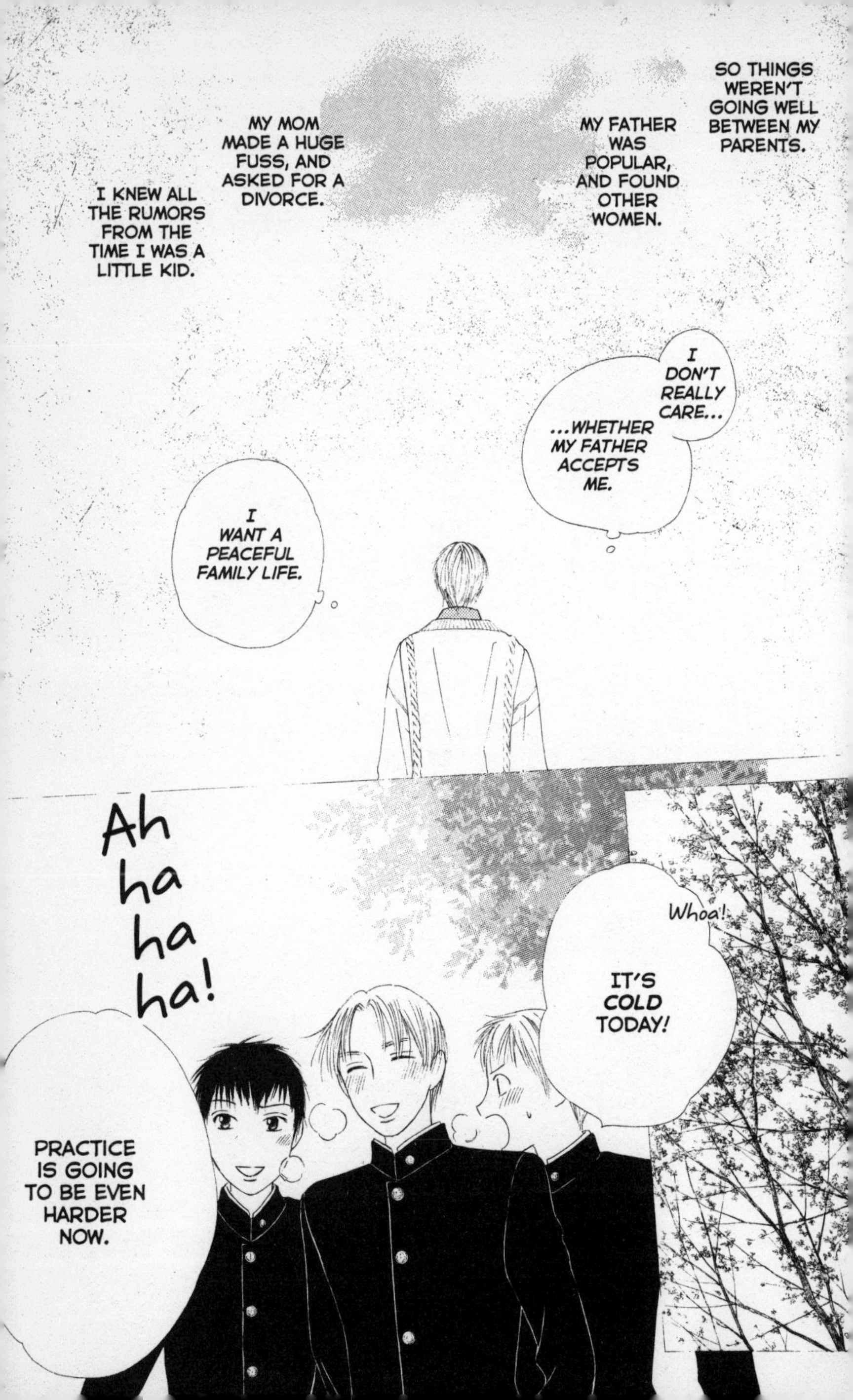
SO THINGS WEREN'T GOING WELL BETWEEN MY PARENTS.
MY FATHER WAS POPULAR, AND FOUND OTHER WOMEN.
MY MOM MADE A HUGE FUSS, AND ASKED FOR A DIVORCE.
I KNEW ALL THE RUMORS FROM THE TIME I WAS A LITTLE KID.
I DON'T REALLY CARE...
...WHETHER MY FATHER ACCEPTS ME.
I WANT A PEACEFUL FAMILY LIFE.
Whoa!
IT'S COLD TODAY!
Ah ha ha ha!
PRACTICE IS GOING TO BE EVEN HARDER NOW.

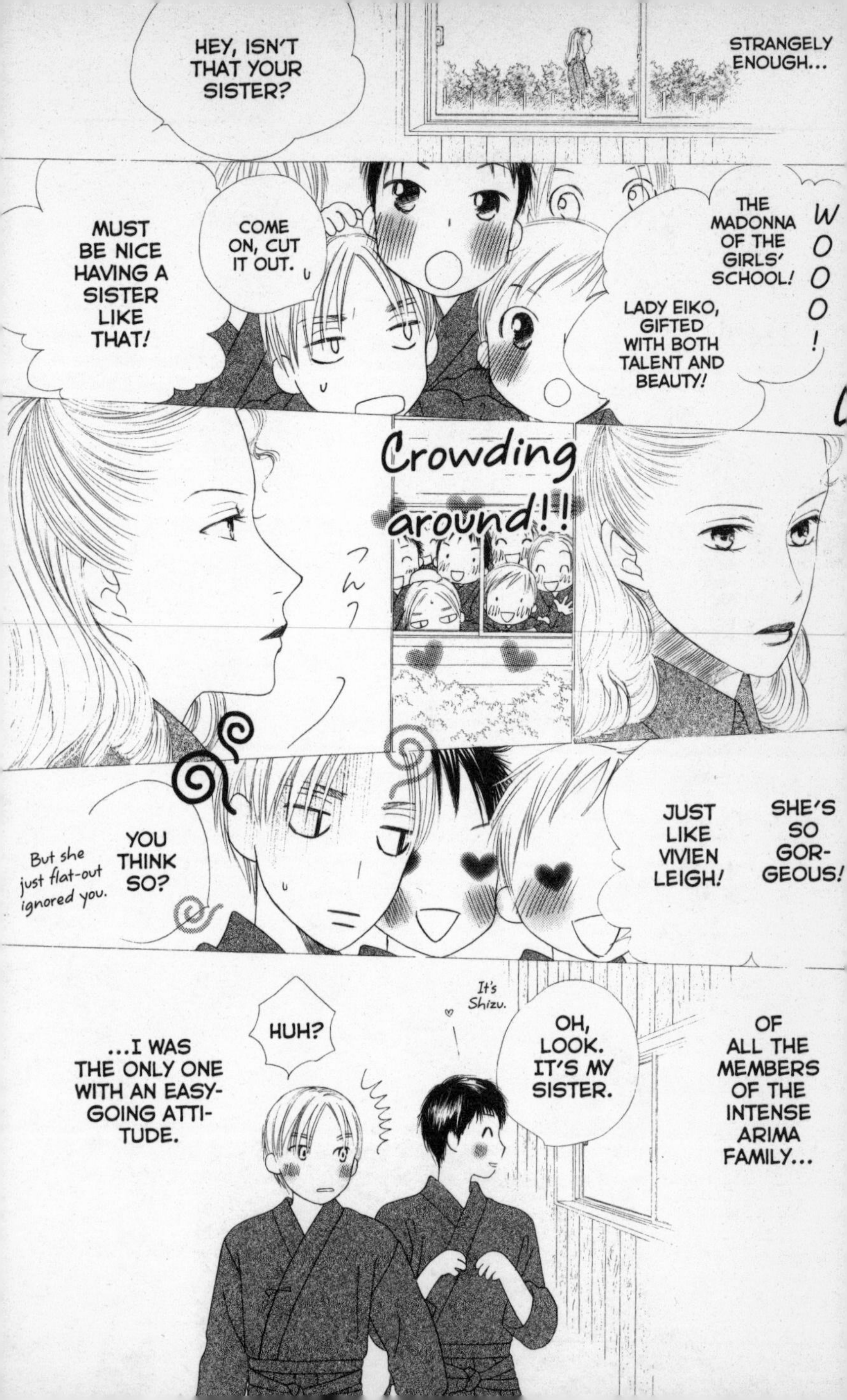
STRANGELY ENOUGH...
HEY, ISN'T THAT YOUR SISTER?
WOOO!
THE MADONNA OF THE GIRLS' SCHOOL!
LADY EIKO, GIFTED WITH BOTH TALENT AND BEAUTY!
COME ON, CUT IT OUT.
MUST BE NICE HAVING A SISTER LIKE THAT!
Crowding around!!
SHE'S SO GORGEOUS!
JUST LIKE VIVIEN LEIGH!
YOU THINK SO?
But she just flat-out ignored you.
OF ALL THE MEMBERS OF THE INTENSE ARIMA FAMILY...
It's Shizu.
OH, LOOK. IT'S MY SISTER.
HUH?
...I WAS THE ONLY ONE WITH AN EASY-GOING ATTITUDE.

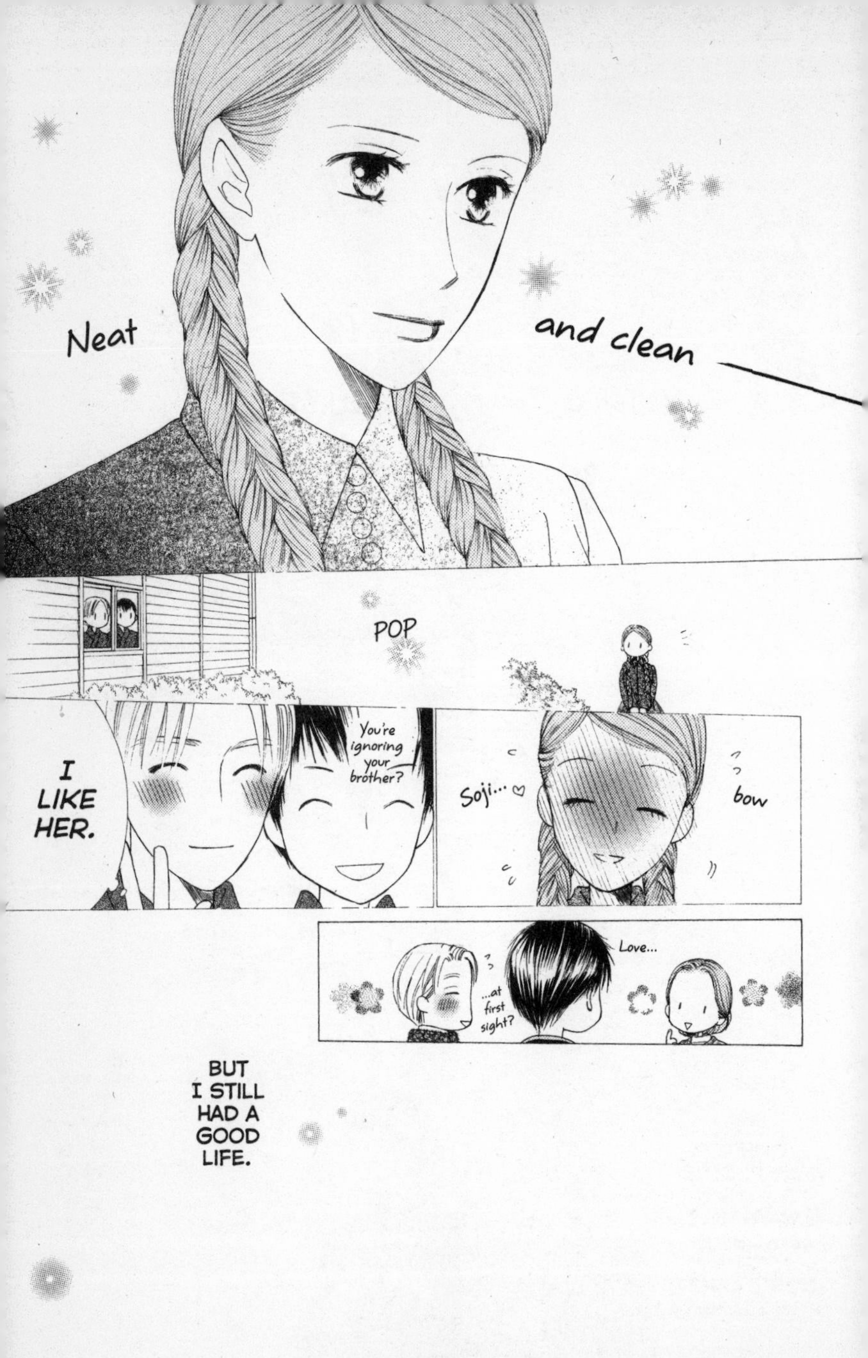
Neat
and clean
POP
Soji... ♡
bow
You're ignoring your brother?
I LIKE HER.
Love...
...at first sight?
BUT I STILL HAD A GOOD LIFE.

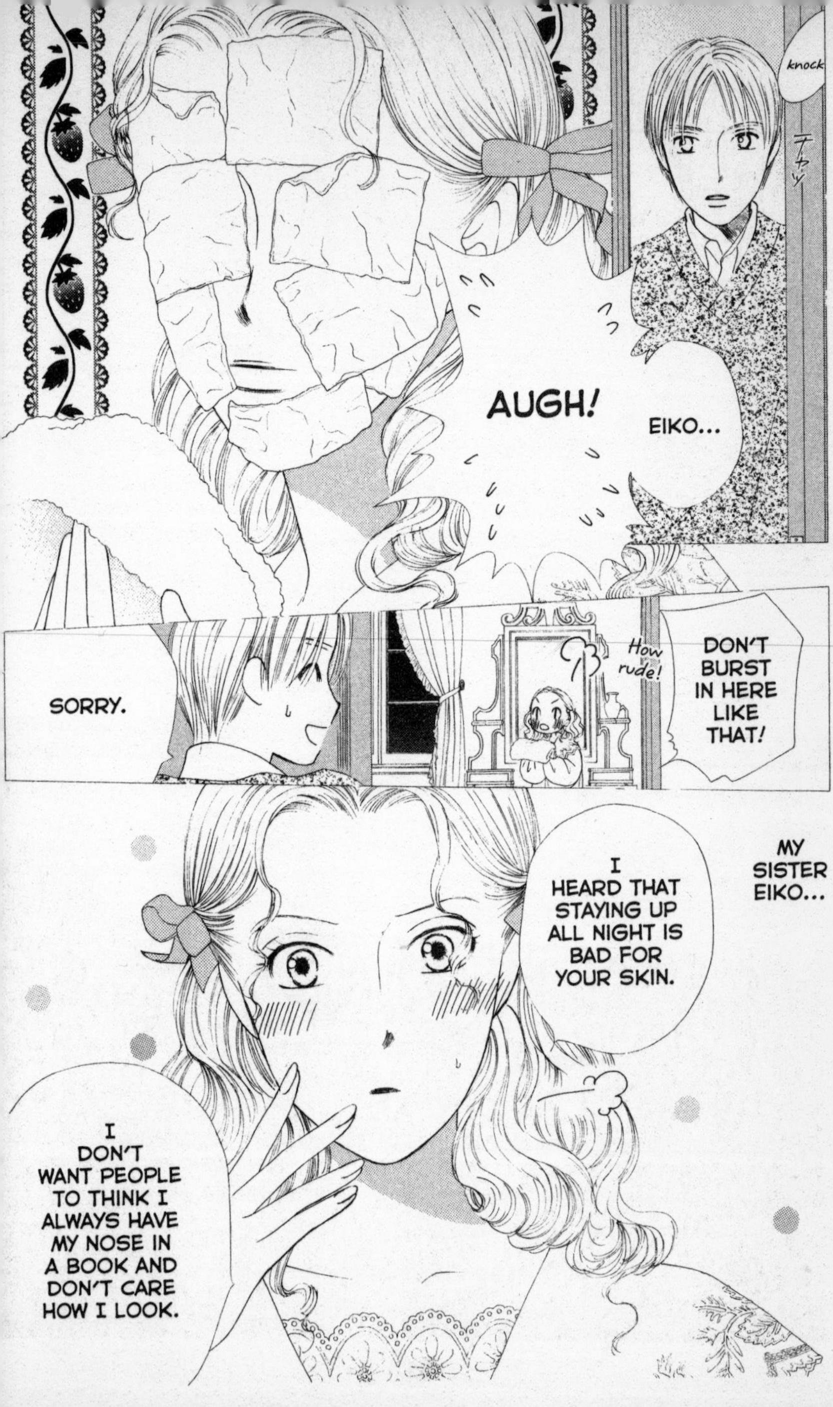
knock
チャッ
EIKO...
AUGH!
DON'T BURST IN HERE LIKE THAT!
How rude!
SORRY.
MY SISTER EIKO...
I HEARD THAT STAYING UP ALL NIGHT IS BAD FOR YOUR SKIN.
I DON'T WANT PEOPLE TO THINK I ALWAYS HAVE MY NOSE IN A BOOK AND DON'T CARE HOW I LOOK.

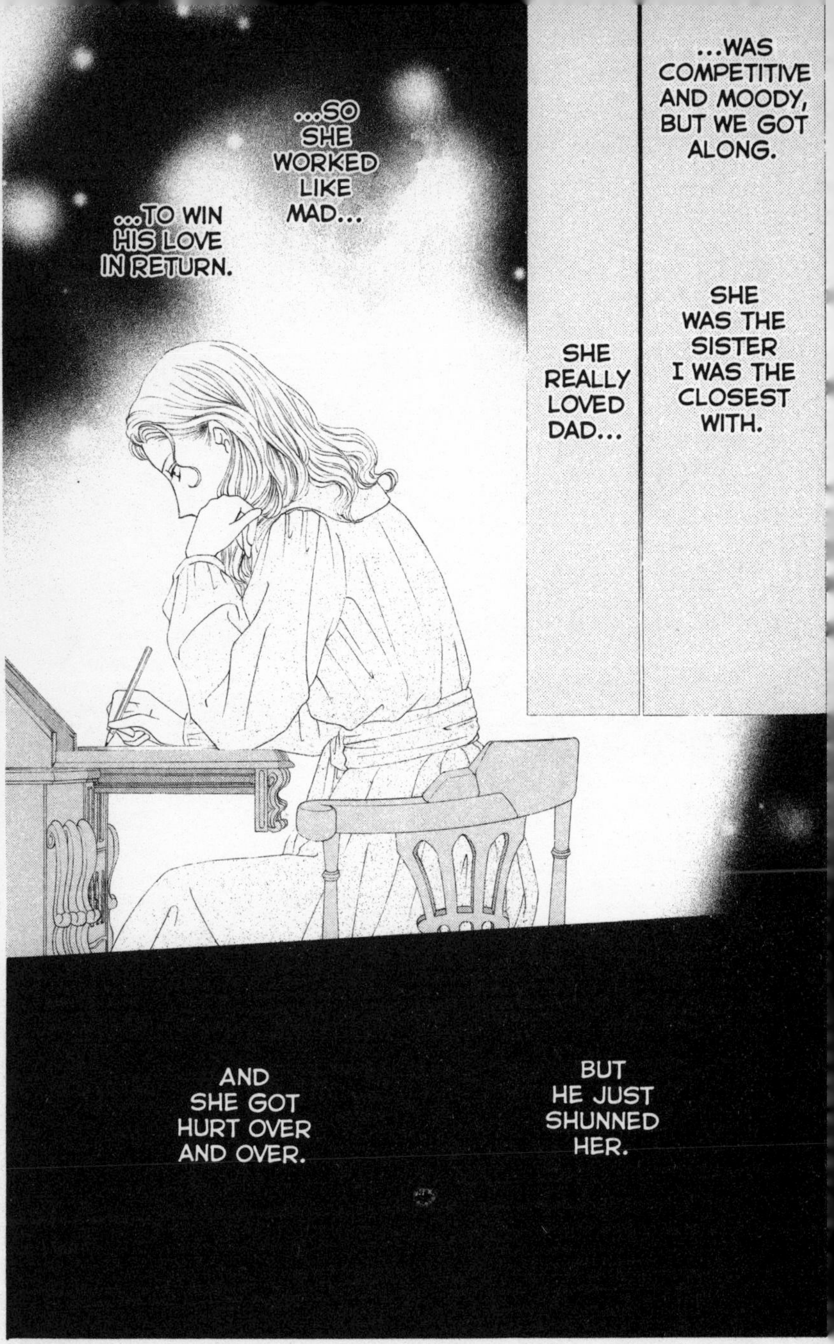
...WAS COMPETITIVE AND MOODY, BUT WE GOT ALONG.
SHE WAS THE SISTER I WAS THE CLOSEST WITH.
SHE REALLY LOVED DAD...
...SO SHE WORKED LIKE MAD...
...TO WIN HIS LOVE IN RETURN.
BUT HE JUST SHUNNED HER.
AND SHE GOT HURT OVER AND OVER.

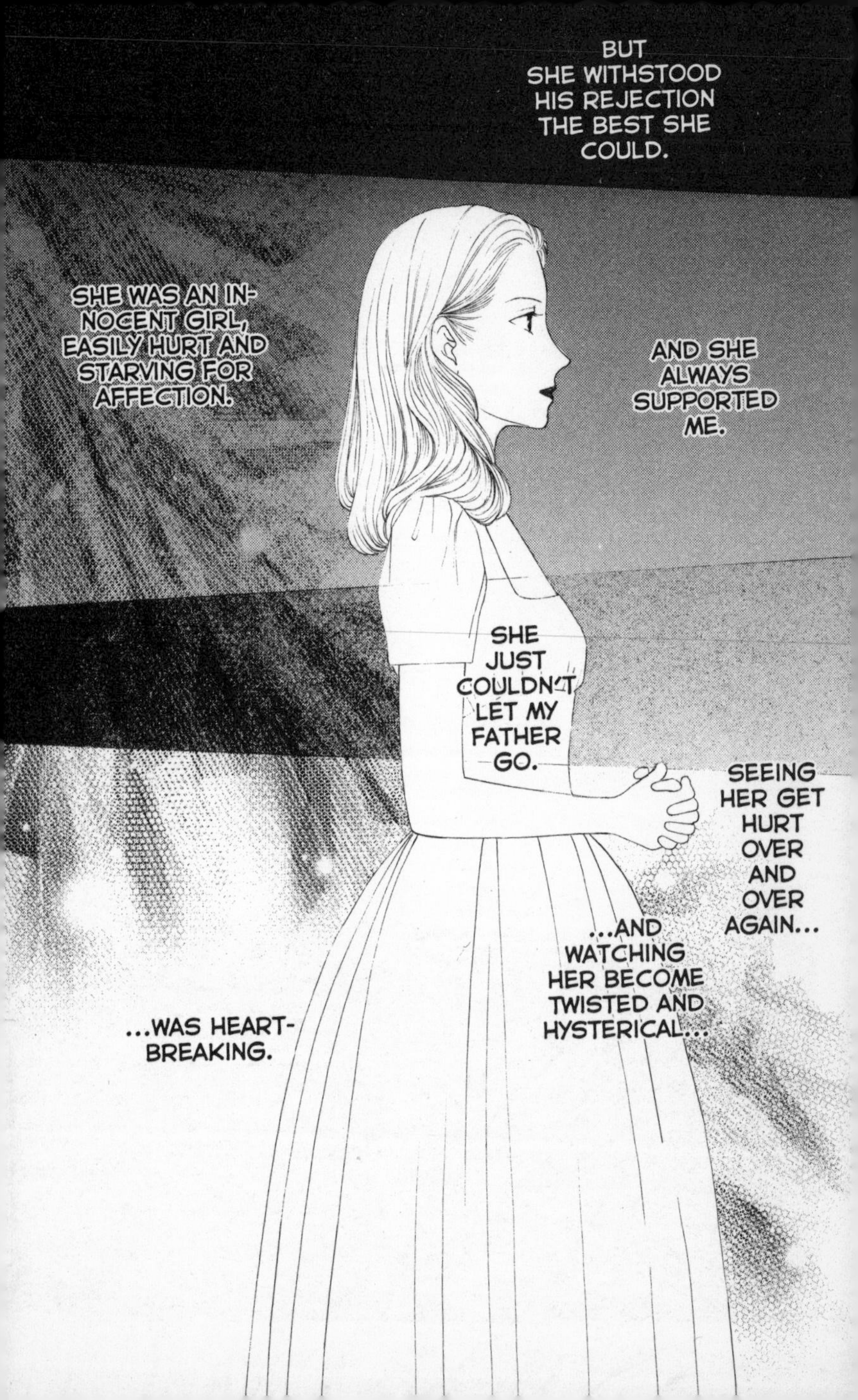
BUT SHE WITHSTOOD HIS REJECTION THE BEST SHE COULD.
AND SHE ALWAYS SUPPORTED ME.
SHE WAS AN INNOCENT GIRL, EASILY HURT AND STARVING FOR AFFECTION.
SHE JUST COULDN'T LET MY FATHER GO.
SEEING HER GET HURT OVER AND OVER AGAIN...
...AND WATCHING HER BECOME TWISTED AND HYSTERICAL...
...WAS HEART-BREAKING.

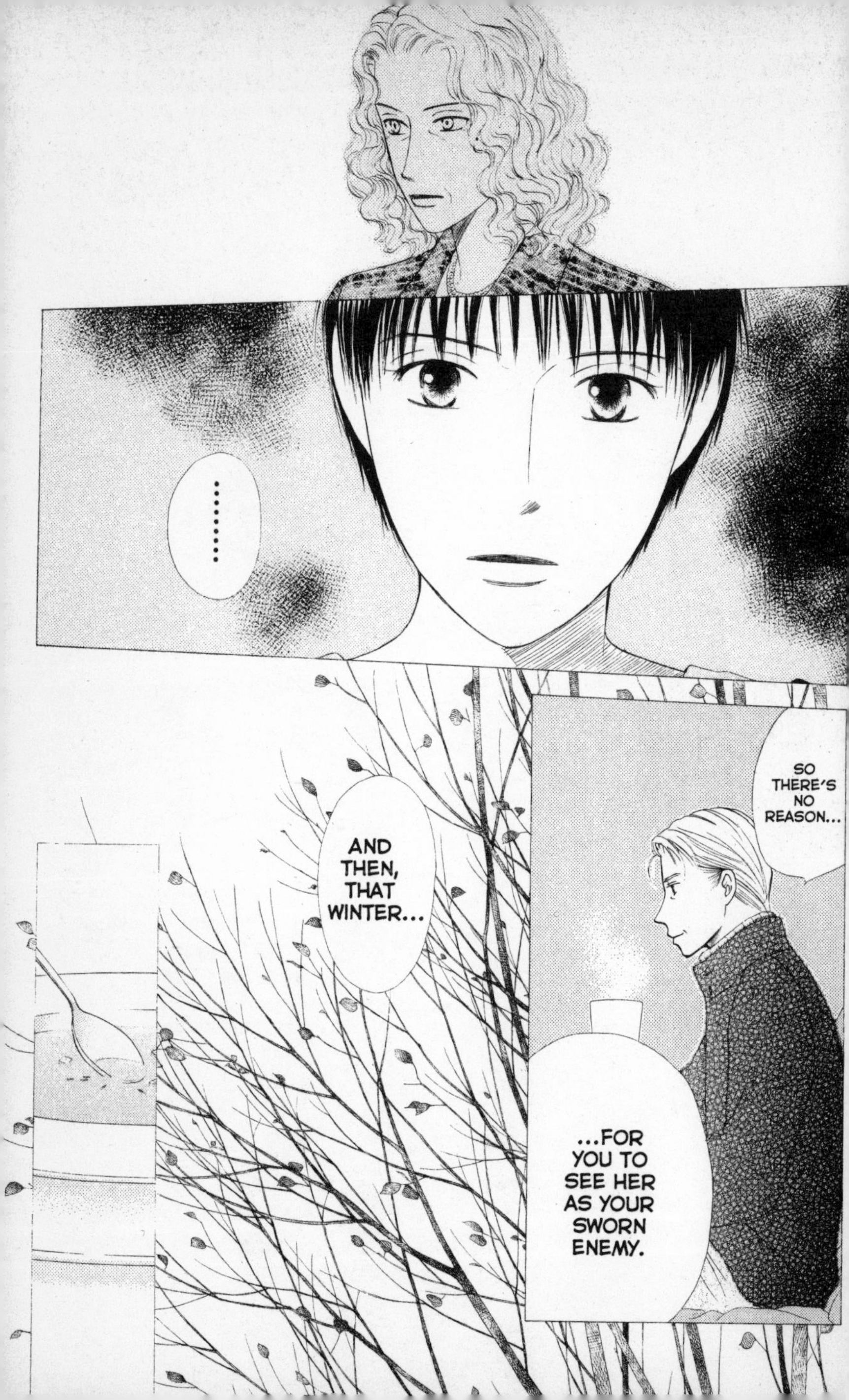
......
SO THERE'S NO REASON...
...FOR YOU TO SEE HER AS YOUR SWORN ENEMY.
AND THEN, THAT WINTER...

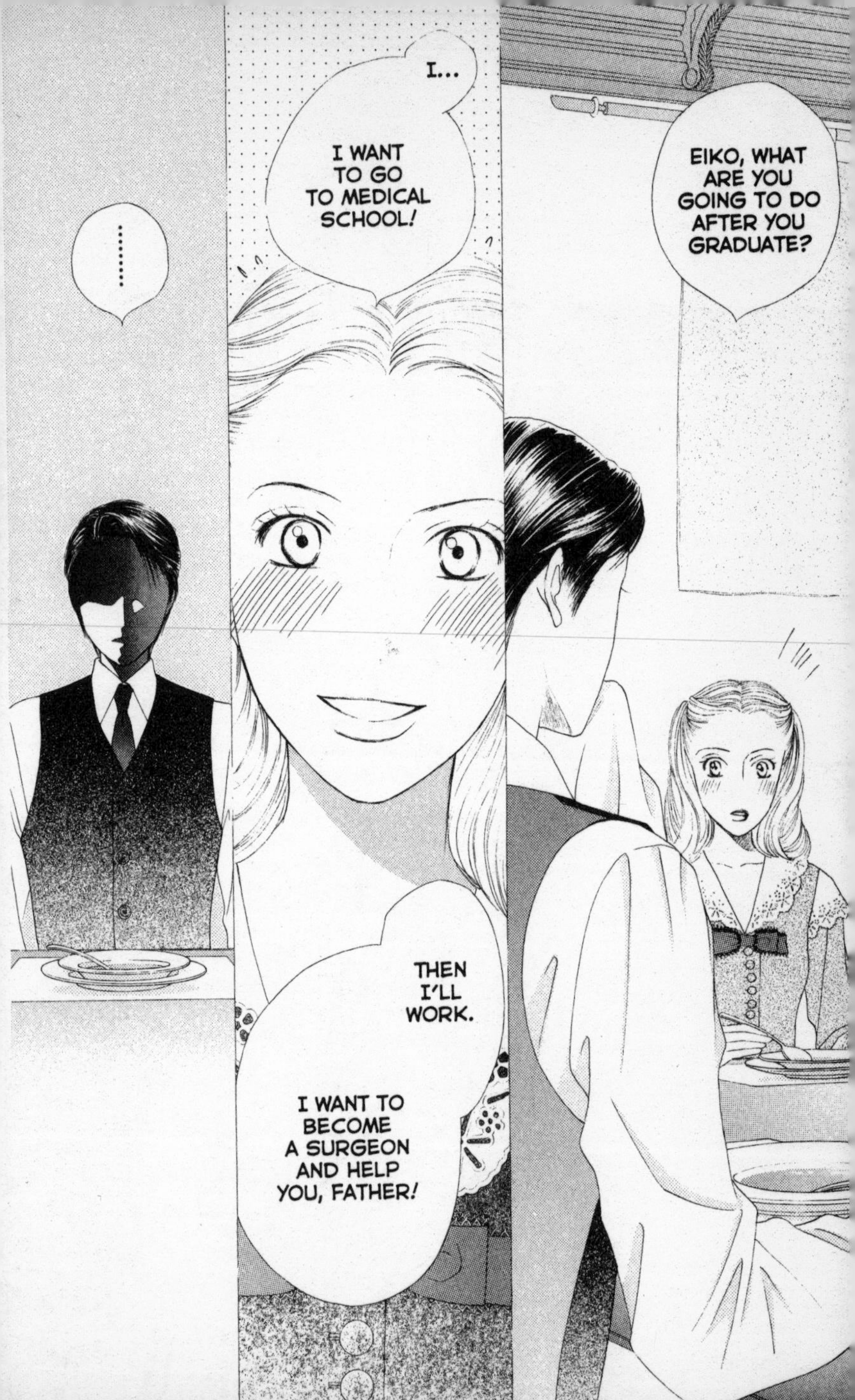
EIKO, WHAT ARE YOU GOING TO DO AFTER YOU GRADUATE?
I...
I WANT TO GO TO MEDICAL SCHOOL!
THEN I'LL WORK.
I WANT TO BECOME A SURGEON AND HELP YOU, FATHER!
......

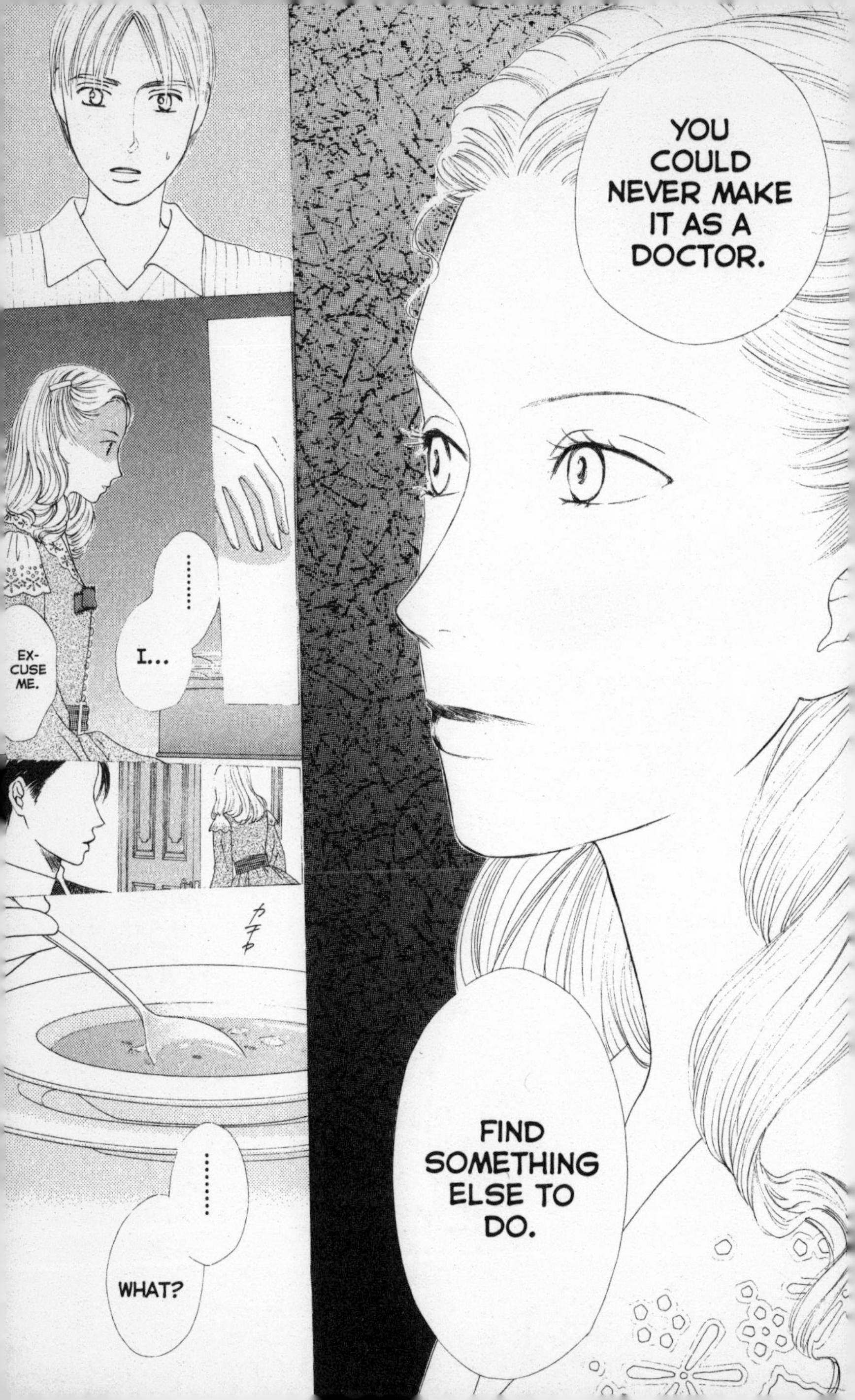
YOU COULD NEVER MAKE IT AS A DOCTOR.
FIND SOMETHING ELSE TO DO.
......
I...
EX-CUSE ME.
カチャ
....
WHAT?

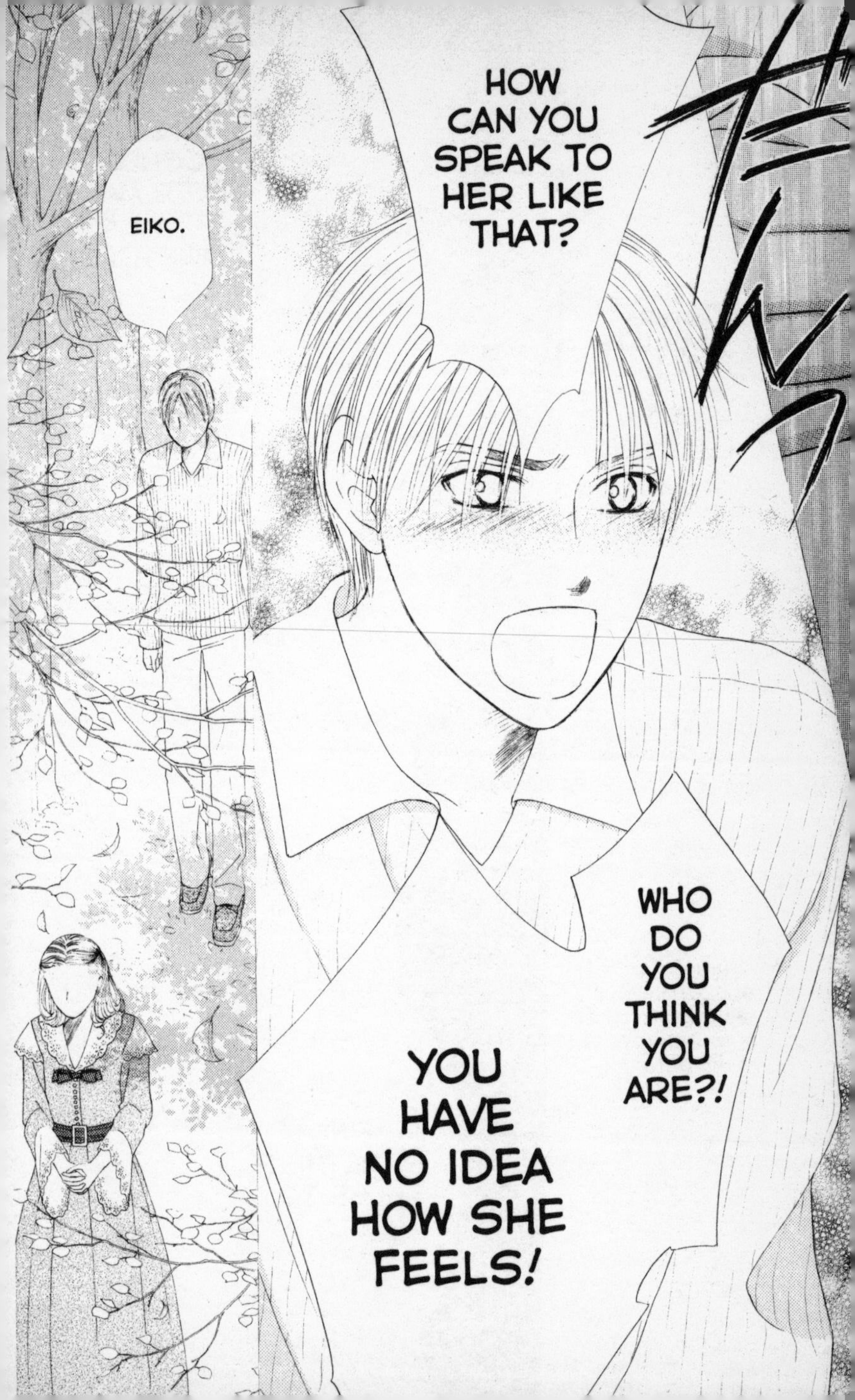
HOW CAN YOU SPEAK TO HER LIKE THAT?
WHO DO YOU THINK YOU ARE?!
YOU HAVE NO IDEA HOW SHE FEELS!
EIKO.

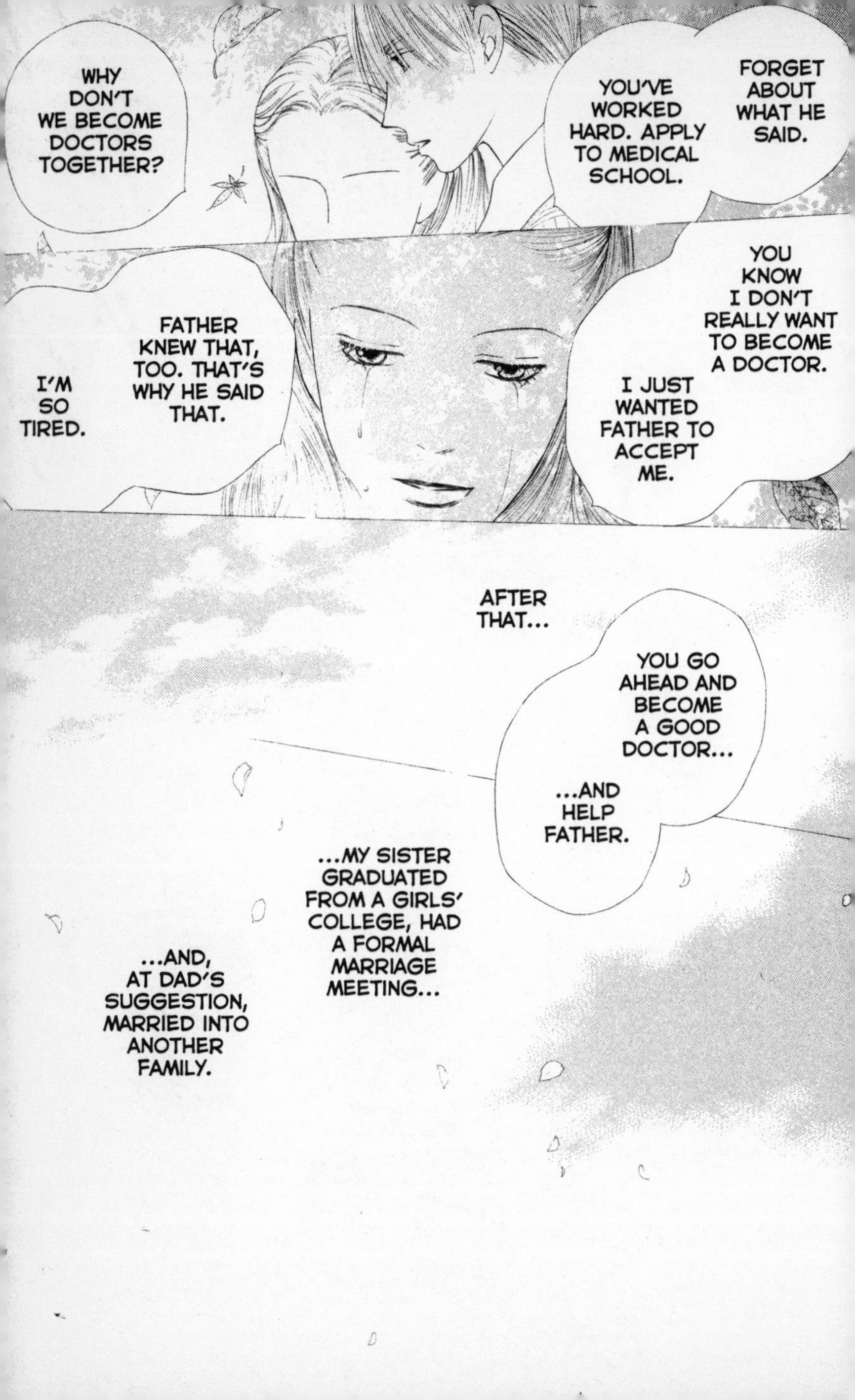
FORGET ABOUT WHAT HE SAID.
YOU'VE WORKED HARD. APPLY TO MEDICAL SCHOOL.
WHY DON'T WE BECOME DOCTORS TOGETHER?
YOU KNOW I DON'T REALLY WANT TO BECOME A DOCTOR.
I JUST WANTED FATHER TO ACCEPT ME.
FATHER KNEW THAT, TOO. THAT'S WHY HE SAID THAT.
I'M SO TIRED.
YOU GO AHEAD AND BECOME A GOOD DOCTOR...
...AND HELP FATHER.
AFTER THAT...
...MY SISTER GRADUATED FROM A GIRLS' COLLEGE, HAD A FORMAL MARRIAGE MEETING...
...AND, AT DAD'S SUGGESTION, MARRIED INTO ANOTHER FAMILY.

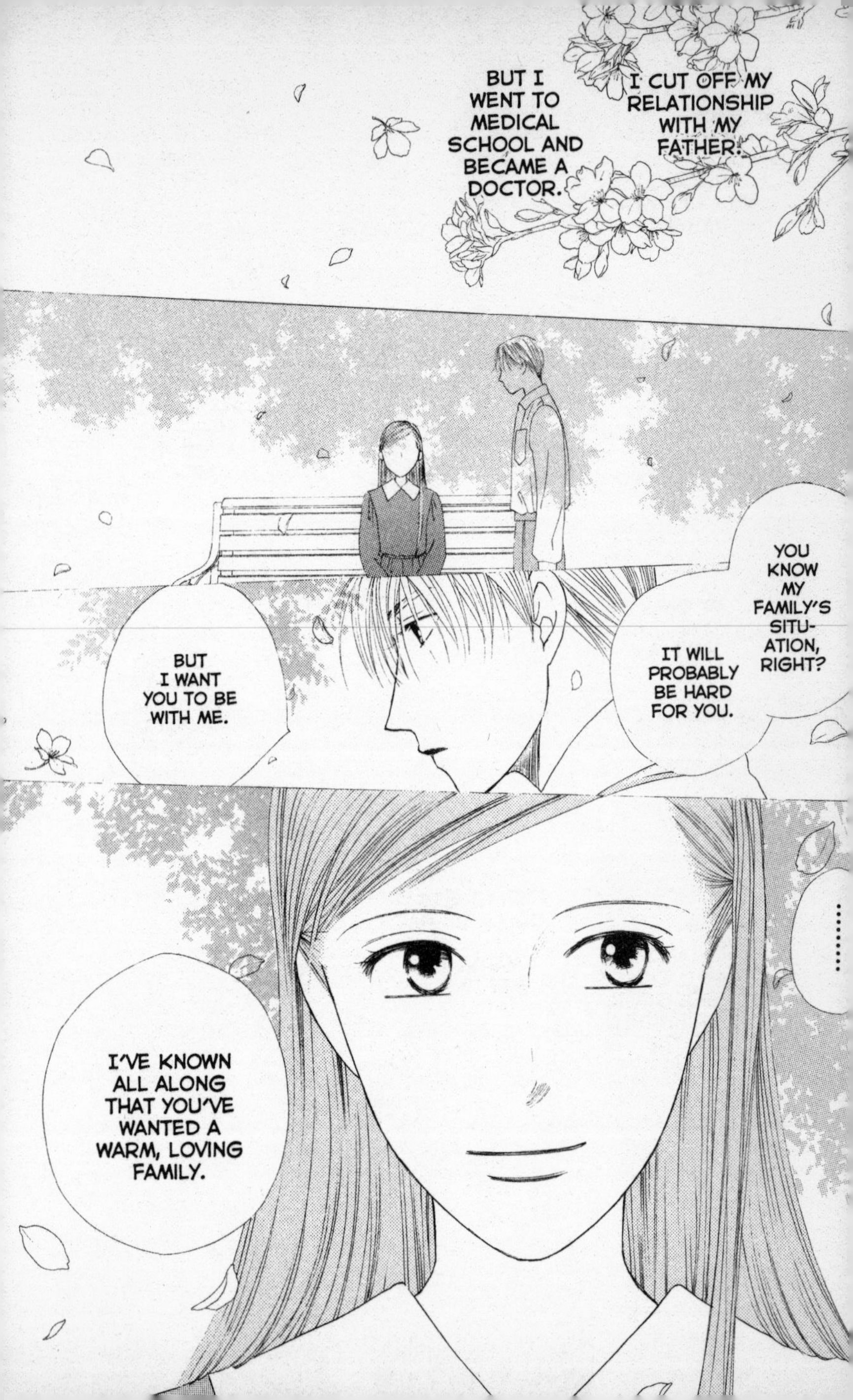
I CUT OFF MY RELATIONSHIP WITH MY FATHER.
BUT I WENT TO MEDICAL SCHOOL AND BECAME A DOCTOR.
YOU KNOW MY FAMILY'S SITUATION, RIGHT?
IT WILL PROBABLY BE HARD FOR YOU.
BUT I WANT YOU TO BE WITH ME.
......
I'VE KNOWN ALL ALONG THAT YOU'VE WANTED A WARM, LOVING FAMILY.

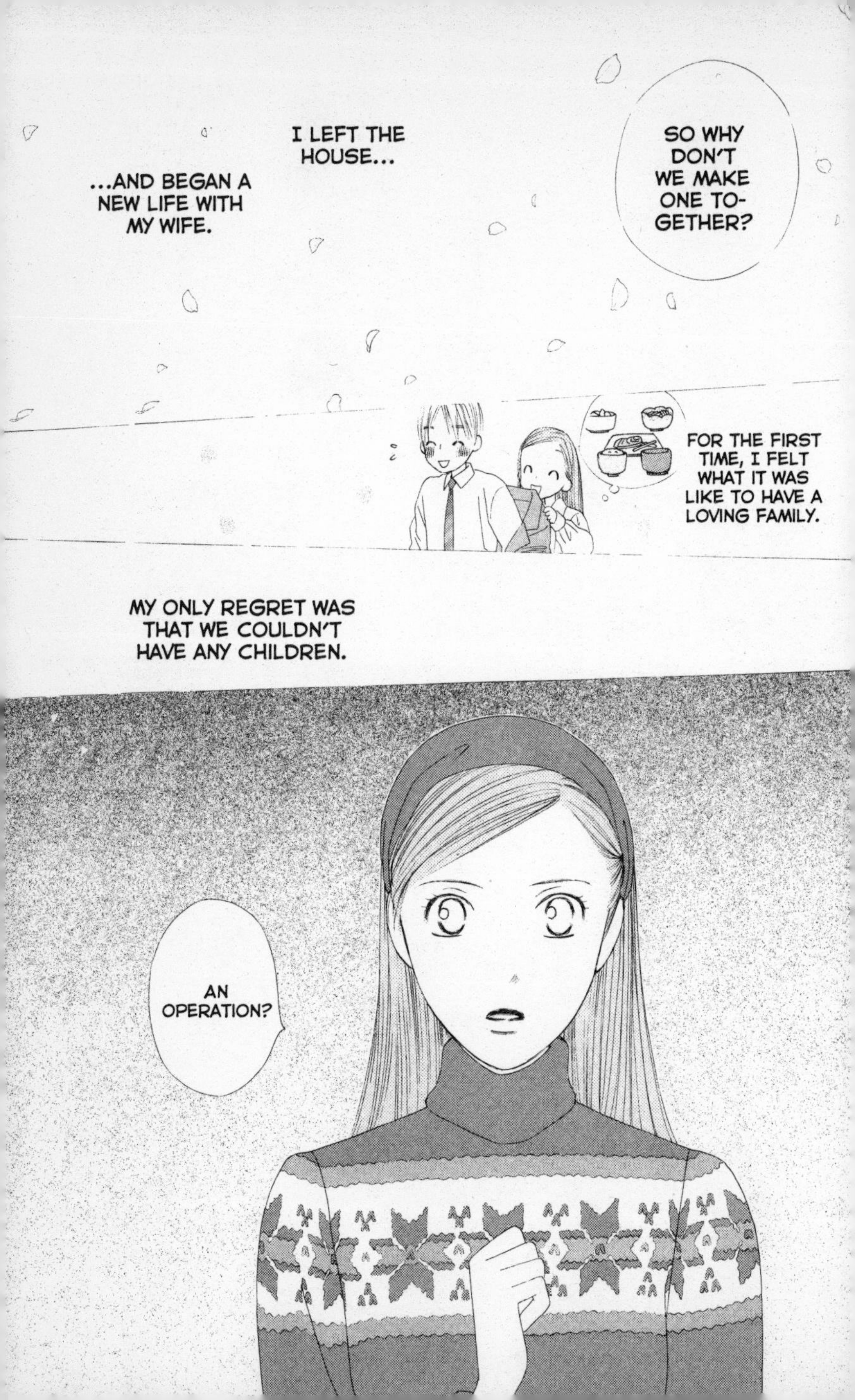
SO WHY DON'T WE MAKE ONE TO-GETHER?
I LEFT THE HOUSE...
...AND BEGAN A NEW LIFE WITH MY WIFE.
FOR THE FIRST TIME, I FELT WHAT IT WAS LIKE TO HAVE A LOVING FAMILY.
MY ONLY REGRET WAS THAT WE COULDN'T HAVE ANY CHILDREN.
AN OPERATION?

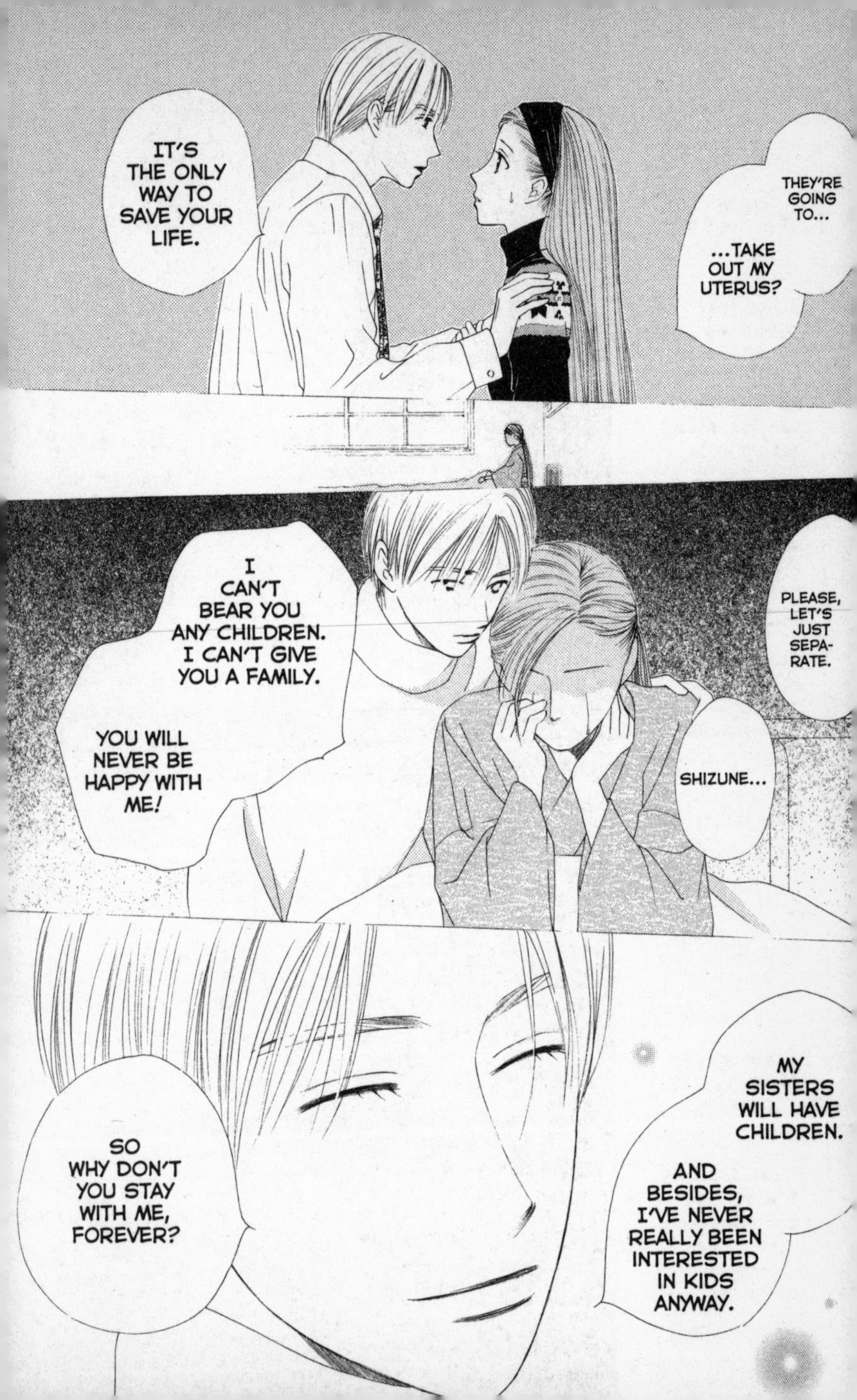
THEY'RE GOING TO...
...TAKE OUT MY UTERUS?
IT'S THE ONLY WAY TO SAVE YOUR LIFE.
PLEASE, LET'S JUST SEPA-RATE.
I CAN'T BEAR YOU ANY CHILDREN. I CAN'T GIVE YOU A FAMILY.
YOU WILL NEVER BE HAPPY WITH ME!
SHIZUNE...
MY SISTERS WILL HAVE CHILDREN.
AND BESIDES, I'VE NEVER REALLY BEEN INTERESTED IN KIDS ANYWAY.
SO WHY DON'T YOU STAY WITH ME, FOREVER?

I FULFILLED MY DUTY.

I LEFT THE FAMILY UP TO MY SISTERS.

I THOUGHT I HAD BEEN RELEASED.

I NEVER EXPECTED...

3

Books on Plates & Bowls

Books that soothe me when I'm tired:

Kohiki Plates,
Lacquer Bowls,
Glass Cups,
Pure White,
Breakfast Sets,
Square Plates,
Wooden Plates,
Porcelain Bowls with Chinese Pictures on Them.

When I see them....

...I get really excited!

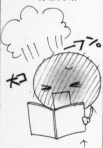

I guess you can't really say this is soothing...

I love thinking, "It'd be nice to eat off plates like those..." I'm such a glutton.

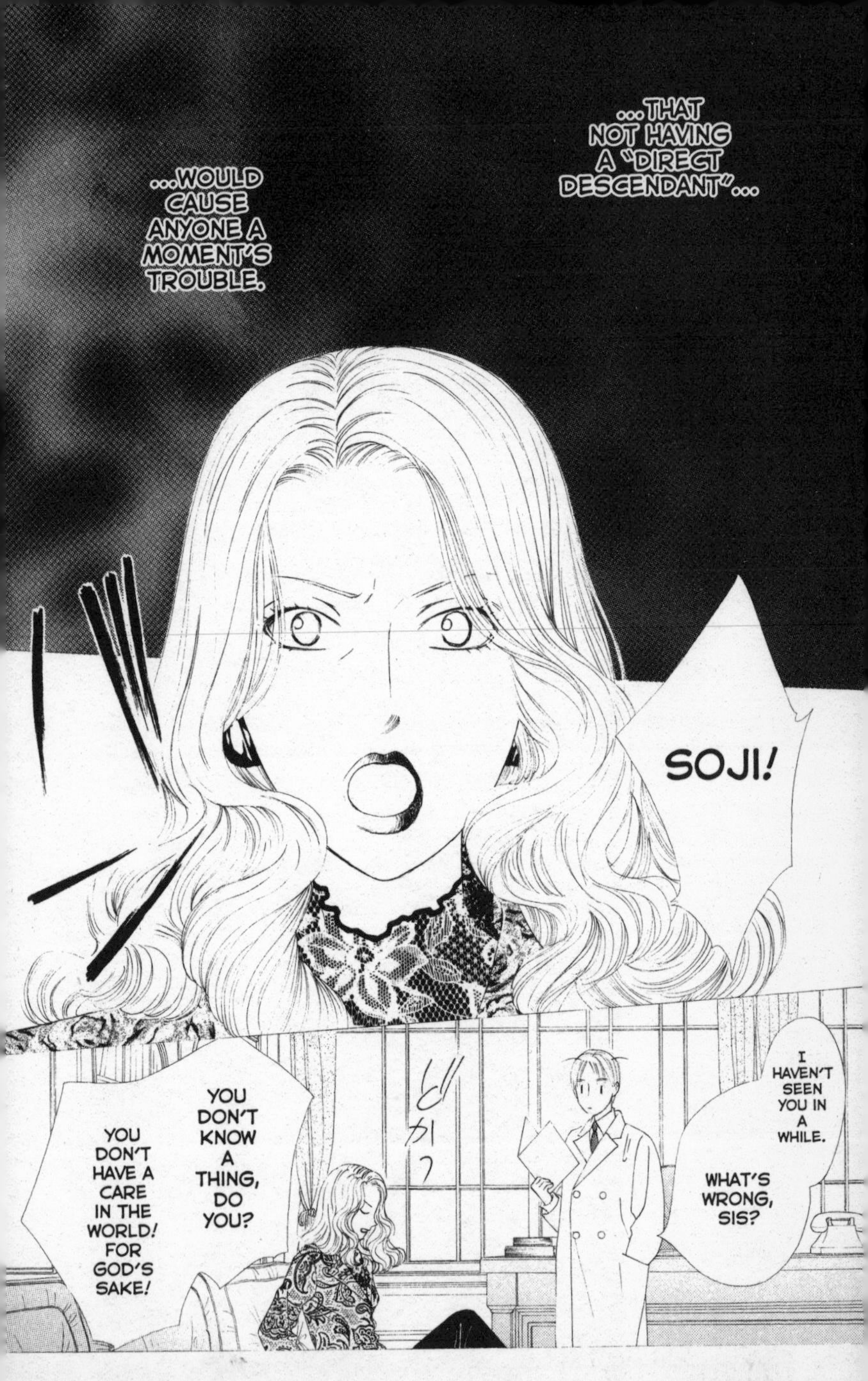
...THAT NOT HAVING A "DIRECT DESCENDANT"...
...WOULD CAUSE ANYONE A MOMENT'S TROUBLE.
SOJI!
I HAVEN'T SEEN YOU IN A WHILE.
WHAT'S WRONG, SIS?
YOU DON'T KNOW A THING, DO YOU?
YOU DON'T HAVE A CARE IN THE WORLD! FOR GOD'S SAKE!

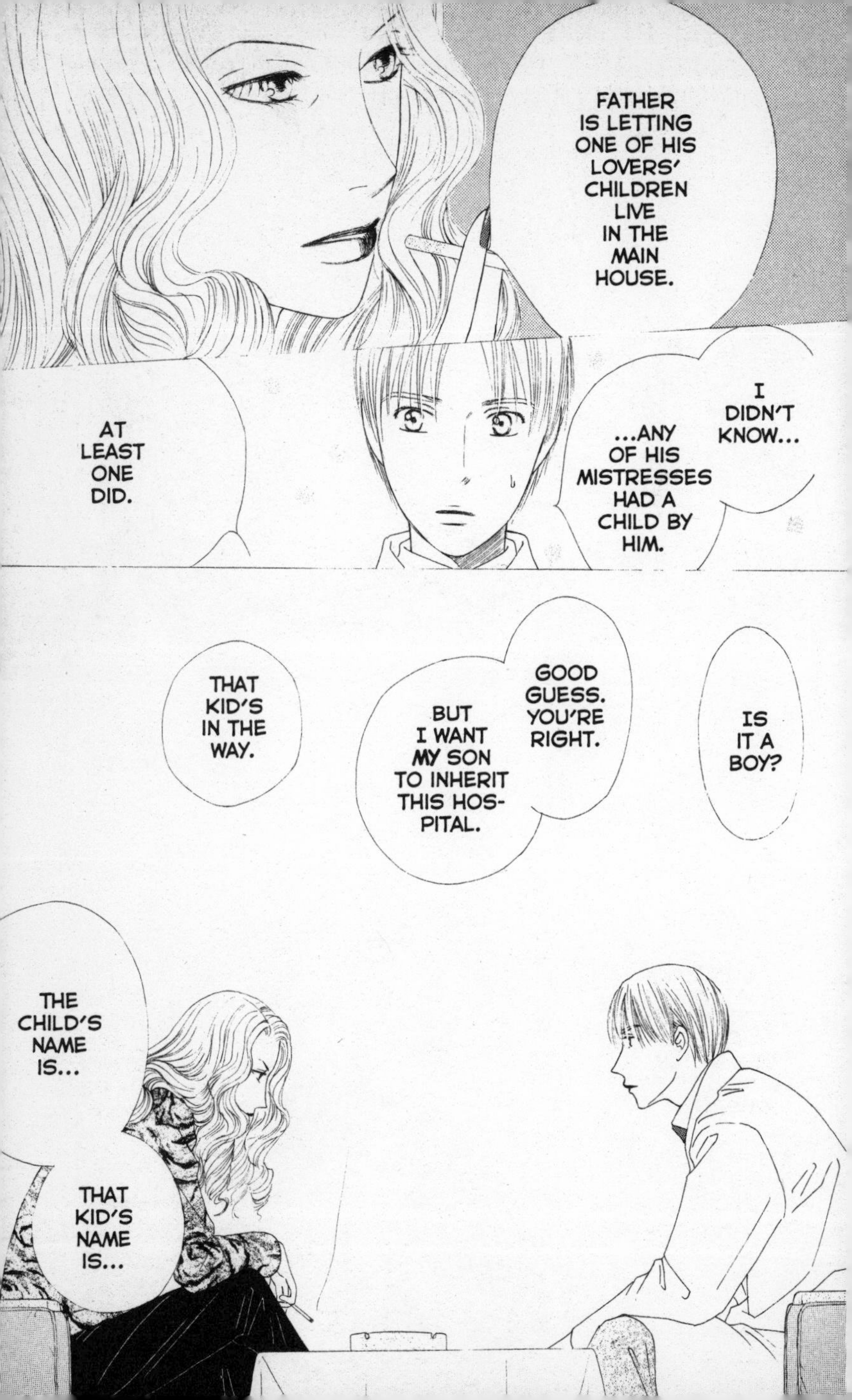
FATHER IS LETTING ONE OF HIS LOVERS' CHILDREN LIVE IN THE MAIN HOUSE.
I DIDN'T KNOW...
...ANY OF HIS MISTRESSES HAD A CHILD BY HIM.
AT LEAST ONE DID.
IS IT A BOY?
GOOD GUESS. YOU'RE RIGHT.
BUT I WANT *MY* SON TO INHERIT THIS HOS-PITAL.
THAT KID'S IN THE WAY.
THE CHILD'S NAME IS...
THAT KID'S NAME IS...

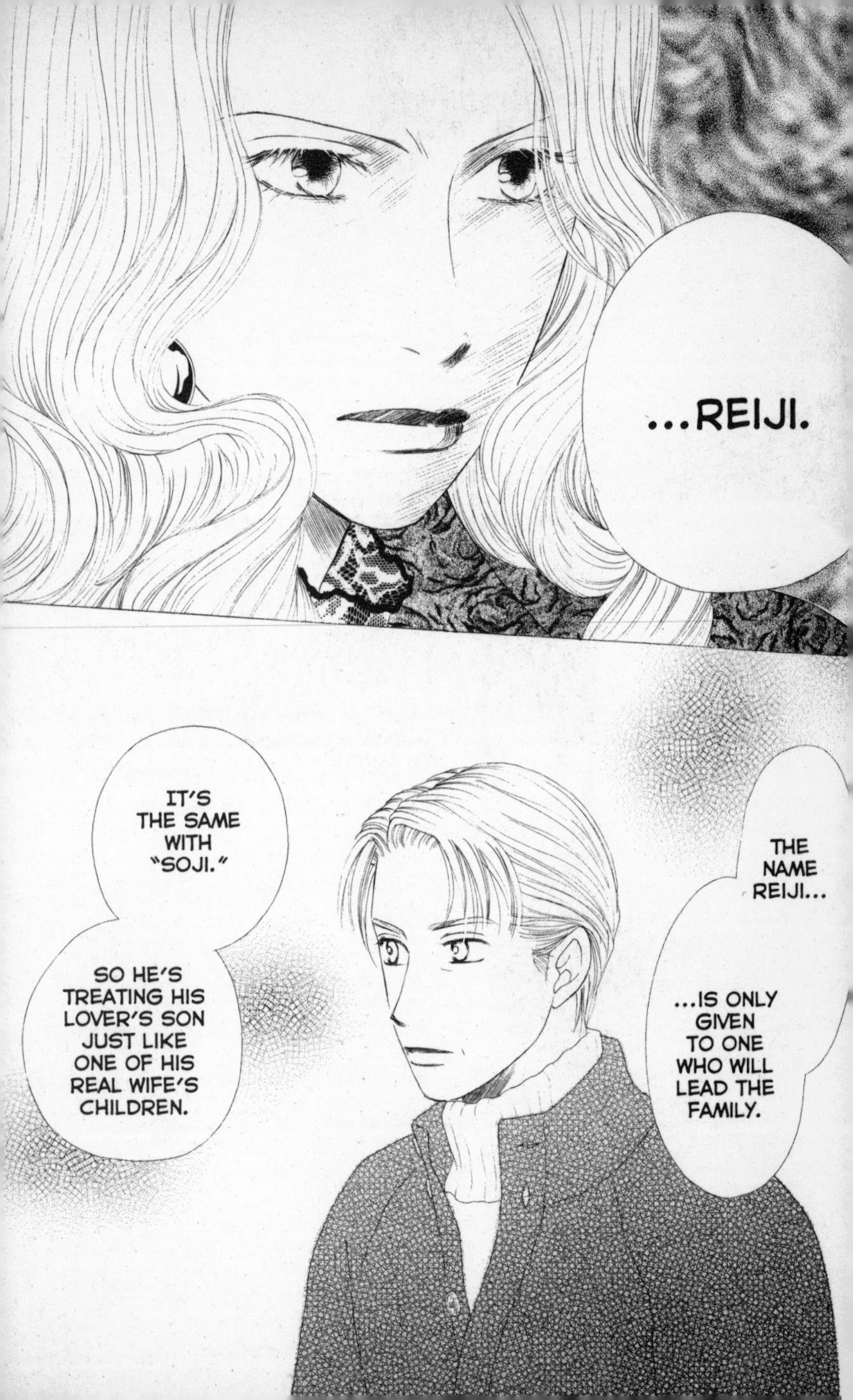
...REIJI.
THE NAME REIJI...
...IS ONLY GIVEN TO ONE WHO WILL LEAD THE FAMILY.
IT'S THE SAME WITH "SOJI."
SO HE'S TREATING HIS LOVER'S SON JUST LIKE ONE OF HIS REAL WIFE'S CHILDREN.

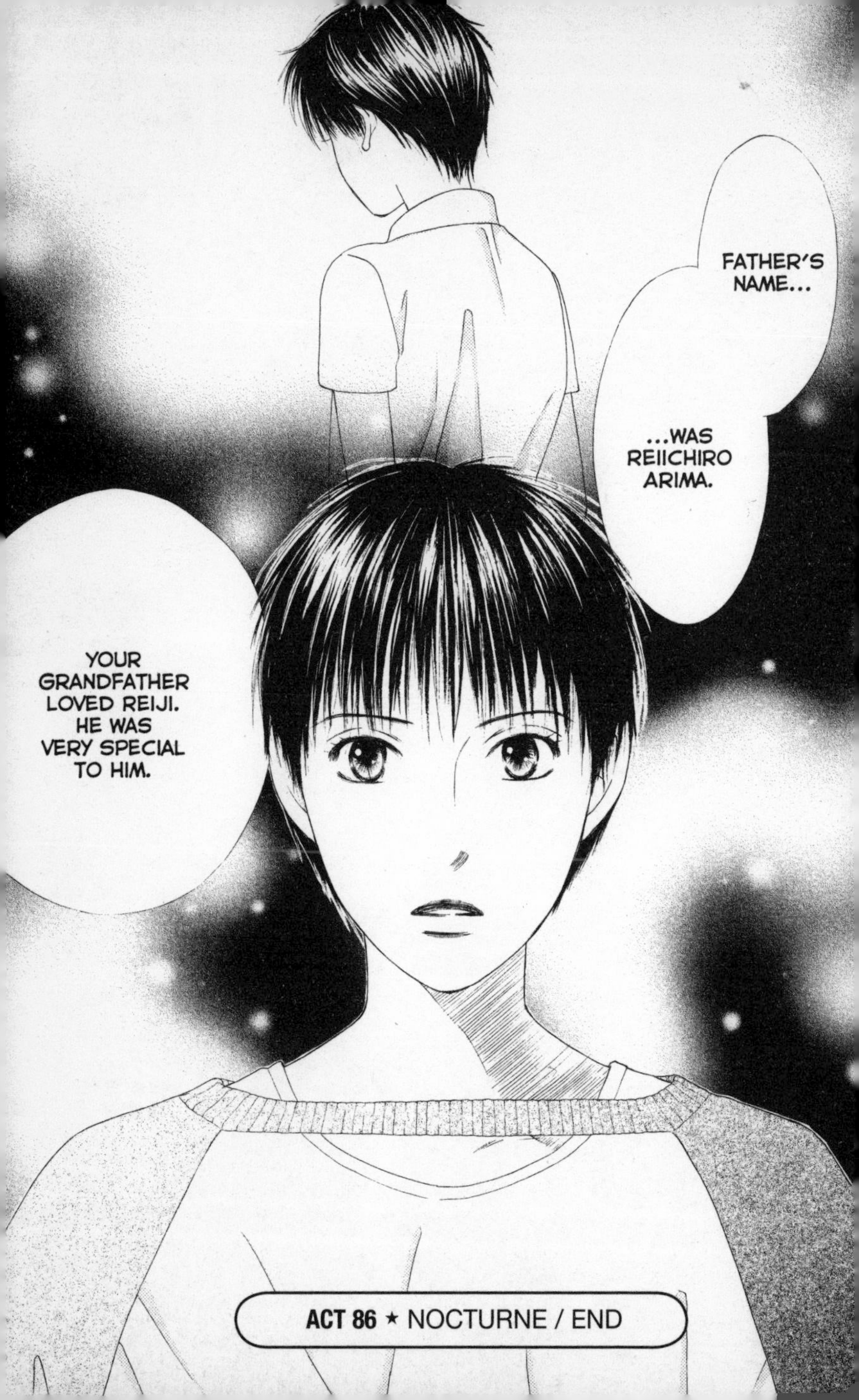
FATHER'S NAME...
...WAS REIICHIRO ARIMA.
YOUR GRANDFATHER LOVED REIJI. HE WAS VERY SPECIAL TO HIM.
ACT 86 ★ NOCTURNE / END

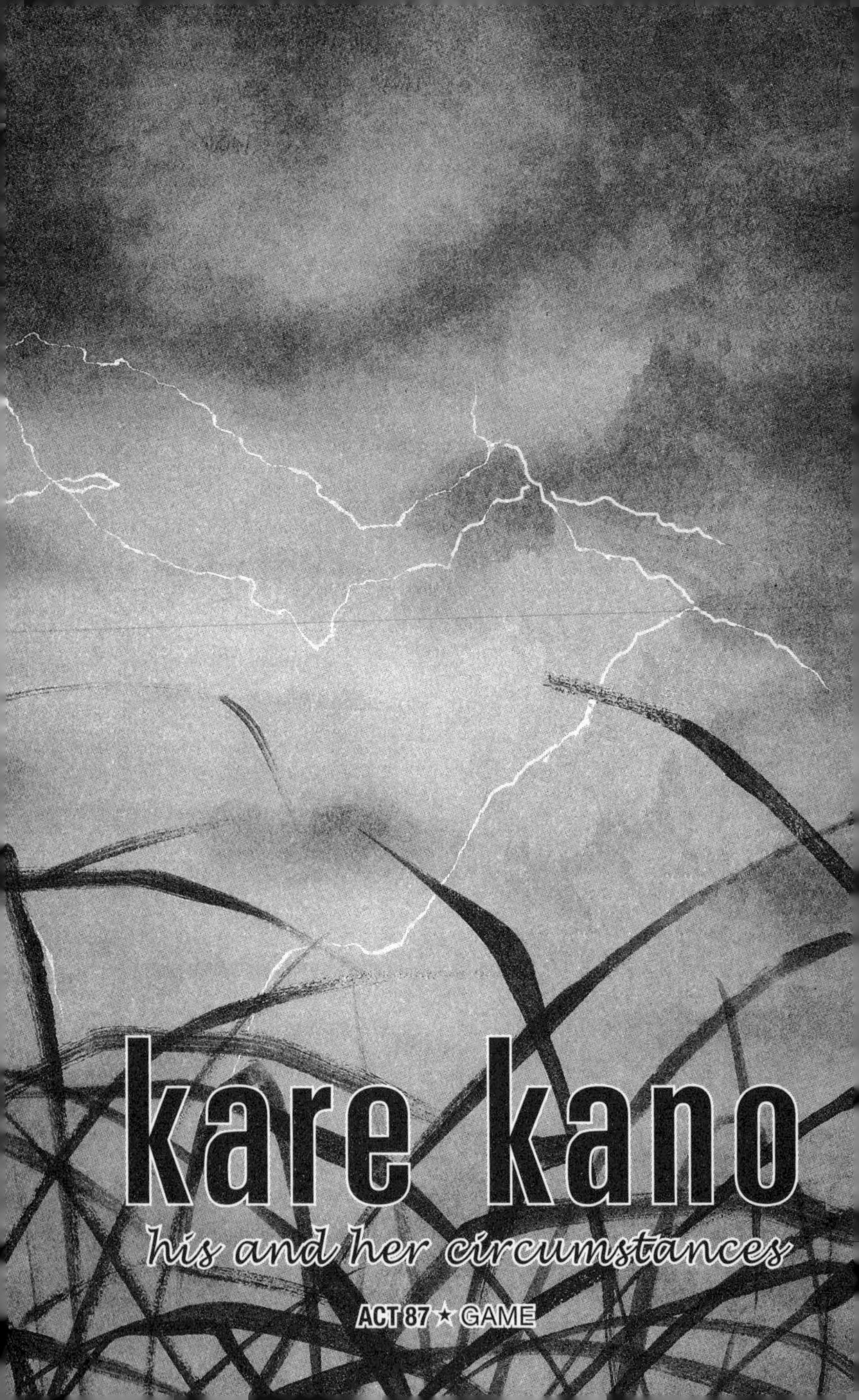
kare kano
his and her circumstances
ACT 87 ★ GAME

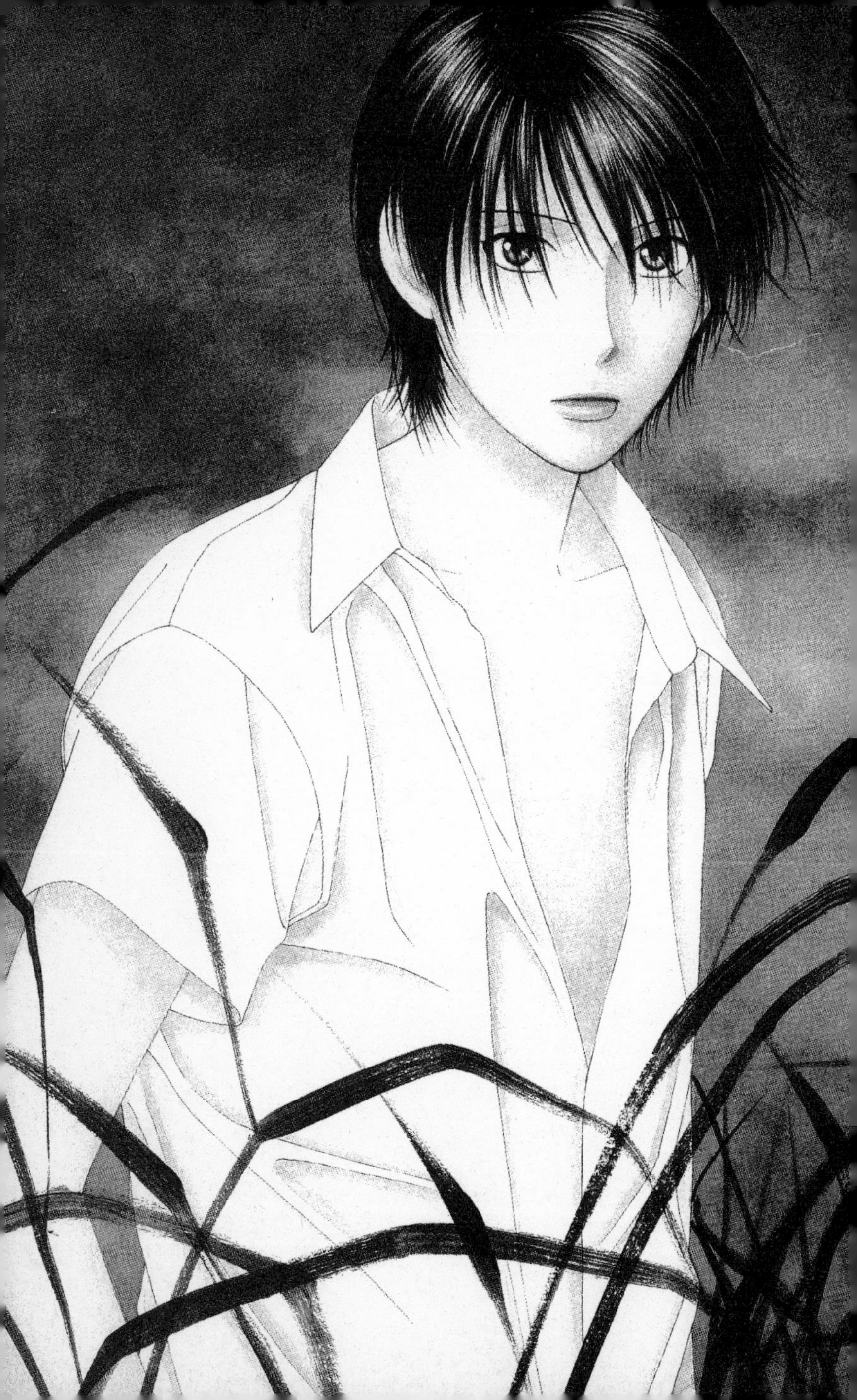

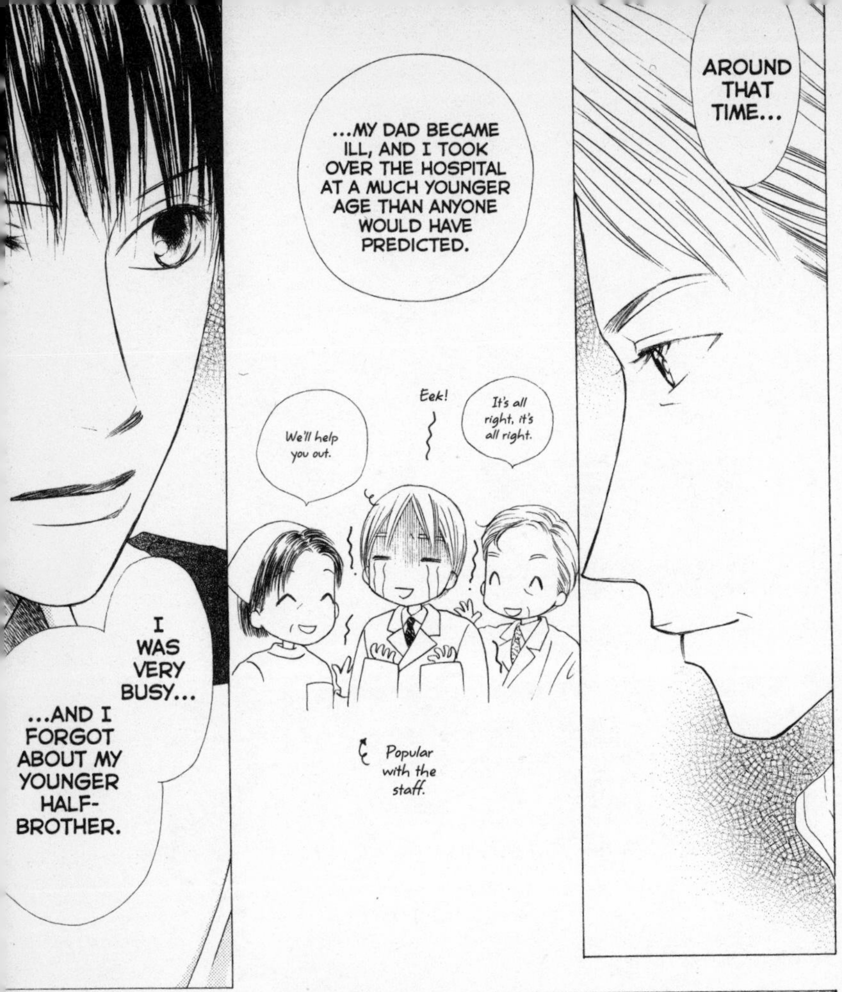
AROUND THAT TIME...
...MY DAD BECAME ILL, AND I TOOK OVER THE HOSPITAL AT A MUCH YOUNGER AGE THAN ANYONE WOULD HAVE PREDICTED.
It's all right, it's all right.
Eek!
We'll help you out.
Popular with the staff.
I WAS VERY BUSY...
...AND I FORGOT ABOUT MY YOUNGER HALF-BROTHER.

Beans.

I've gotten into beans lately. They're delicious! I separate out some beans and put them in the refrigerator.

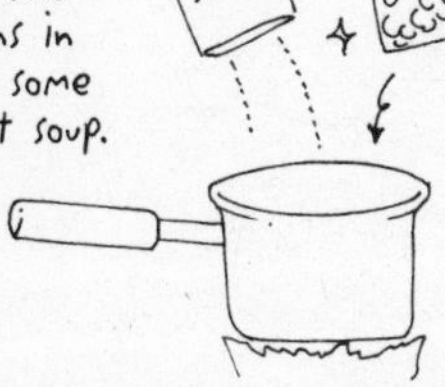
soup

I boil some water and put the beans in with some instant soup.

That's what I've been having for breakfast lately.

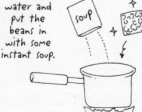

I want to try different bean variations.

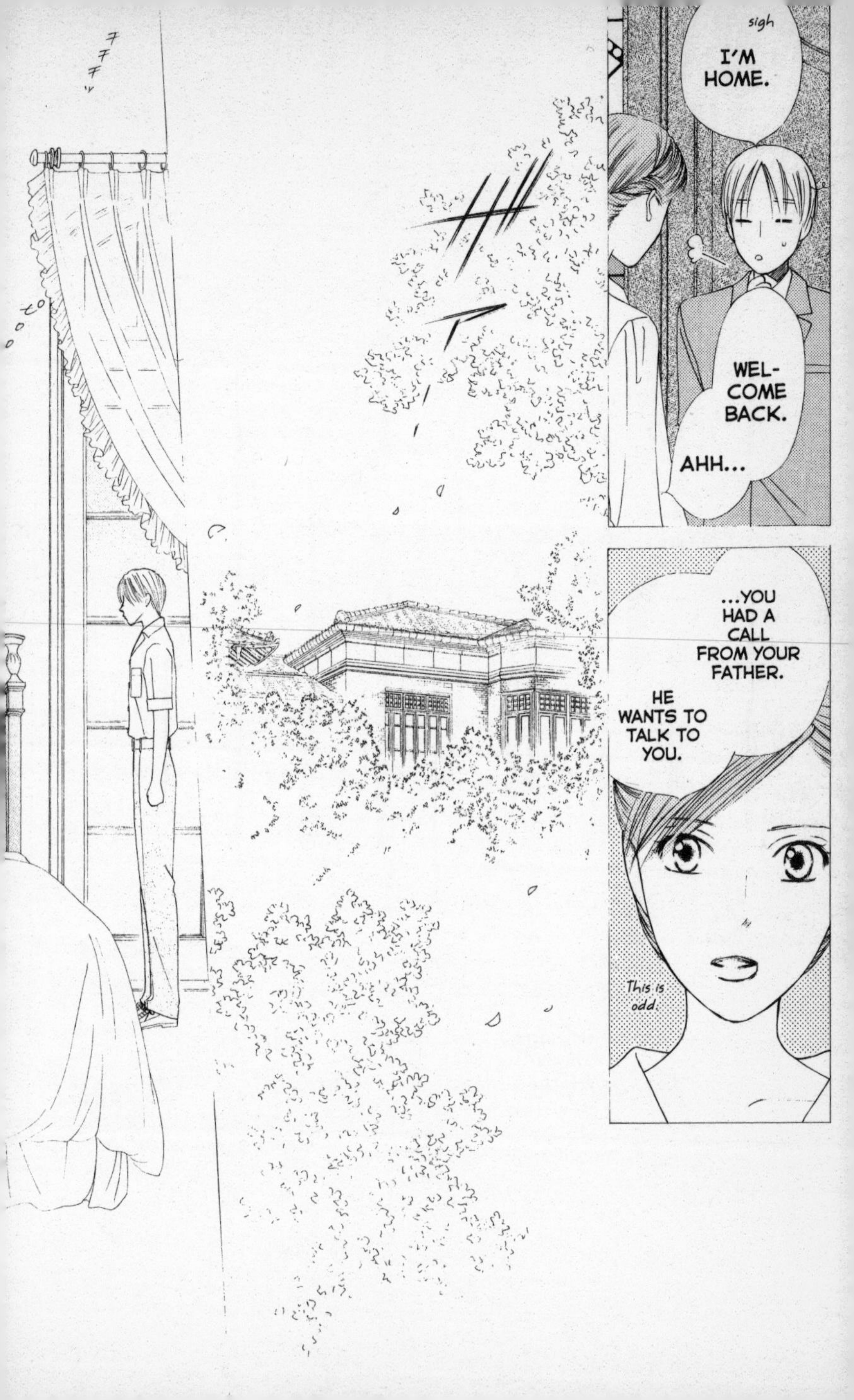
sigh
I'M HOME.
WEL-COME BACK.
AHH...
...YOU HAD A CALL FROM YOUR FATHER.
HE WANTS TO TALK TO YOU.
This is odd.
チチチッ

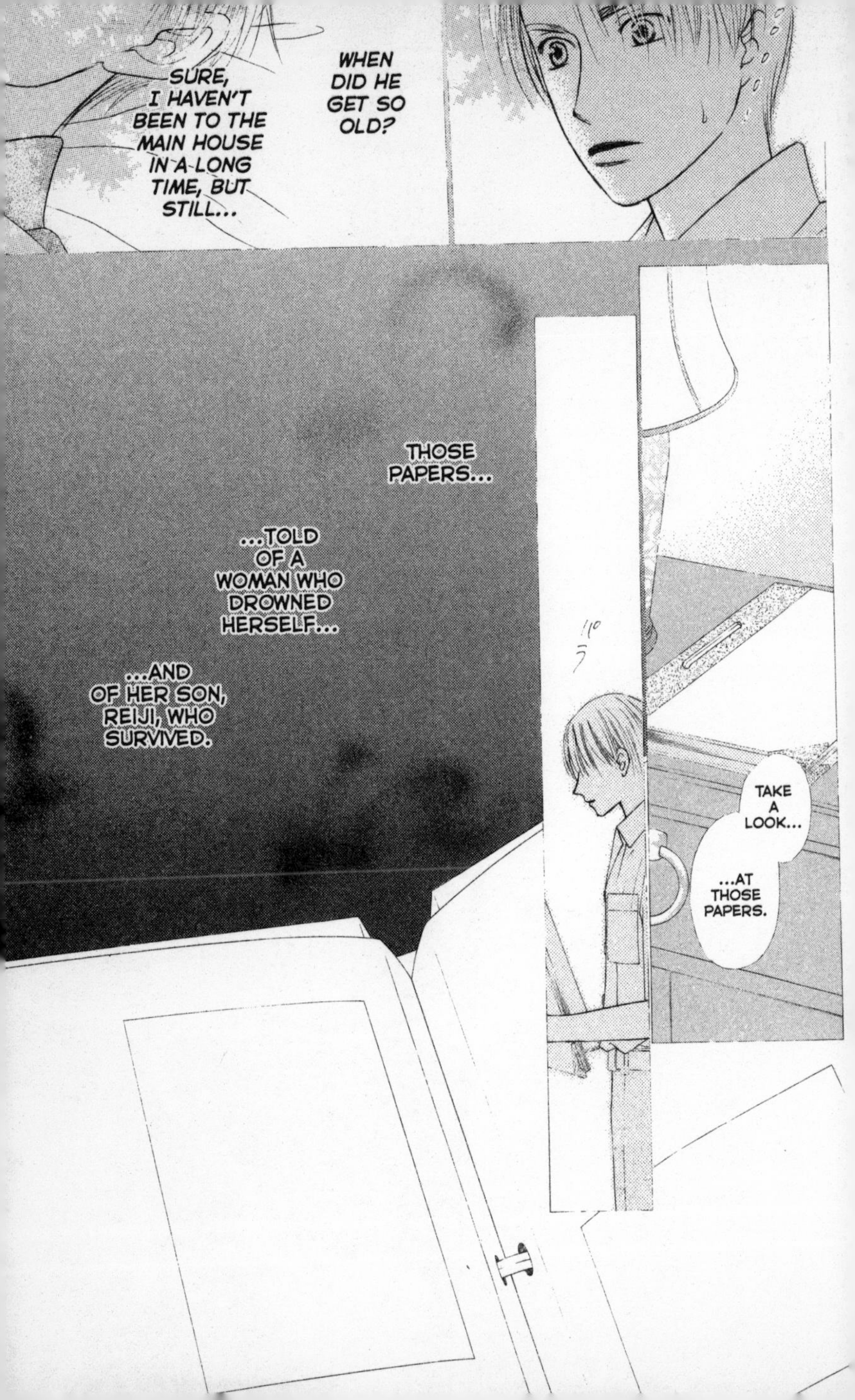
WHEN DID HE GET SO OLD?
SURE, I HAVEN'T BEEN TO THE MAIN HOUSE IN A LONG TIME, BUT STILL...
TAKE A LOOK...
...AT THOSE PAPERS.
THOSE PAPERS...
...TOLD OF A WOMAN WHO DROWNED HERSELF...
...AND OF HER SON, REIJI, WHO SURVIVED.

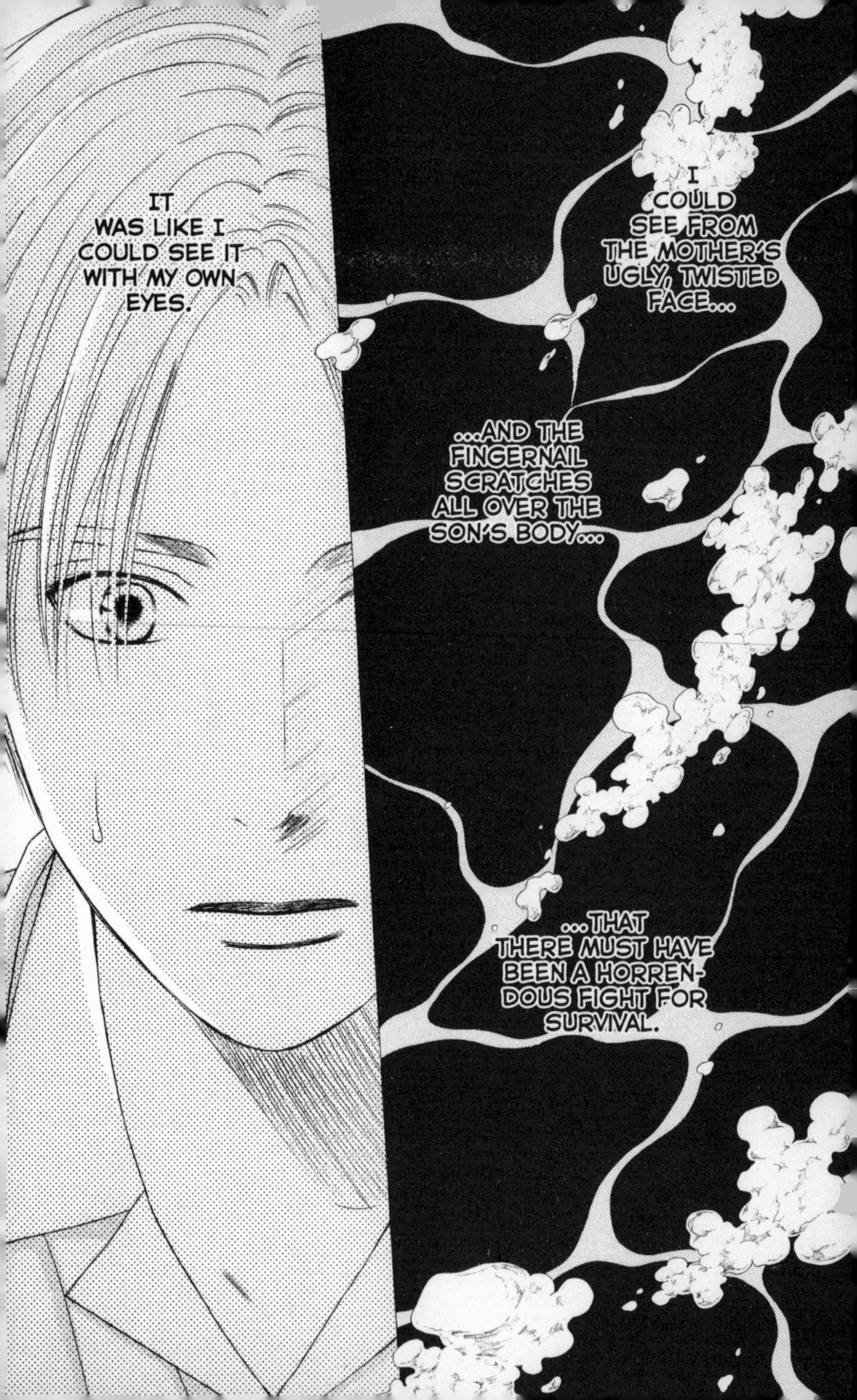
I COULD SEE FROM THE MOTHER'S UGLY, TWISTED FACE...
...AND THE FINGERNAIL SCRATCHES ALL OVER THE SON'S BODY...
...THAT THERE MUST HAVE BEEN A HORRENDOUS FIGHT FOR SURVIVAL.
IT WAS LIKE I COULD SEE IT WITH MY OWN EYES.

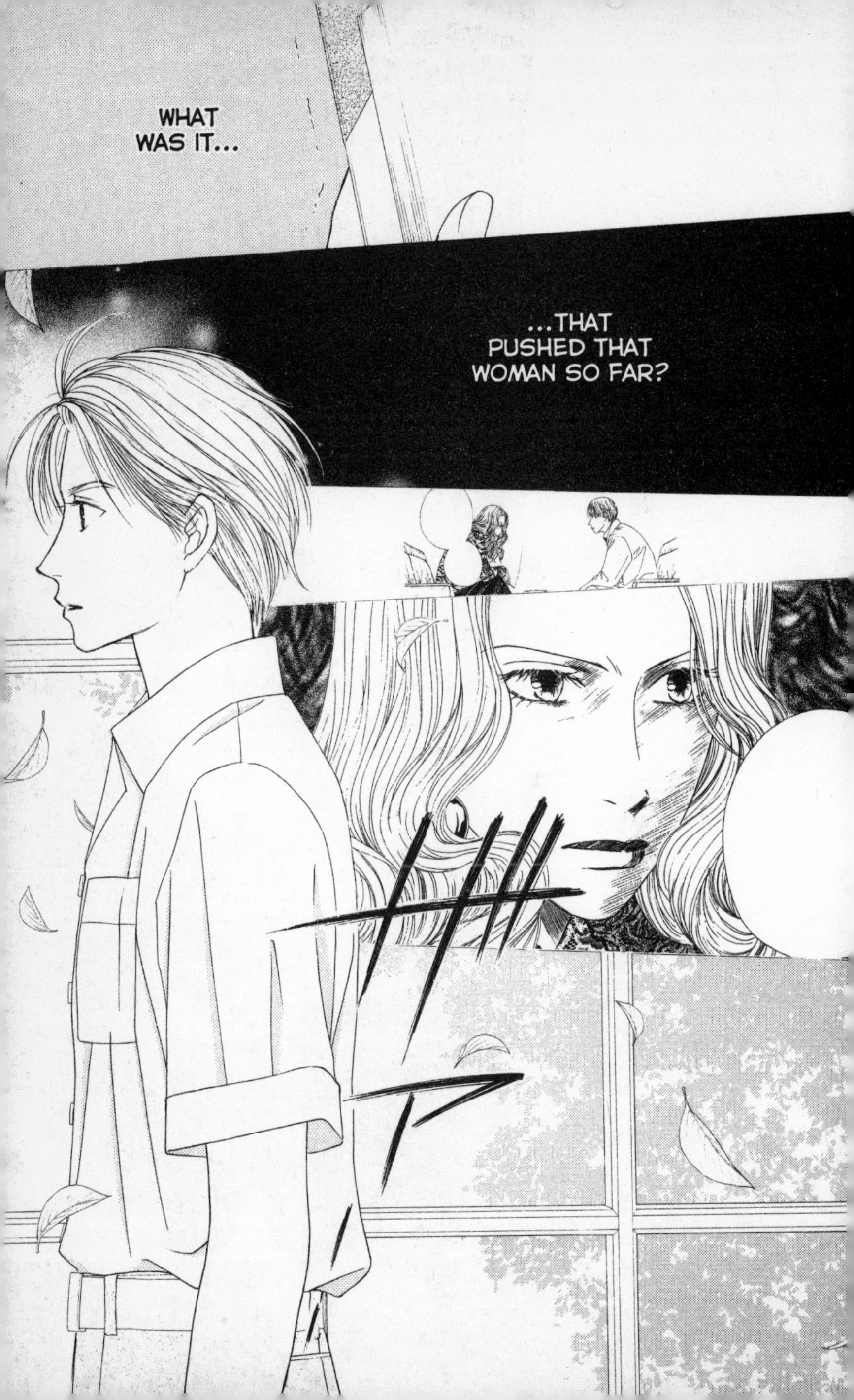
WHAT WAS IT...
...THAT PUSHED THAT WOMAN SO FAR?

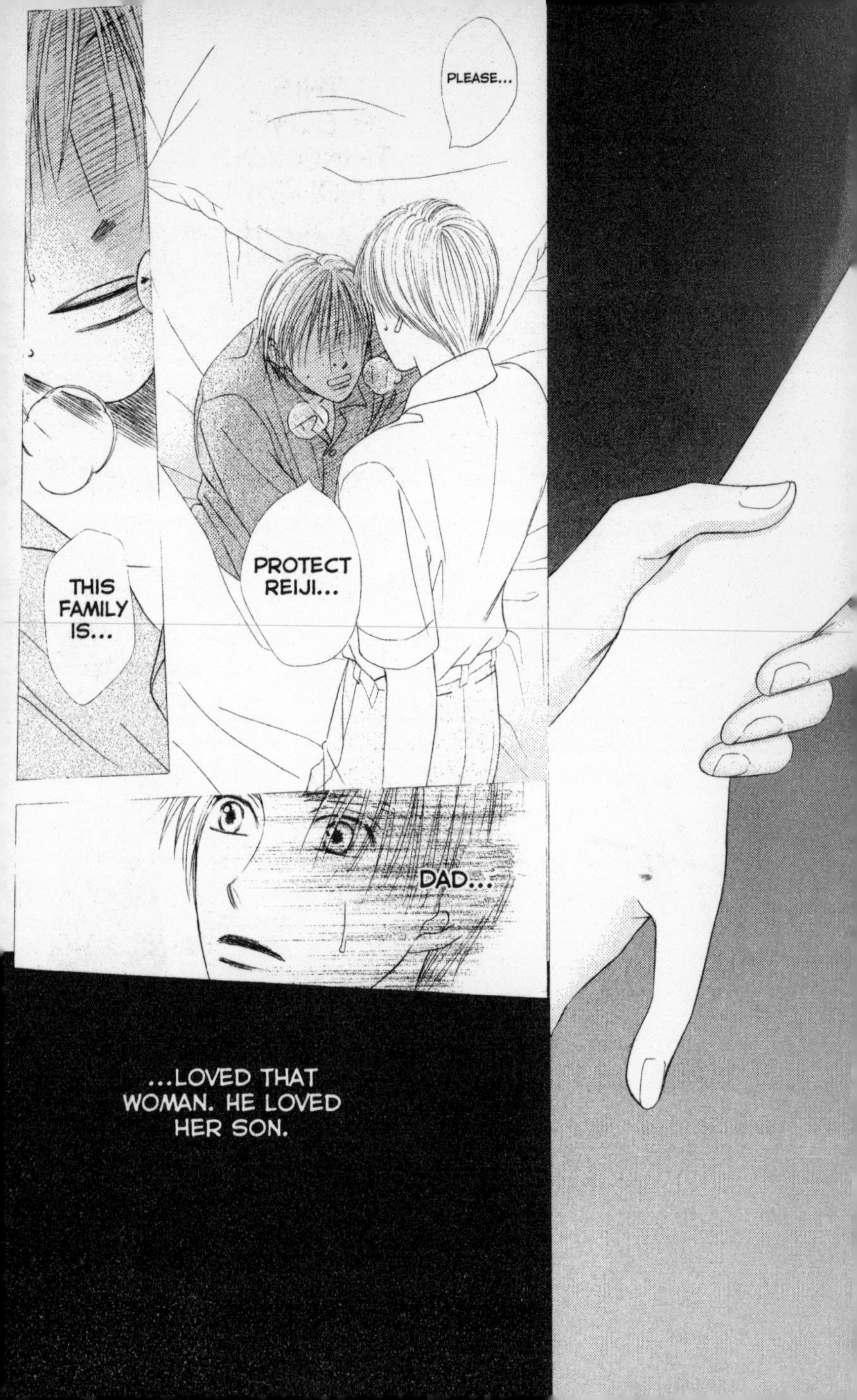
PLEASE...
PROTECT REIJI...
THIS FAMILY IS...
DAD...
...LOVED THAT WOMAN. HE LOVED HER SON.

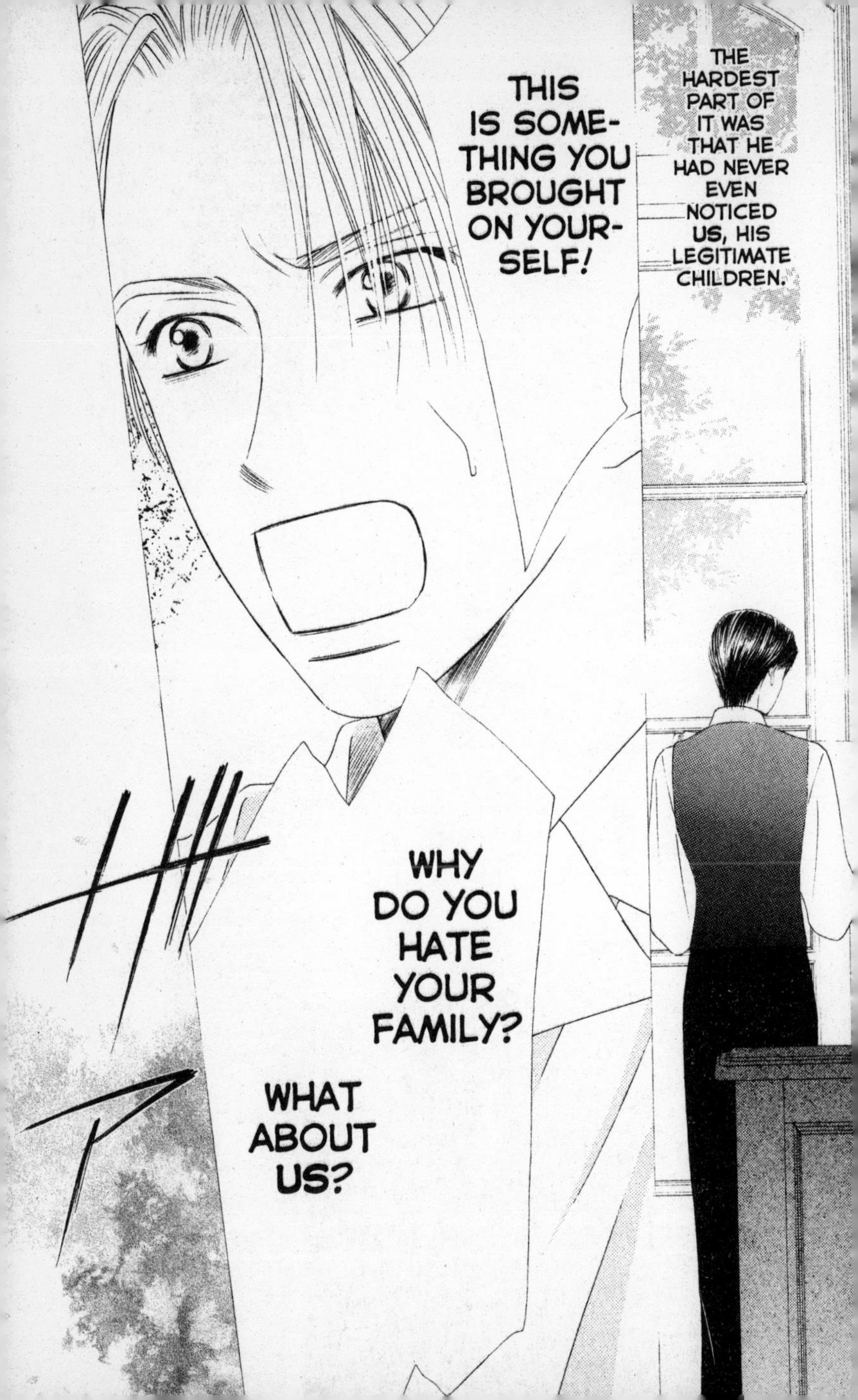
THE HARDEST PART OF IT WAS THAT HE HAD NEVER EVEN NOTICED US, HIS LEGITIMATE CHILDREN.
THIS IS SOME-THING YOU BROUGHT ON YOUR-SELF!
WHY DO YOU HATE YOUR FAMILY?
WHAT ABOUT US?

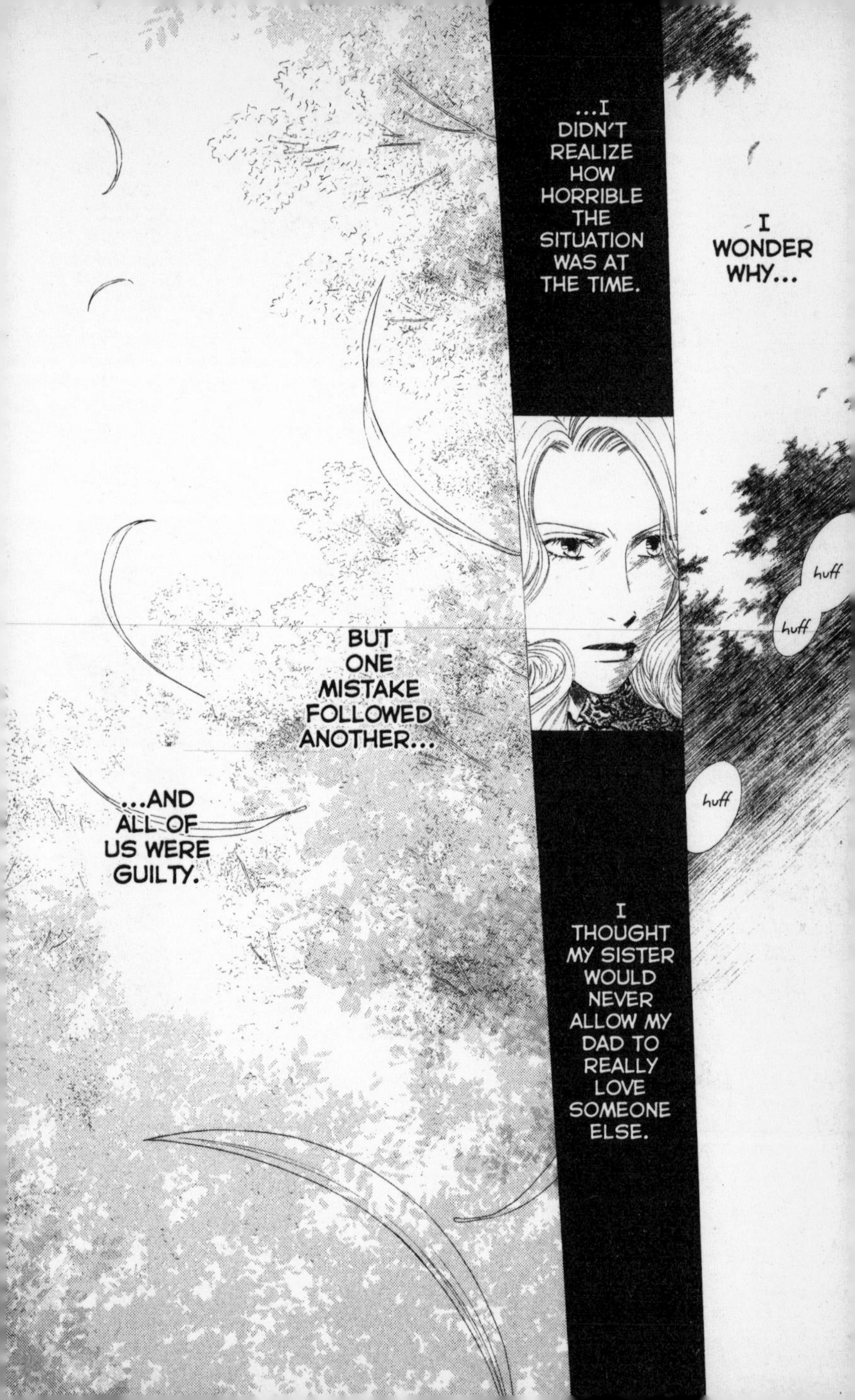
I WONDER WHY...
...I DIDN'T REALIZE HOW HORRIBLE THE SITUATION WAS AT THE TIME.
huff
huff
huff
I THOUGHT MY SISTER WOULD NEVER ALLOW MY DAD TO REALLY LOVE SOMEONE ELSE.
BUT ONE MISTAKE FOLLOWED ANOTHER...
...AND ALL OF US WERE GUILTY.

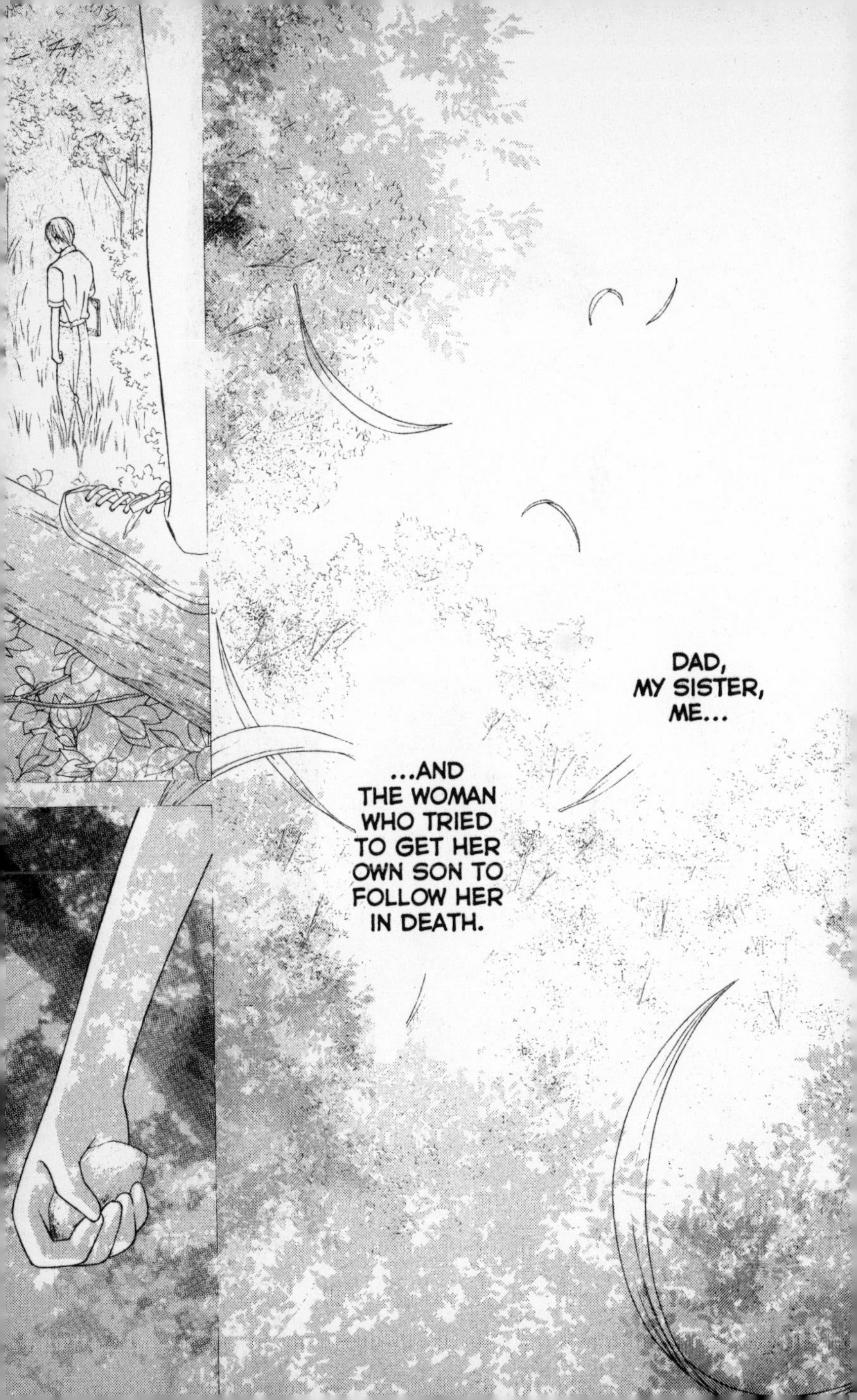
DAD, MY SISTER, ME...
...AND THE WOMAN WHO TRIED TO GET HER OWN SON TO FOLLOW HER IN DEATH.

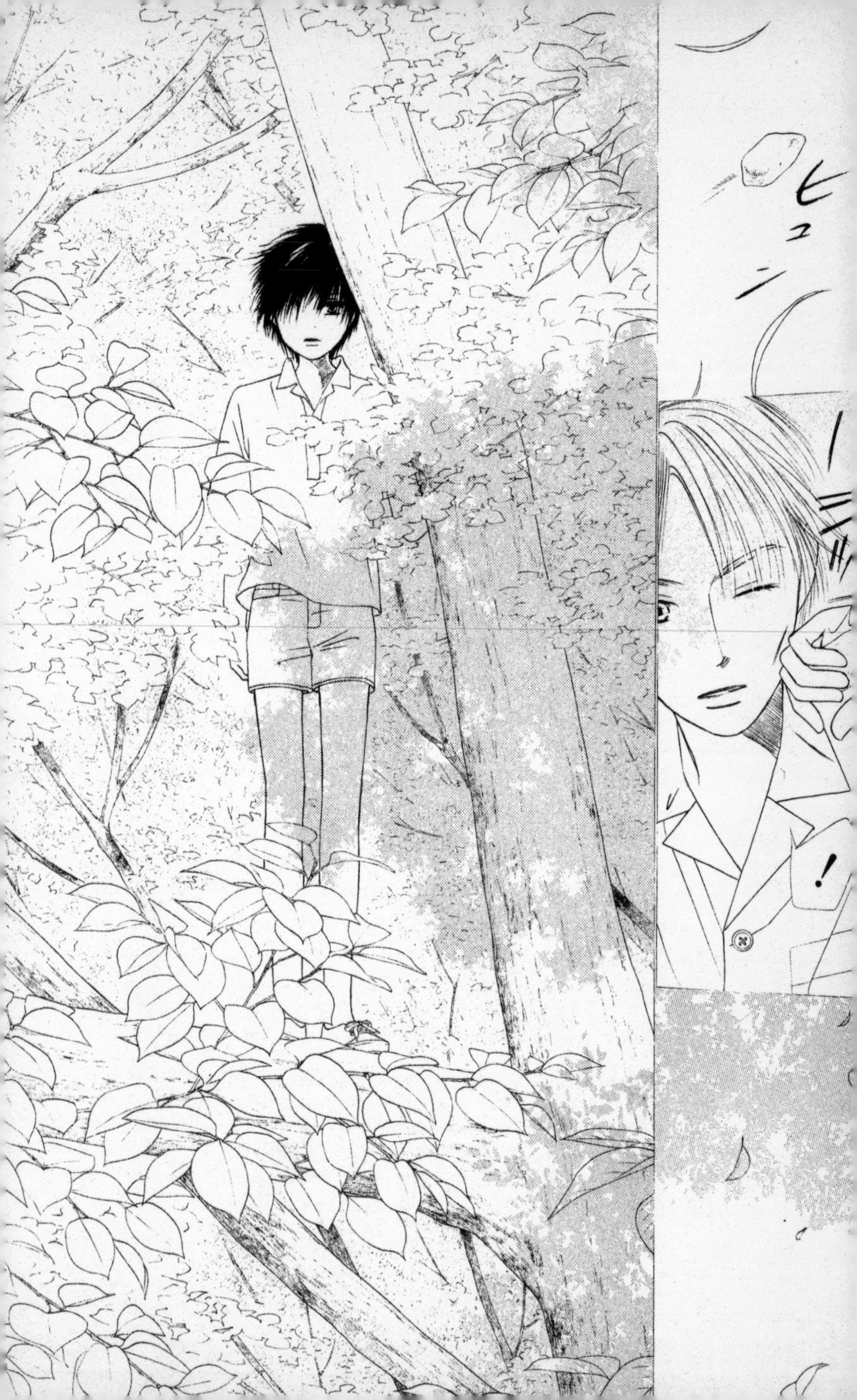
ヒュン
!

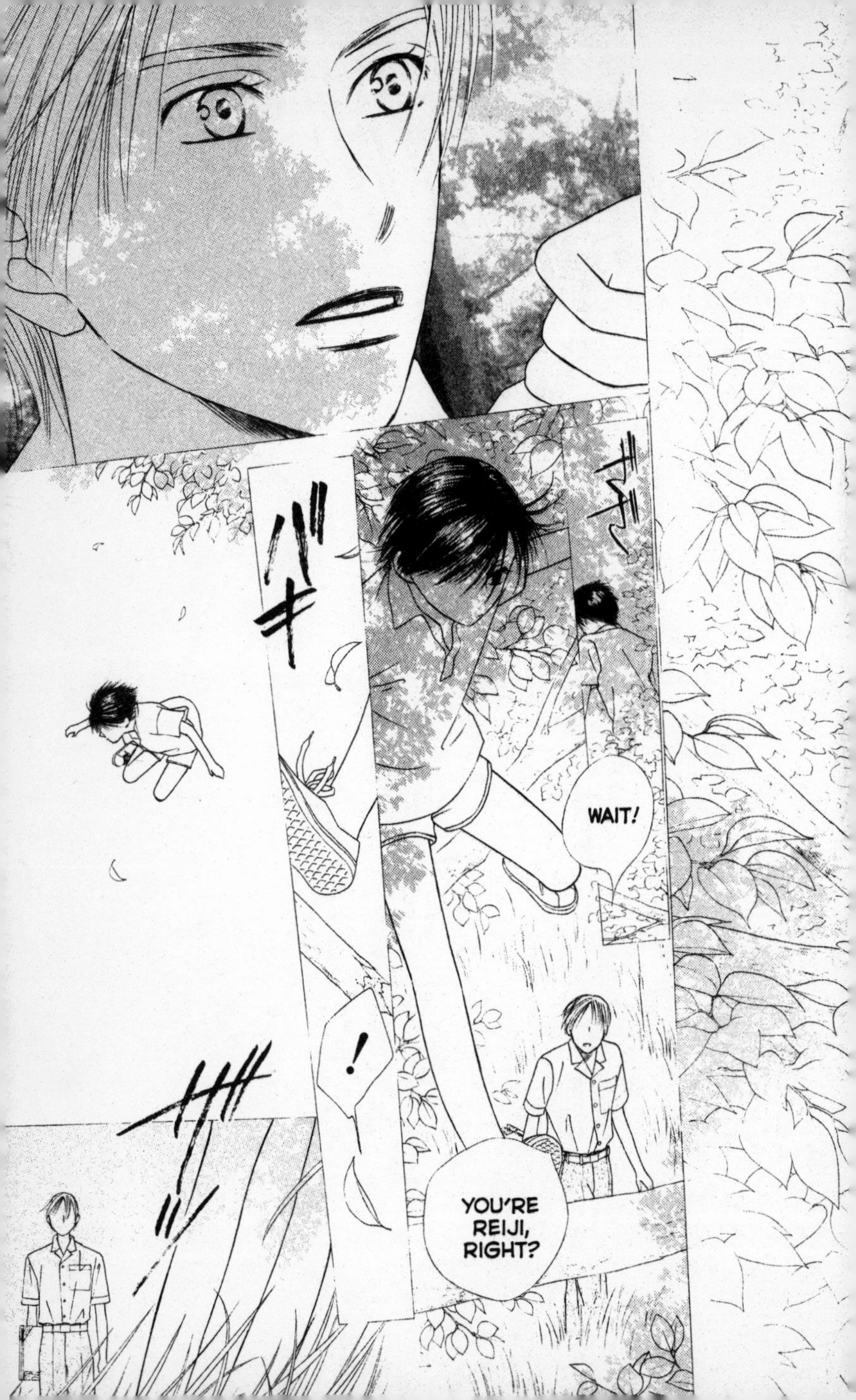
WAIT!
!
YOU'RE REIJI, RIGHT?

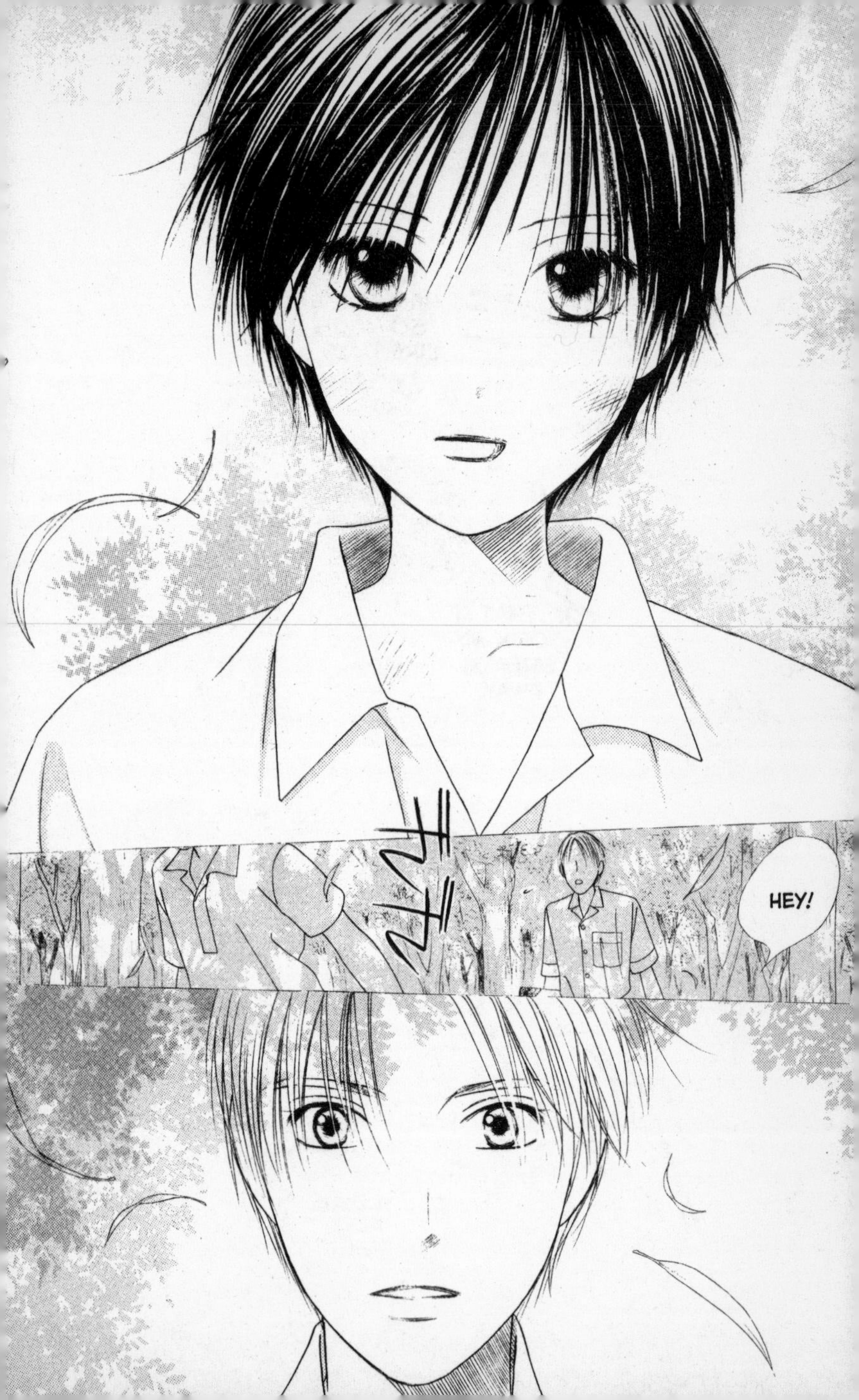
HEY!

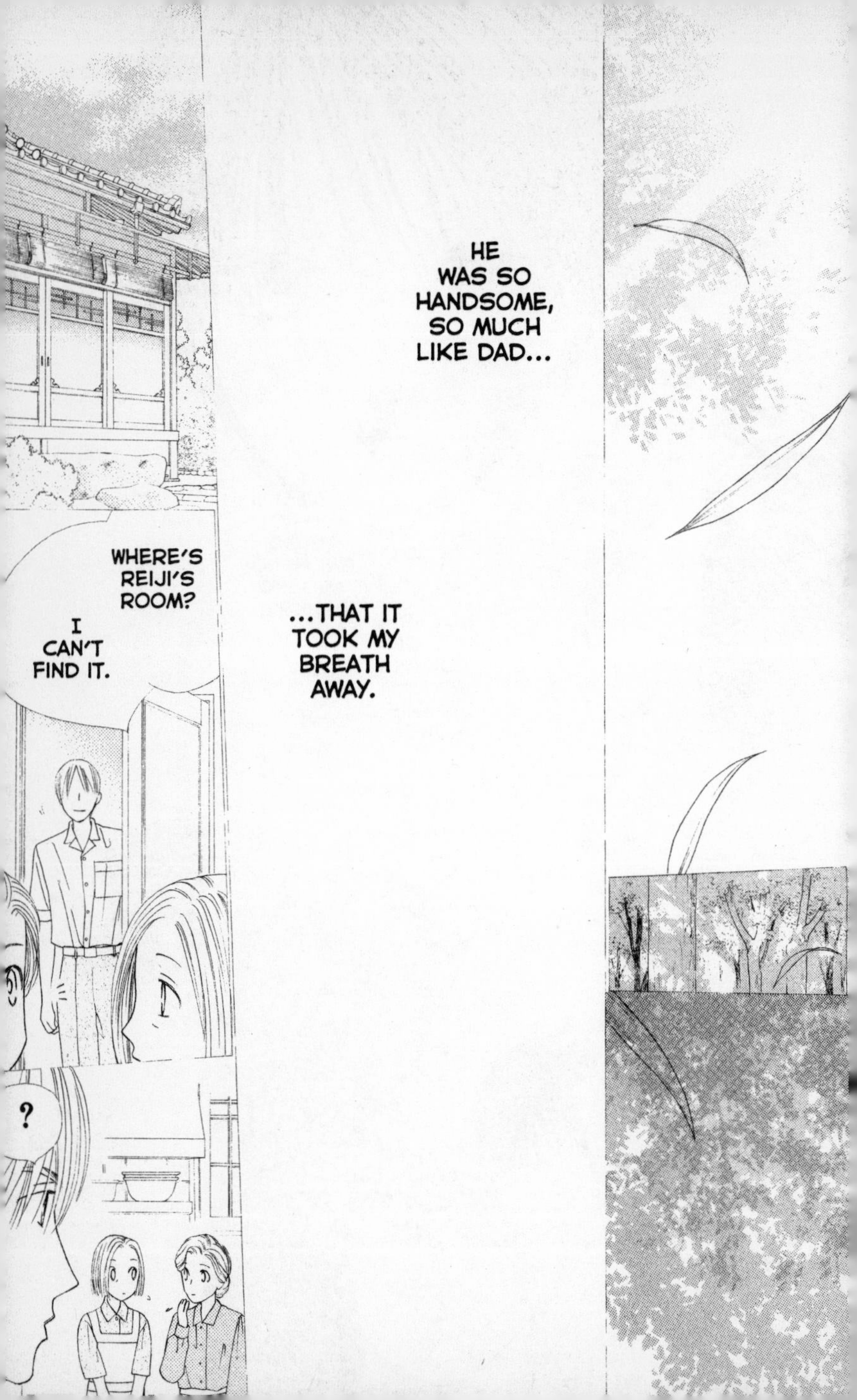
HE WAS SO HANDSOME, SO MUCH LIKE DAD...
...THAT IT TOOK MY BREATH AWAY.
WHERE'S REIJI'S ROOM?
I CAN'T FIND IT.
?

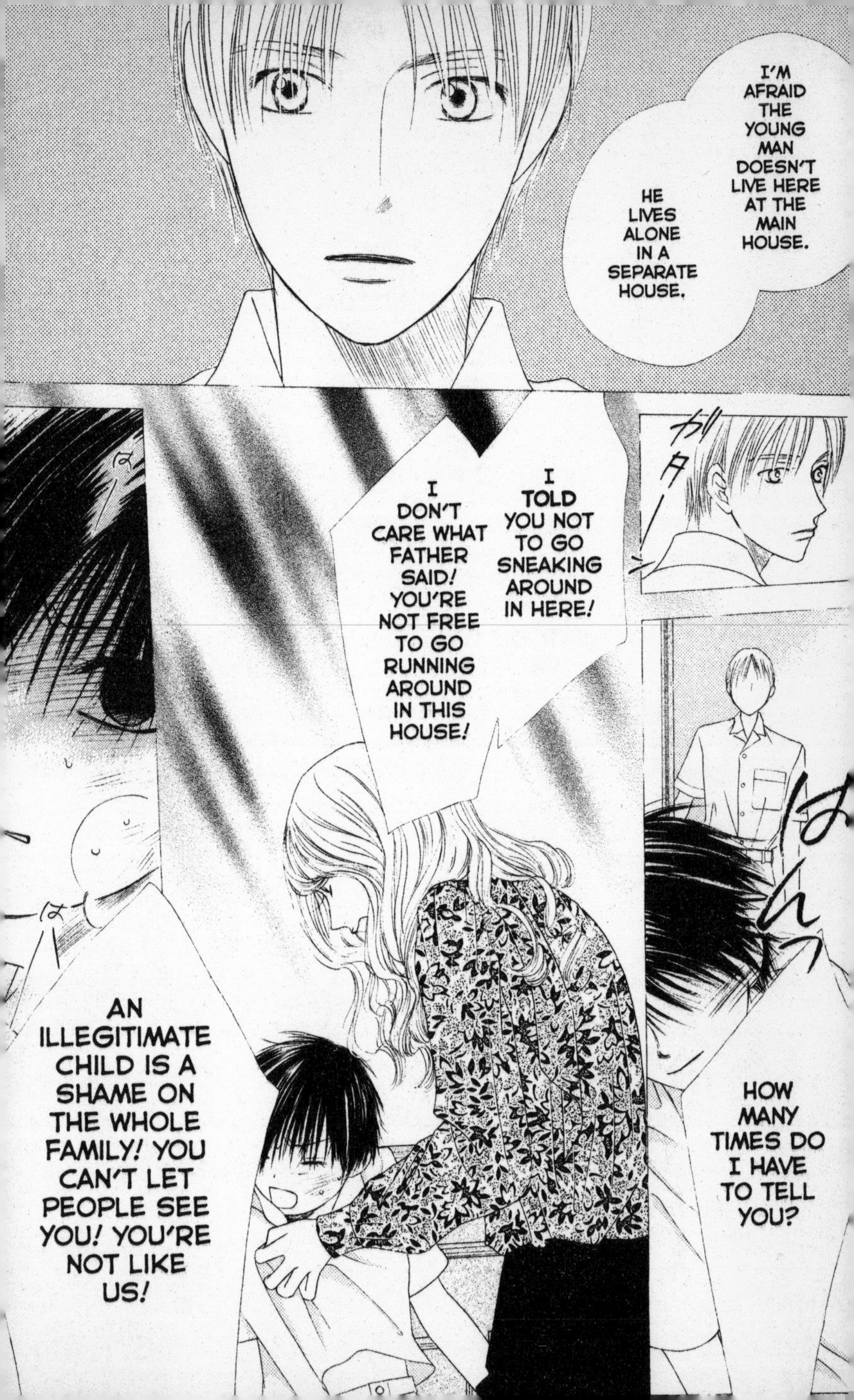
I'M AFRAID THE YOUNG MAN DOESN'T LIVE HERE AT THE MAIN HOUSE.
HE LIVES ALONE IN A SEPARATE HOUSE.
I TOLD YOU NOT TO GO SNEAKING AROUND IN HERE!
I DON'T CARE WHAT FATHER SAID! YOU'RE NOT FREE TO GO RUNNING AROUND IN THIS HOUSE!
HOW MANY TIMES DO I HAVE TO TELL YOU?
AN ILLEGITIMATE CHILD IS A SHAME ON THE WHOLE FAMILY! YOU CAN'T LET PEOPLE SEE YOU! YOU'RE NOT LIKE US!

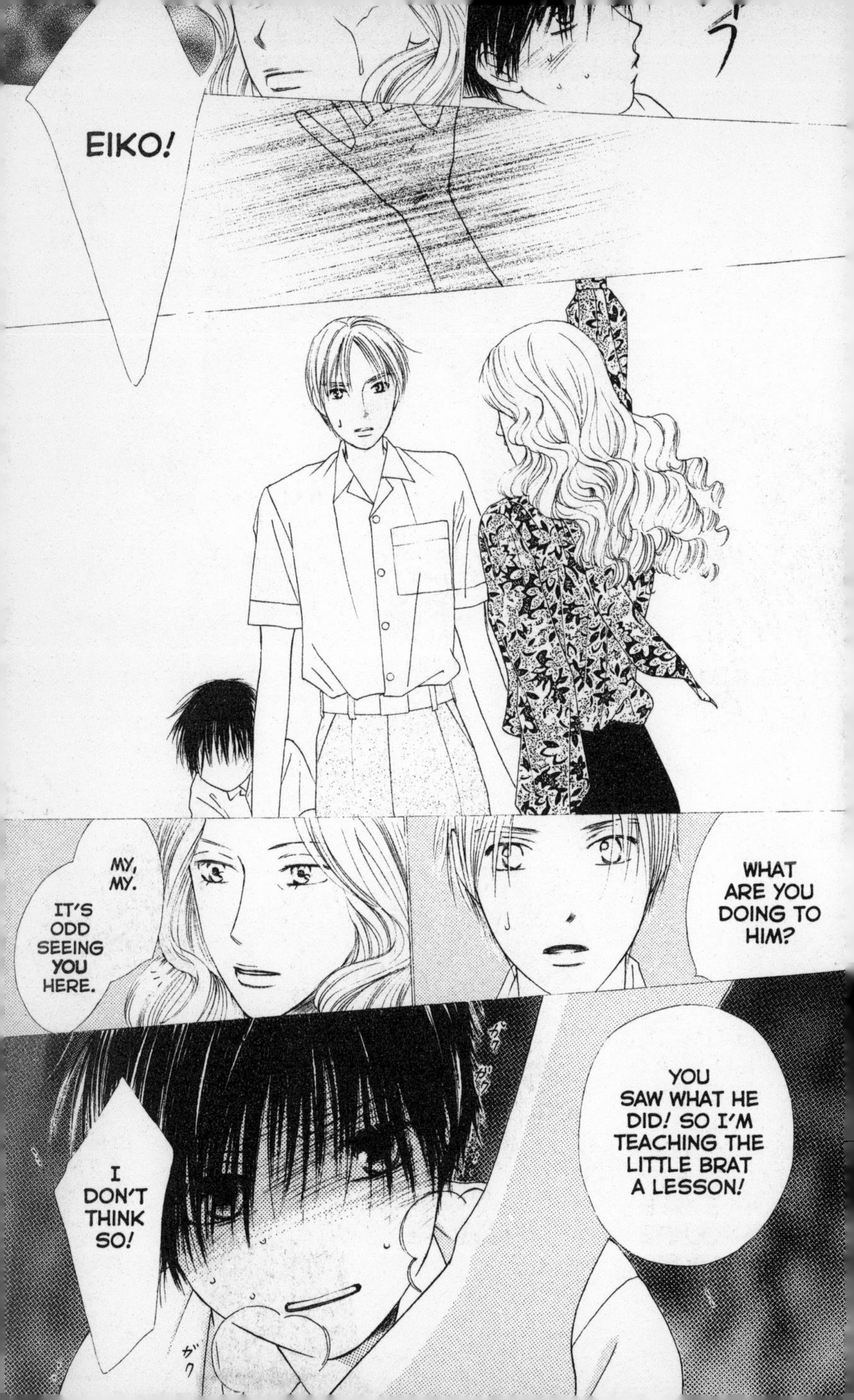
EIKO!
WHAT ARE YOU DOING TO HIM?
MY, MY. IT'S ODD SEEING YOU HERE.
YOU SAW WHAT HE DID! SO I'M TEACHING THE LITTLE BRAT A LESSON!
I DON'T THINK SO!

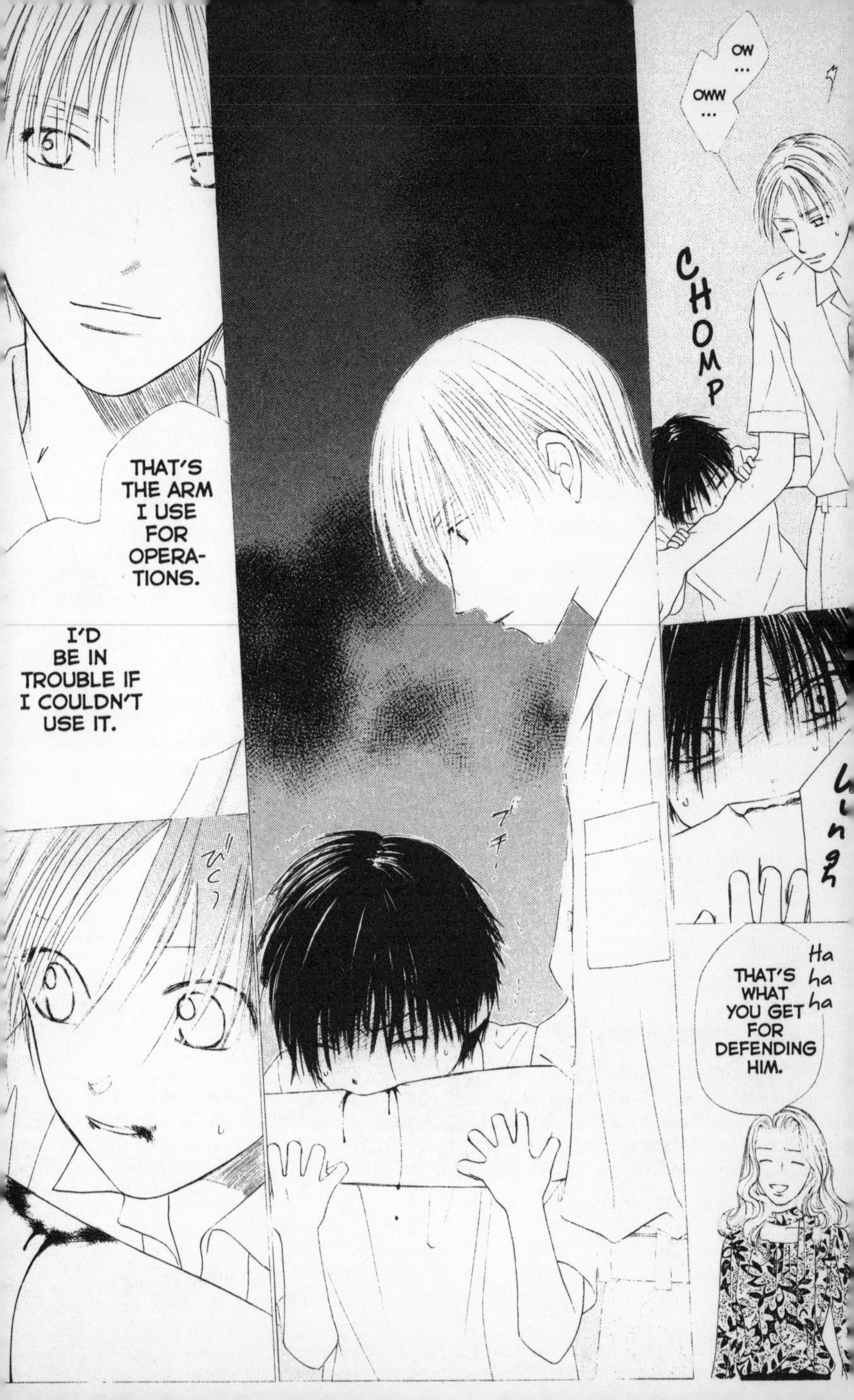
OW ...
OWW ...
CHOMP
Ungh
THAT'S WHAT YOU GET FOR DEFENDING HIM.
Ha ha ha
THAT'S THE ARM I USE FOR OPERA-TIONS.
I'D BE IN TROUBLE IF I COULDN'T USE IT.

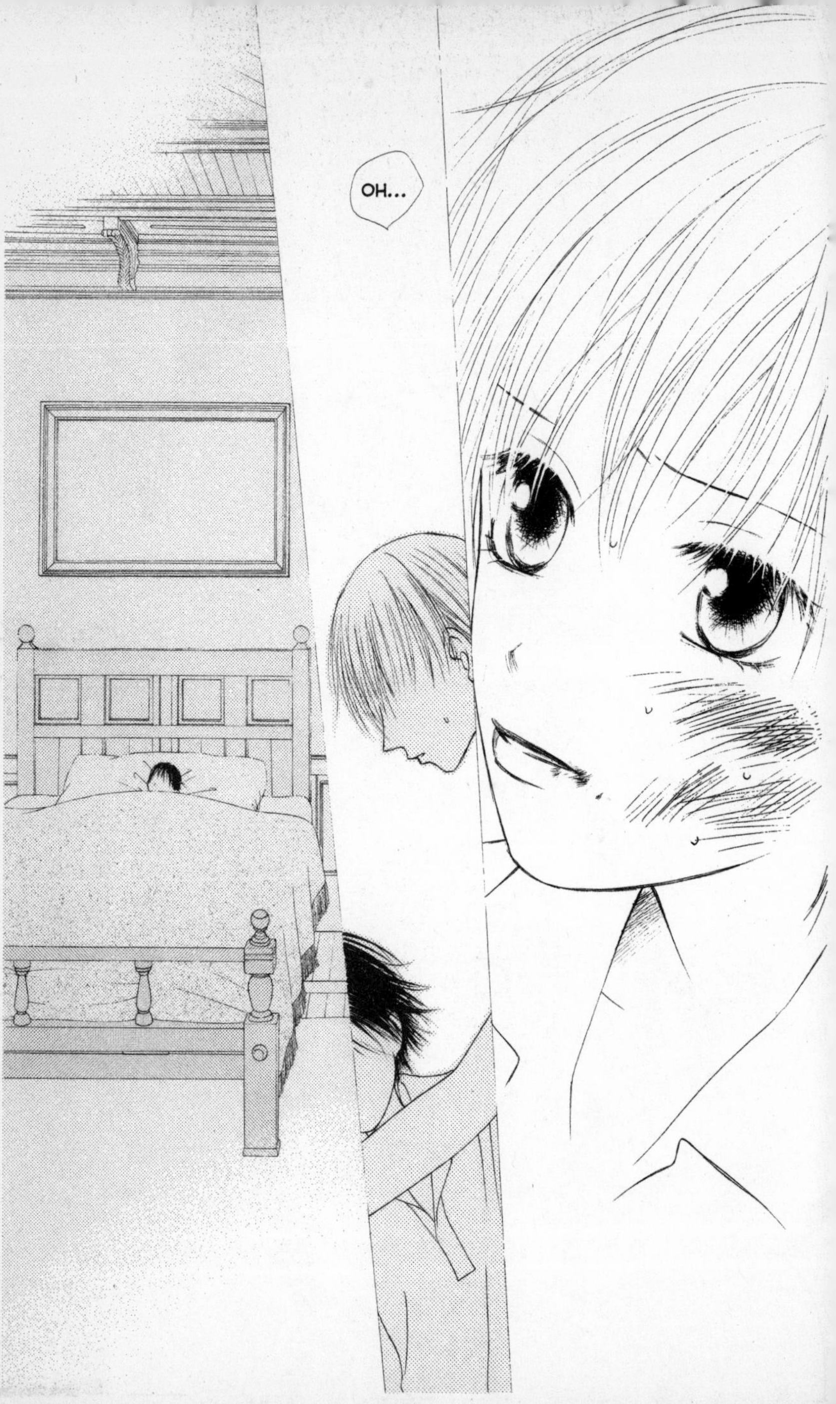
OH...

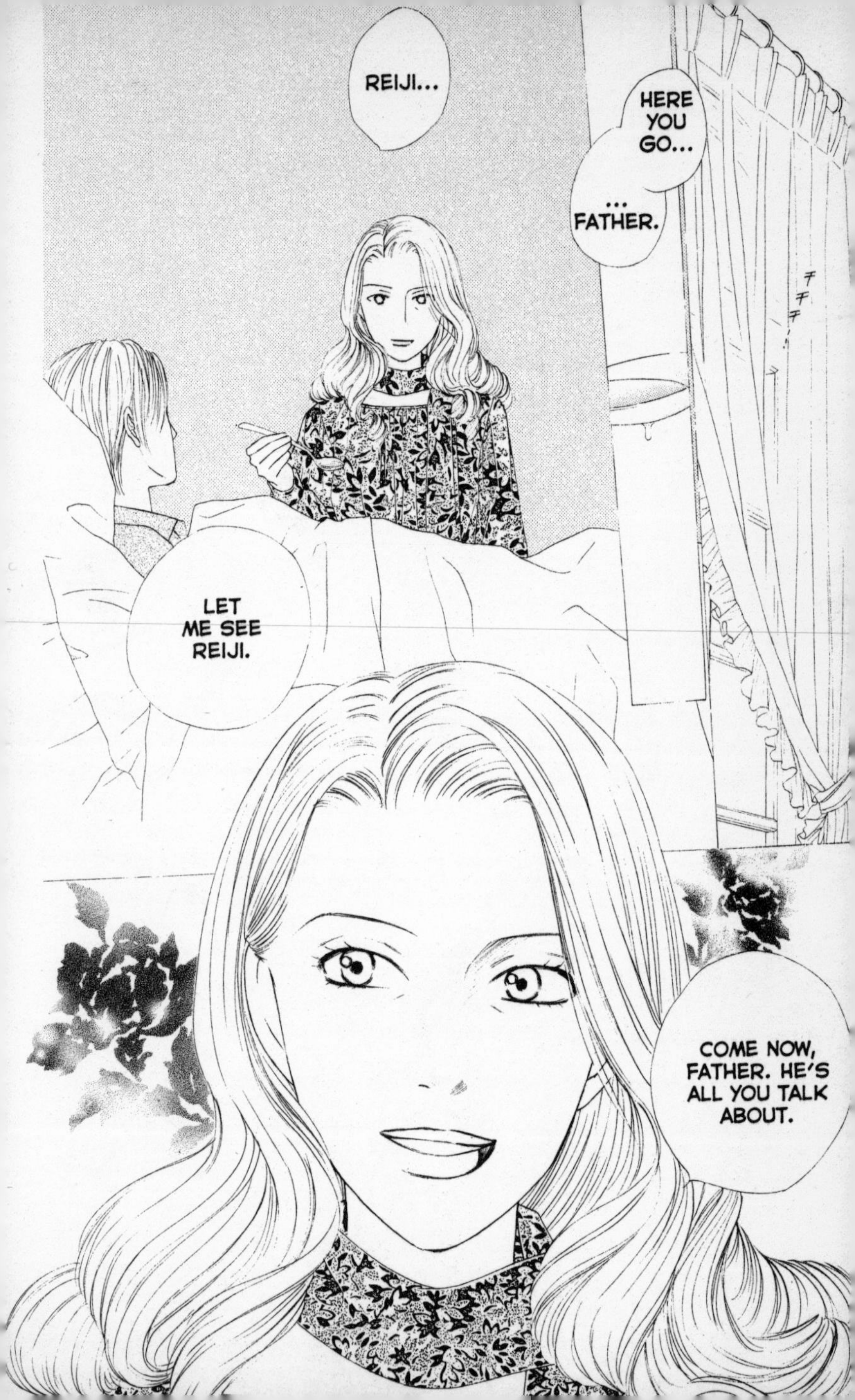
HERE YOU GO...
...FATHER.
REIJI...
LET ME SEE REIJI.
COME NOW, FATHER. HE'S ALL YOU TALK ABOUT.

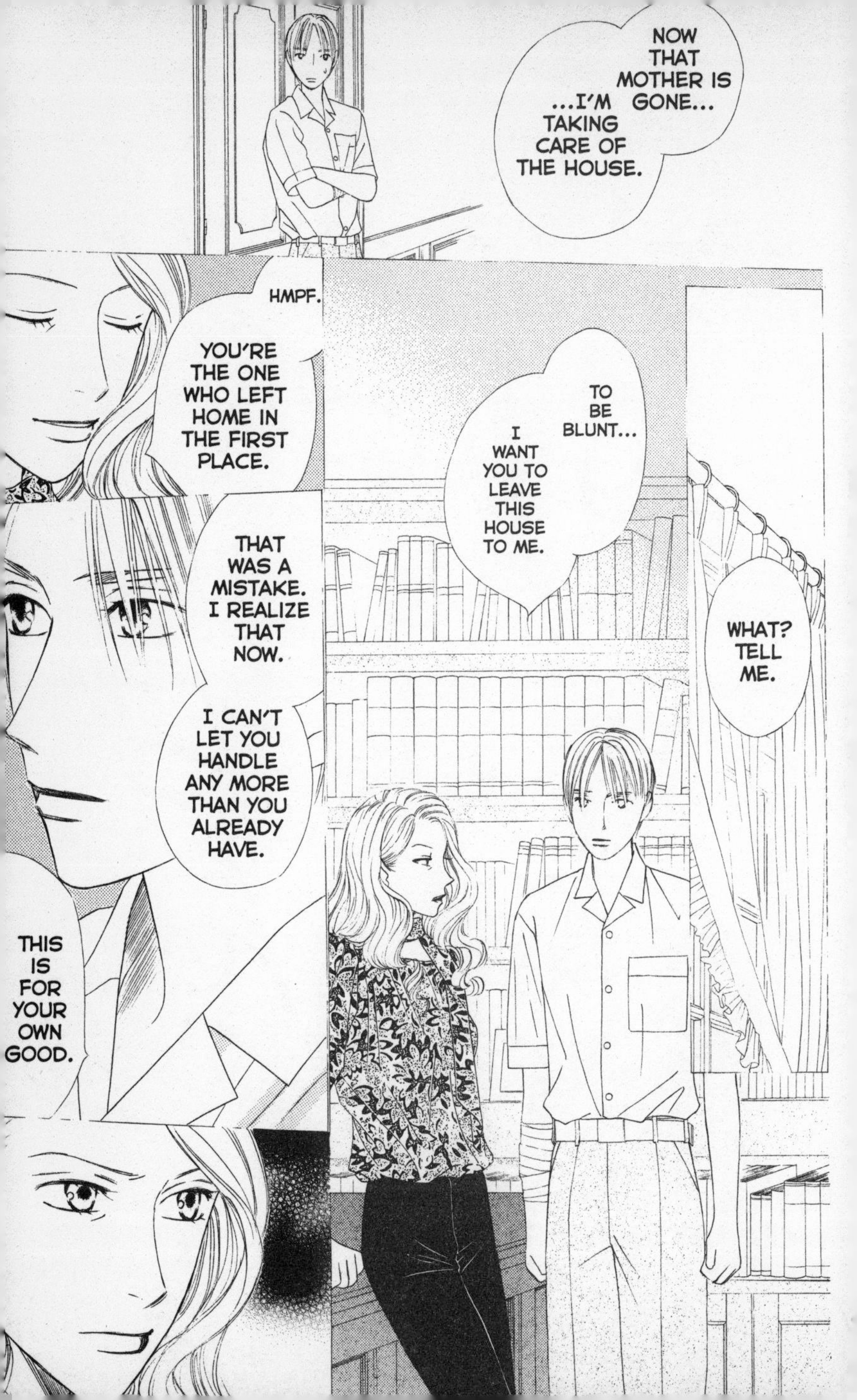
NOW THAT MOTHER IS GONE...
...I'M TAKING CARE OF THE HOUSE.
TO BE BLUNT...
I WANT YOU TO LEAVE THIS HOUSE TO ME.
WHAT? TELL ME.
HMPF.
YOU'RE THE ONE WHO LEFT HOME IN THE FIRST PLACE.
THAT WAS A MISTAKE. I REALIZE THAT NOW.
I CAN'T LET YOU HANDLE ANY MORE THAN YOU ALREADY HAVE.
THIS IS FOR YOUR OWN GOOD.

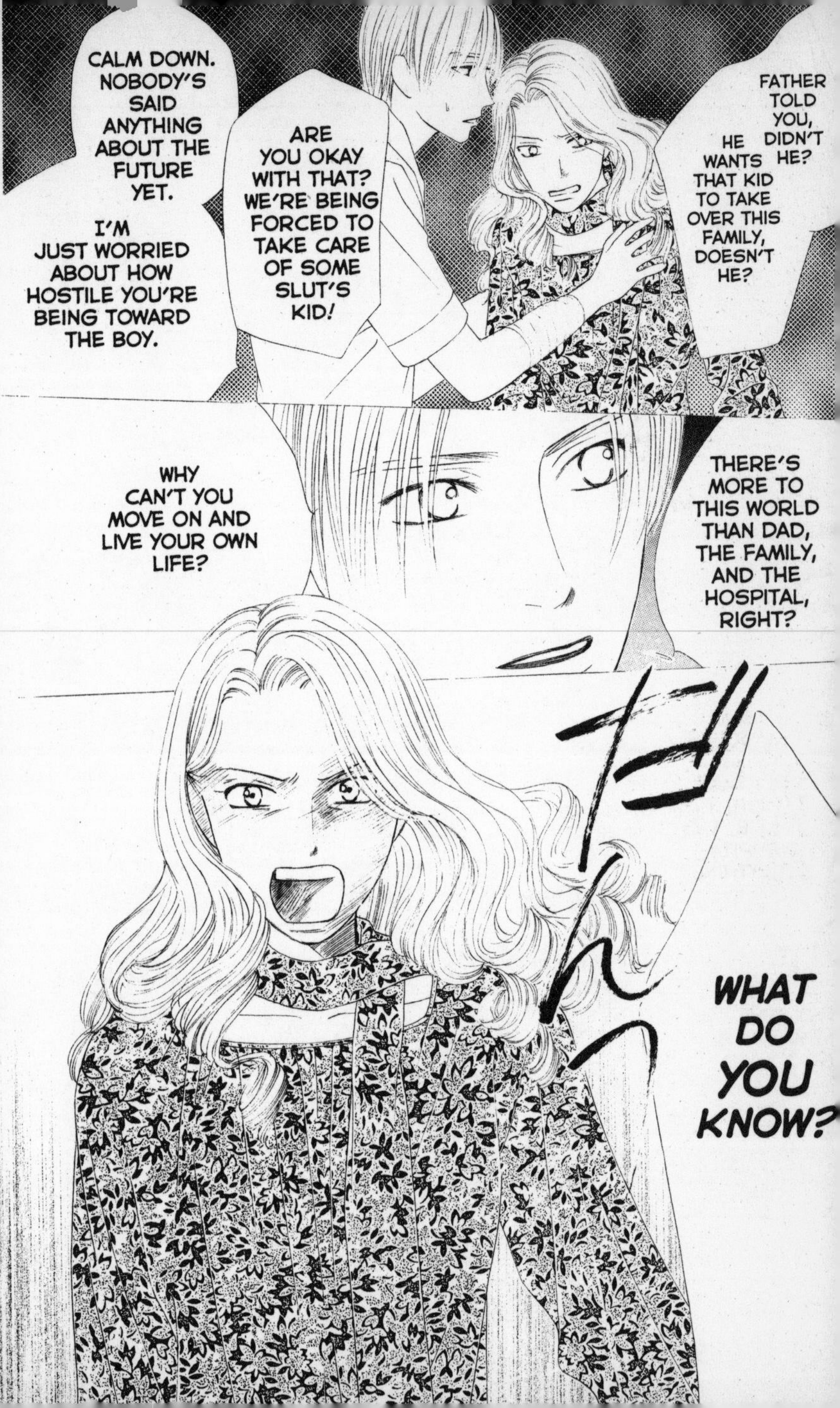
FATHER TOLD YOU, DIDN'T HE?
HE WANTS THAT KID TO TAKE OVER THIS FAMILY, DOESN'T HE?
ARE YOU OKAY WITH THAT? WE'RE BEING FORCED TO TAKE CARE OF SOME SLUT'S KID!
CALM DOWN. NOBODY'S SAID ANYTHING ABOUT THE FUTURE YET.
I'M JUST WORRIED ABOUT HOW HOSTILE YOU'RE BEING TOWARD THE BOY.
THERE'S MORE TO THIS WORLD THAN DAD, THE FAMILY, AND THE HOSPITAL, RIGHT?
WHY CAN'T YOU MOVE ON AND LIVE YOUR OWN LIFE?
WHAT DO YOU KNOW?

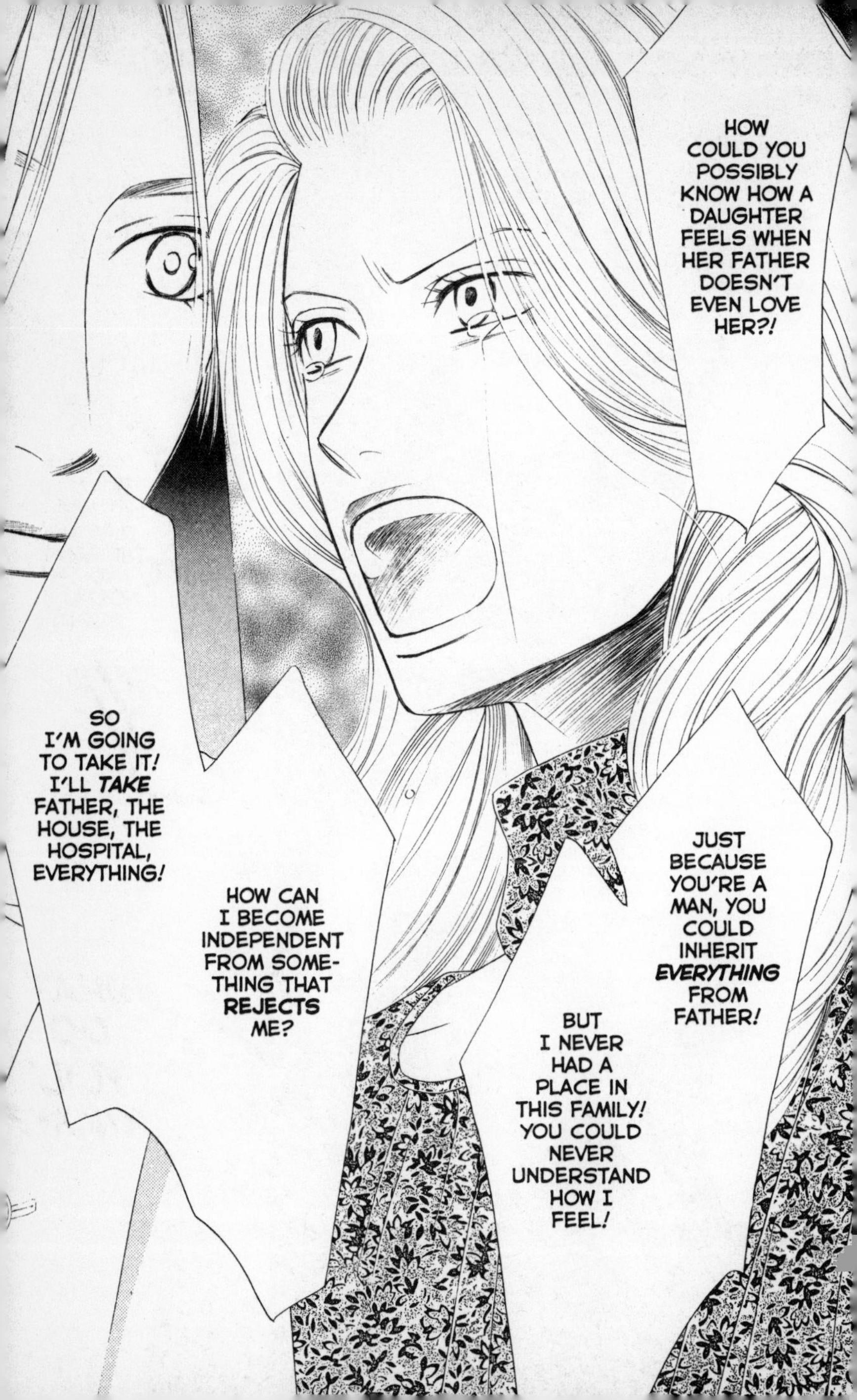
HOW COULD YOU POSSIBLY KNOW HOW A DAUGHTER FEELS WHEN HER FATHER DOESN'T EVEN LOVE HER?!
JUST BECAUSE YOU'RE A MAN, YOU COULD INHERIT *EVERYTHING* FROM FATHER!
BUT I NEVER HAD A PLACE IN THIS FAMILY! YOU COULD NEVER UNDERSTAND HOW I FEEL!
HOW CAN I BECOME INDEPENDENT FROM SOME-THING THAT **REJECTS** ME?
SO I'M GOING TO TAKE IT! I'LL *TAKE* FATHER, THE HOUSE, THE HOSPITAL, EVERYTHING!

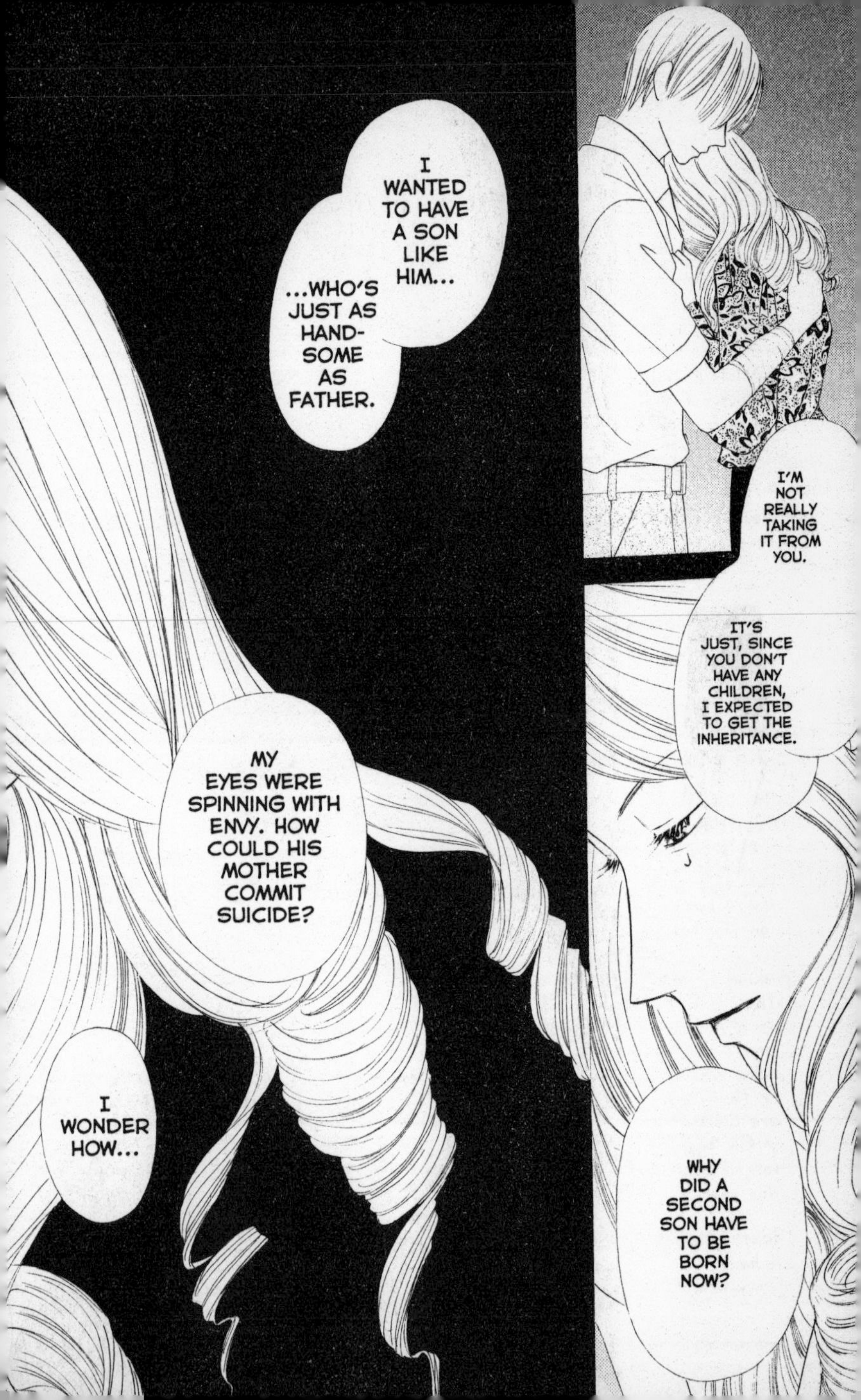
I'M NOT REALLY TAKING IT FROM YOU.
IT'S JUST, SINCE YOU DON'T HAVE ANY CHILDREN, I EXPECTED TO GET THE INHERITANCE.
WHY DID A SECOND SON HAVE TO BE BORN NOW?
I WANTED TO HAVE A SON LIKE HIM...
...WHO'S JUST AS HAND-SOME AS FATHER.
MY EYES WERE SPINNING WITH ENVY. HOW COULD HIS MOTHER COMMIT SUICIDE?
I WONDER HOW...

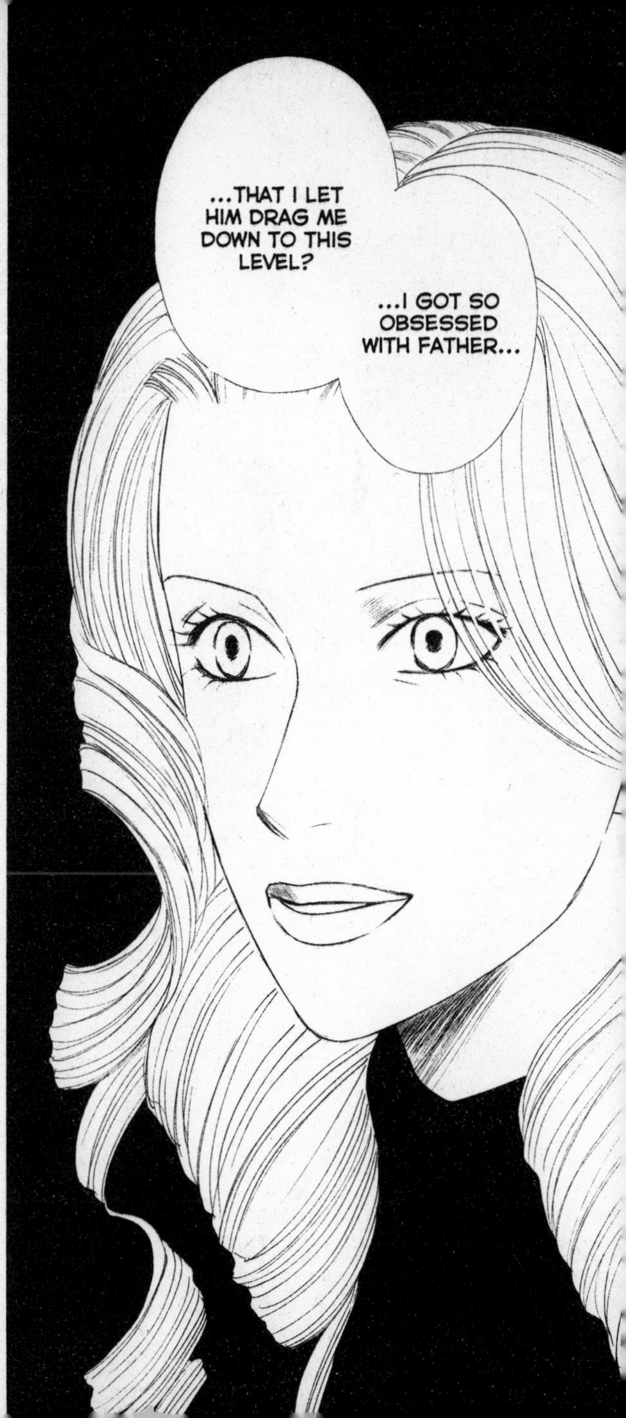
...I GOT SO OBSESSED WITH FATHER...
...THAT I LET HIM DRAG ME DOWN TO THIS LEVEL?

4

50s, 60s & 70s Mode

This part was so fun to draw!♡ The clothes are so cute! Like the "parachute" one-piece dress, and the one-piece with the flower print. Just looking at them still gets me excited.

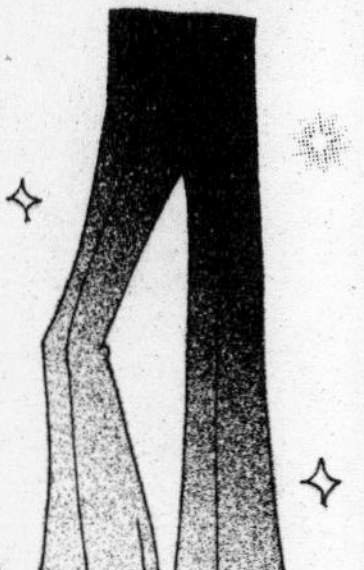

They're really wide on the bottom!

Speaking of 70s clothes, you've got to have bell-bottoms! I really wanted Eiko to wear them, but there weren't any full body shots of her. Too bad...

♡ Next volume will be in 80s mode!♡

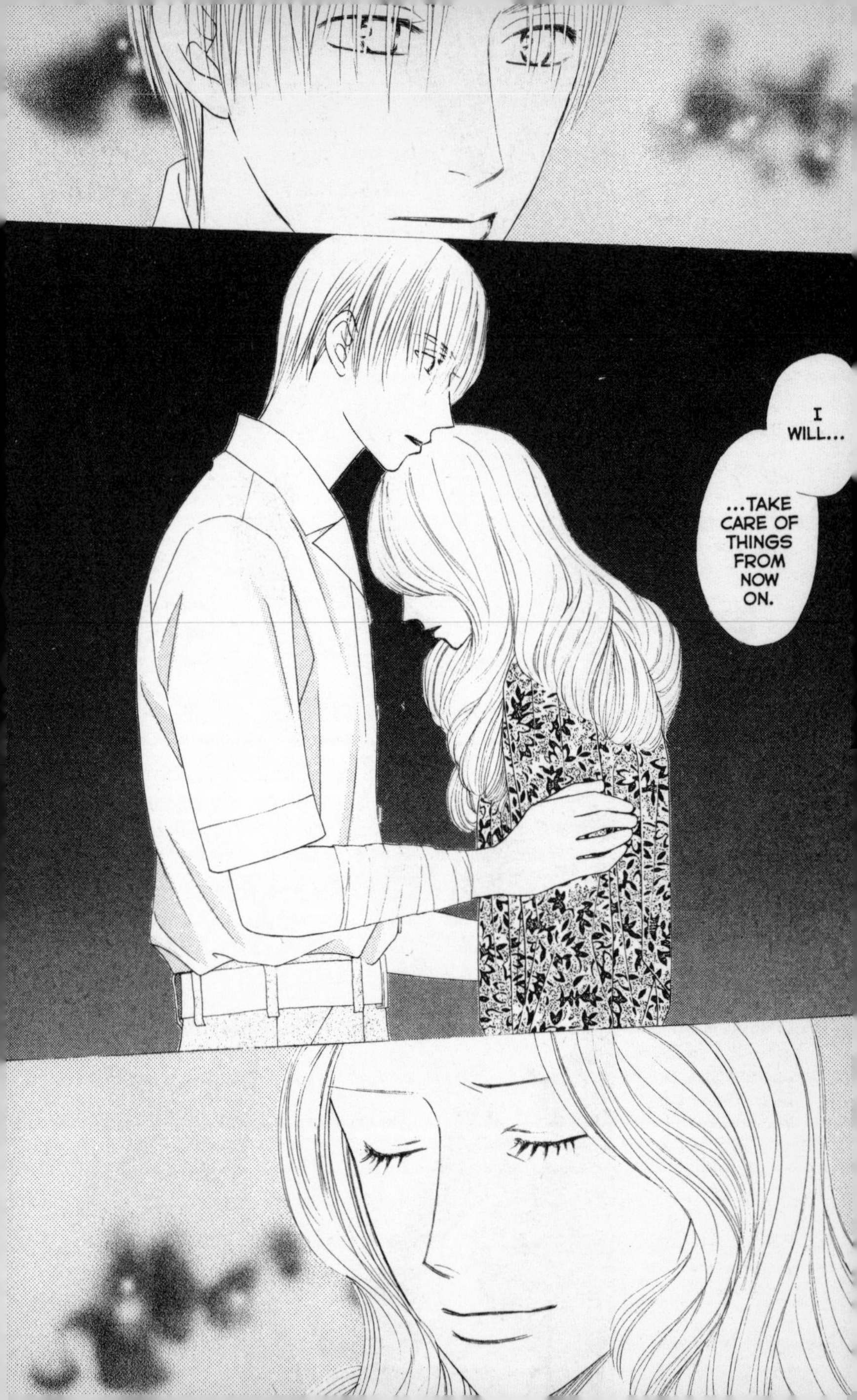
I WILL... ...TAKE CARE OF THINGS FROM NOW ON.

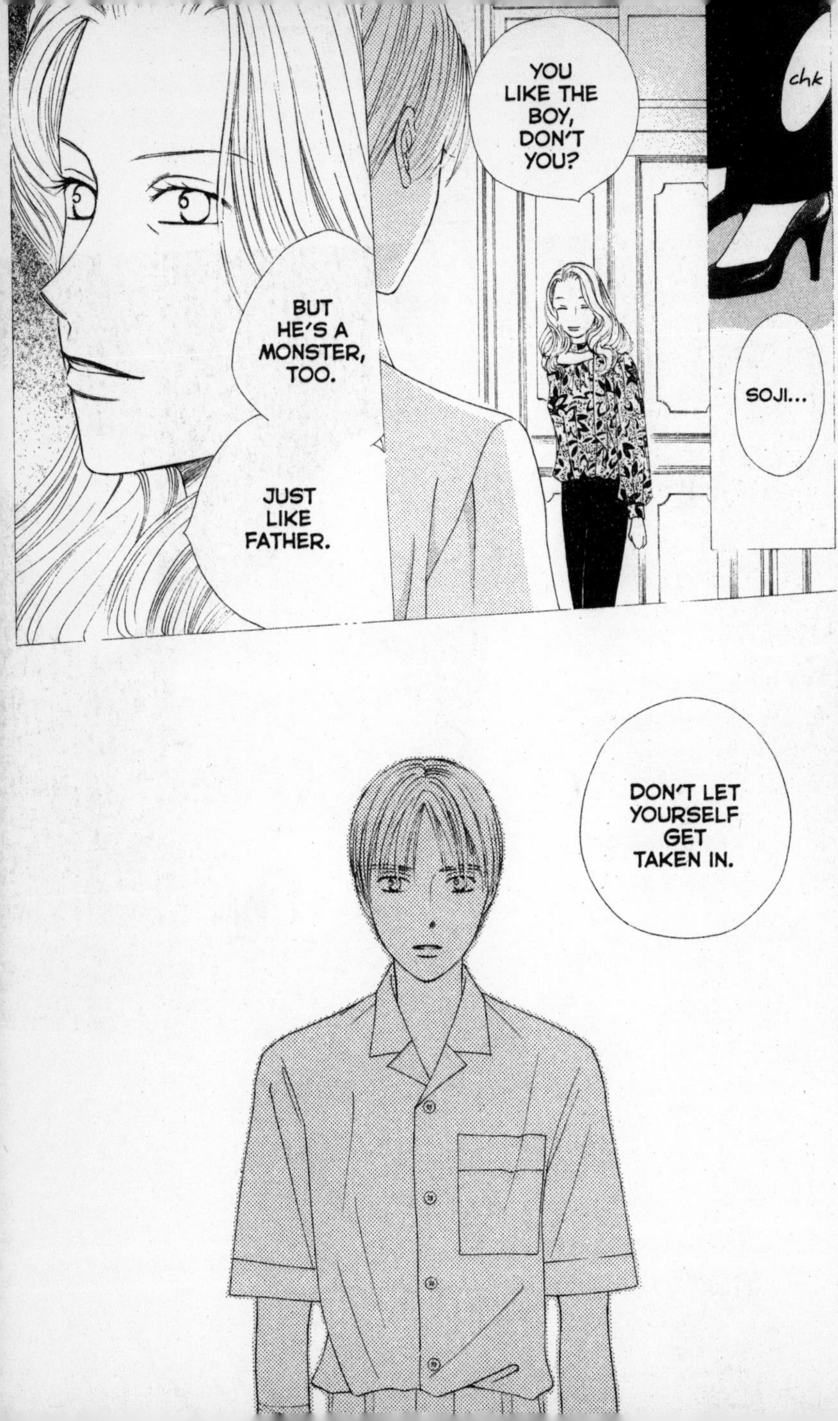
chk
SOJI...
YOU LIKE THE BOY, DON'T YOU?
BUT HE'S A MONSTER, TOO.
JUST LIKE FATHER.
DON'T LET YOURSELF GET TAKEN IN.

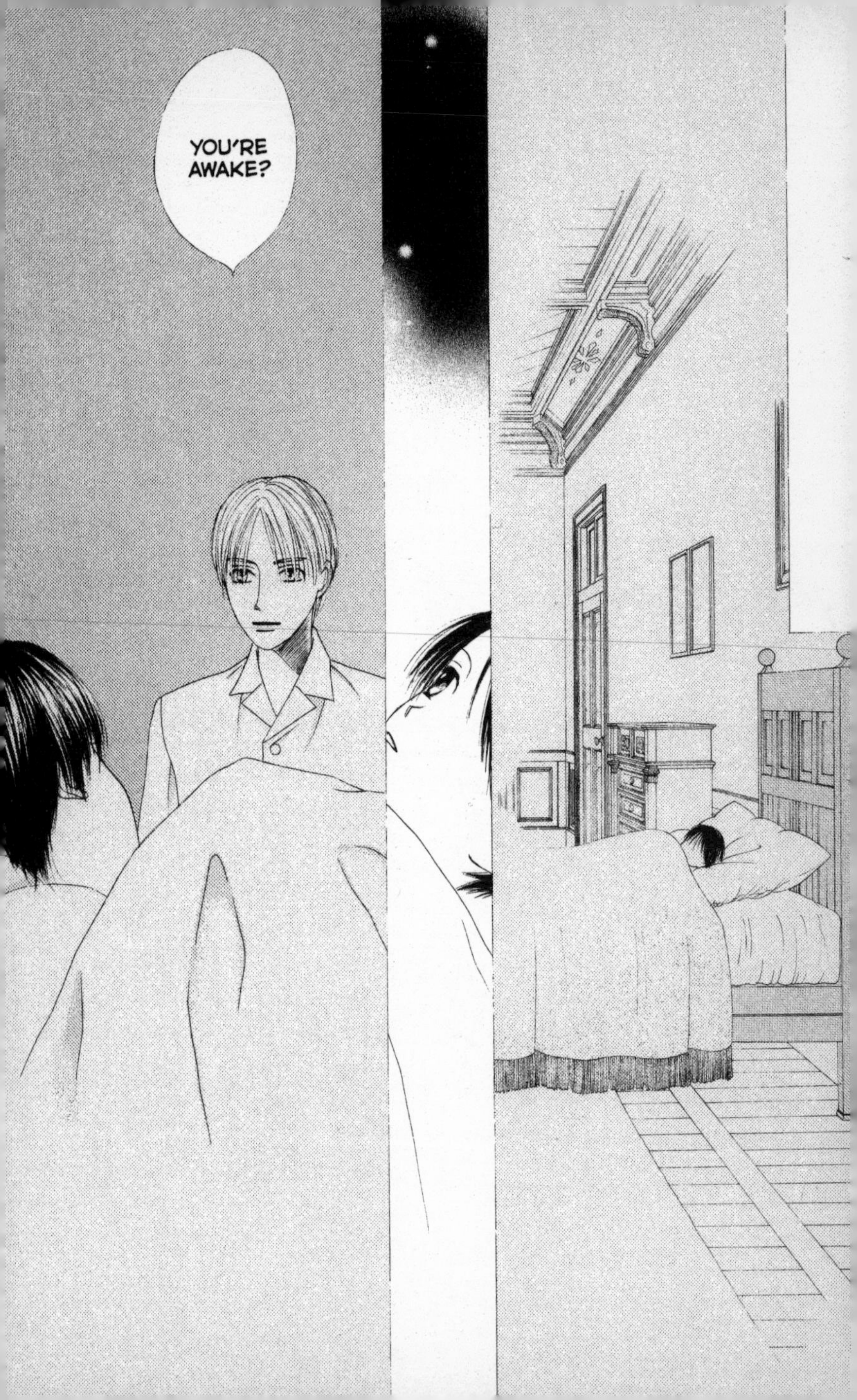
YOU'RE AWAKE?

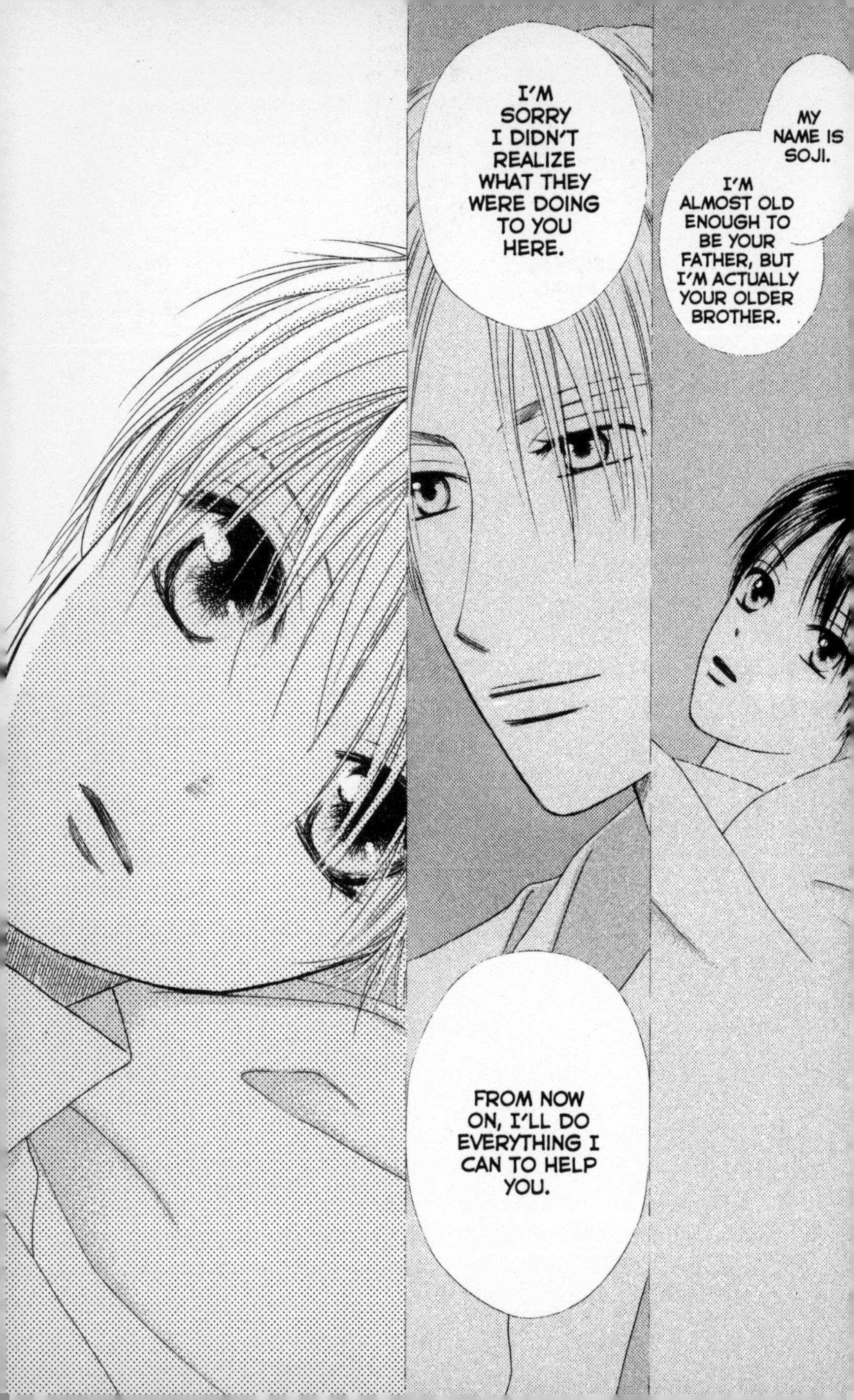
MY NAME IS SOJI.
I'M ALMOST OLD ENOUGH TO BE YOUR FATHER, BUT I'M ACTUALLY YOUR OLDER BROTHER.
I'M SORRY I DIDN'T REALIZE WHAT THEY WERE DOING TO YOU HERE.
FROM NOW ON, I'LL DO EVERYTHING I CAN TO HELP YOU.

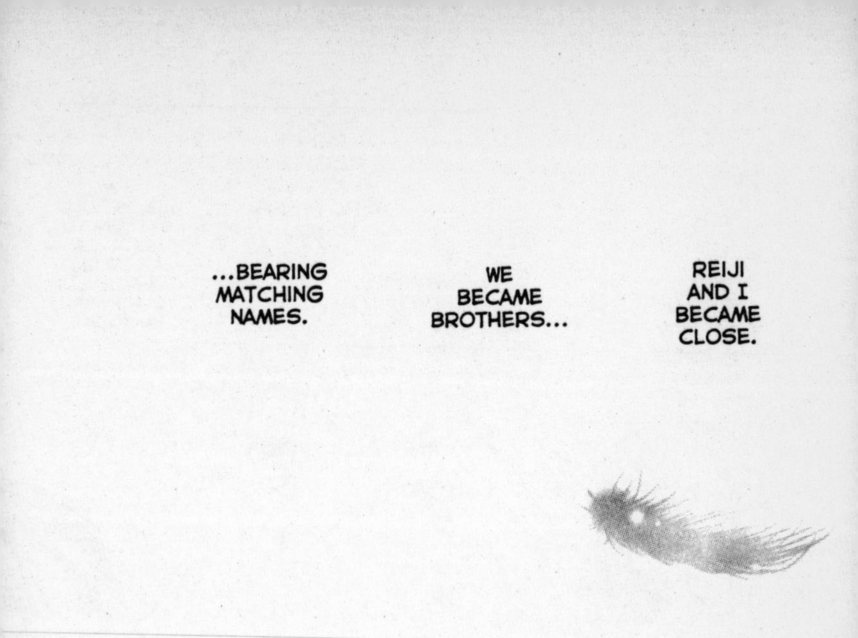
REIJI AND I BECAME CLOSE.
WE BECAME BROTHERS...
...BEARING MATCHING NAMES.

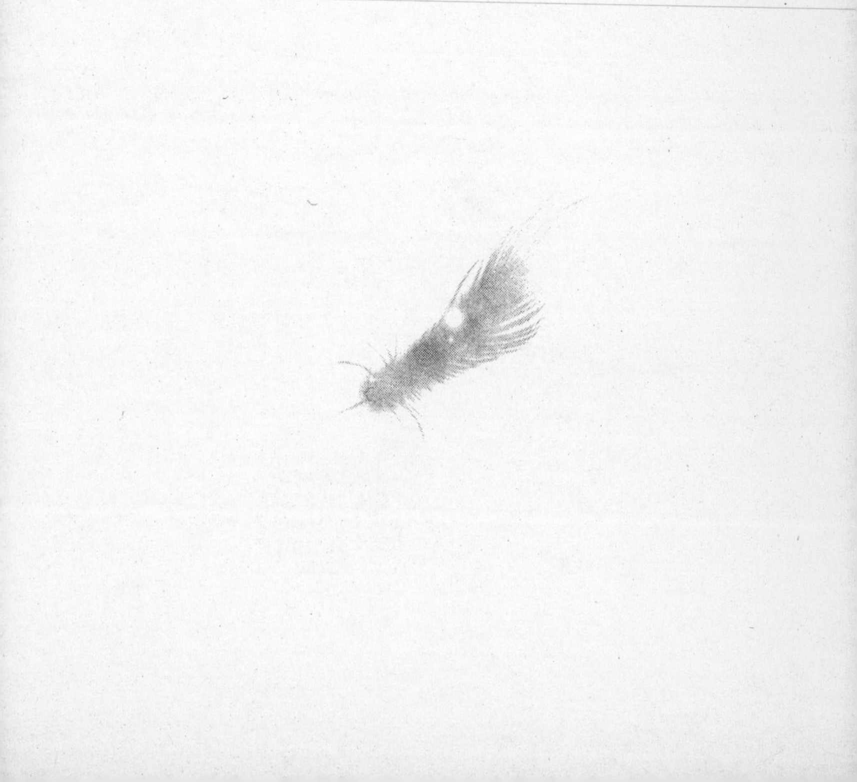

OUR AGES, CIRCUMSTANCES, AND PERSONALITIES DID NOT MATCH.
BUT WE HAD A FATHER IN COMMON.

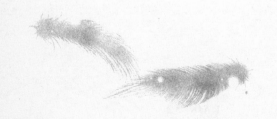

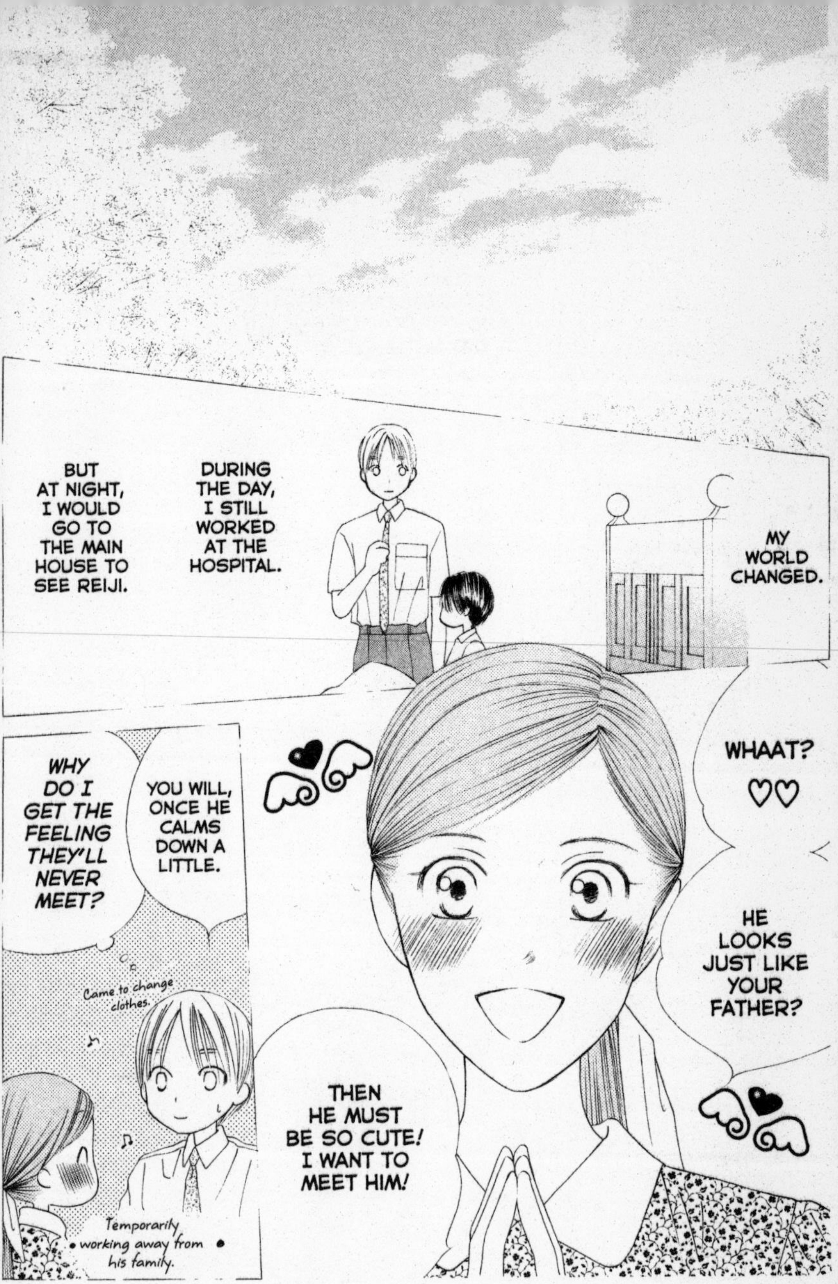
MY WORLD CHANGED.
DURING THE DAY, I STILL WORKED AT THE HOSPITAL.
BUT AT NIGHT, I WOULD GO TO THE MAIN HOUSE TO SEE REIJI.
WHAAT? ♡♡
HE LOOKS JUST LIKE YOUR FATHER?
THEN HE MUST BE SO CUTE! I WANT TO MEET HIM!
YOU WILL, ONCE HE CALMS DOWN A LITTLE.
WHY DO I GET THE FEELING THEY'LL NEVER MEET?
Came to change clothes.
Temporarily working away from his family.

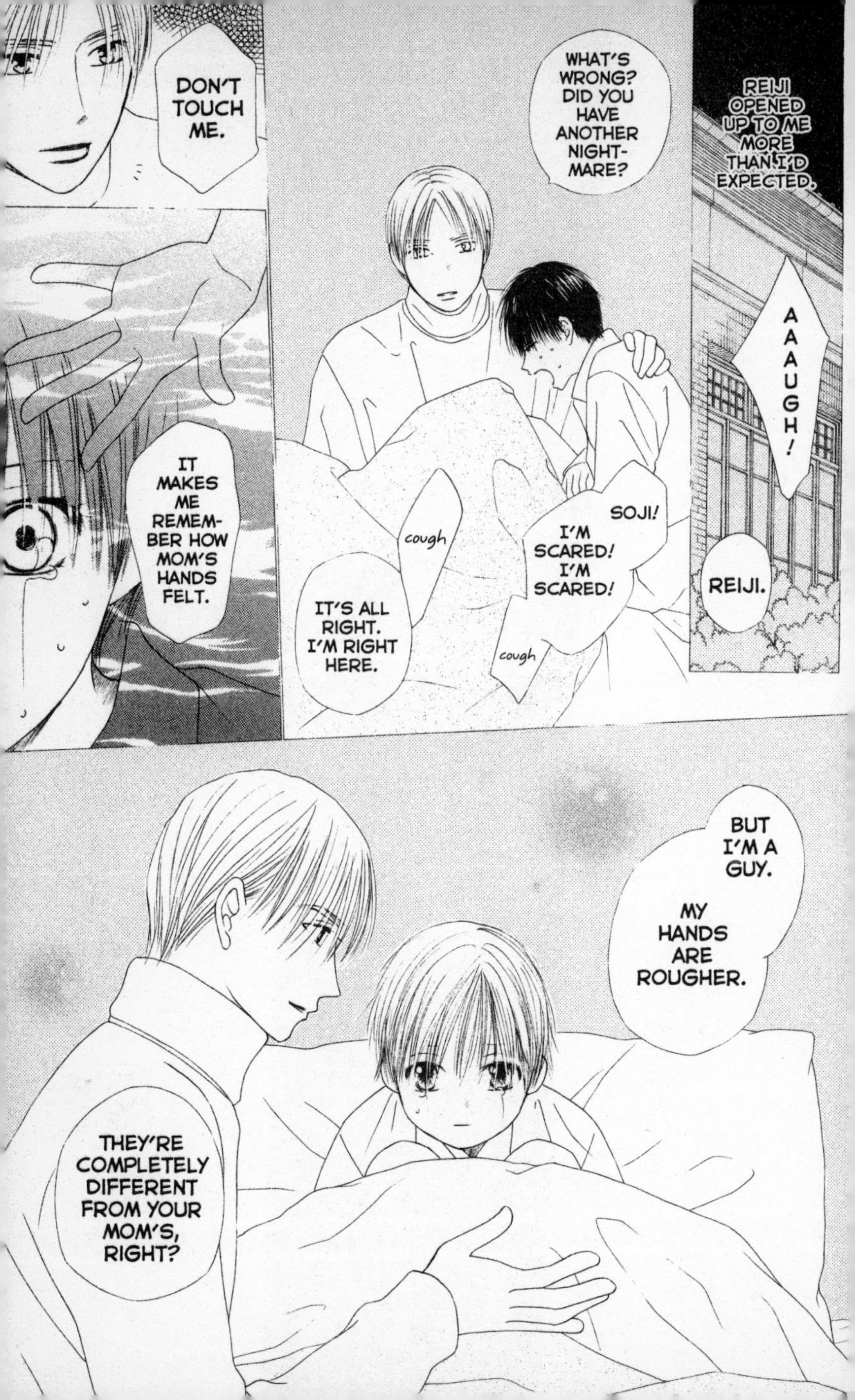
REIJI OPENED UP TO ME MORE THAN I'D EXPECTED.
AAAAUGH!
REIJI.
WHAT'S WRONG? DID YOU HAVE ANOTHER NIGHT-MARE?
SOJI! I'M SCARED! I'M SCARED!
cough
cough
IT'S ALL RIGHT. I'M RIGHT HERE.
DON'T TOUCH ME.
IT MAKES ME REMEMBER HOW MOM'S HANDS FELT.
BUT I'M A GUY.
MY HANDS ARE ROUGHER.
THEY'RE COMPLETELY DIFFERENT FROM YOUR MOM'S, RIGHT?

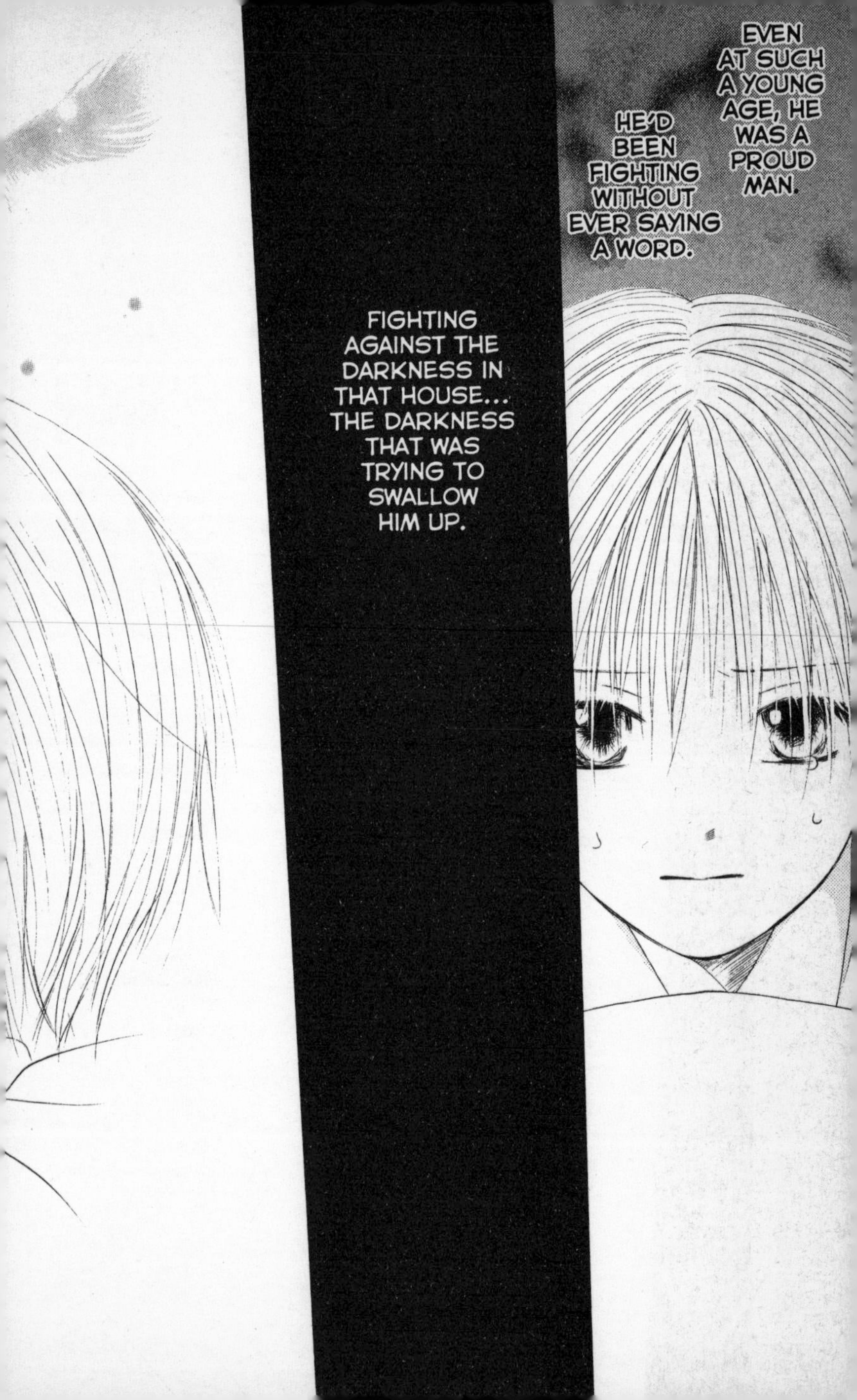
EVEN AT SUCH A YOUNG AGE, HE WAS A PROUD MAN.
HE'D BEEN FIGHTING WITHOUT EVER SAYING A WORD.
FIGHTING AGAINST THE DARKNESS IN THAT HOUSE... THE DARKNESS THAT WAS TRYING TO SWALLOW HIM UP.

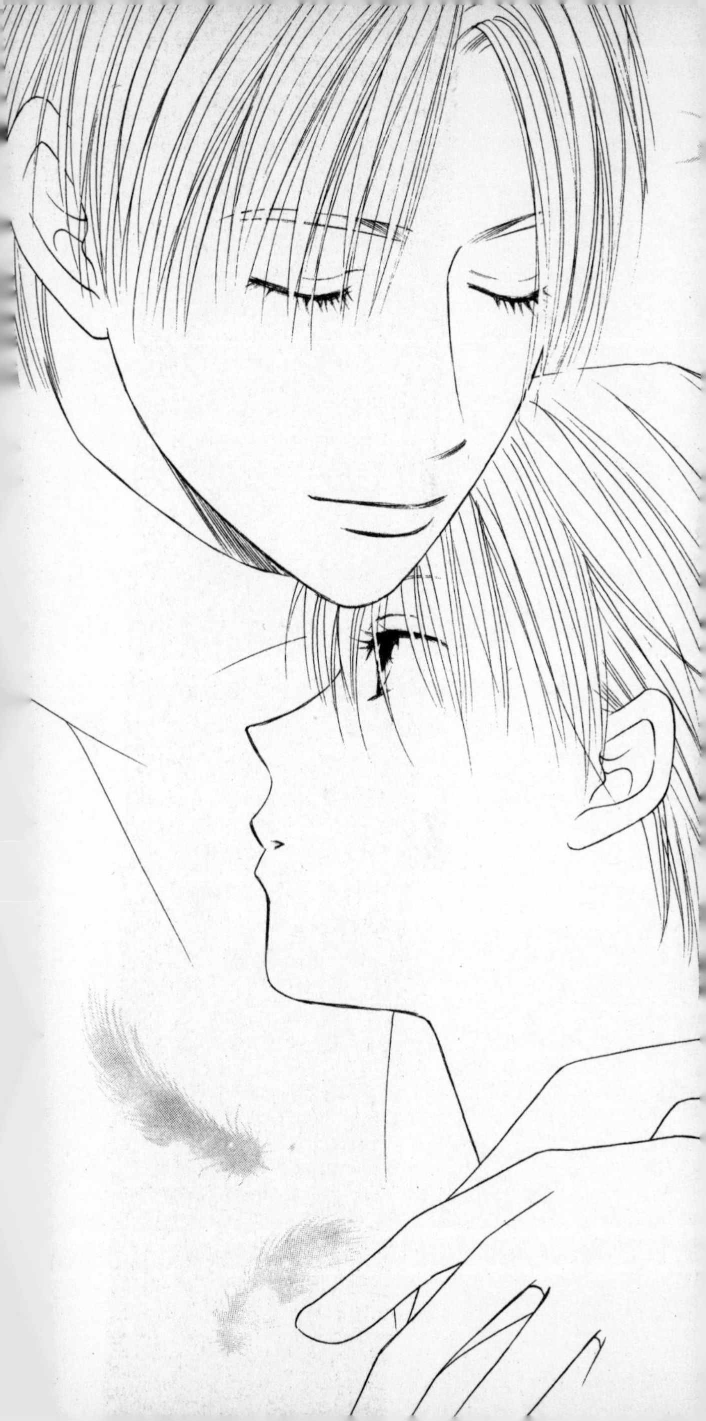

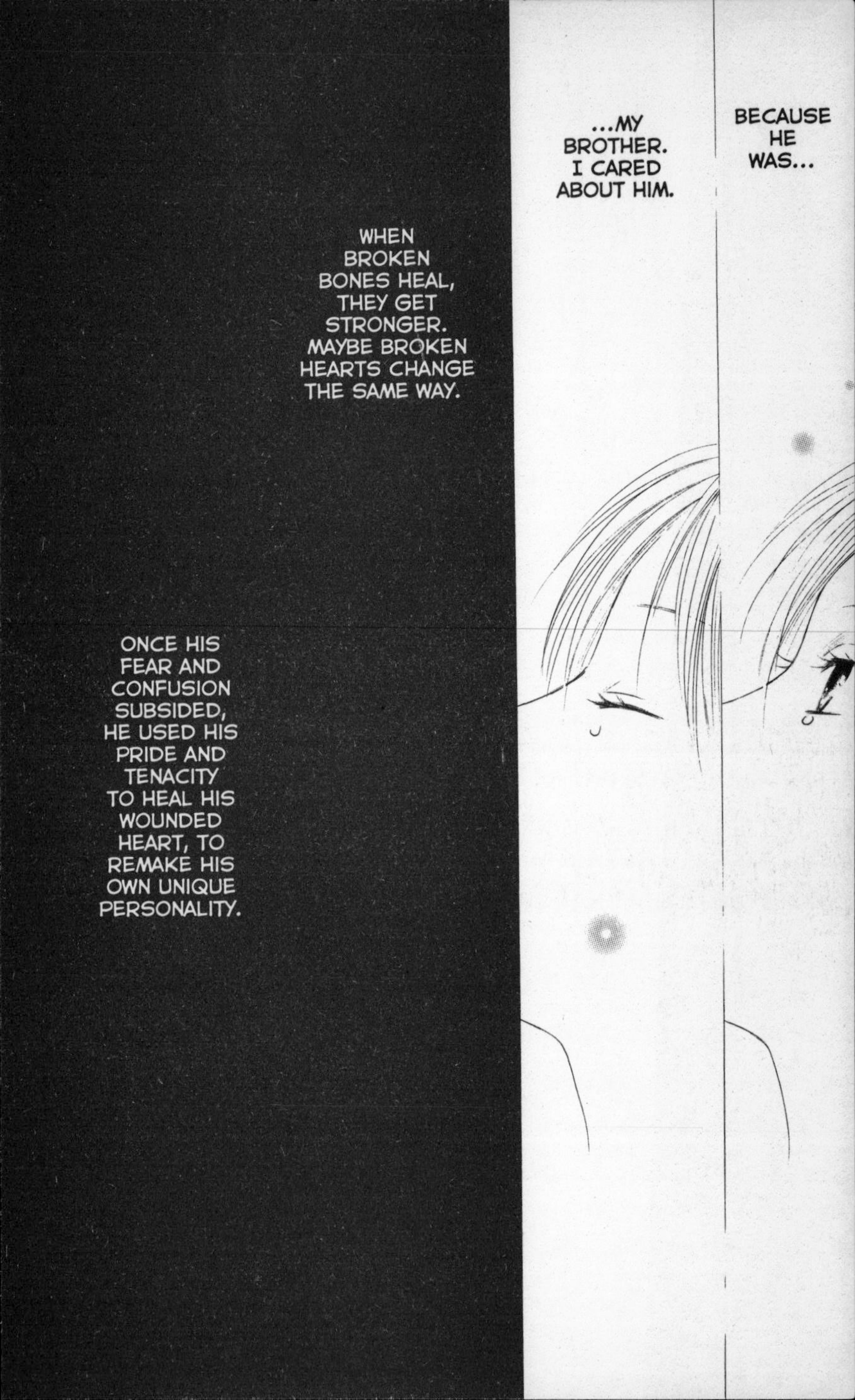
BECAUSE HE WAS...
...MY BROTHER. I CARED ABOUT HIM.
WHEN BROKEN BONES HEAL, THEY GET STRONGER. MAYBE BROKEN HEARTS CHANGE THE SAME WAY.
ONCE HIS FEAR AND CONFUSION SUBSIDED, HE USED HIS PRIDE AND TENACITY TO HEAL HIS WOUNDED HEART, TO REMAKE HIS OWN UNIQUE PERSONALITY.

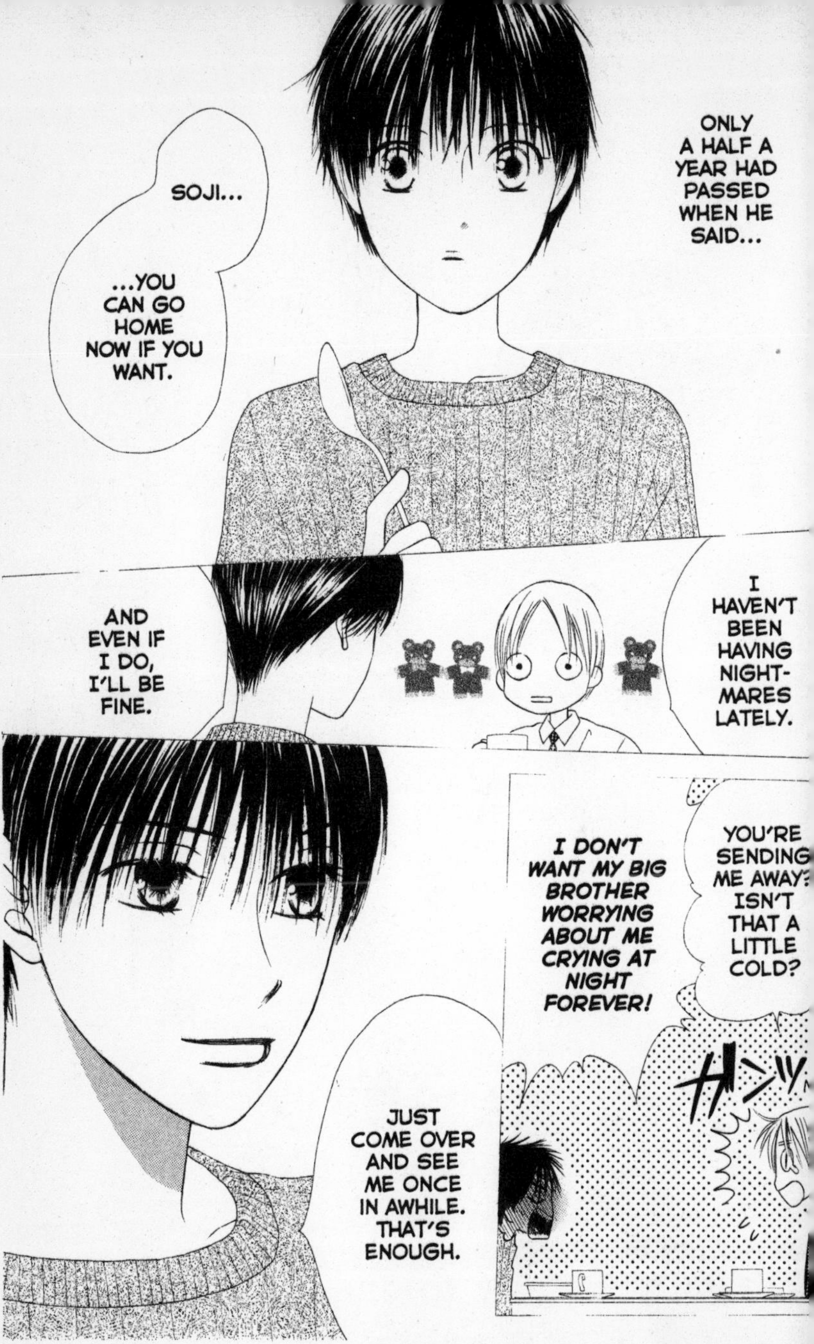
ONLY A HALF A YEAR HAD PASSED WHEN HE SAID...
SOJI...
...YOU CAN GO HOME NOW IF YOU WANT.
I HAVEN'T BEEN HAVING NIGHT-MARES LATELY.
AND EVEN IF I DO, I'LL BE FINE.
YOU'RE SENDING ME AWAY? ISN'T THAT A LITTLE COLD?
I DON'T WANT MY BIG BROTHER WORRYING ABOUT ME CRYING AT NIGHT FOREVER!
JUST COME OVER AND SEE ME ONCE IN AWHILE. THAT'S ENOUGH.

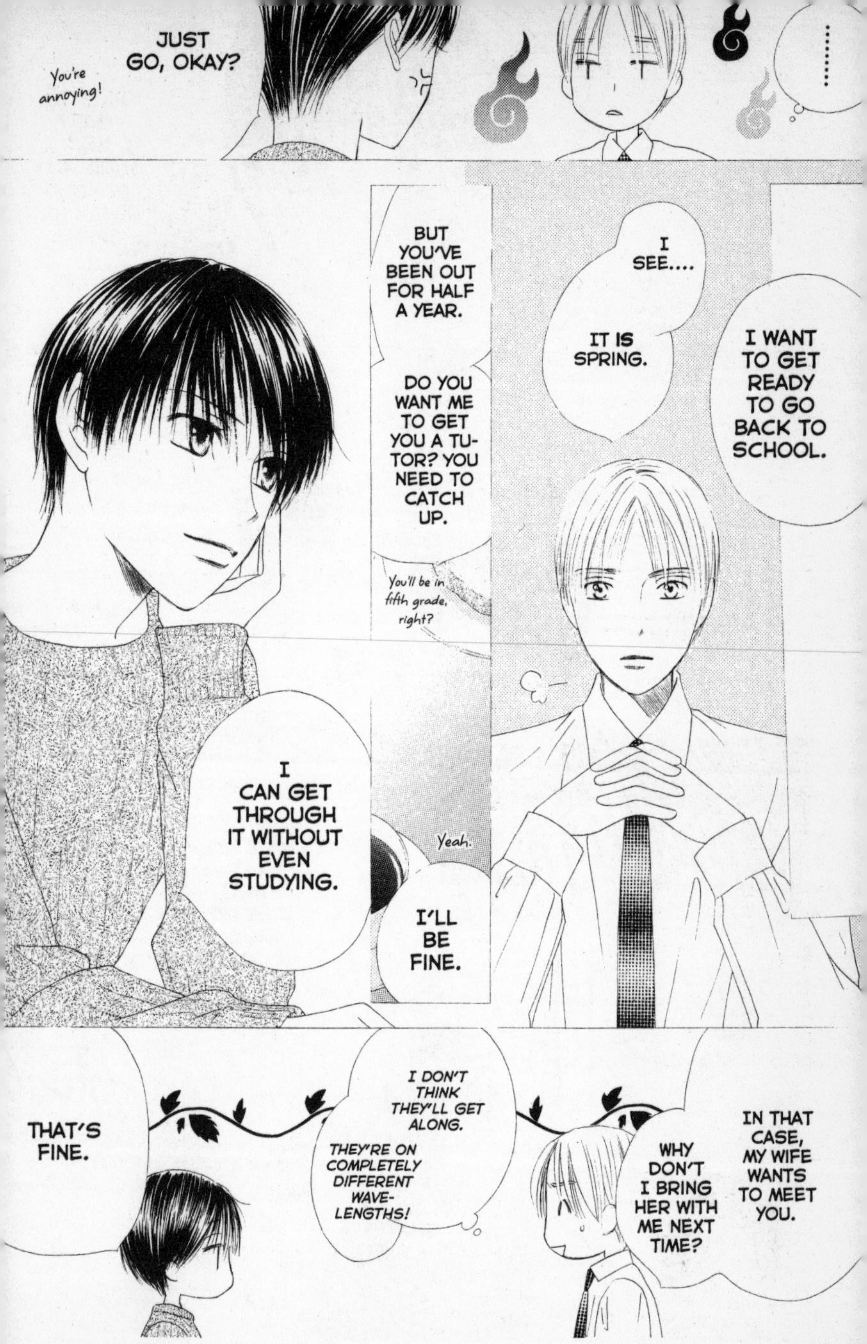

......
JUST GO, OKAY?
You're annoying!
I WANT TO GET READY TO GO BACK TO SCHOOL.
I SEE.... IT IS SPRING.
BUT YOU'VE BEEN OUT FOR HALF A YEAR.
DO YOU WANT ME TO GET YOU A TUTOR? YOU NEED TO CATCH UP.
You'll be in fifth grade, right?
Yeah.
I'LL BE FINE.
I CAN GET THROUGH IT WITHOUT EVEN STUDYING.
IN THAT CASE, MY WIFE WANTS TO MEET YOU.
WHY DON'T I BRING HER WITH ME NEXT TIME?
I DON'T THINK THEY'LL GET ALONG.
THEY'RE ON COMPLETELY DIFFERENT WAVE-LENGTHS!
THAT'S FINE.

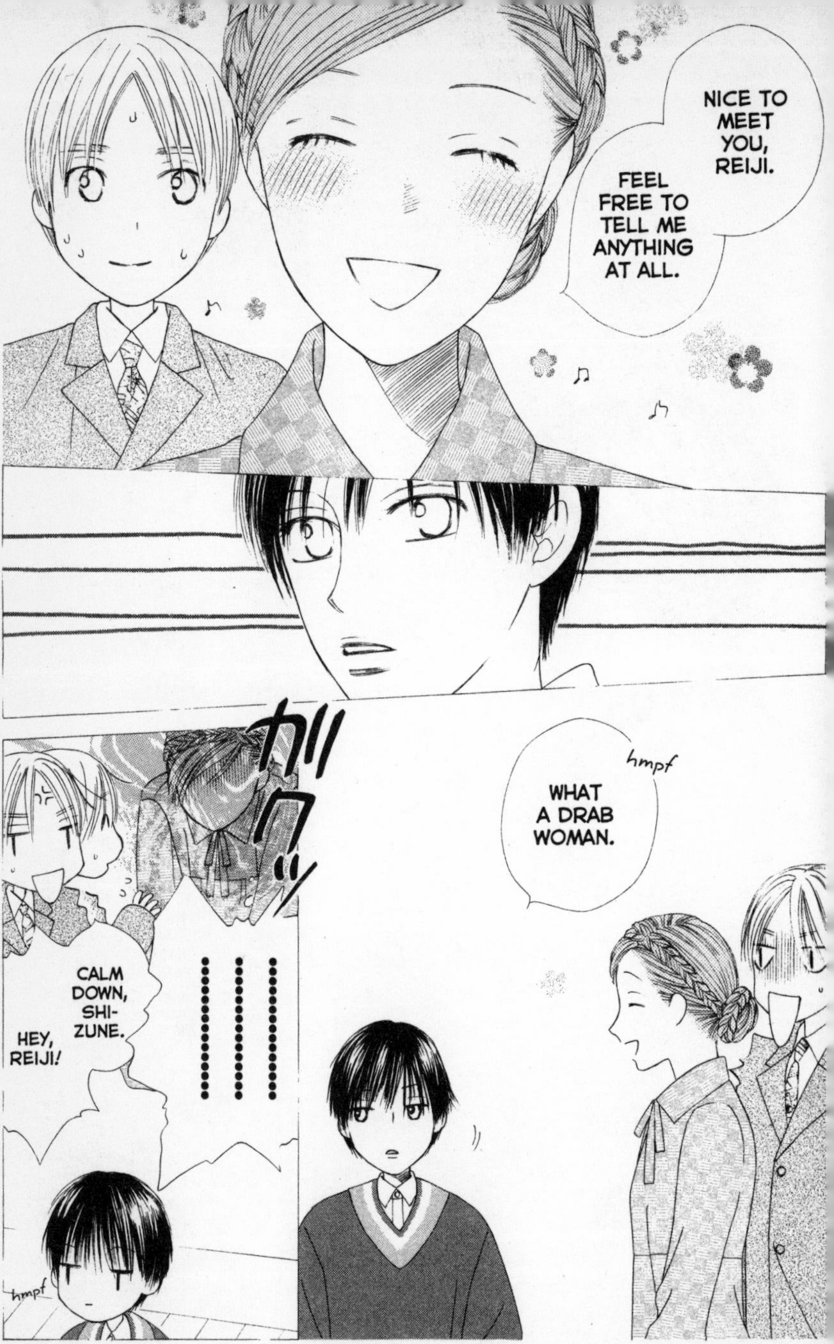
NICE TO MEET YOU, REIJI.
FEEL FREE TO TELL ME ANYTHING AT ALL.
hmpf
WHAT A DRAB WOMAN.
ガクッ
CALM DOWN, SHI-ZUNE.
HEY, REIJI!
hmpf

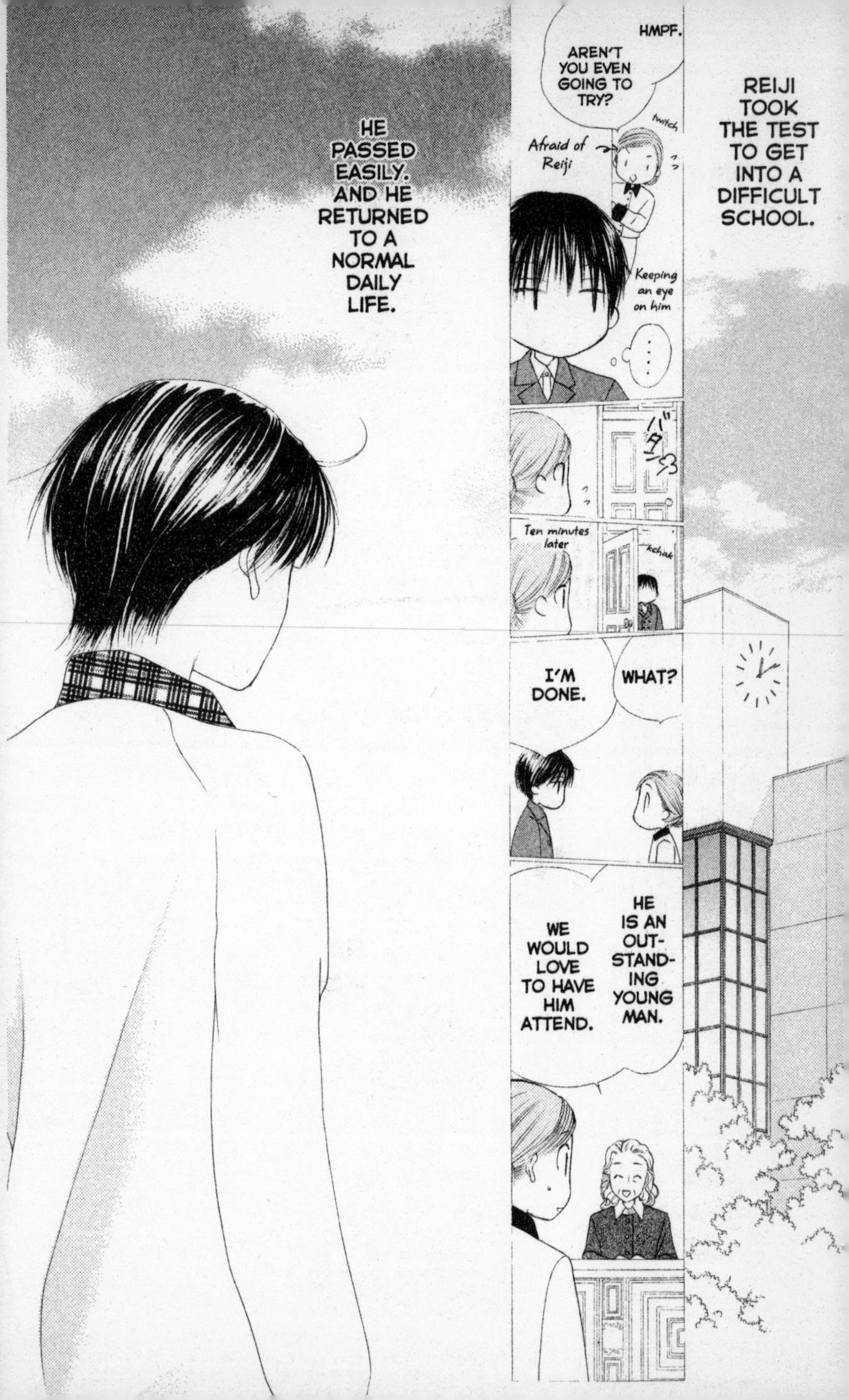
REIJI TOOK THE TEST TO GET INTO A DIFFICULT SCHOOL.
HMPF.
AREN'T YOU EVEN GOING TO TRY?
twitch
Afraid of Reiji
Keeping an eye on him
....
バタン
Ten minutes later
kchak
WHAT?
I'M DONE.
HE IS AN OUT-STAND-ING YOUNG MAN.
WE WOULD LOVE TO HAVE HIM ATTEND.
HE PASSED EASILY. AND HE RETURNED TO A NORMAL DAILY LIFE.

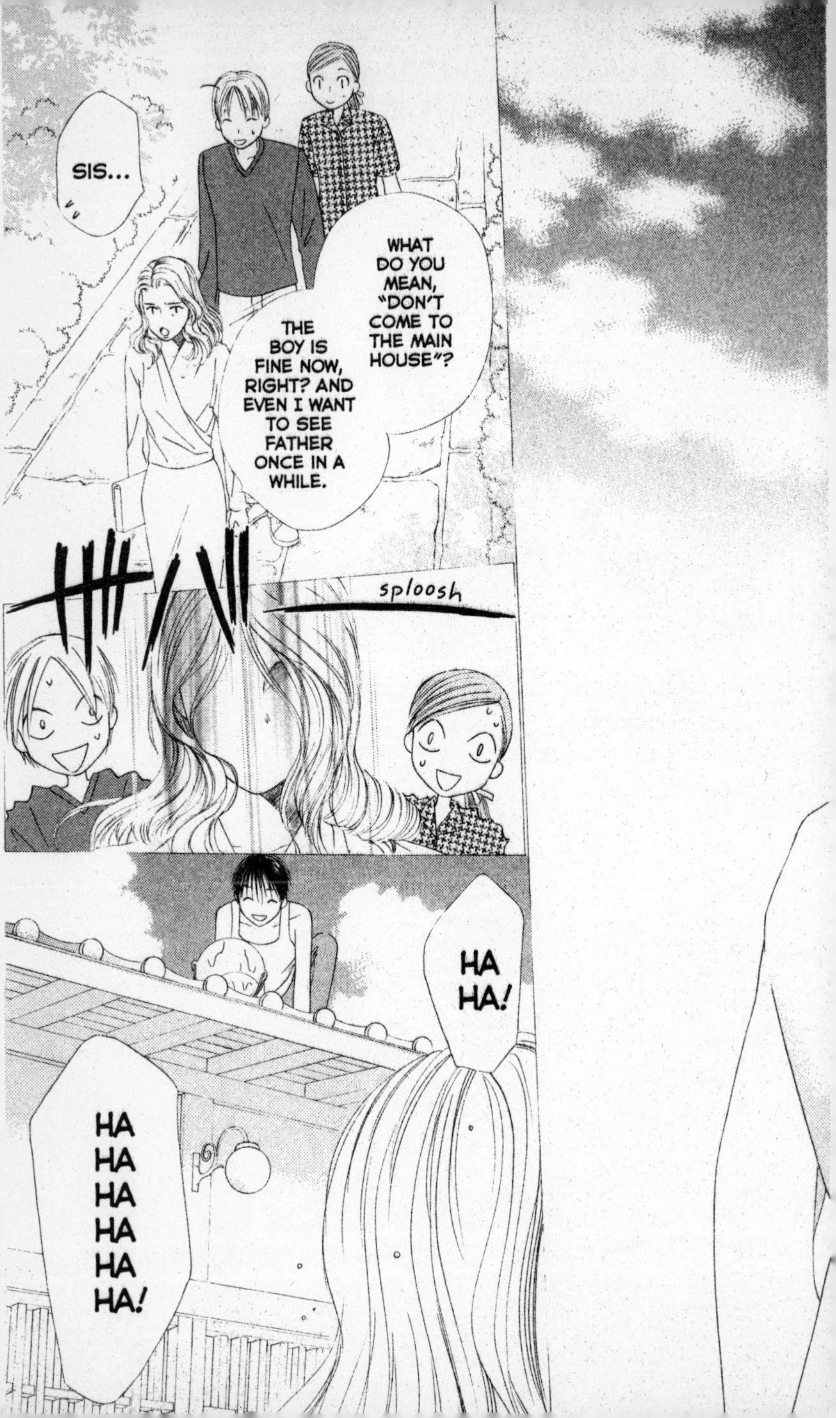
WHAT DO YOU MEAN, "DON'T COME TO THE MAIN HOUSE"?
THE BOY IS FINE NOW, RIGHT? AND EVEN I WANT TO SEE FATHER ONCE IN A WHILE.
SIS...
sploosh
HA HA!
HA HA HA HA HA HA HA!

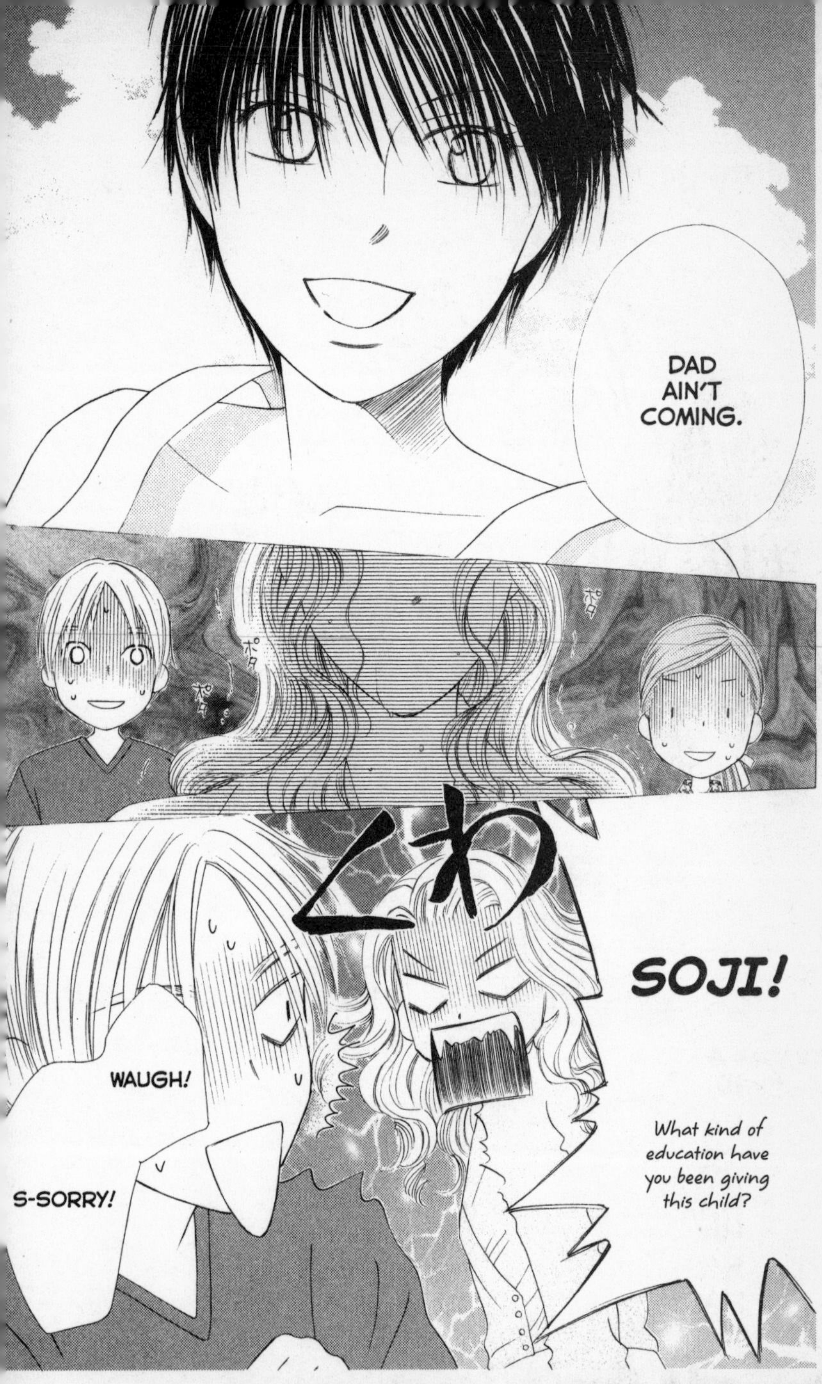

DAD AIN'T COMING.
くわ
SOJI!
What kind of education have you been giving this child?
WAUGH!
S-SORRY!

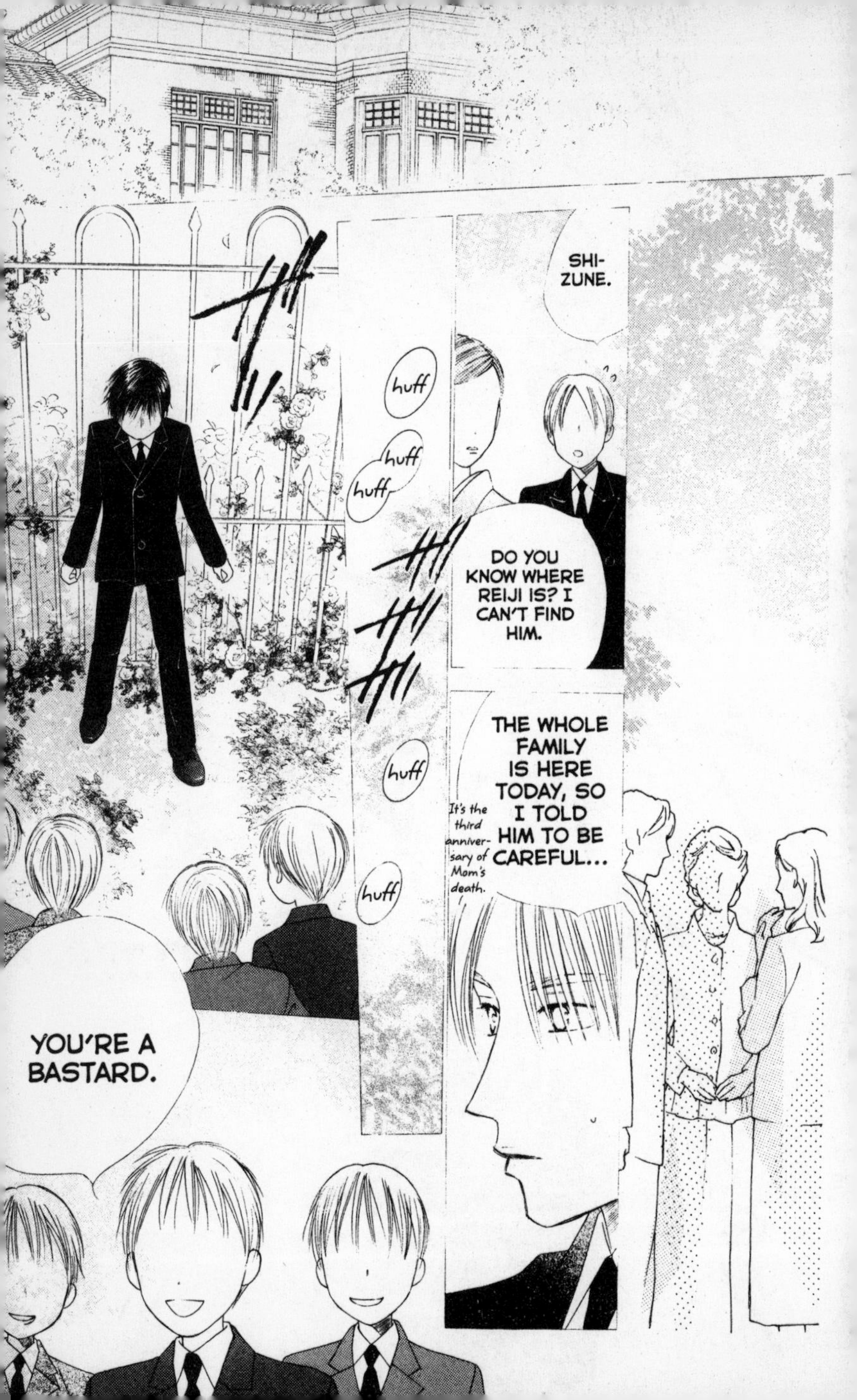
SHI-ZUNE.
DO YOU KNOW WHERE REIJI IS? I CAN'T FIND HIM.
THE WHOLE FAMILY IS HERE TODAY, SO I TOLD HIM TO BE CAREFUL...
It's the third anniversary of Mom's death.
huff
huff
huff
huff
huff
YOU'RE A BASTARD.

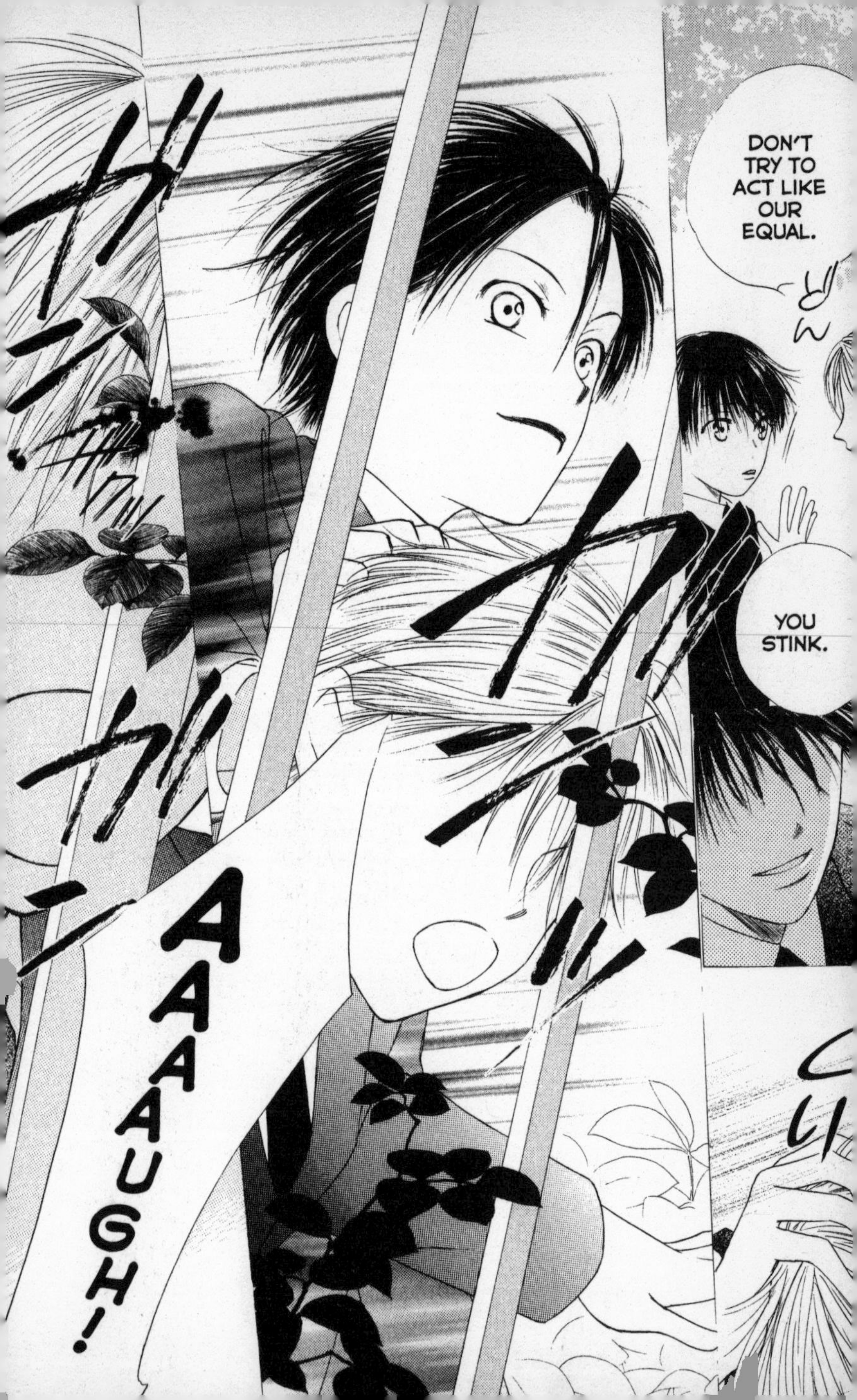
DON'T TRY TO ACT LIKE OUR EQUAL.
YOU STINK.
AAAAUGH!

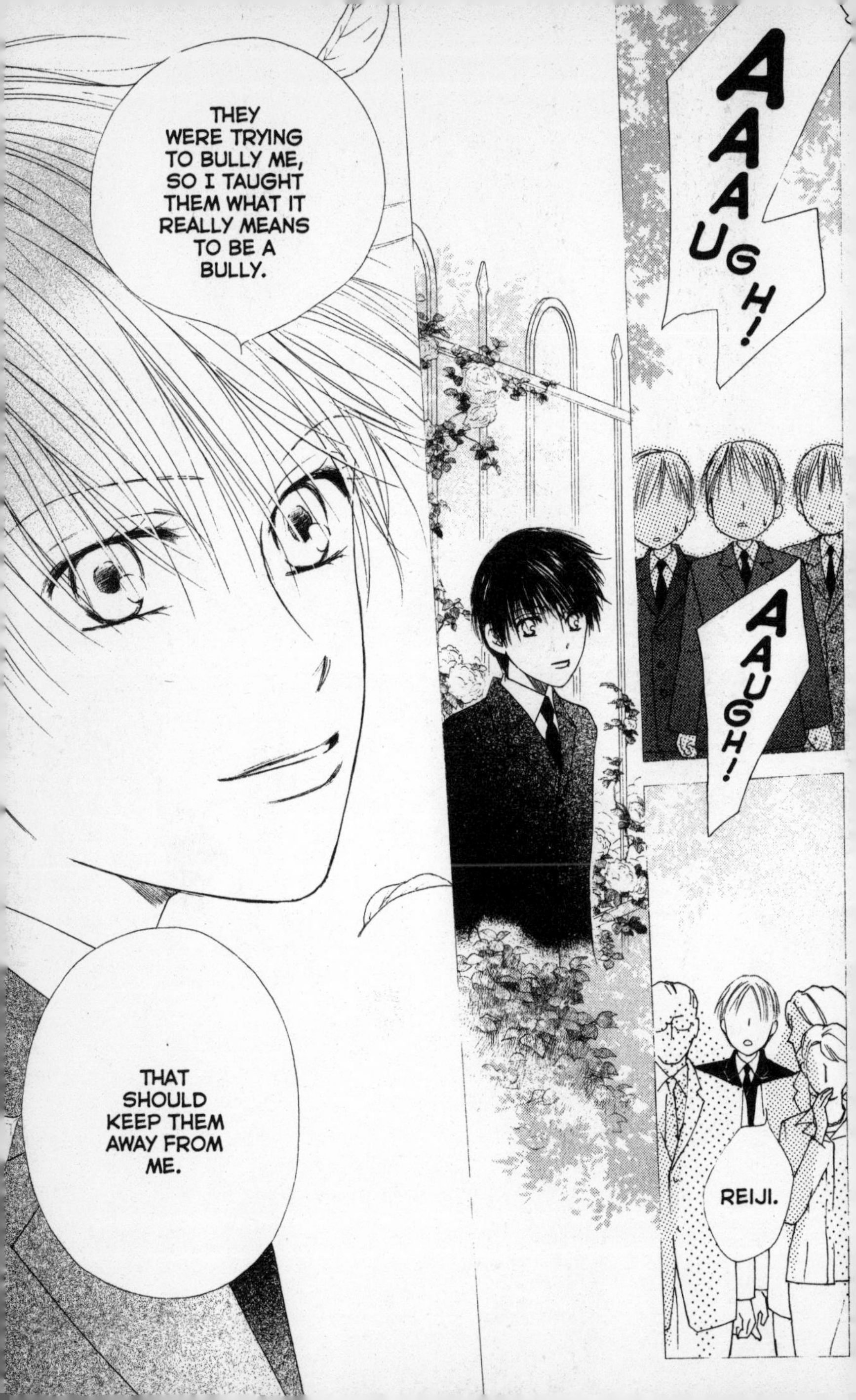
AAAAUGH!
AAAUGH!
REIJI.
THEY WERE TRYING TO BULLY ME, SO I TAUGHT THEM WHAT IT REALLY MEANS TO BE A BULLY.
THAT SHOULD KEEP THEM AWAY FROM ME.

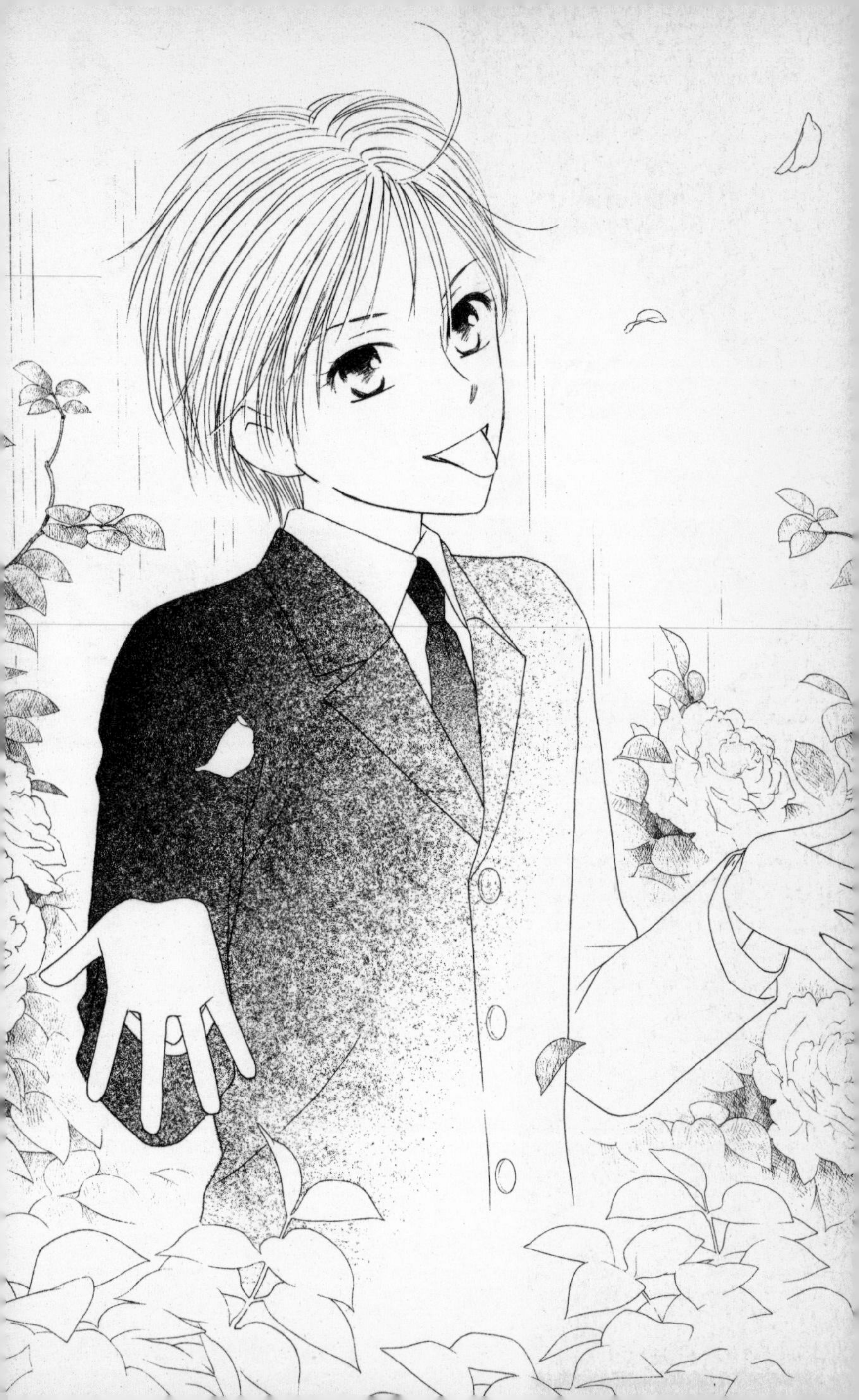

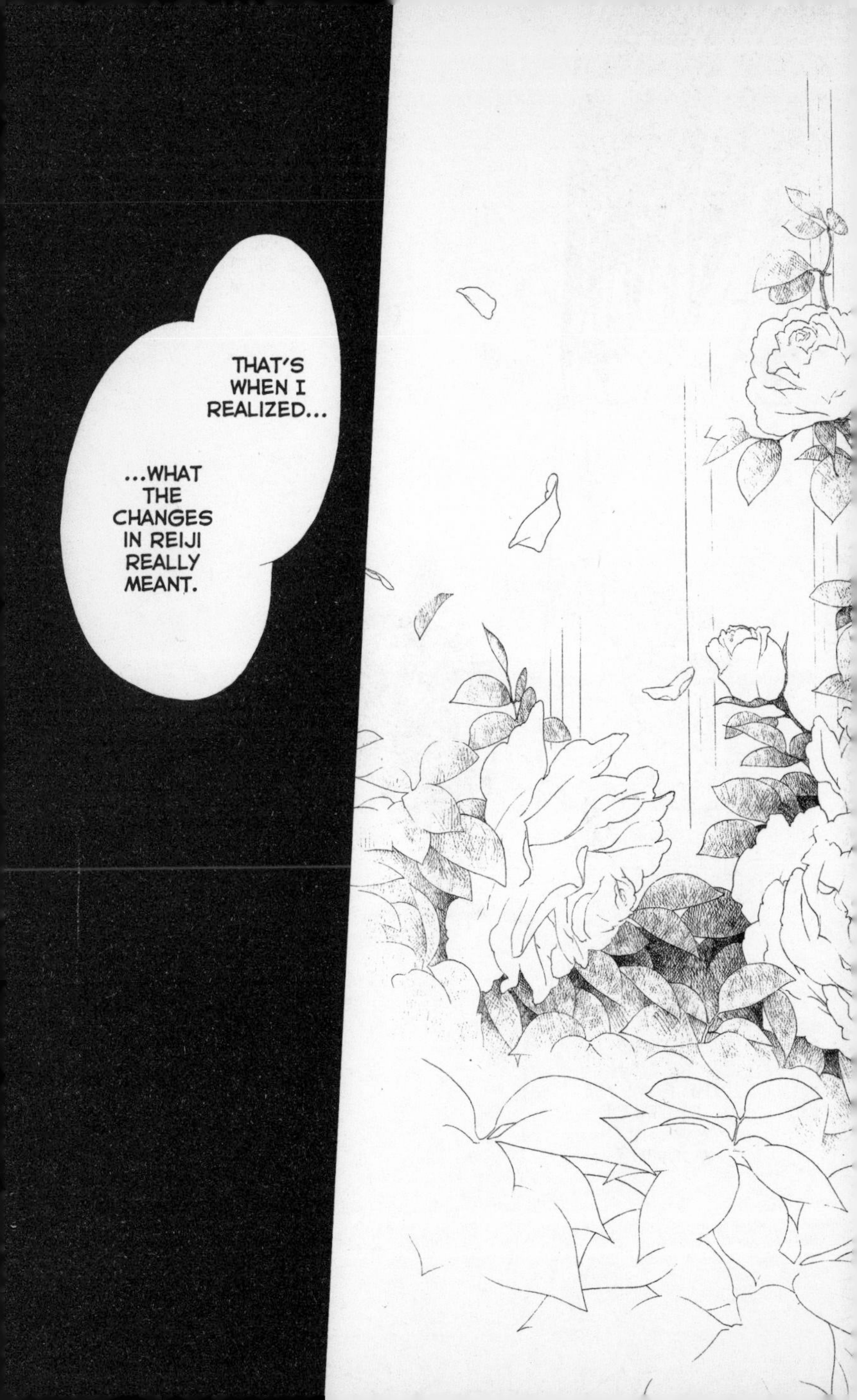
THAT'S WHEN I REALIZED...
...WHAT THE CHANGES IN REIJI REALLY MEANT.

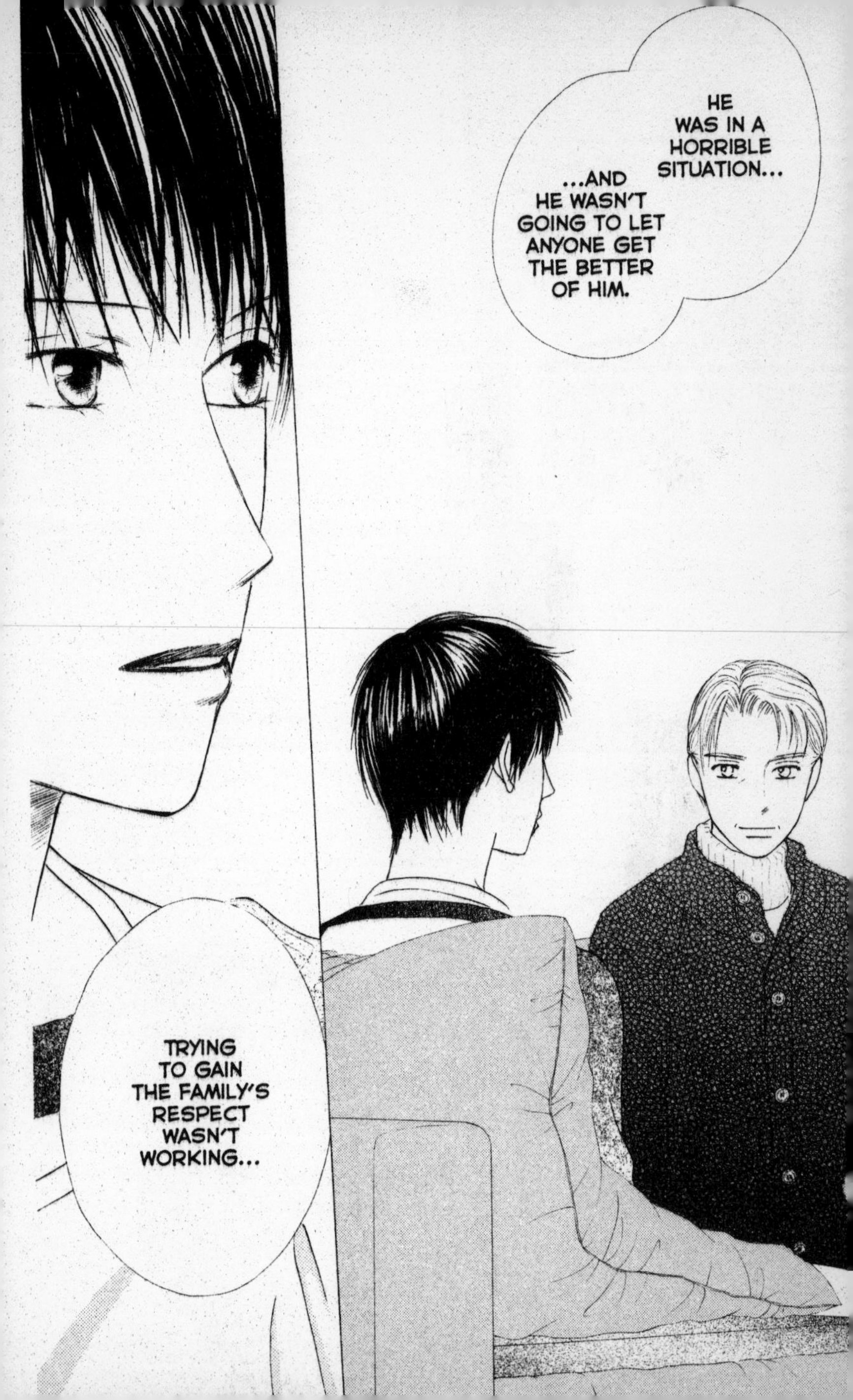
HE WAS IN A HORRIBLE SITUATION...
...AND HE WASN'T GOING TO LET ANYONE GET THE BETTER OF HIM.
TRYING TO GAIN THE FAMILY'S RESPECT WASN'T WORKING...

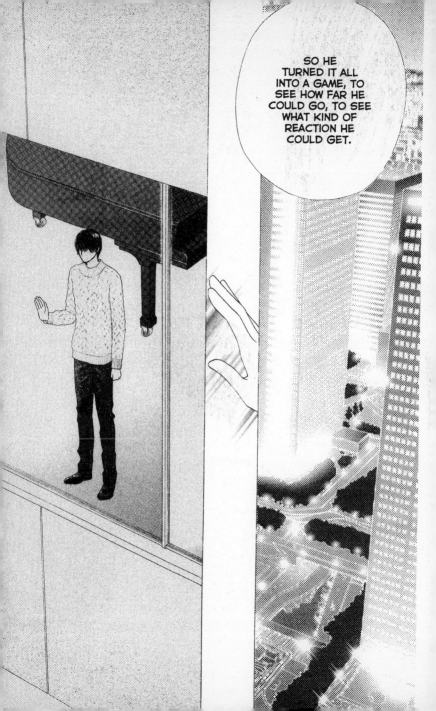

SO HE TURNED IT ALL INTO A GAME, TO SEE HOW FAR HE COULD GO, TO SEE WHAT KIND OF REACTION HE COULD GET.

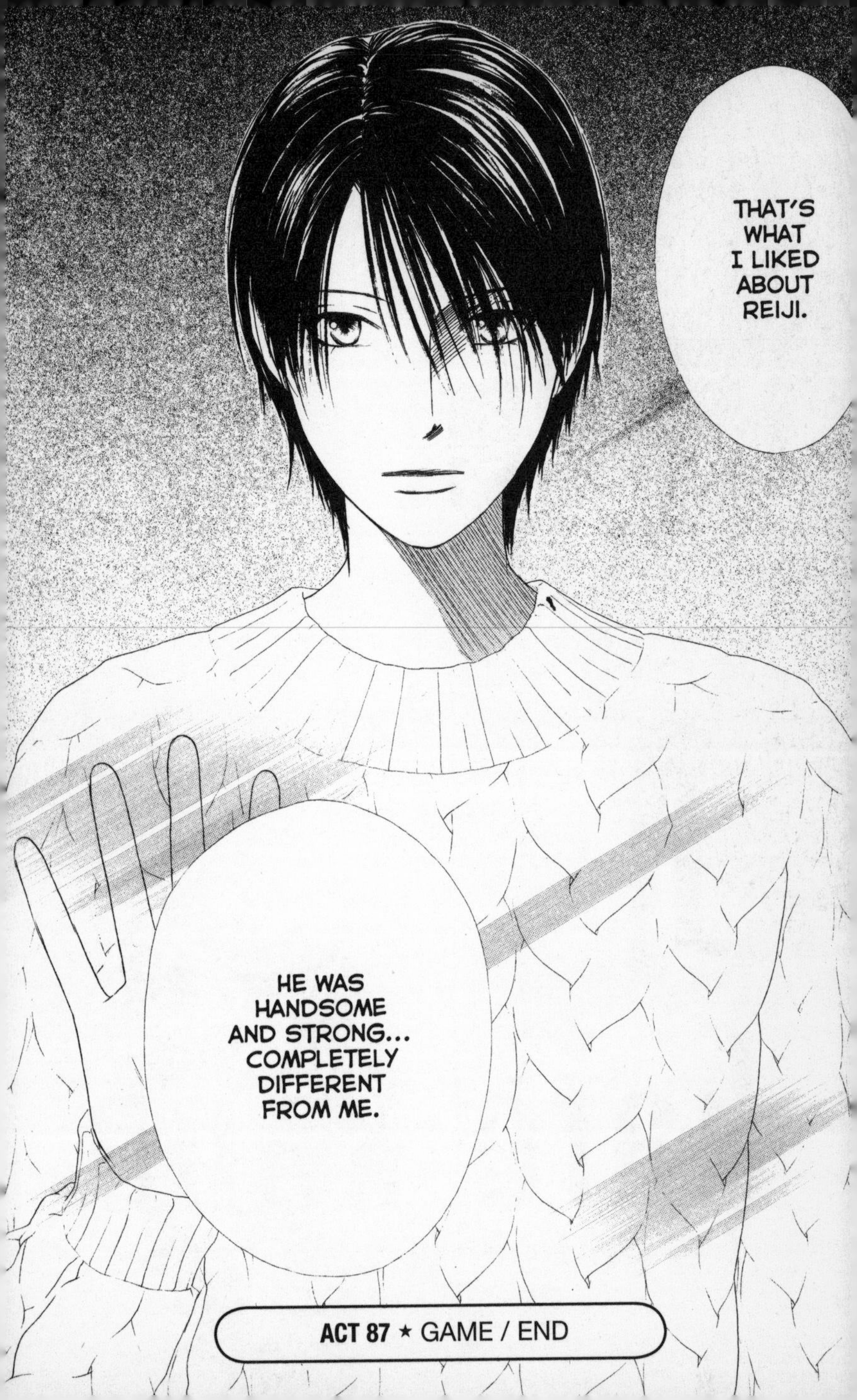
THAT'S WHAT I LIKED ABOUT REIJI.
HE WAS HANDSOME AND STRONG... COMPLETELY DIFFERENT FROM ME.
ACT 87 ★ GAME / END

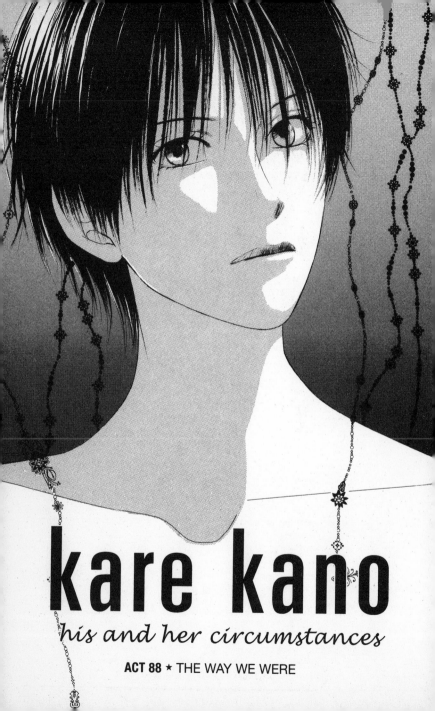

kare kano
his and her circumstances

ACT 88 ★ THE WAY WE WERE

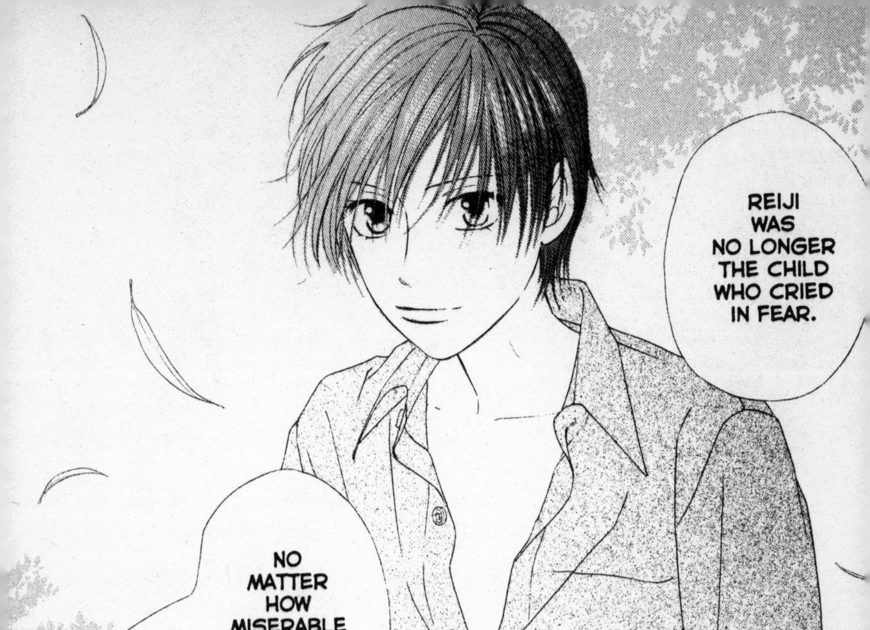
REIJI WAS NO LONGER THE CHILD WHO CRIED IN FEAR.
NO MATTER HOW MISERABLE OTHERS TRIED TO MAKE HIM...
...HE JUST KEPT THAT SMIRK ON HIS FACE.

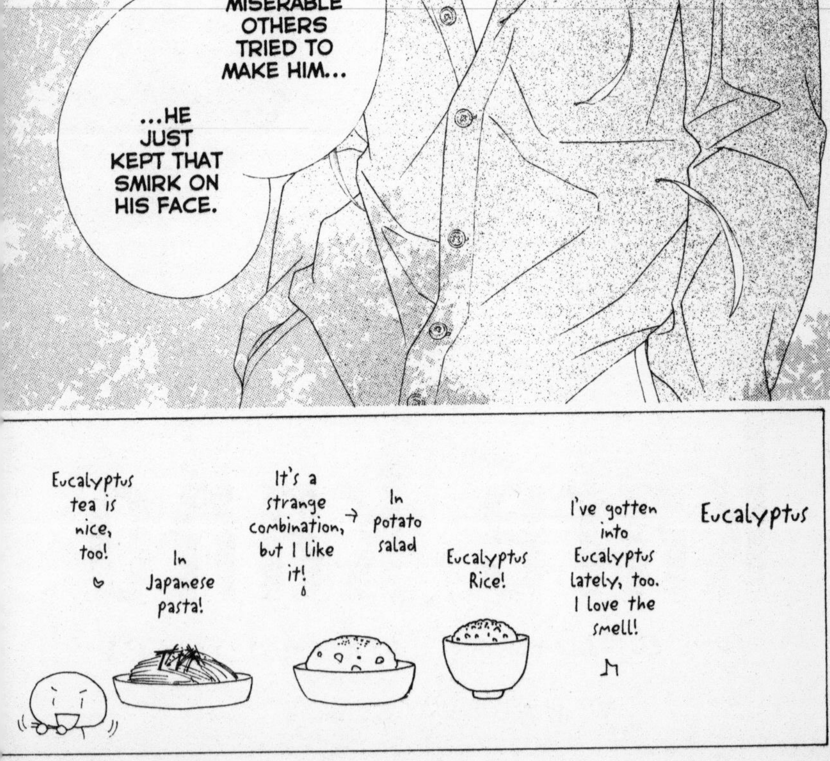
Eucalyptus
I've gotten into Eucalyptus lately, too. I love the smell! ♪
Eucalyptus Rice!
In potato salad
It's a strange combination, but I like it!
In Japanese pasta!
Eucalyptus tea is nice, too!

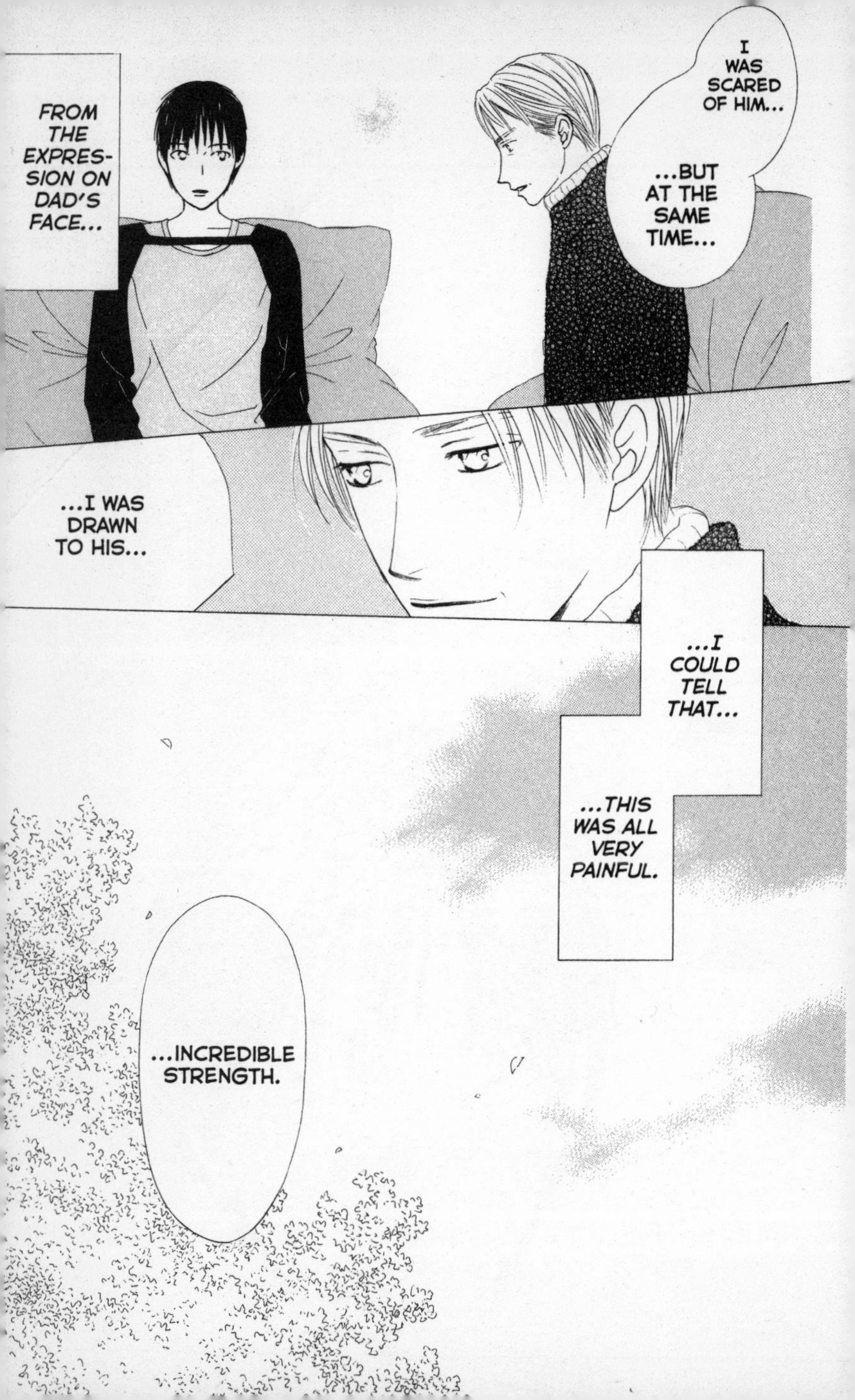
I WAS SCARED OF HIM...
...BUT AT THE SAME TIME...
FROM THE EXPRES-SION ON DAD'S FACE...
...I WAS DRAWN TO HIS...
...I COULD TELL THAT...
...THIS WAS ALL VERY PAINFUL.
...INCREDIBLE STRENGTH.

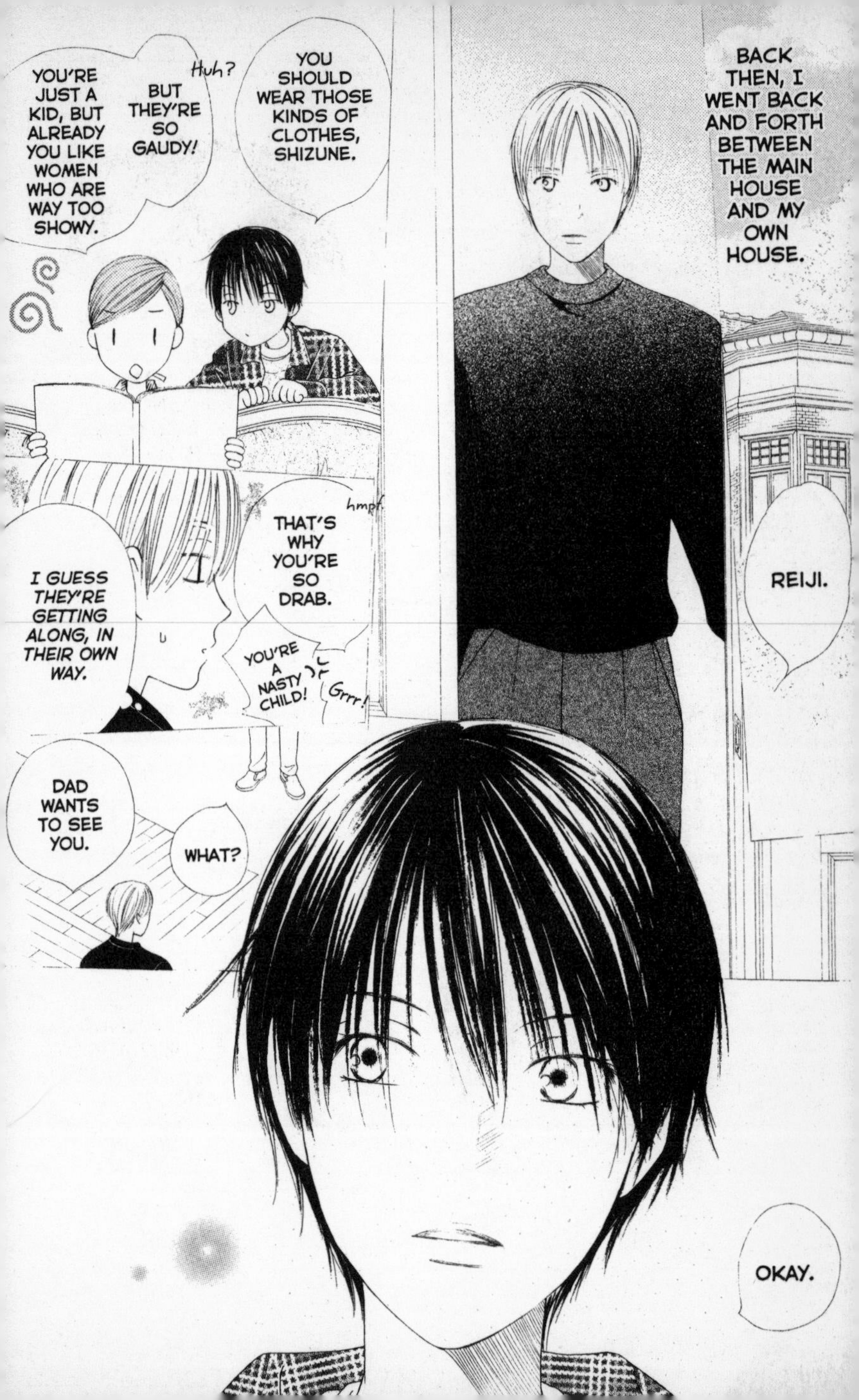
BACK THEN, I WENT BACK AND FORTH BETWEEN THE MAIN HOUSE AND MY OWN HOUSE.
REIJI.
YOU SHOULD WEAR THOSE KINDS OF CLOTHES, SHIZUNE.
Huh?
BUT THEY'RE SO GAUDY!
YOU'RE JUST A KID, BUT ALREADY YOU LIKE WOMEN WHO ARE WAY TOO SHOWY.
hmpf.
THAT'S WHY YOU'RE SO DRAB.
YOU'RE A NASTY CHILD!
Grrr!
I GUESS THEY'RE GETTING ALONG, IN THEIR OWN WAY.
DAD WANTS TO SEE YOU.
WHAT?
OKAY.

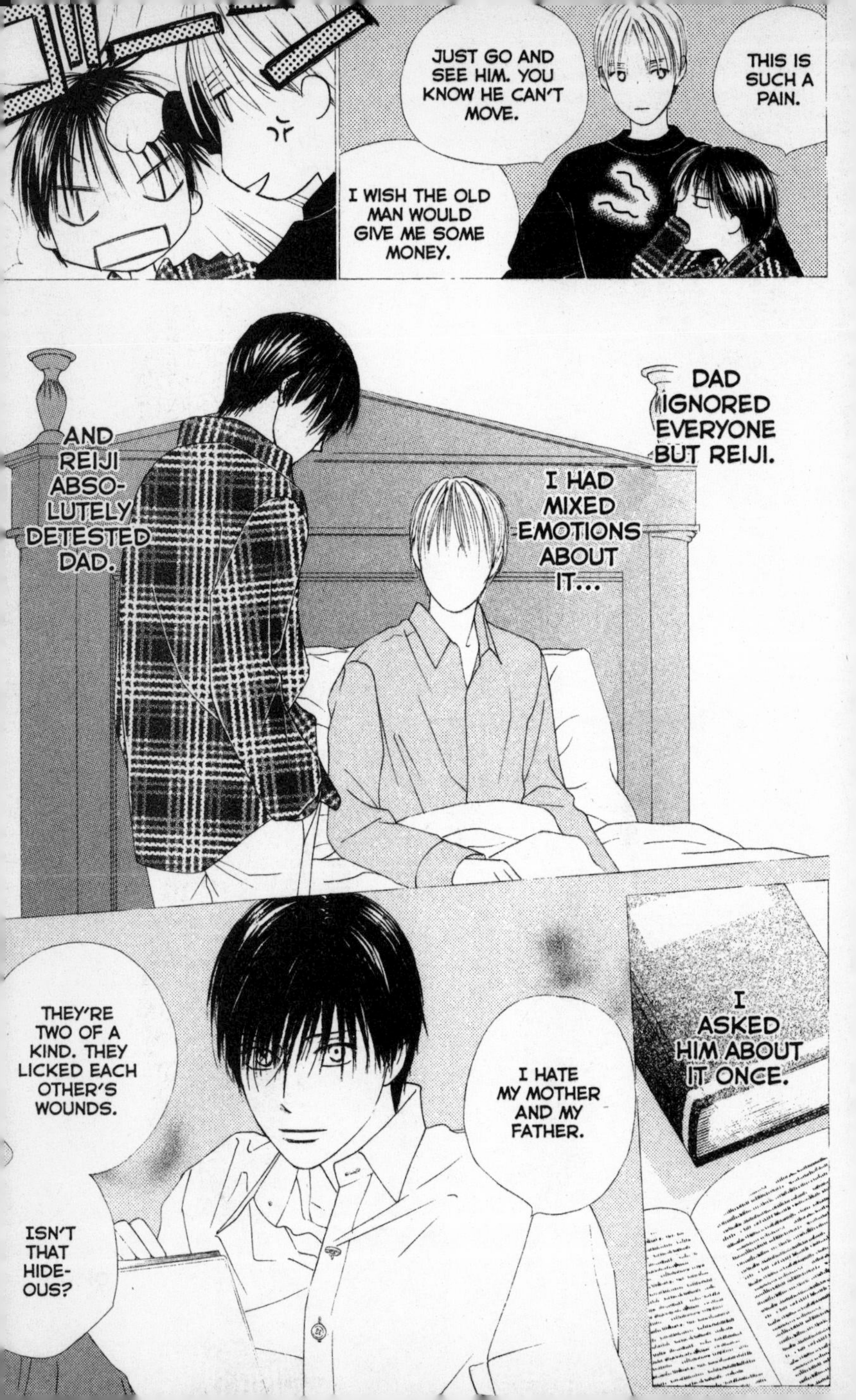
THIS IS SUCH A PAIN.
JUST GO AND SEE HIM. YOU KNOW HE CAN'T MOVE.
I WISH THE OLD MAN WOULD GIVE ME SOME MONEY.
DAD IGNORED EVERYONE BUT REIJI.
I HAD MIXED EMOTIONS ABOUT IT...
AND REIJI ABSOLUTELY DETESTED DAD.
I ASKED HIM ABOUT IT ONCE.
I HATE MY MOTHER AND MY FATHER.
THEY'RE TWO OF A KIND. THEY LICKED EACH OTHER'S WOUNDS.
ISN'T THAT HIDEOUS?

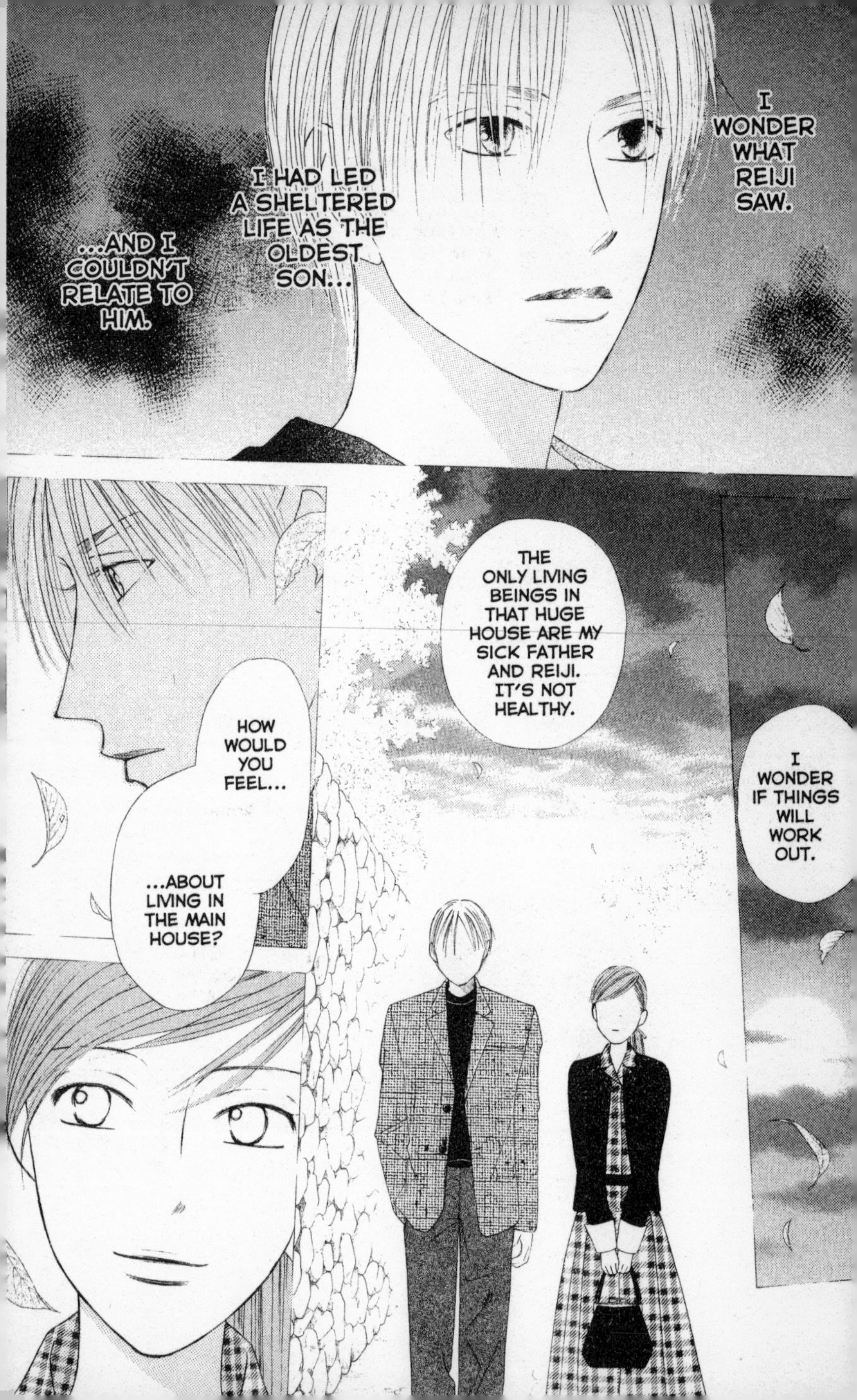
I WONDER WHAT REIJI SAW.
I HAD LED A SHELTERED LIFE AS THE OLDEST SON...
...AND I COULDN'T RELATE TO HIM.
I WONDER IF THINGS WILL WORK OUT.
THE ONLY LIVING BEINGS IN THAT HUGE HOUSE ARE MY SICK FATHER AND REIJI. IT'S NOT HEALTHY.
HOW WOULD YOU FEEL...
...ABOUT LIVING IN THE MAIN HOUSE?

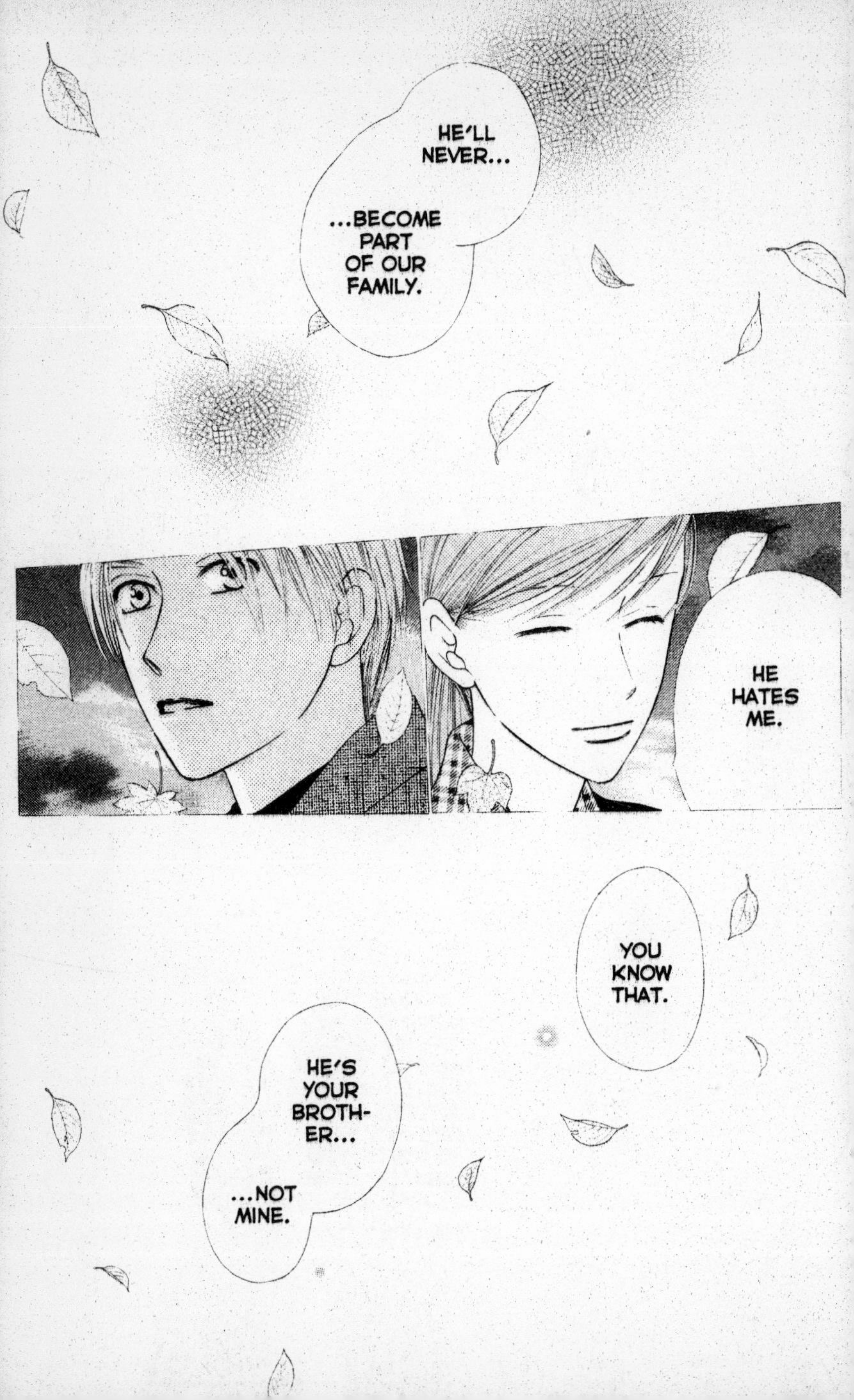
HE'LL NEVER...
...BECOME PART OF OUR FAMILY.
HE HATES ME.
YOU KNOW THAT.
HE'S YOUR BROTH-ER...
...NOT MINE.

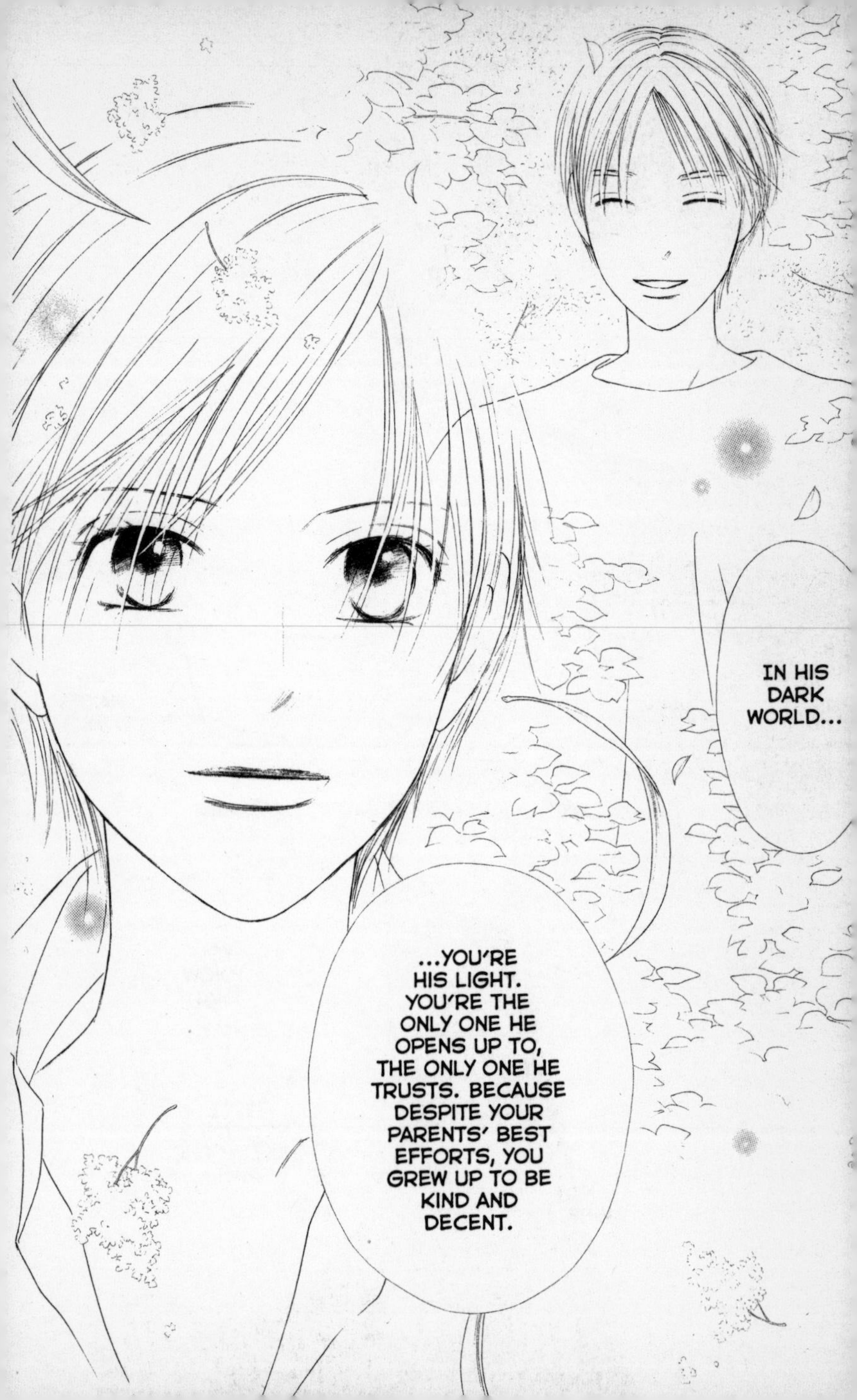
IN HIS DARK WORLD...
...YOU'RE HIS LIGHT. YOU'RE THE ONLY ONE HE OPENS UP TO, THE ONLY ONE HE TRUSTS. BECAUSE DESPITE YOUR PARENTS' BEST EFFORTS, YOU GREW UP TO BE KIND AND DECENT.

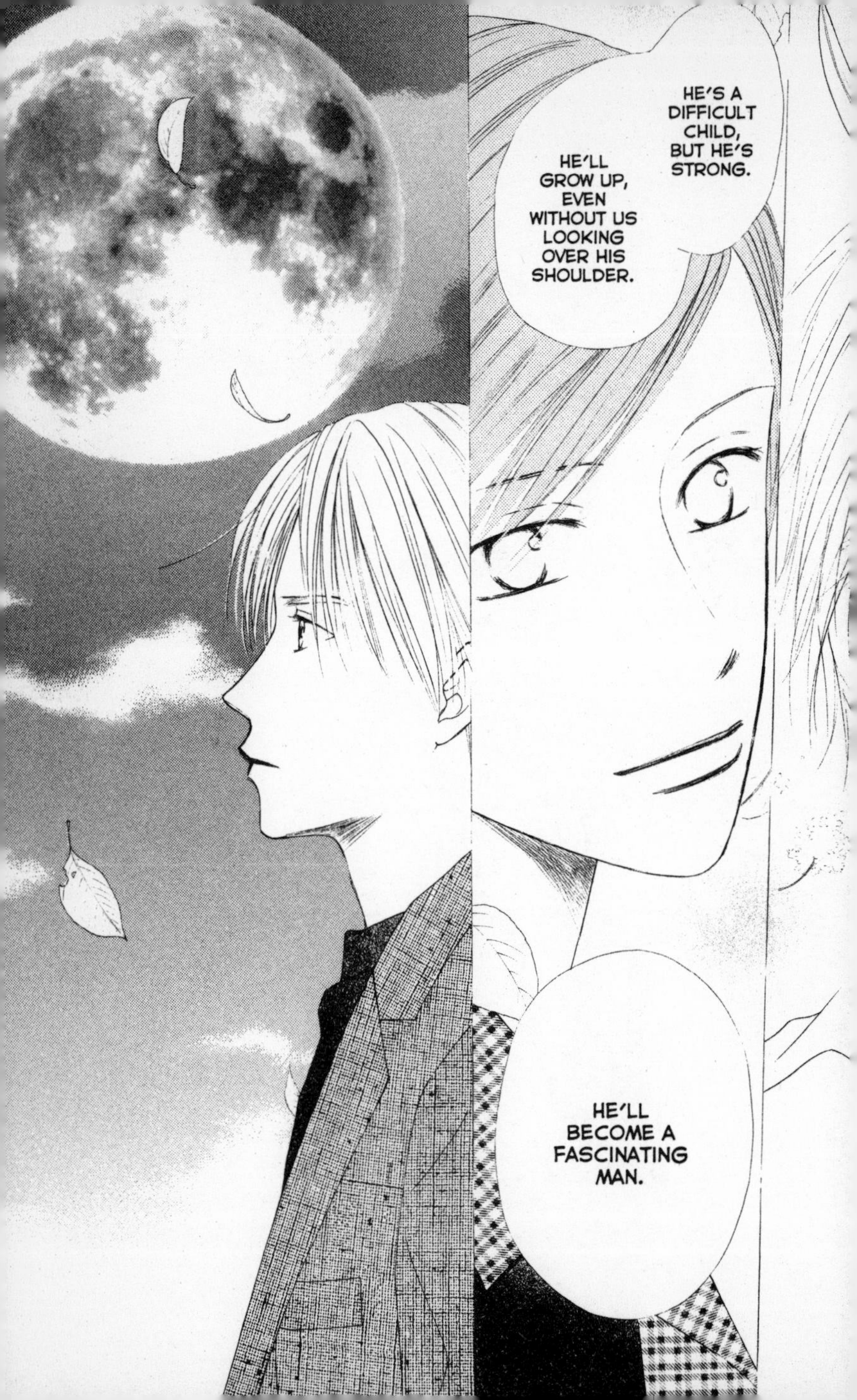
HE'S A DIFFICULT CHILD, BUT HE'S STRONG.
HE'LL GROW UP, EVEN WITHOUT US LOOKING OVER HIS SHOULDER.
HE'LL BECOME A FASCINATING MAN.

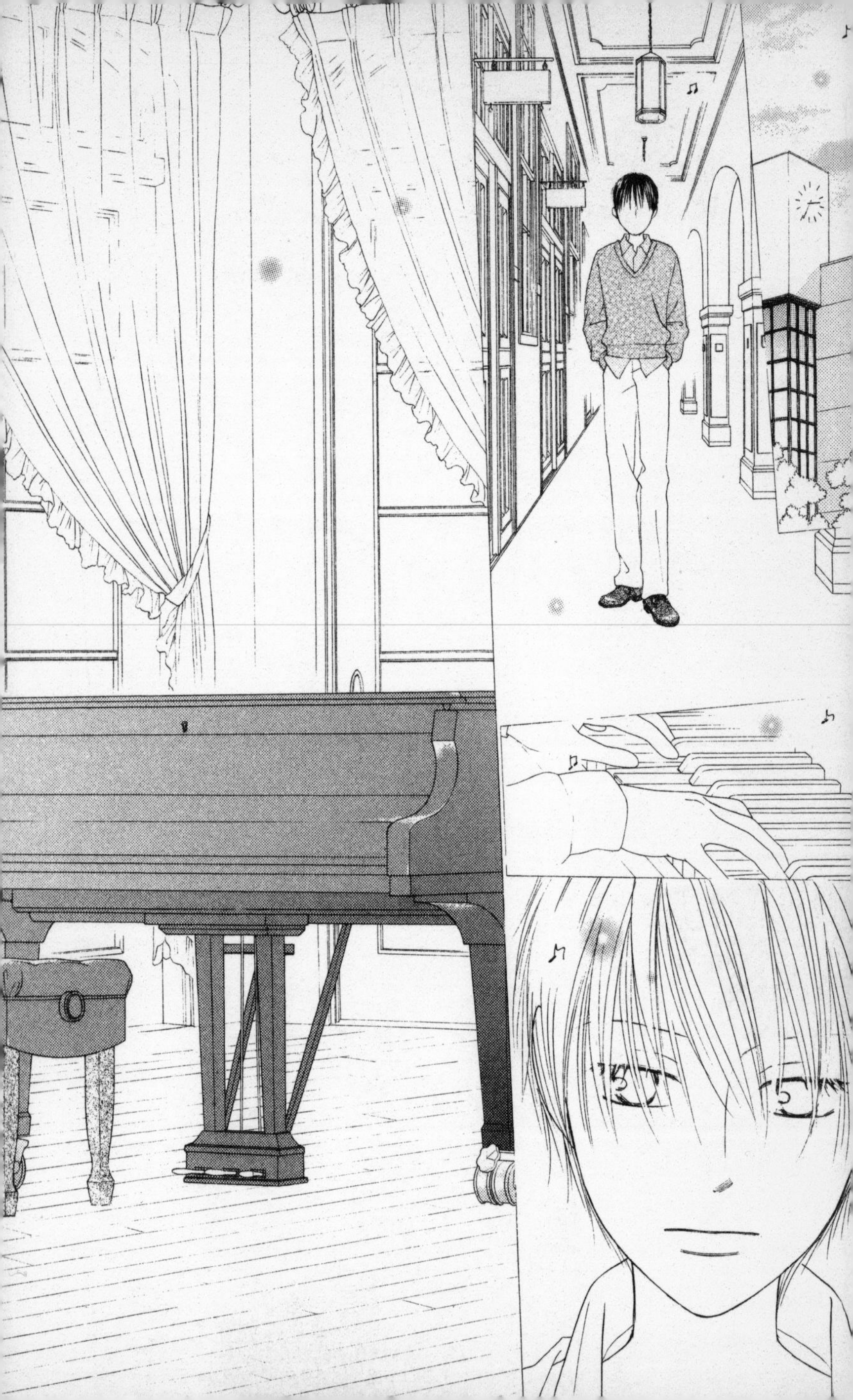

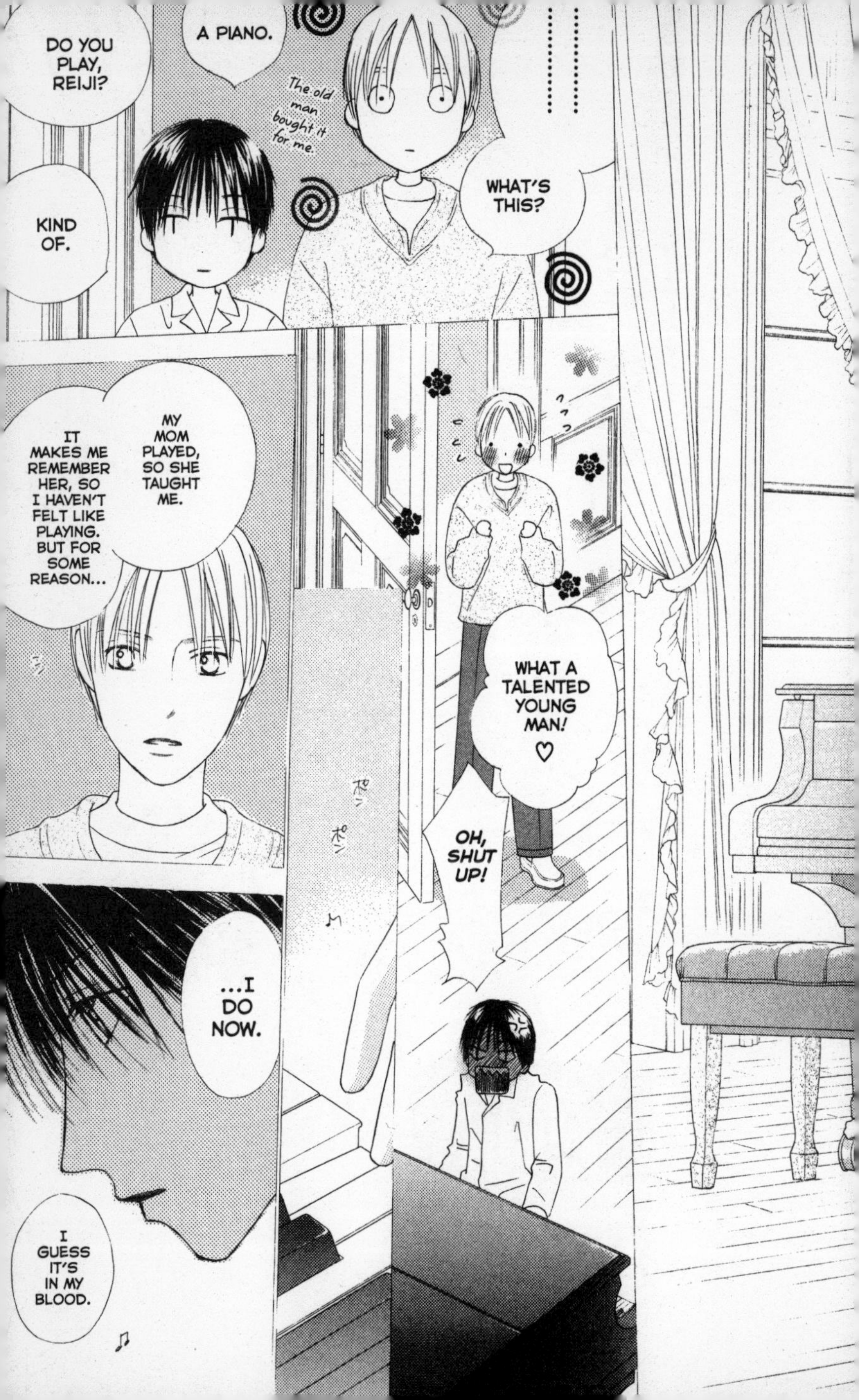
WHAT'S THIS?
......
A PIANO.
The old man bought it for me.
DO YOU PLAY, REIJI?
KIND OF.
MY MOM PLAYED, SO SHE TAUGHT ME.
IT MAKES ME REMEMBER HER, SO I HAVEN'T FELT LIKE PLAYING. BUT FOR SOME REASON...
...I DO NOW.
I GUESS IT'S IN MY BLOOD.
ポン
ポン
WHAT A TALENTED YOUNG MAN! ♡
OH, SHUT UP!

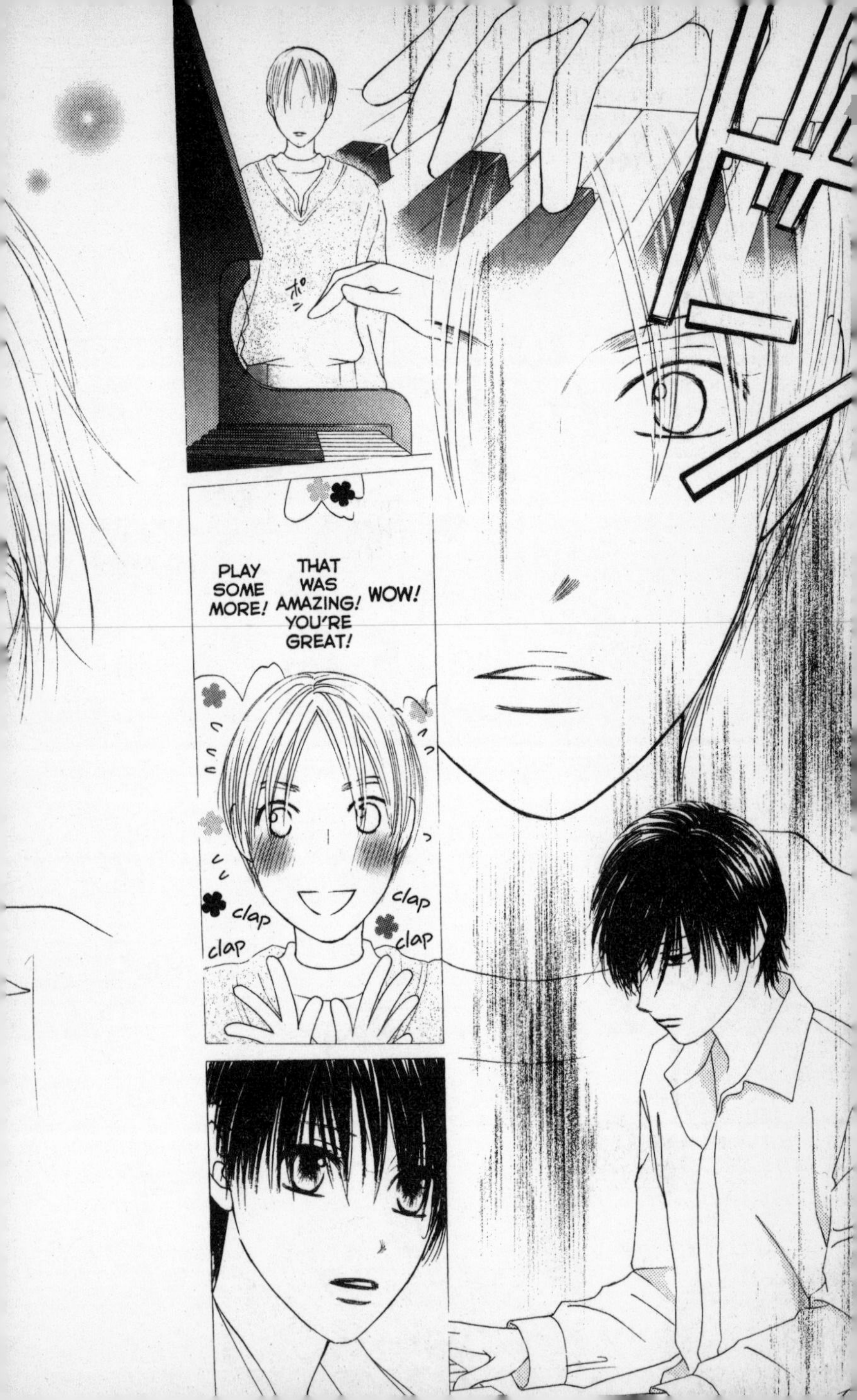
WOW!
THAT WAS AMAZING! YOU'RE GREAT!
PLAY SOME MORE!
clap
clap
clap
clap

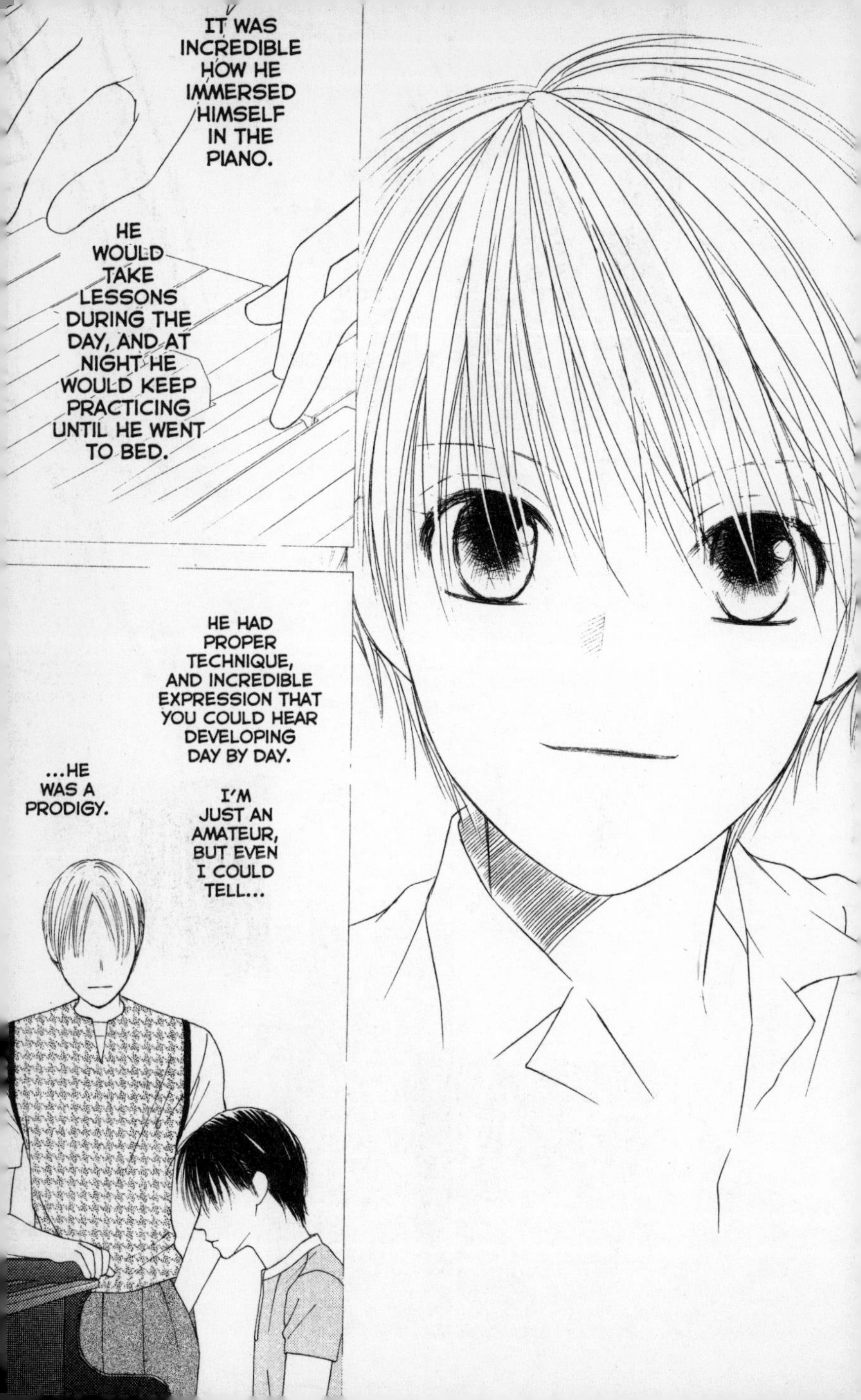
IT WAS INCREDIBLE HOW HE IMMERSED HIMSELF IN THE PIANO.
HE WOULD TAKE LESSONS DURING THE DAY, AND AT NIGHT HE WOULD KEEP PRACTICING UNTIL HE WENT TO BED.
HE HAD PROPER TECHNIQUE, AND INCREDIBLE EXPRESSION THAT YOU COULD HEAR DEVELOPING DAY BY DAY.
I'M JUST AN AMATEUR, BUT EVEN I COULD TELL...
...HE WAS A PRODIGY.

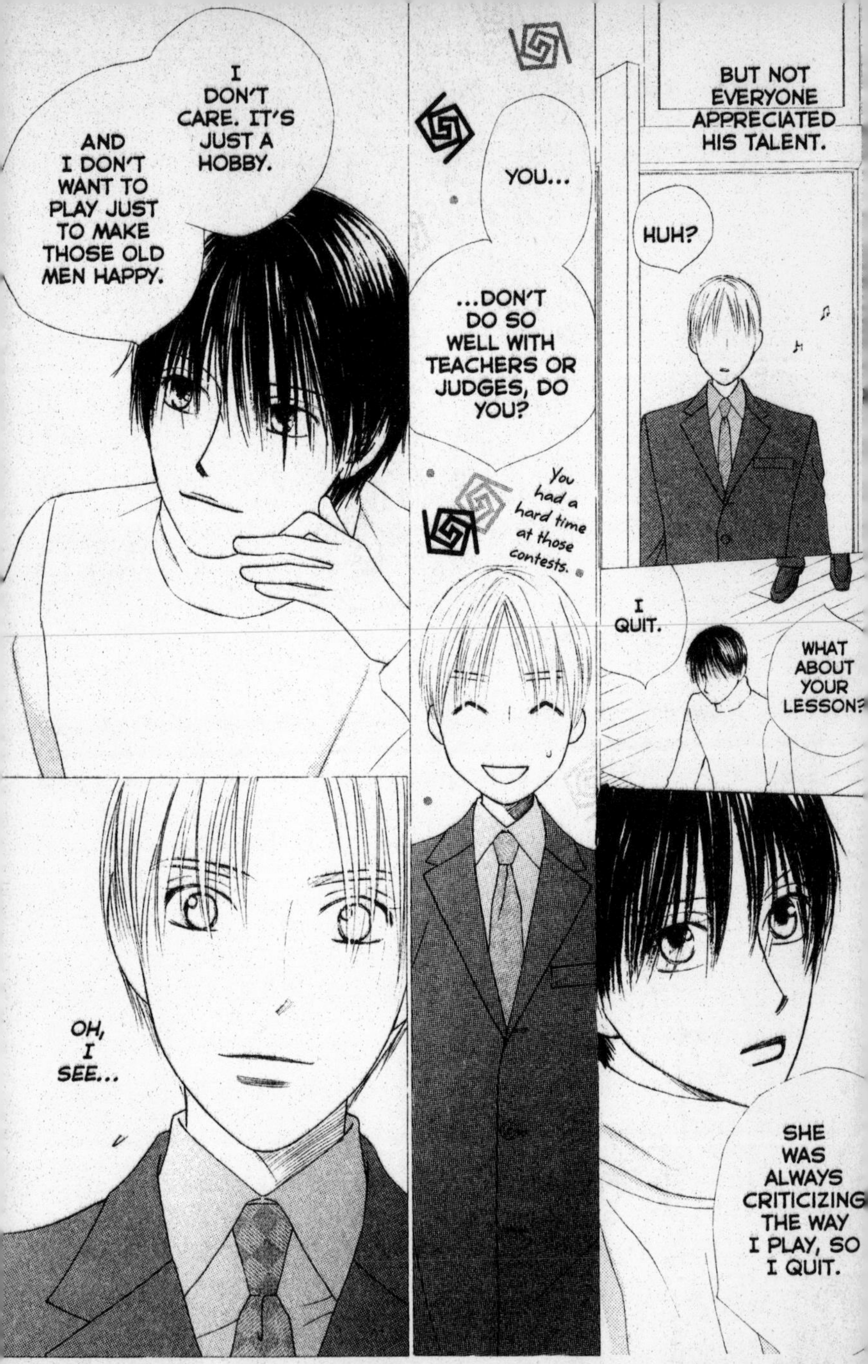
BUT NOT EVERYONE APPRECIATED HIS TALENT.
HUH?
WHAT ABOUT YOUR LESSON?
I QUIT.
SHE WAS ALWAYS CRITICIZING THE WAY I PLAY, SO I QUIT.
YOU...
...DON'T DO SO WELL WITH TEACHERS OR JUDGES, DO YOU?
You had a hard time at those contests.
I DON'T CARE. IT'S JUST A HOBBY.
AND I DON'T WANT TO PLAY JUST TO MAKE THOSE OLD MEN HAPPY.
OH, I SEE...

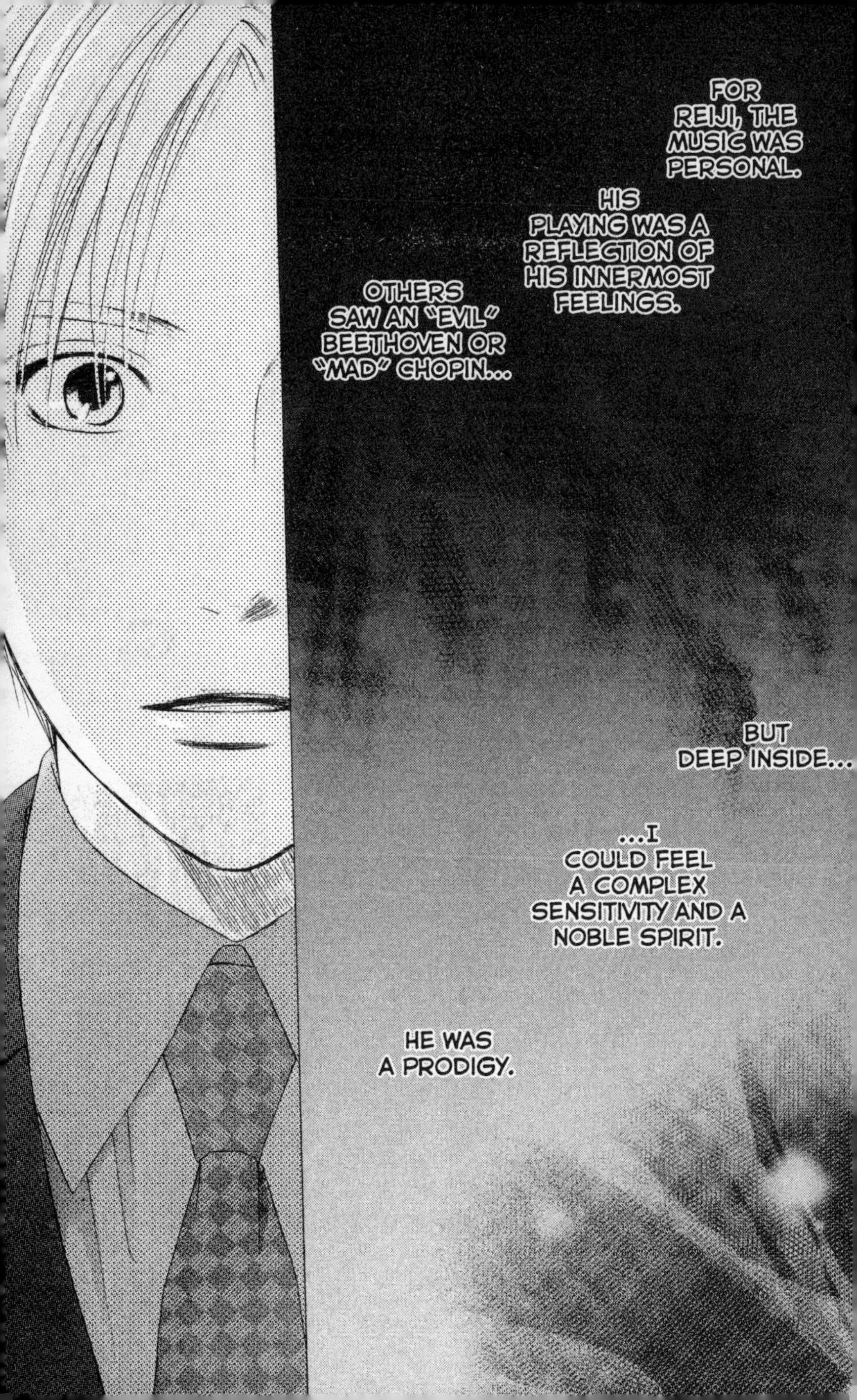
FOR REIJI, THE MUSIC WAS PERSONAL.
HIS PLAYING WAS A REFLECTION OF HIS INNERMOST FEELINGS.
OTHERS SAW AN "EVIL" BEETHOVEN OR "MAD" CHOPIN...
BUT DEEP INSIDE...
...I COULD FEEL A COMPLEX SENSITIVITY AND A NOBLE SPIRIT.
HE WAS A PRODIGY.

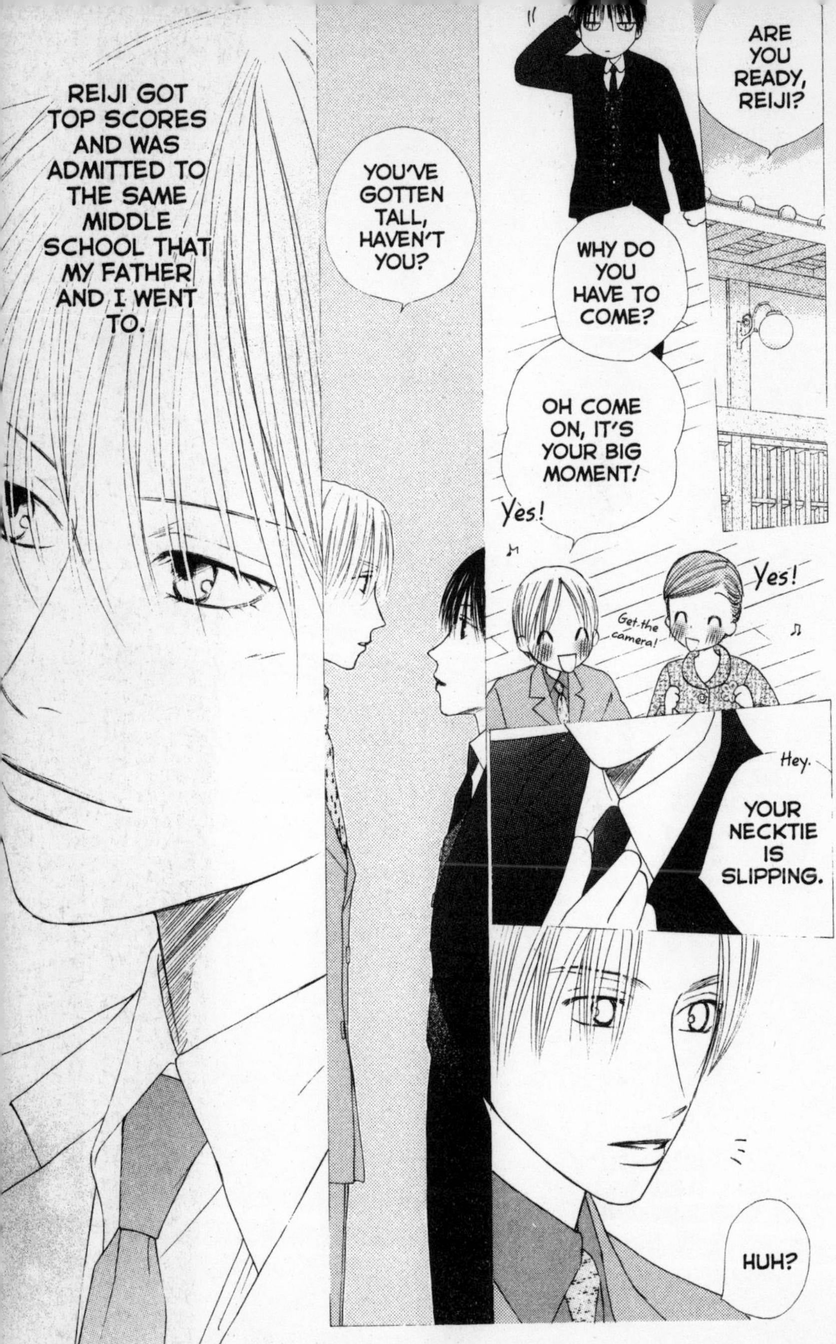
ARE YOU READY, REIJI?
WHY DO YOU HAVE TO COME?
OH COME ON, IT'S YOUR BIG MOMENT!
Yes!
Get the camera!
Yes!
Hey.
YOUR NECKTIE IS SLIPPING.
HUH?
YOU'VE GOTTEN TALL, HAVEN'T YOU?
REIJI GOT TOP SCORES AND WAS ADMITTED TO THE SAME MIDDLE SCHOOL THAT MY FATHER AND I WENT TO.

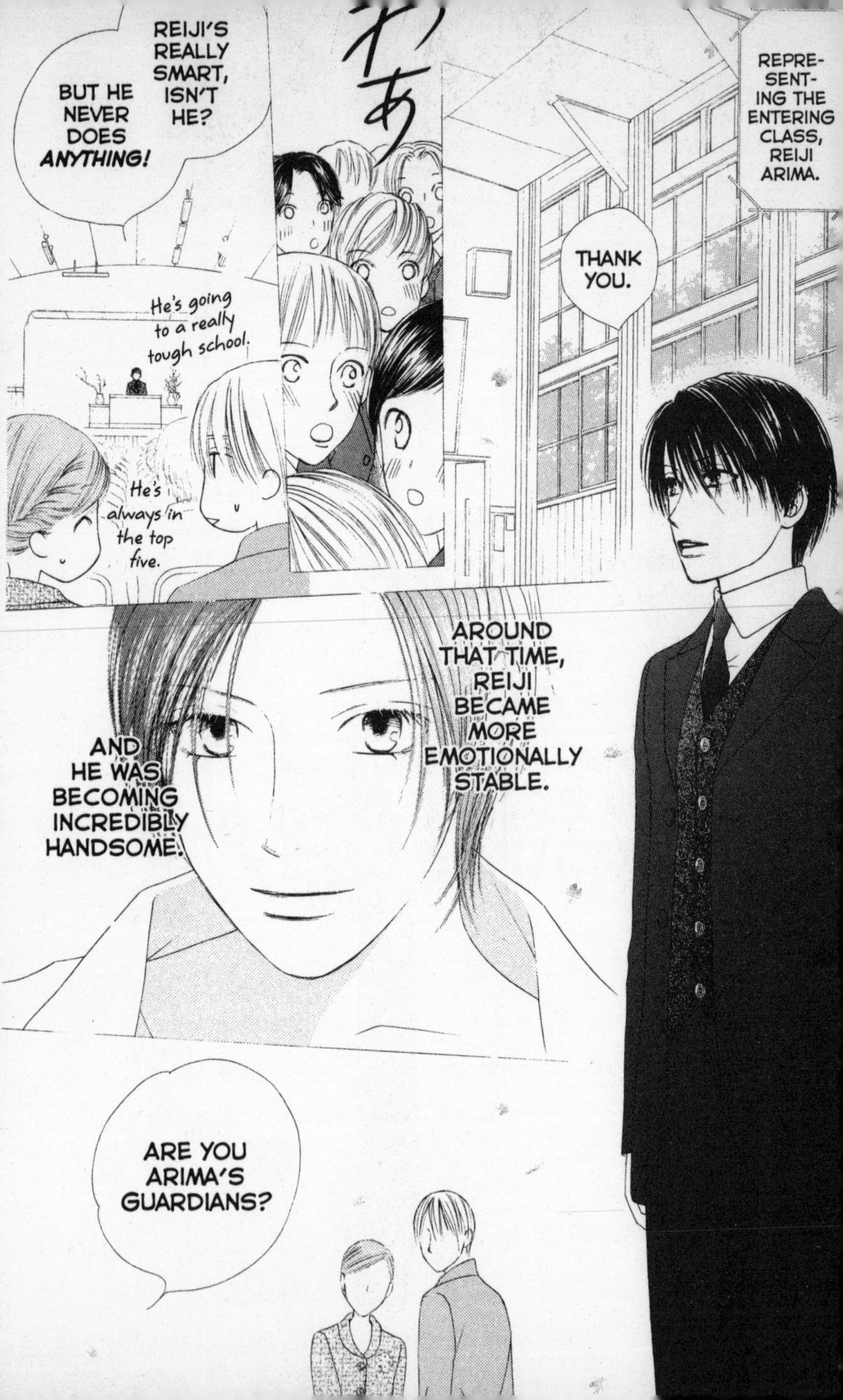
REPRESENTING THE ENTERING CLASS, REIJI ARIMA.
THANK YOU.
わあ
REIJI'S REALLY SMART, ISN'T HE?
BUT HE NEVER DOES ANYTHING!
He's going to a really tough school.
He's always in the top five.
AROUND THAT TIME, REIJI BECAME MORE EMOTIONALLY STABLE.
AND HE WAS BECOMING INCREDIBLY HANDSOME.
ARE YOU ARIMA'S GUARDIANS?

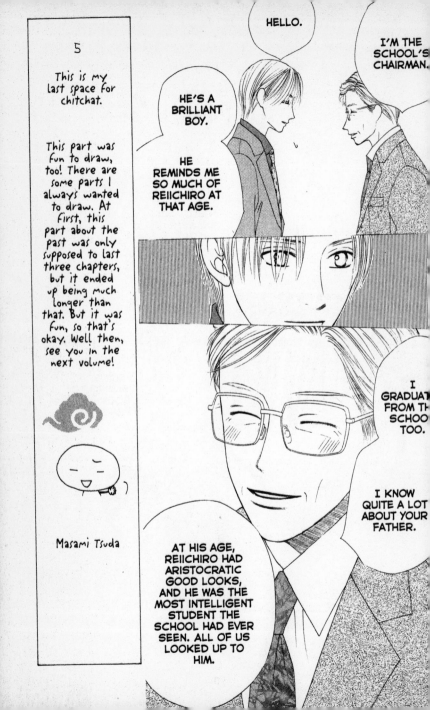

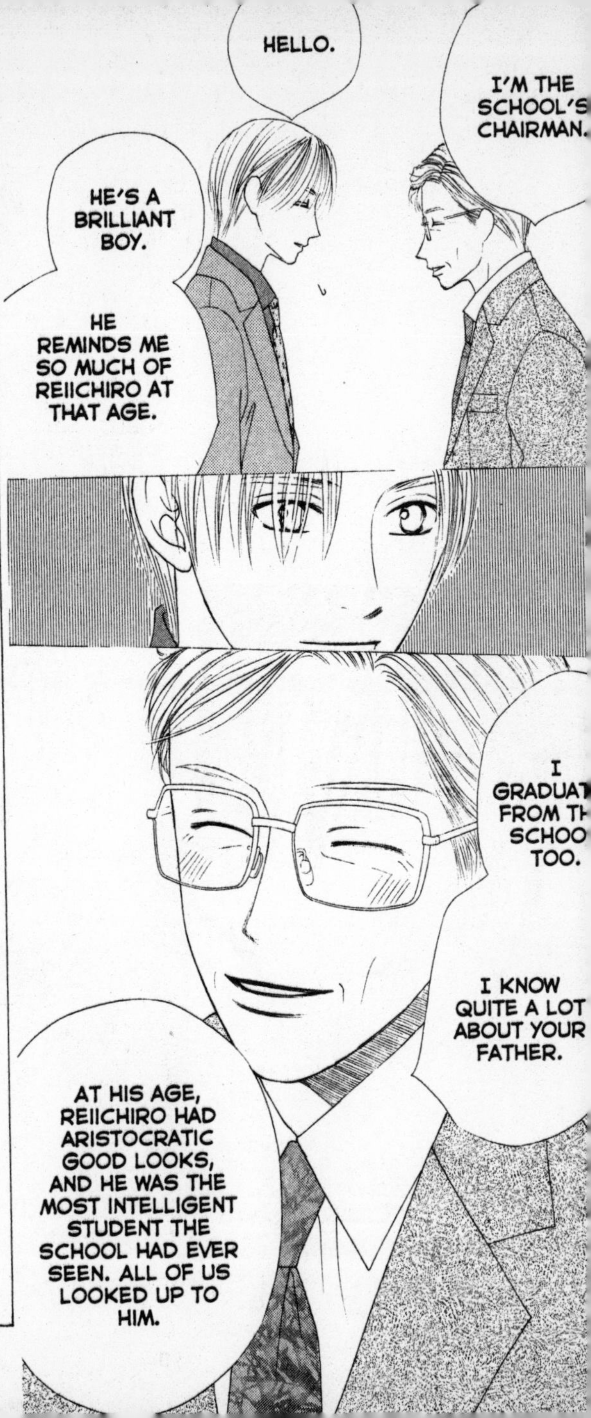
I'M THE SCHOOL'S CHAIRMAN.
HELLO.
HE'S A BRILLIANT BOY.
HE REMINDS ME SO MUCH OF REIICHIRO AT THAT AGE.
I GRADUAT FROM TH SCHOO TOO.
I KNOW QUITE A LOT ABOUT YOUR FATHER.
AT HIS AGE, REIICHIRO HAD ARISTOCRATIC GOOD LOOKS, AND HE WAS THE MOST INTELLIGENT STUDENT THE SCHOOL HAD EVER SEEN. ALL OF US LOOKED UP TO HIM.

5

This is my last space for chitchat.

This part was fun to draw, too! There are some parts I always wanted to draw. At first, this part about the past was only supposed to last three chapters, but it ended up being much longer than that. But it was fun, so that's okay. Well then, see you in the next volume!

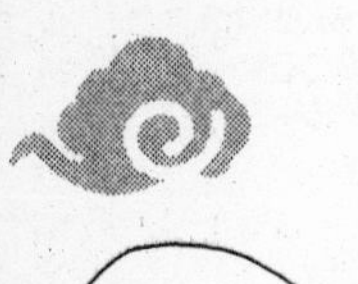

Masami Tsuda

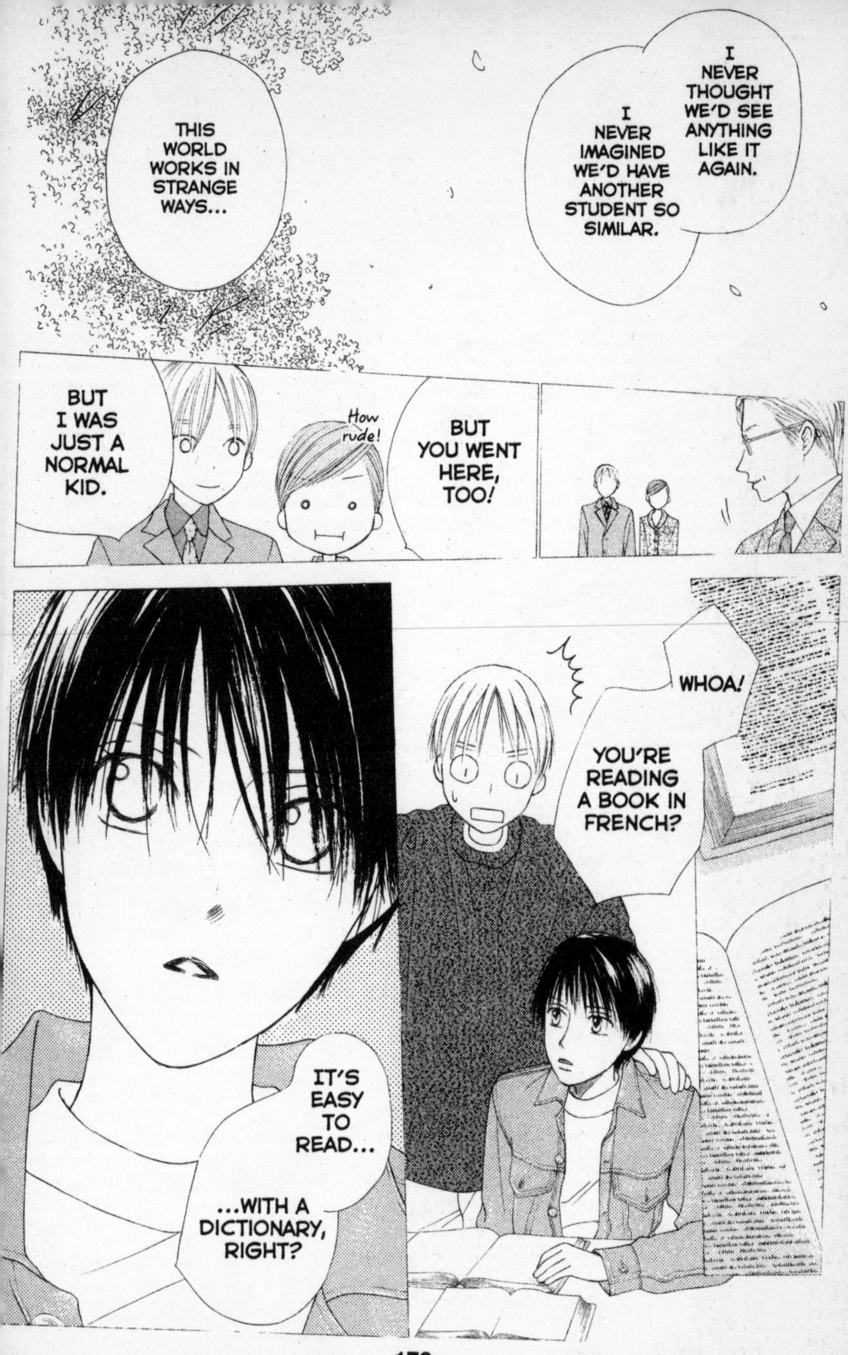
I NEVER THOUGHT WE'D SEE ANYTHING LIKE IT AGAIN.
I NEVER IMAGINED WE'D HAVE ANOTHER STUDENT SO SIMILAR.
THIS WORLD WORKS IN STRANGE WAYS...
BUT YOU WENT HERE, TOO!
How rude!
BUT I WAS JUST A NORMAL KID.
WHOA!
YOU'RE READING A BOOK IN FRENCH?
IT'S EASY TO READ...
...WITH A DICTIONARY, RIGHT?

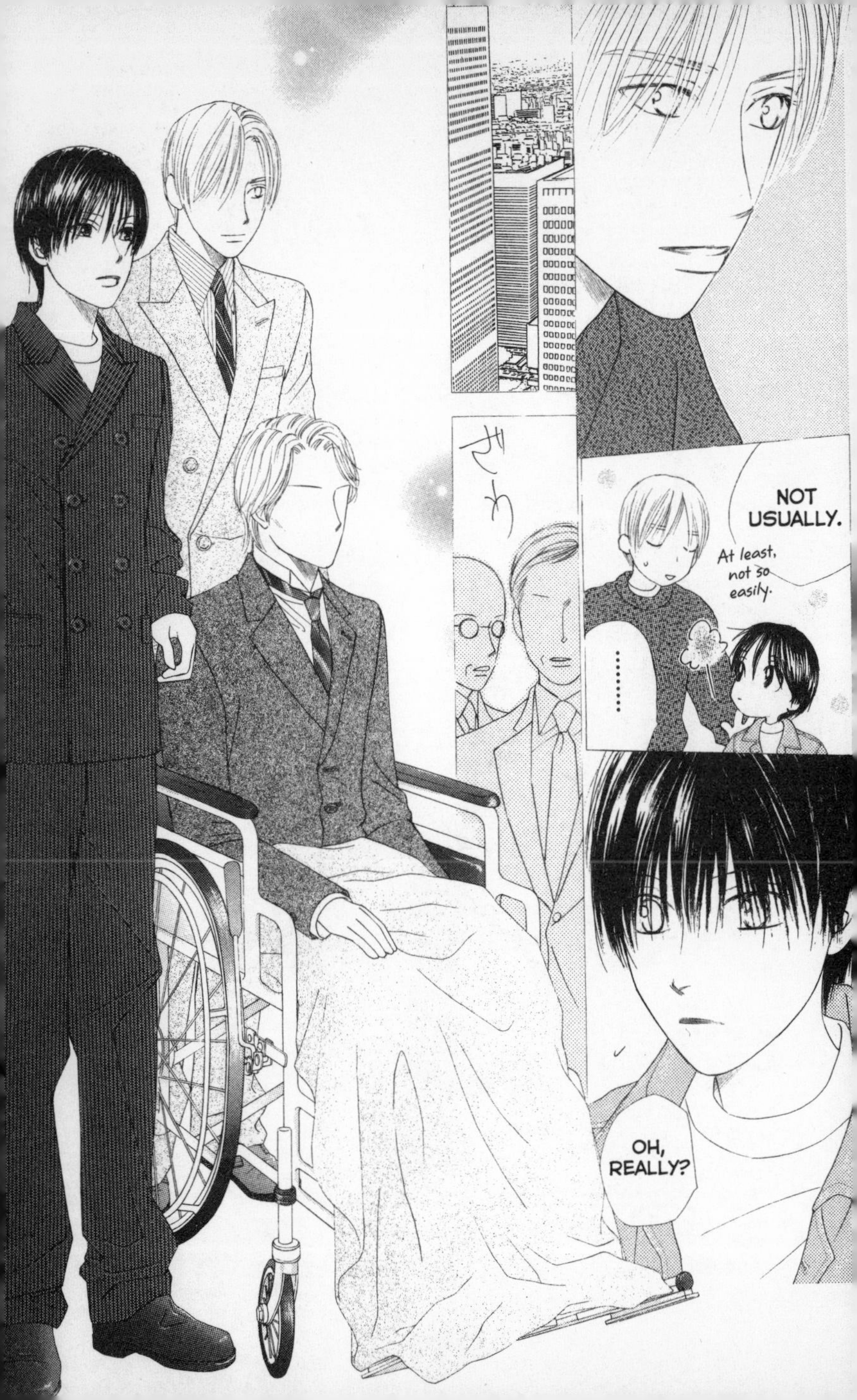
NOT USUALLY.
At least, not so easily.
……
OH, REALLY?
ざわ

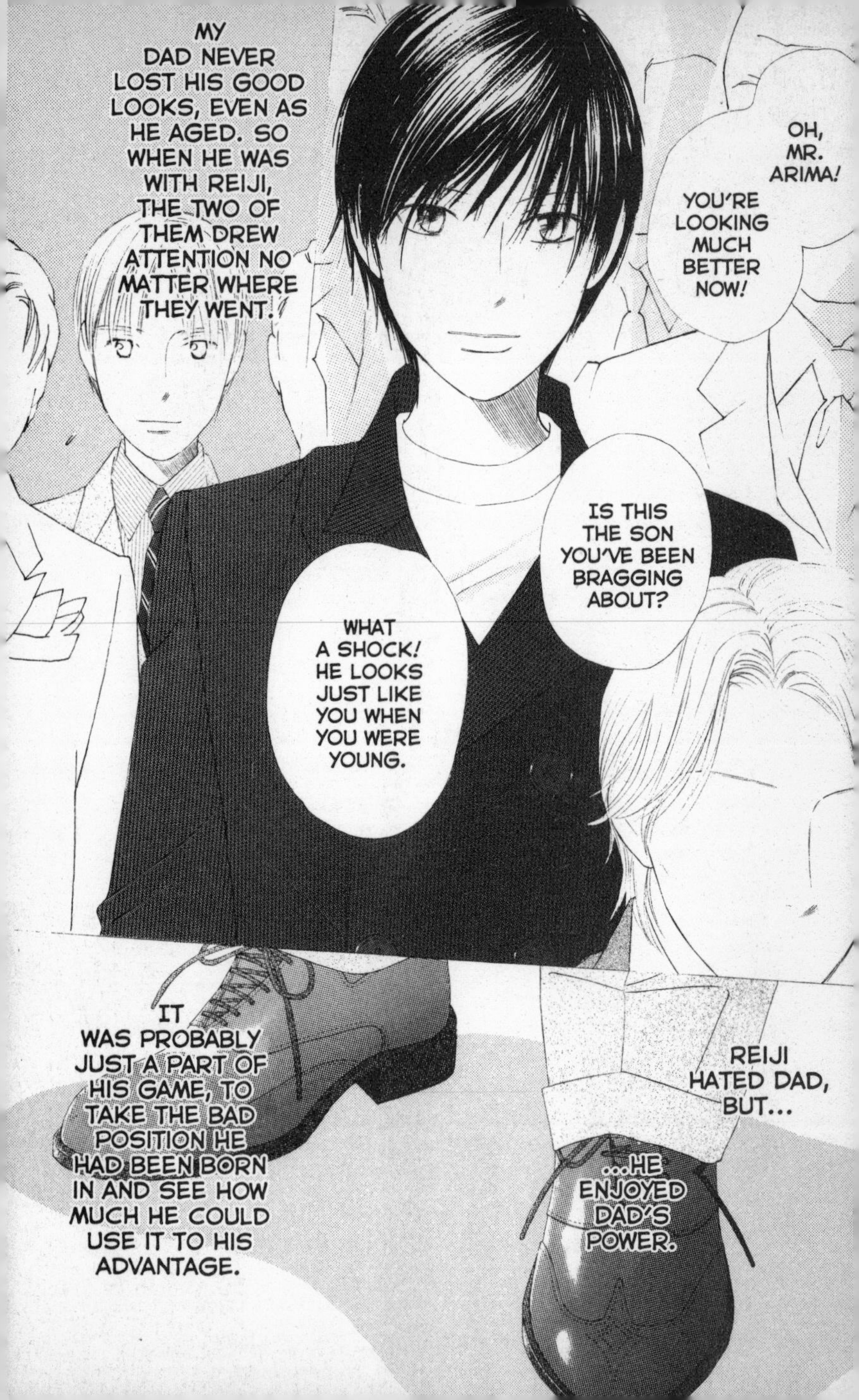
OH, MR. ARIMA!
YOU'RE LOOKING MUCH BETTER NOW!
MY DAD NEVER LOST HIS GOOD LOOKS, EVEN AS HE AGED. SO WHEN HE WAS WITH REIJI, THE TWO OF THEM DREW ATTENTION NO MATTER WHERE THEY WENT.
IS THIS THE SON YOU'VE BEEN BRAGGING ABOUT?
WHAT A SHOCK! HE LOOKS JUST LIKE YOU WHEN YOU WERE YOUNG.
REIJI HATED DAD, BUT...
...HE ENJOYED DAD'S POWER.
IT WAS PROBABLY JUST A PART OF HIS GAME, TO TAKE THE BAD POSITION HE HAD BEEN BORN IN AND SEE HOW MUCH HE COULD USE IT TO HIS ADVANTAGE.

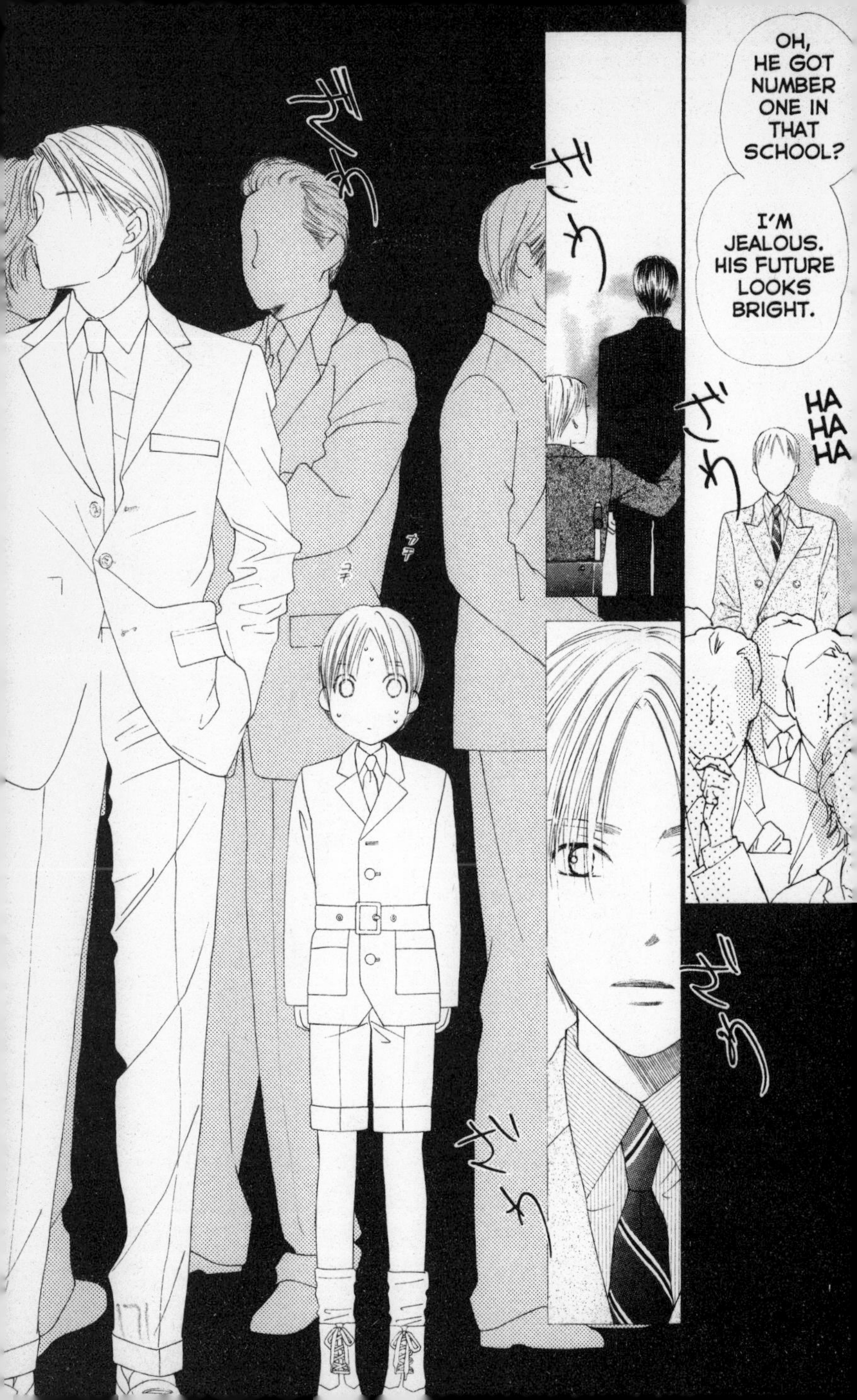
OH, HE GOT NUMBER ONE IN THAT SCHOOL?
I'M JEALOUS. HIS FUTURE LOOKS BRIGHT.
HA HA HA

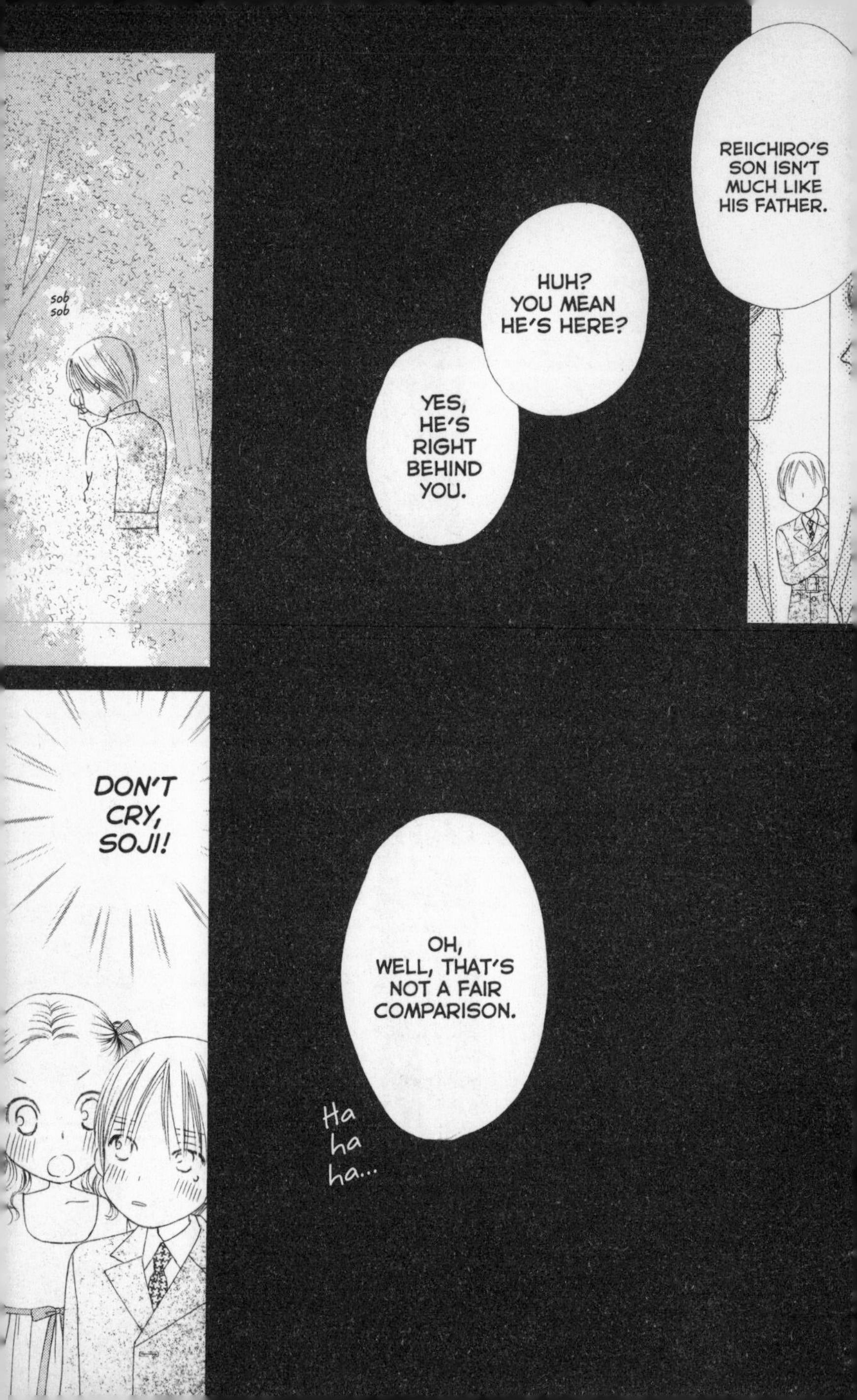
REIICHIRO'S SON ISN'T MUCH LIKE HIS FATHER.
HUH? YOU MEAN HE'S HERE?
YES, HE'S RIGHT BEHIND YOU.
sob sob
OH, WELL, THAT'S NOT A FAIR COMPARISON.
Ha ha ha...
DON'T CRY, SOJI!

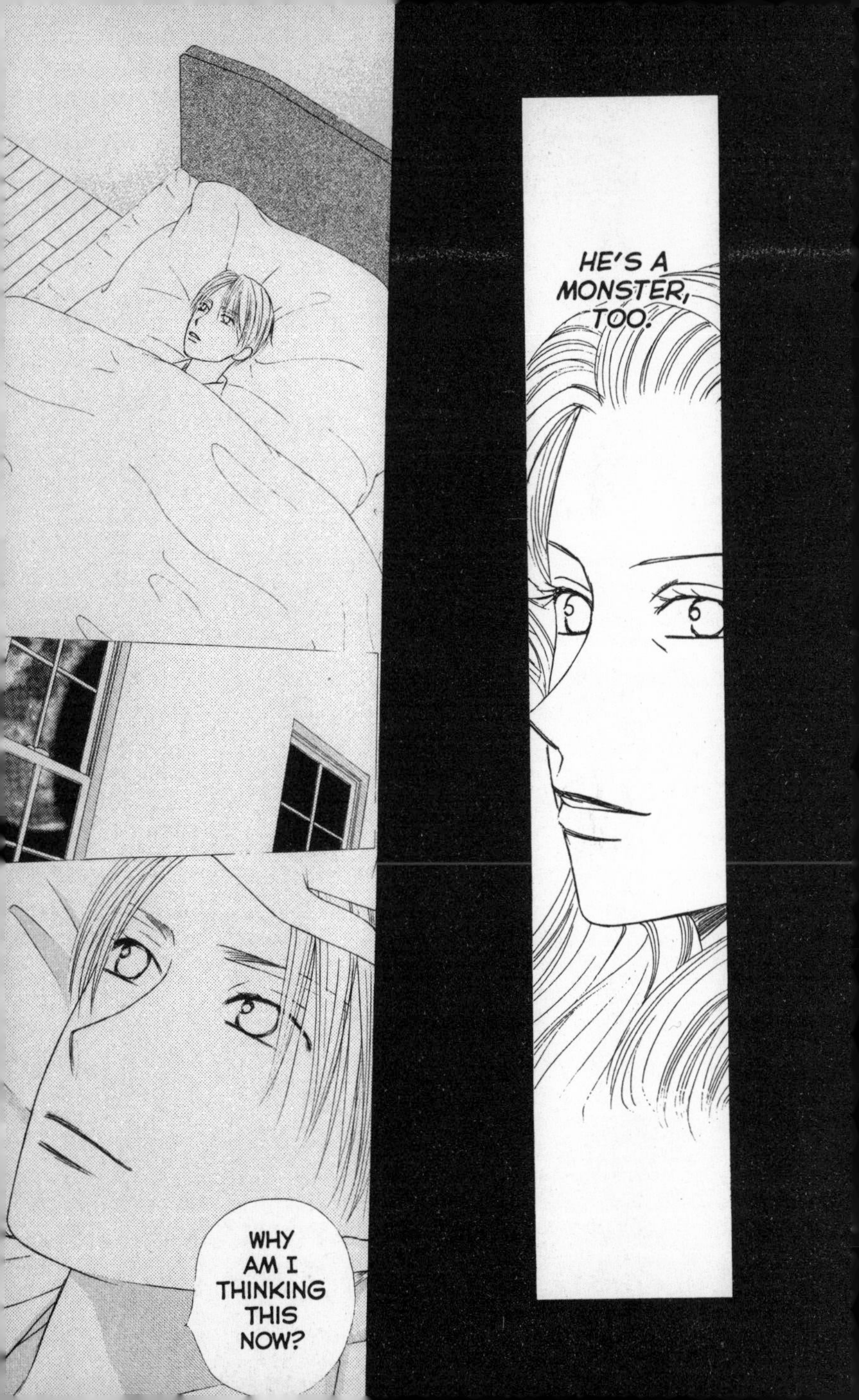
HE'S A MONSTER, TOO.
WHY AM I THINKING THIS NOW?

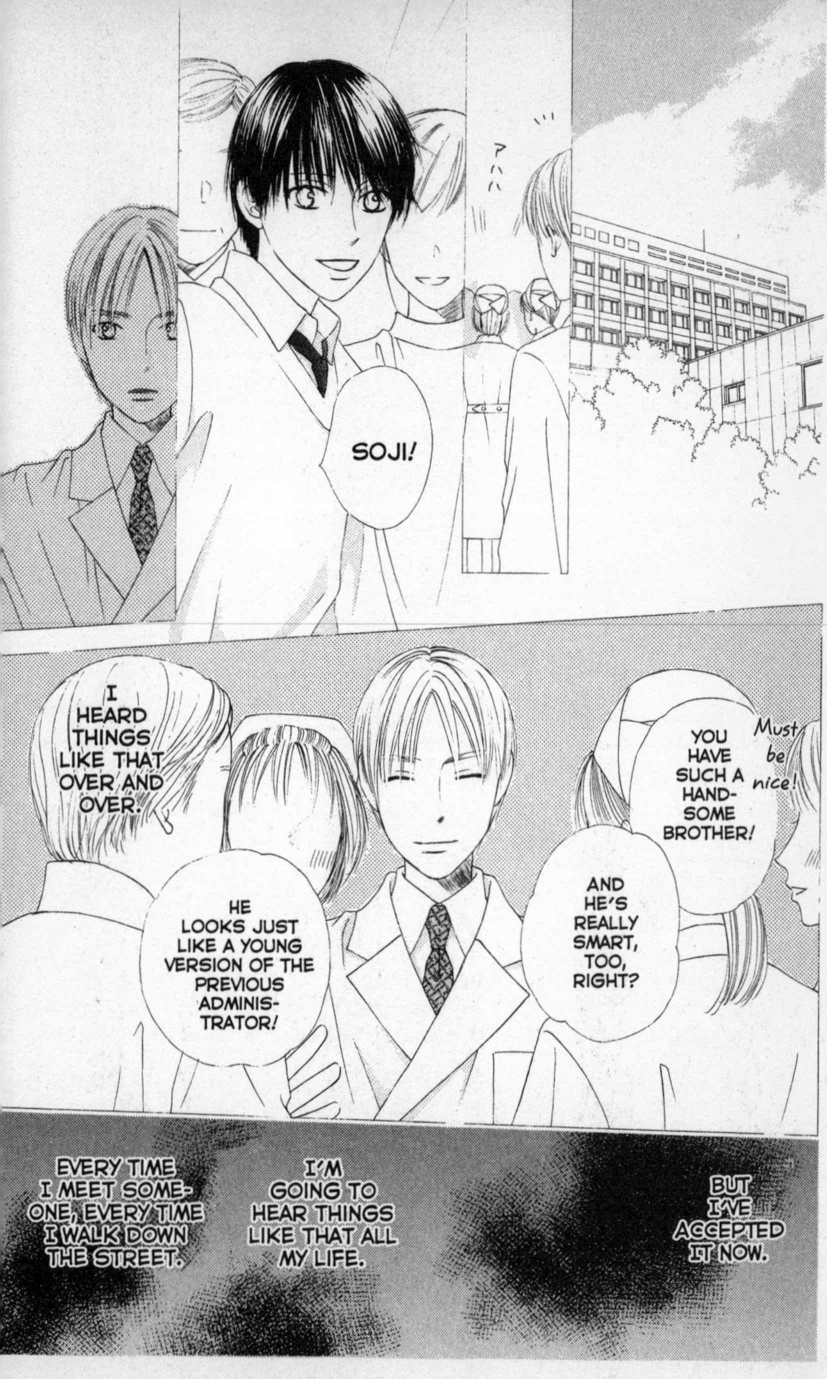
アハハ
SOJI!
YOU HAVE SUCH A HANDSOME BROTHER!
Must be nice!
AND HE'S REALLY SMART, TOO, RIGHT?
HE LOOKS JUST LIKE A YOUNG VERSION OF THE PREVIOUS ADMINISTRATOR!
I HEARD THINGS LIKE THAT OVER AND OVER.
EVERY TIME I MEET SOMEONE, EVERY TIME I WALK DOWN THE STREET.
I'M GOING TO HEAR THINGS LIKE THAT ALL MY LIFE.
BUT I'VE ACCEPTED IT NOW.

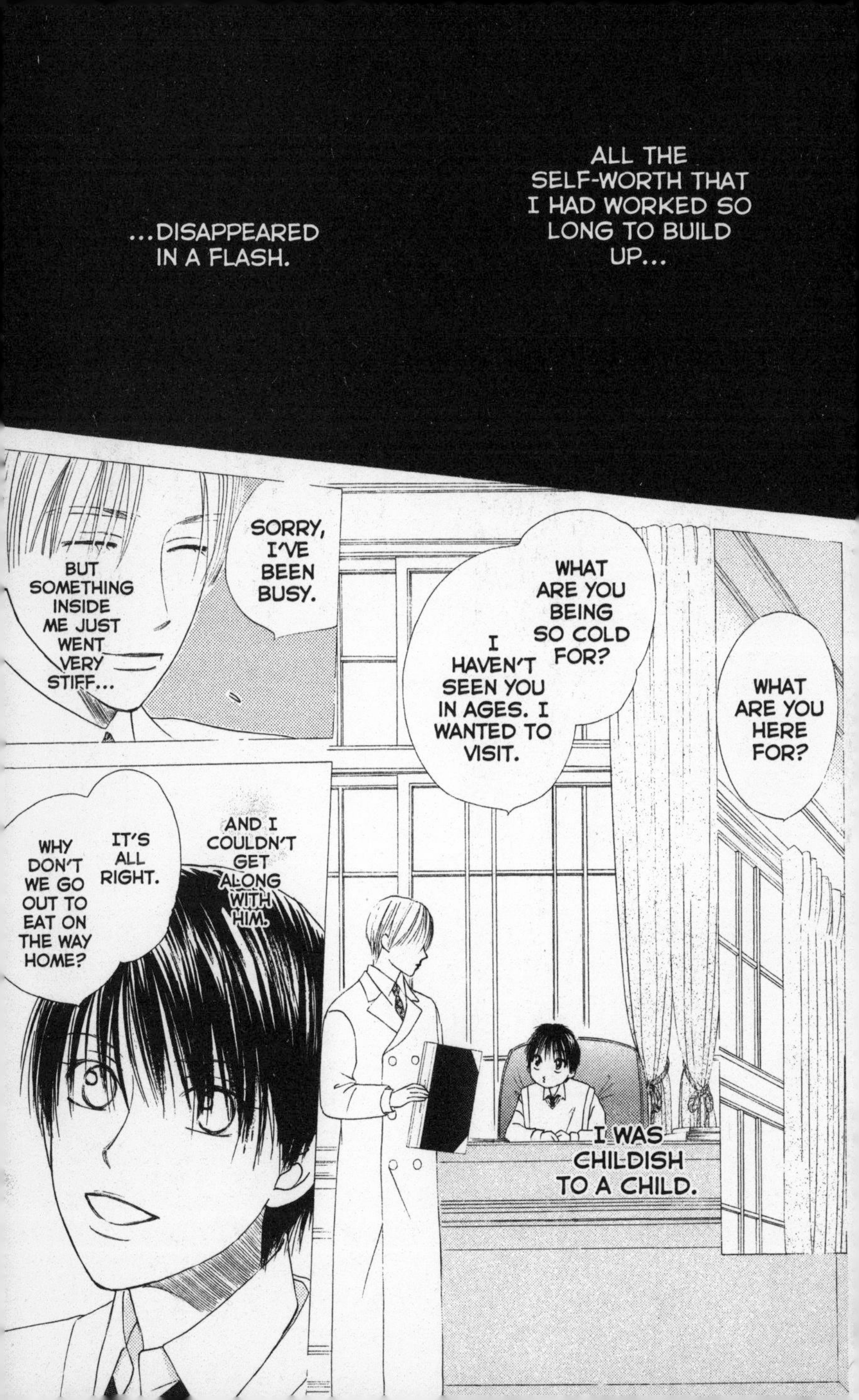
ALL THE SELF-WORTH THAT I HAD WORKED SO LONG TO BUILD UP...
...DISAPPEARED IN A FLASH.
WHAT ARE YOU HERE FOR?
WHAT ARE YOU BEING SO COLD FOR?
I HAVEN'T SEEN YOU IN AGES. I WANTED TO VISIT.
I WAS CHILDISH TO A CHILD.
SORRY, I'VE BEEN BUSY.
BUT SOMETHING INSIDE ME JUST WENT VERY STIFF...
AND I COULDN'T GET ALONG WITH HIM.
IT'S ALL RIGHT.
WHY DON'T WE GO OUT TO EAT ON THE WAY HOME?

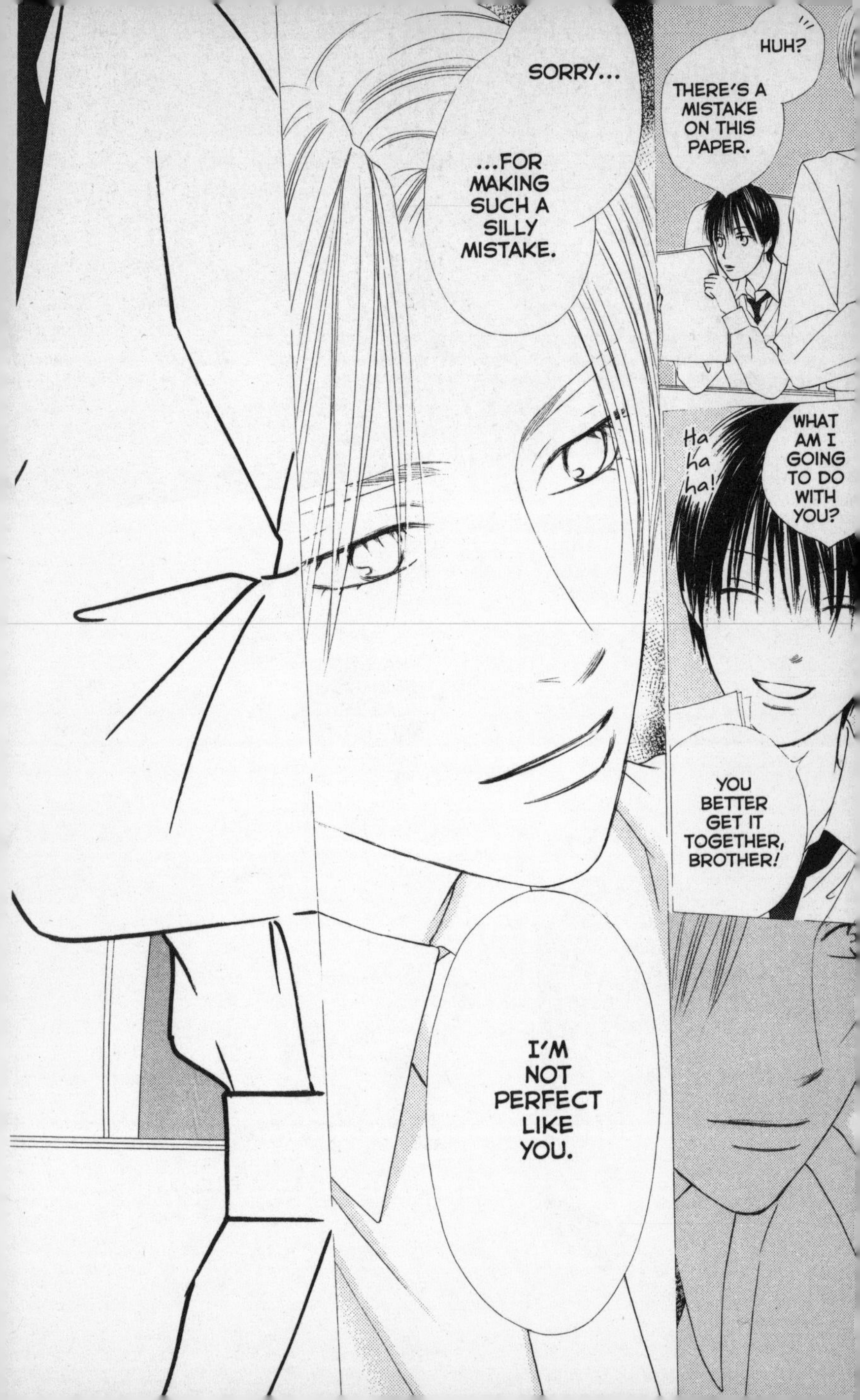
HUH?
THERE'S A MISTAKE ON THIS PAPER.
WHAT AM I GOING TO DO WITH YOU?
Ha ha ha!
YOU BETTER GET IT TOGETHER, BROTHER!
SORRY...
...FOR MAKING SUCH A SILLY MISTAKE.
I'M NOT PERFECT LIKE YOU.

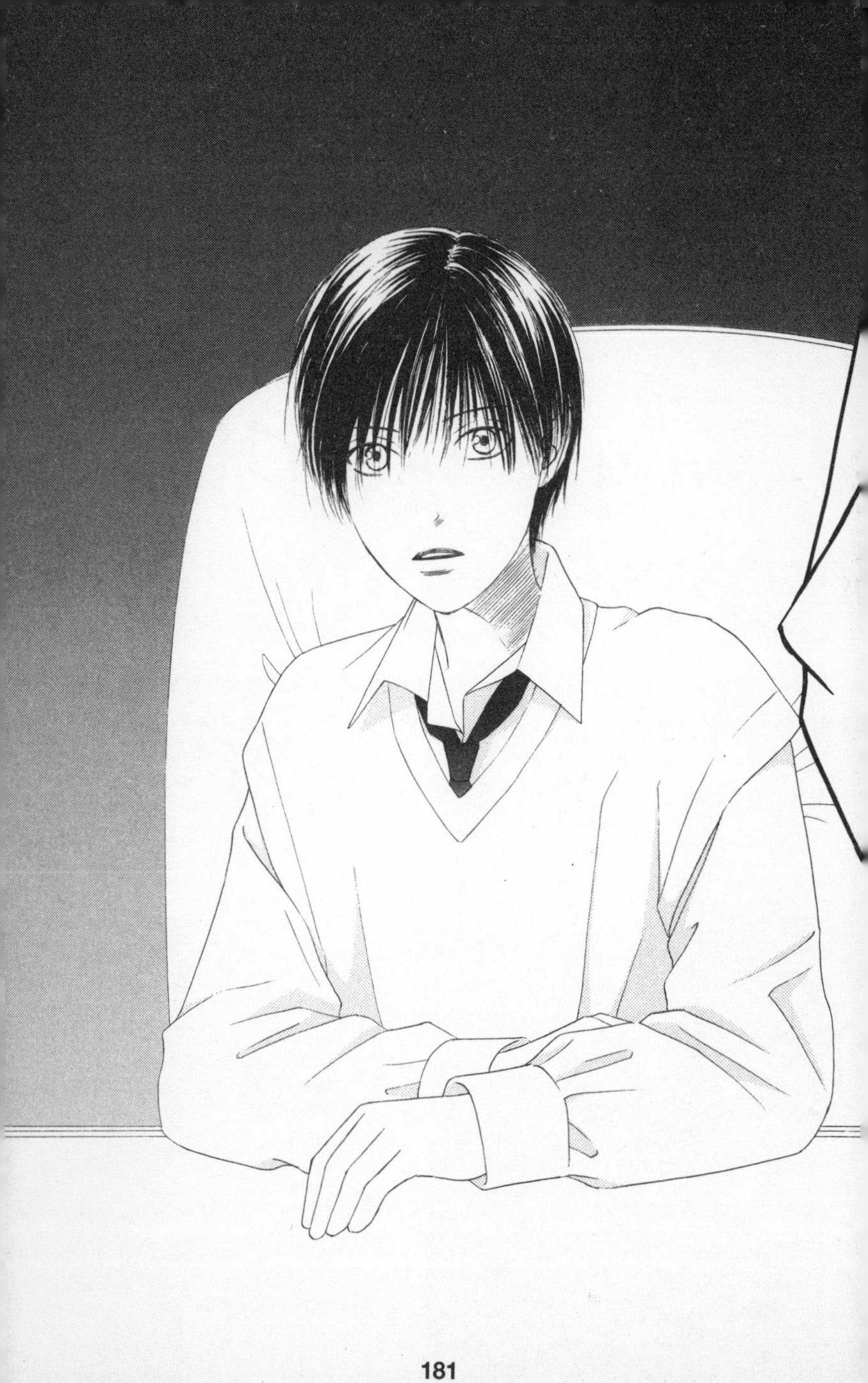

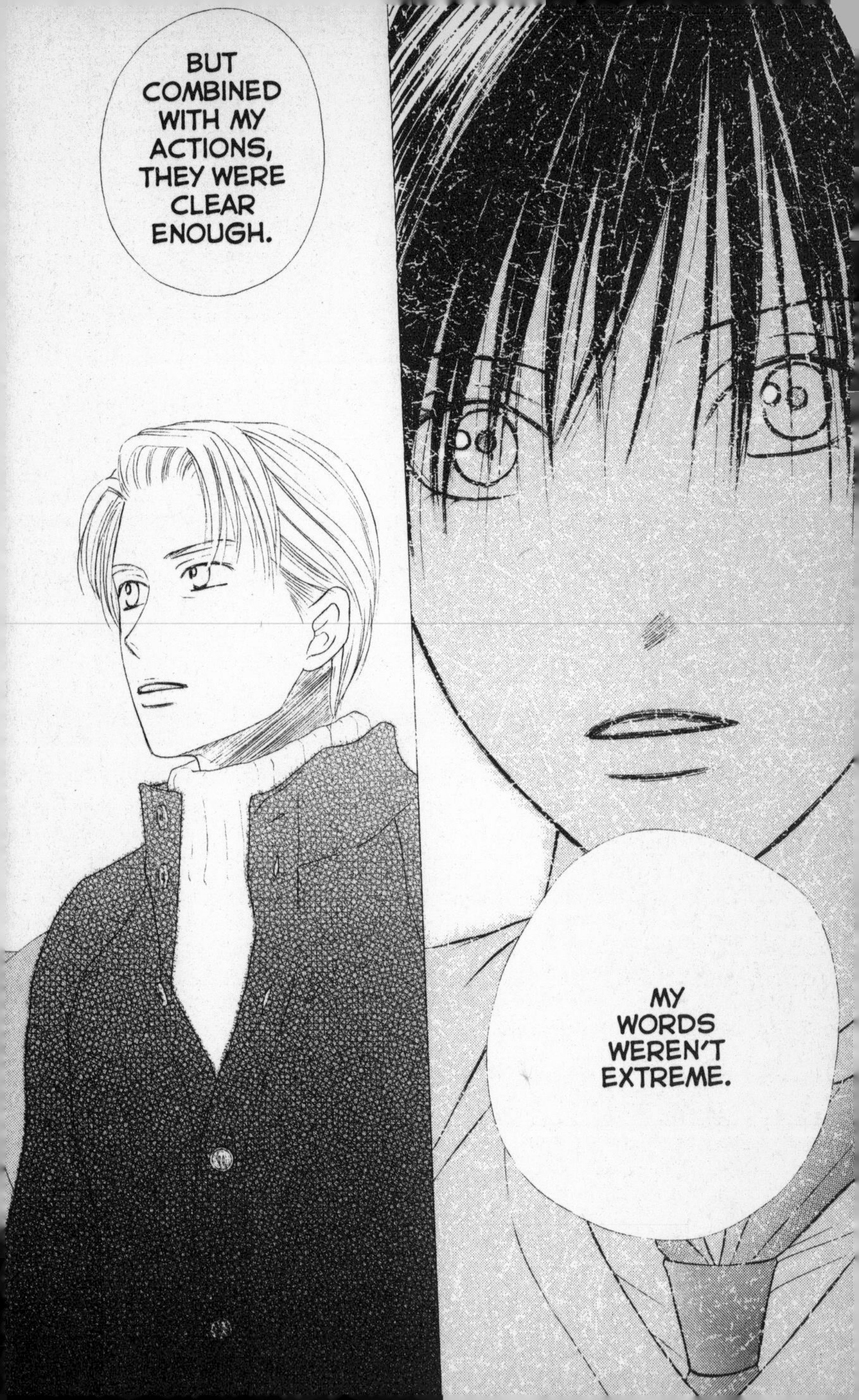
MY WORDS WEREN'T EXTREME.
BUT COMBINED WITH MY ACTIONS, THEY WERE CLEAR ENOUGH.

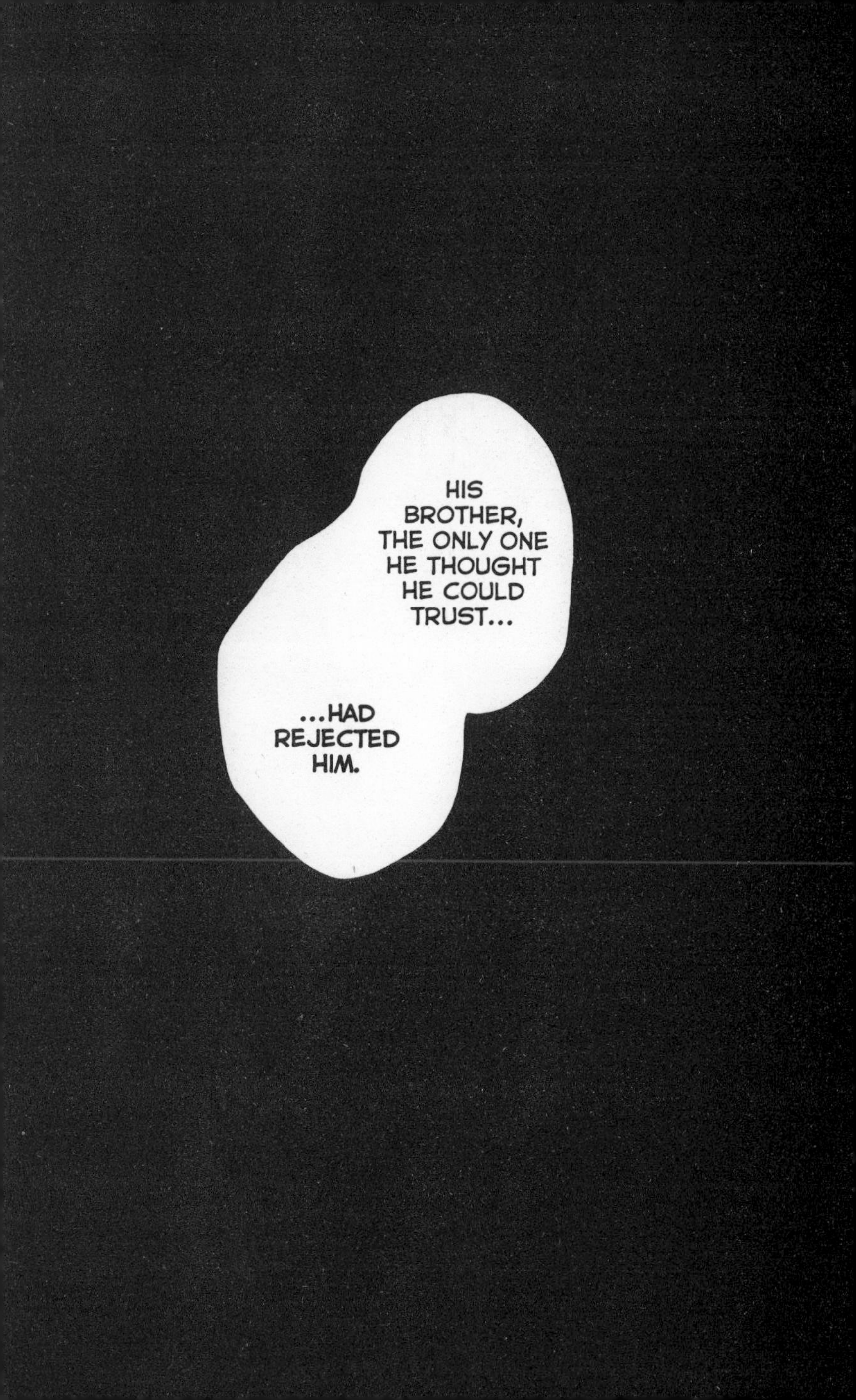
HIS BROTHER, THE ONLY ONE HE THOUGHT HE COULD TRUST...
...HAD REJECTED HIM.

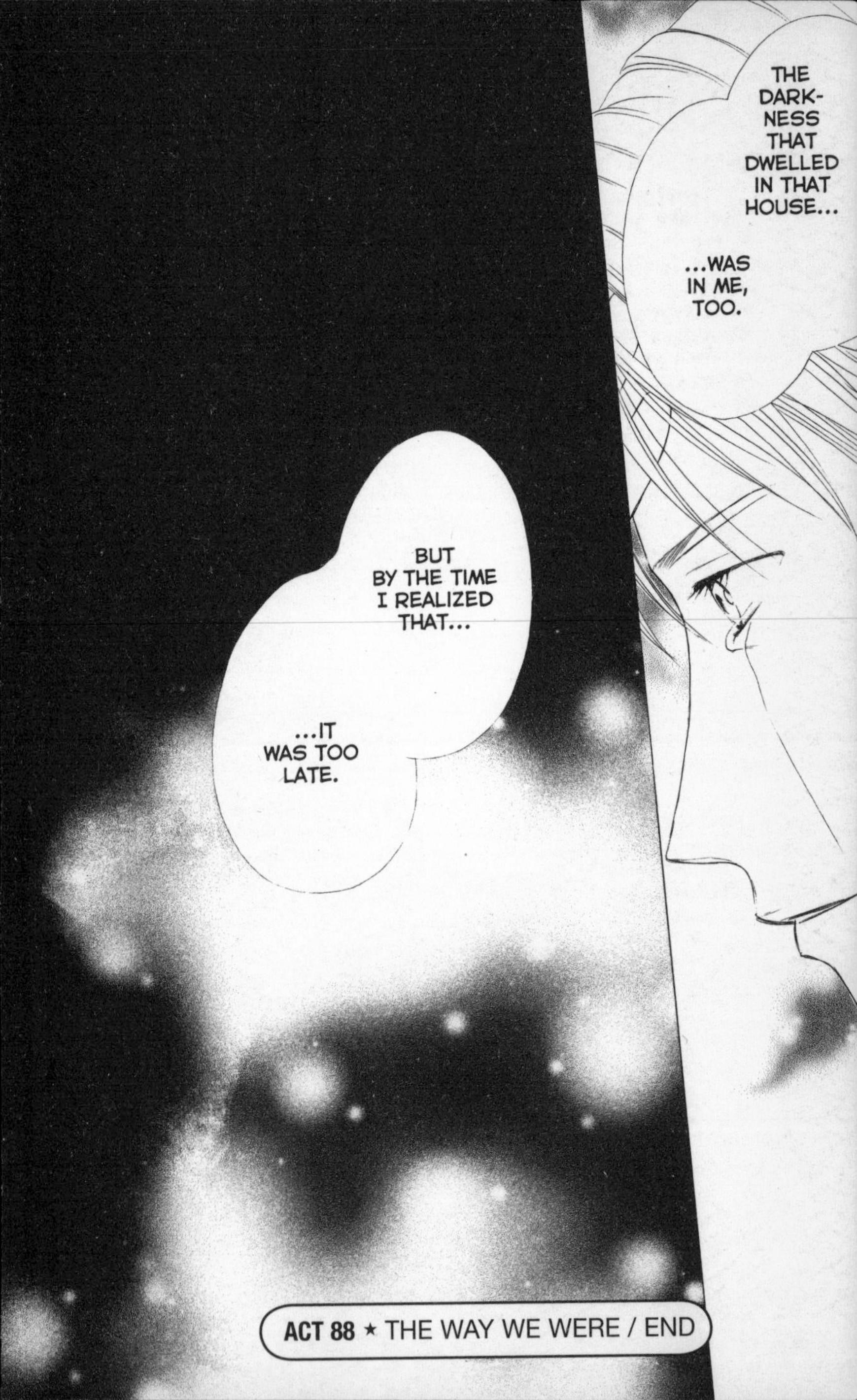
THE DARKNESS THAT DWELLED IN THAT HOUSE...
...WAS IN ME, TOO.
BUT BY THE TIME I REALIZED THAT...
...IT WAS TOO LATE.
ACT 88 ★ THE WAY WE WERE / END

TSUDA'S DIARY

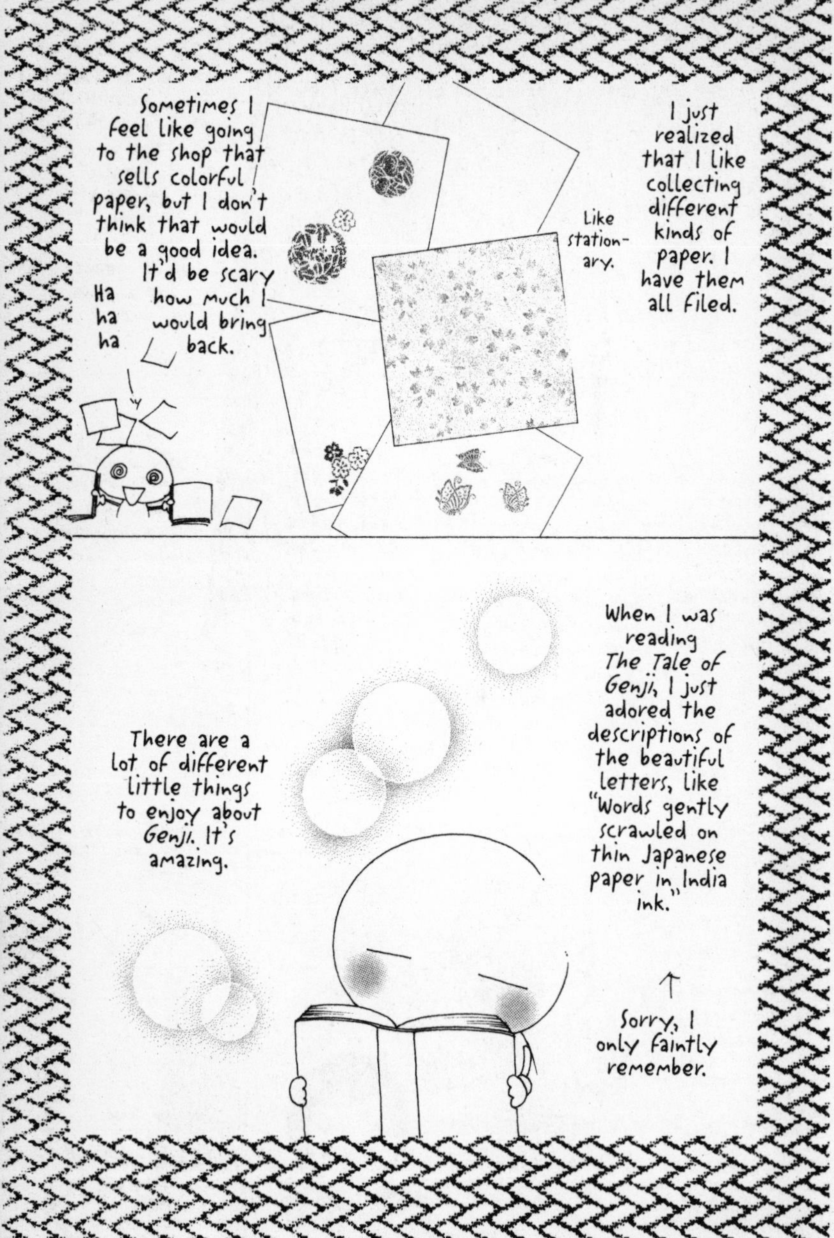
I just realized that I like collecting different kinds of paper. I have them all filed.
Like station-ary.
Sometimes I feel like going to the shop that sells colorful paper, but I don't think that would be a good idea. It'd be scary how much I would bring back.
Ha ha ha
When I was reading The Tale of Genji, I just adored the descriptions of the beautiful letters, like "Words gently scrawled on thin Japanese paper in India ink."
Sorry, I only faintly remember.
There are a lot of different little things to enjoy about Genji. It's amazing.

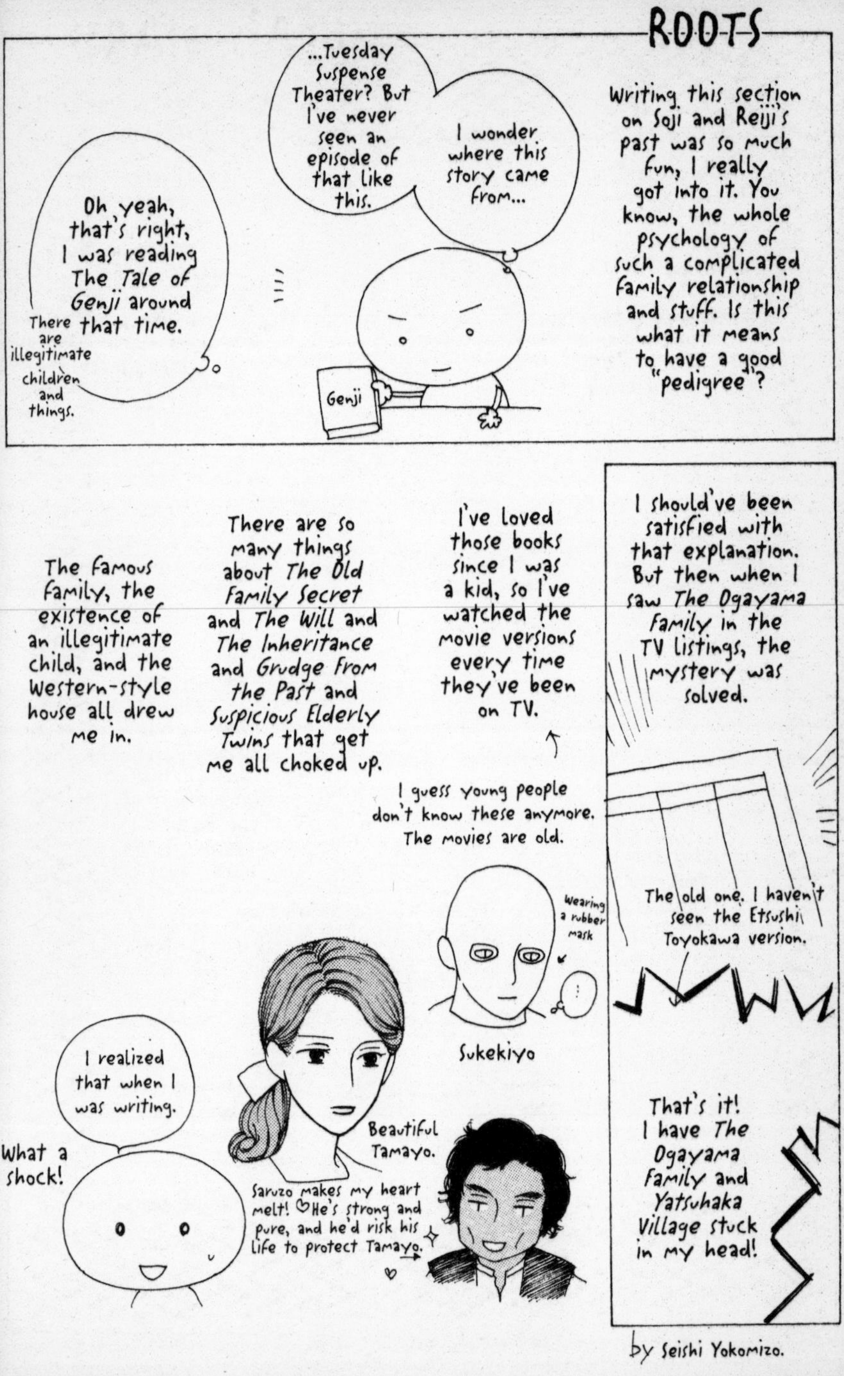
ROOTS
Writing this section on Soji and Reiji's past was so much fun, I really got into it. You know, the whole psychology of such a complicated family relationship and stuff. Is this what it means to have a good "pedigree"?
I wonder where this story came from...
...Tuesday Suspense Theater? But I've never seen an episode of that like this.
Oh yeah, that's right, I was reading The Tale of Genji around that time.
There are illegitimate children and things.
Genji
I should've been satisfied with that explanation. But then when I saw The Ogayama Family in the TV listings, the mystery was solved.
The old one. I haven't seen the Etsushi Toyokawa version.
That's it! I have The Ogayama Family and Yatsuhaka Village stuck in my head!
by Seishi Yokomizo.
I've loved those books since I was a kid, so I've watched the movie versions every time they've been on TV.
There are so many things about The Old Family Secret and The Will and The Inheritance and Grudge From the Past and Suspicious Elderly Twins that get me all choked up.
The famous family, the existence of an illegitimate child, and the Western-style house all drew me in.
I guess young people don't know these anymore. The movies are old.
Wearing a rubber mask
Sukekiyo
Beautiful Tamayo.
Saruzo makes my heart melt! ♡ He's strong and pure, and he'd risk his life to protect Tamayo.
I realized that when I was writing.
What a shock!

Retro Fever

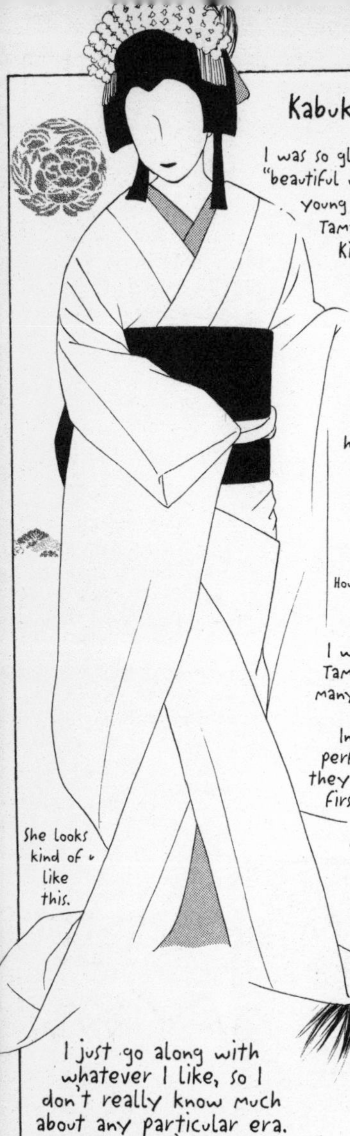
She looks kind of like this.

Kabuki

I was so glad I got to see the "beautiful woman" and "beautiful young woman" combination of Tamasaburo and Kikunosuke. Kikunosuke is so cute as Konami in *Yamashina Kankyo*. And her kimono was gorgeous. There was such a great balance of colors... Her kimono and skin were pure white, her hair decoration was white, her hair, eyes, and sash were black, and there was just a splash of red.

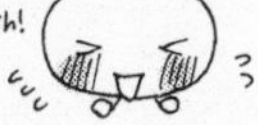
How stylish!

I went mainly to check out Tamasaburo, but there are so many other great actresses as well!
In *Sakura Gimin-Den*, the performances were so moving they made me cry. (That's the first time that's happened.)
I like Fukusuke's portrayal of the wife. When she's in that role, I never miss a performance!

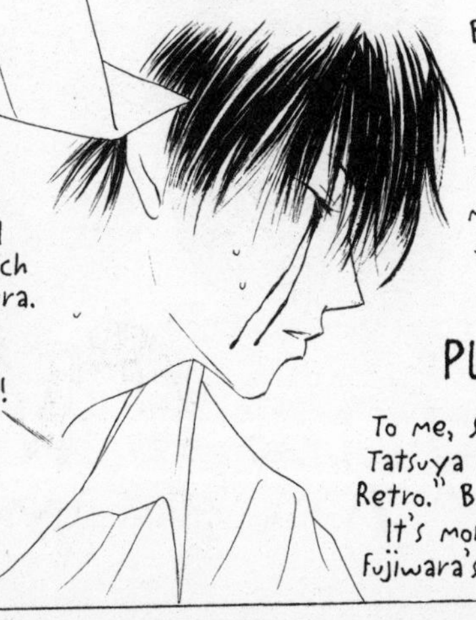

I just go along with whatever I like, so I don't really know much about any particular era. Well, that's okay, because I'm a manga artist, not a student! (Self-affirmation)

I've always sort of liked this kind of thing, but as I saw more and more of it while I was doing my research, my interest heated up.
I like stuff from the Meiji, Taisho, and Showa eras. And even older things too, like from the Edo period, the Heian period, or even older. It's hard to keep track of all of it!

Novels

I like Izumi Kyoka's novel "The Surgery." It's so intense, it makes me want to yell, "It's just TOO good!" The set-up and the names are too cool!
The platonic love between the Countess and the surgeon is just so.... Damn you, Kyoka!

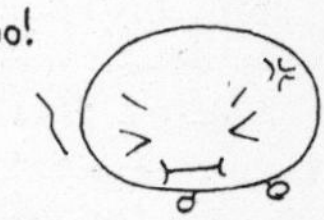
Boo!

"The Surgery" is also a movie by Tamasaburo. It's just as beautiful as the original book, so I like this version, too.

Plays

To me, *Shintokumaru*, with Tatsuya Fujiwara is "Showa Retro." But it's not really... It's more like it's sexy. Fujiwara's really sexy, too!

Building up my strength

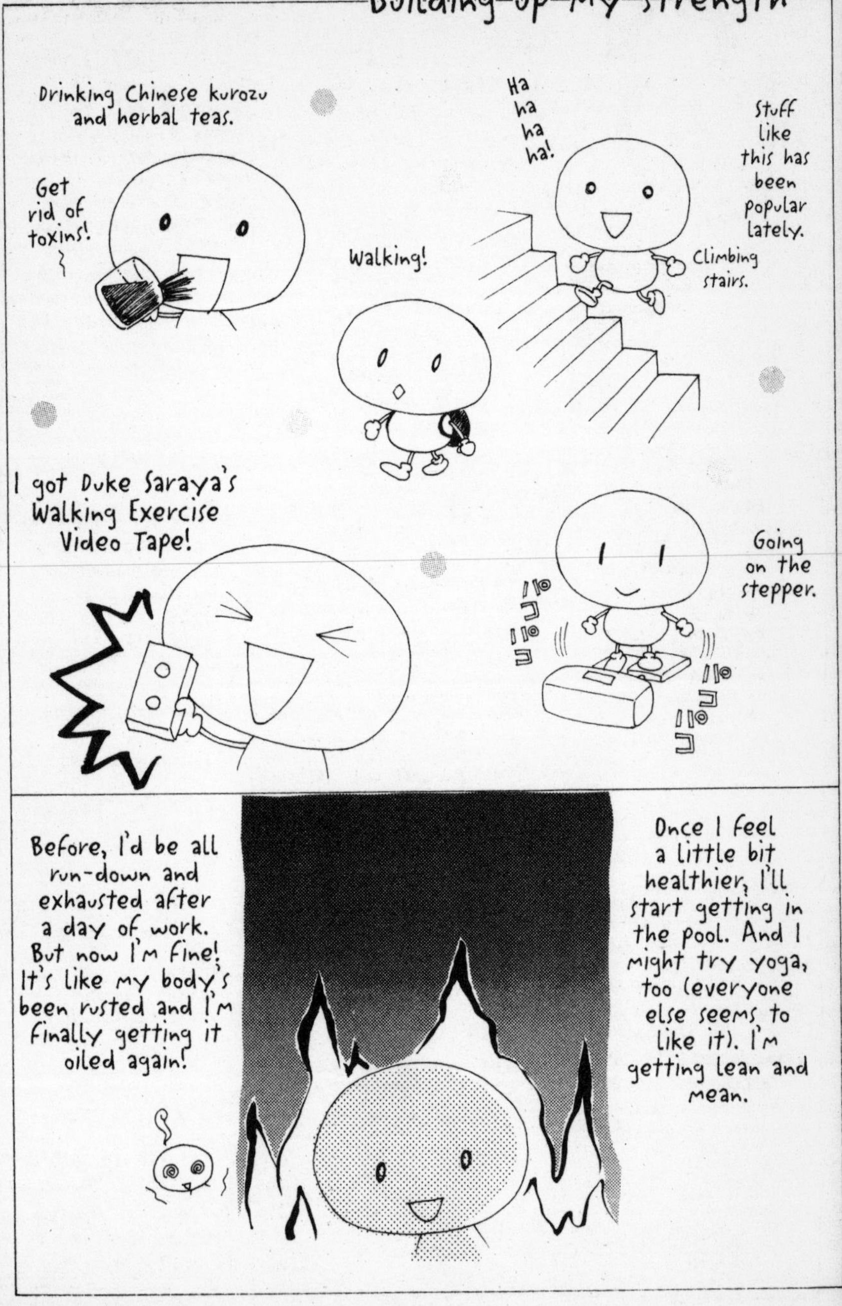
Stuff like this has been popular lately.
Ha ha ha ha!
Climbing stairs.
Drinking Chinese kurozu and herbal teas.
Get rid of toxins!
Walking!
Going on the stepper.
パコ パコ
パコ パコ
I got Duke Saraya's Walking Exercise Video Tape!
Once I feel a little bit healthier, I'll start getting in the pool. And I might try yoga, too (everyone else seems to like it). I'm getting lean and mean.
Before, I'd be all run-down and exhausted after a day of work. But now I'm fine! It's like my body's been rusted and I'm finally getting it oiled again!

JAZZ

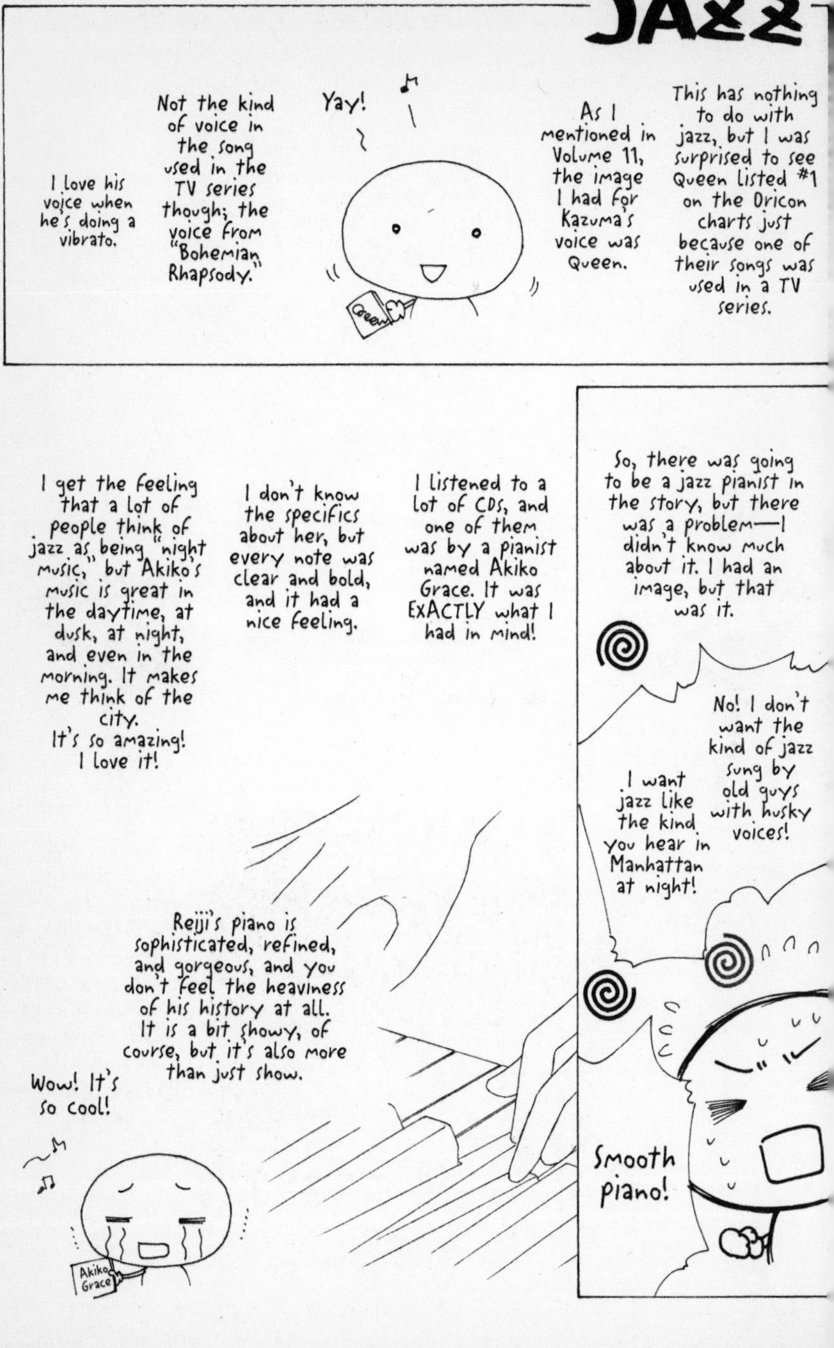

This has nothing to do with jazz, but I was surprised to see Queen listed #1 on the Oricon charts just because one of their songs was used in a TV series.
As I mentioned in Volume 11, the image I had for Kazuma's voice was Queen.
Yay!
Queen
Not the kind of voice in the song used in the TV series though; the voice from "Bohemian Rhapsody."
I love his voice when he's doing a vibrato.
So, there was going to be a jazz pianist in the story, but there was a problem—I didn't know much about it. I had an image, but that was it.
No! I don't want the kind of jazz sung by old guys with husky voices!
I want jazz like the kind you hear in Manhattan at night!
Smooth piano!
I listened to a lot of CDs, and one of them was by a pianist named Akiko Grace. It was EXACTLY what I had in mind!
I don't know the specifics about her, but every note was clear and bold, and it had a nice feeling.
I get the feeling that a lot of people think of jazz as being "night music," but Akiko's music is great in the daytime, at dusk, at night, and even in the morning. It makes me think of the city.
It's so amazing! I love it!
Reiji's piano is sophisticated, refined, and gorgeous, and you don't feel the heaviness of his history at all. It is a bit showy, of course, but it's also more than just show.
Wow! It's so cool!
Akiko Grace

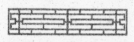

Thanks to the following people:

Editor	S. Taneoka
Staff	N. Shimizu
	R. Ogawa
	Y. Etou
	R. Takahashi

Maintenance   The therapists at the massage parlor

AND   K. U

coming soon

kare kano
his and her circumstances

volume nineteen

Soichiro tells Yukino what he's learned from his adoptive father. Yukino reflects on how mature Soichiro has become... but will he only repeat his forebears' mistakes? Then Ryoko resurfaces in Soichiro's life...and Reiji reveals the real reason he came to Japan.

TOKYOPOP PRESENTS
MANGA 漫画
THE NEW SIZZLING HOT
MANGA
MAGAZINE
ZELDA AND FRIEND FROM
WAR ON FLESH
©2005 Justin Boring, Greg Hildebrandt and TOKYOPOP
SIGN UP FOR FREE WWW.TOKYOPOP.COM

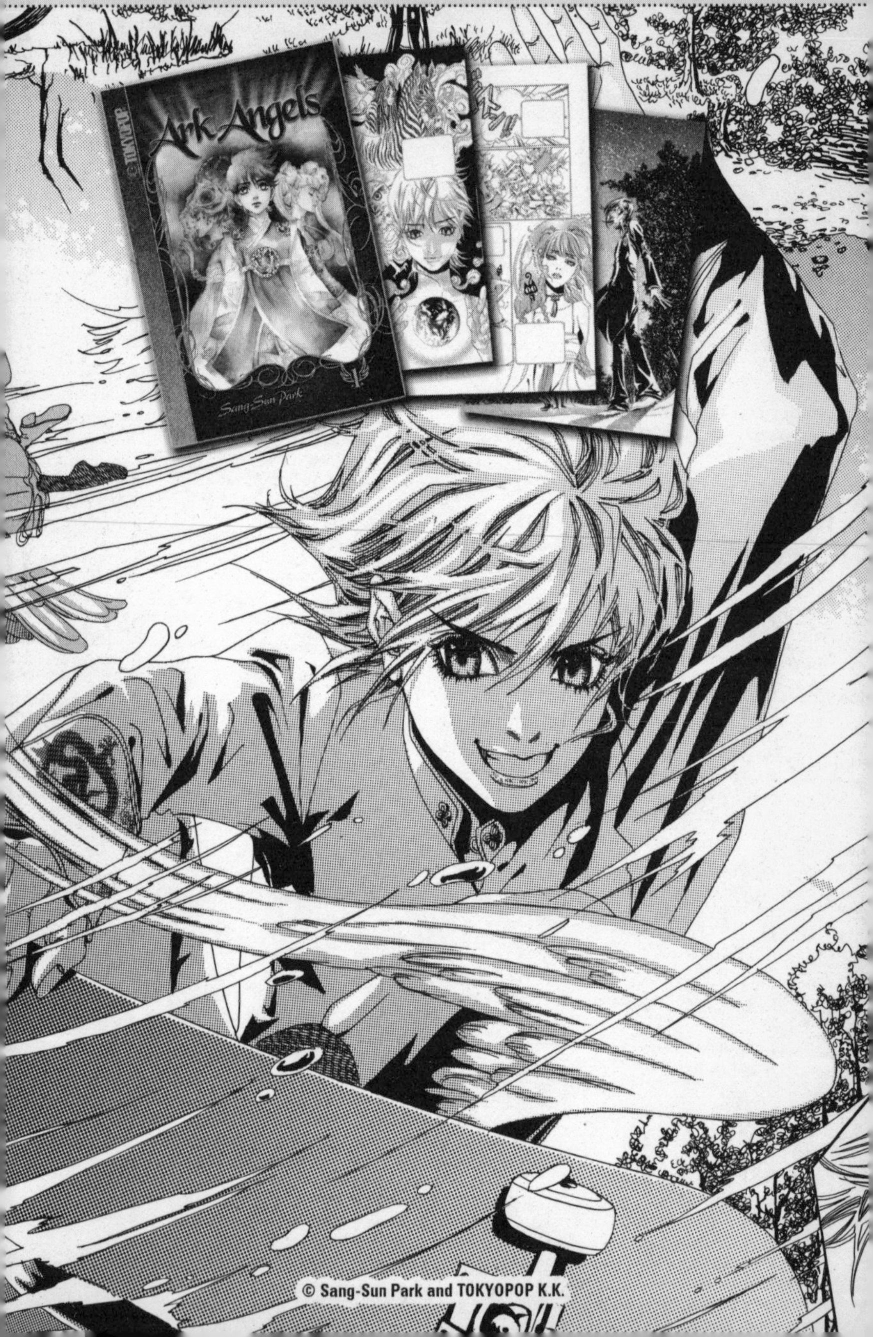
Ark Angels
TOKYOPOP
Sang-Sun Park

ARK ANGELS

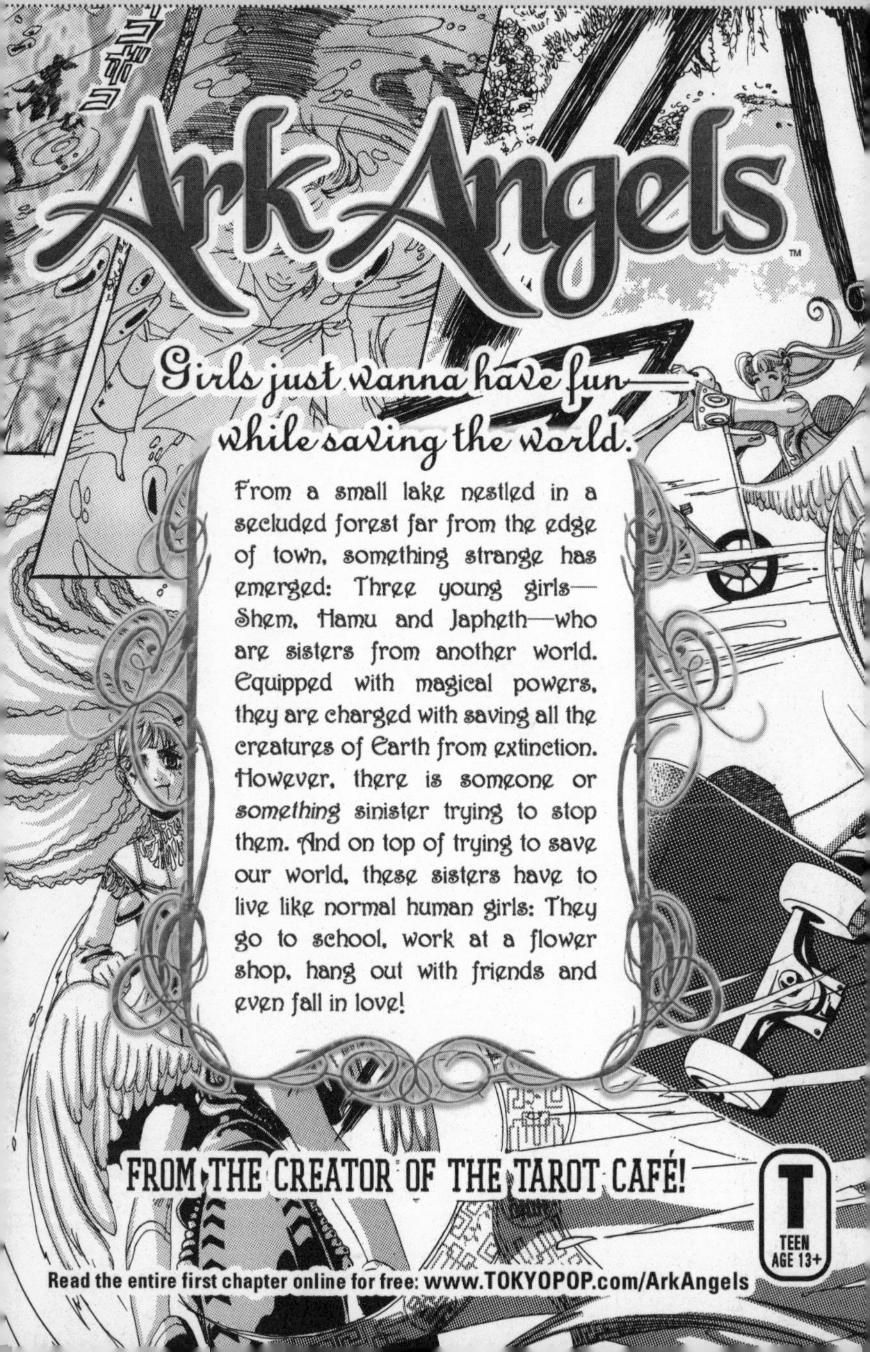
Ark Angels™
Girls just wanna have fun—
while saving the world.
From a small lake nestled in a secluded forest far from the edge of town, something strange has emerged: Three young girls—Shem, Hamu and Japheth—who are sisters from another world. Equipped with magical powers, they are charged with saving all the creatures of Earth from extinction. However, there is someone or *something* sinister trying to stop them. And on top of trying to save our world, these sisters have to live like normal human girls: They go to school, work at a flower shop, hang out with friends and even fall in love!
FROM THE CREATOR OF THE TAROT CAFÉ!
T
TEEN
AGE 13+
Read the entire first chapter online for free: www.TOKYOPOP.com/ArkAngels

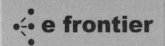

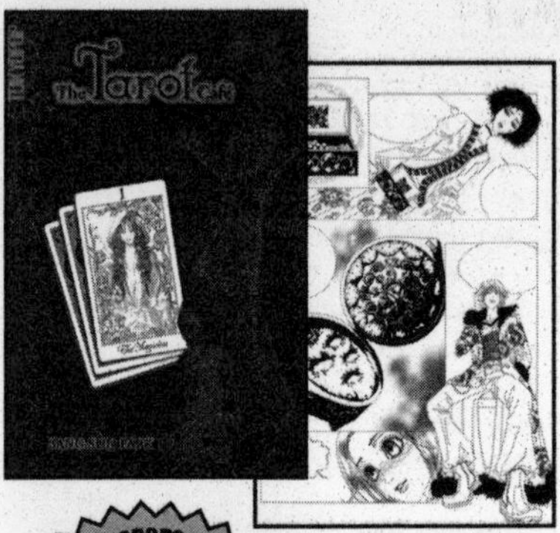
The Tarot Café

BY SANG-SUN PARK

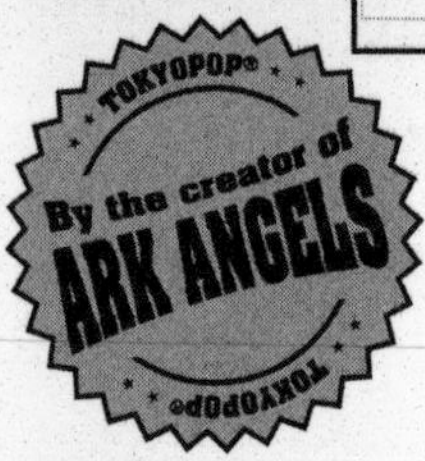
TOKYOPOP®
By the creator of
ARK ANGELS
TOKYOPOP®

THE TAROT CAFÉ

I was always kind of fond of *Petshop of Horrors,* and then along comes *The Tarot Café* and blows me away. It's like *Petshop,* but with a bishonen factor that goes through the roof and into the stratosphere! Sang-Sun Park's art is just unreal. It's beautifully detailed, all the characters are stunning and unique, and while at first the story seems to be yet another Gothy episodic piece of fluff, there is a dark side to Pamela and her powers that I can't wait to read more about. I'm a sucker for teenage werewolves, too.

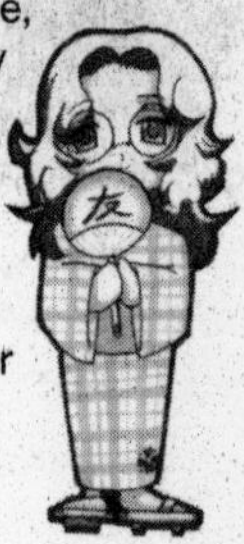

~Lillian Diaz-Pryzbyl, Editor

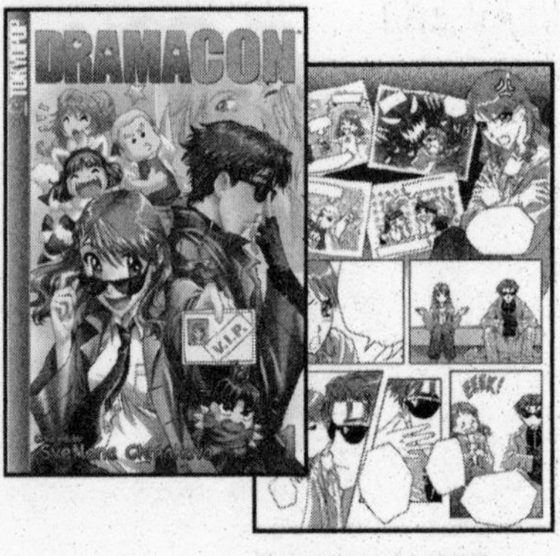
DRAMACON
V.I.P.
EEK!

BY SVETLANA CHMAKOVA

DRAMACON

I love this manga! First of all, Svetlana is amazing. She's the artist who creates "The Adventures of CosmoGIRL!" manga feature in *CosmoGIRL!* magazine, and she totally rules. *Dramacon* is a juicy romance about a guy and a girl who meet up every year at a crazy anime convention. It grabbed me from the first panel and just wouldn't let go. If you love shojo as much as I do, this book will rock your world.

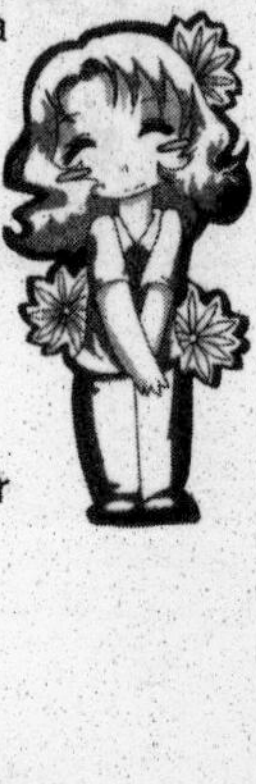

~Julie Taylor, Senior Editor

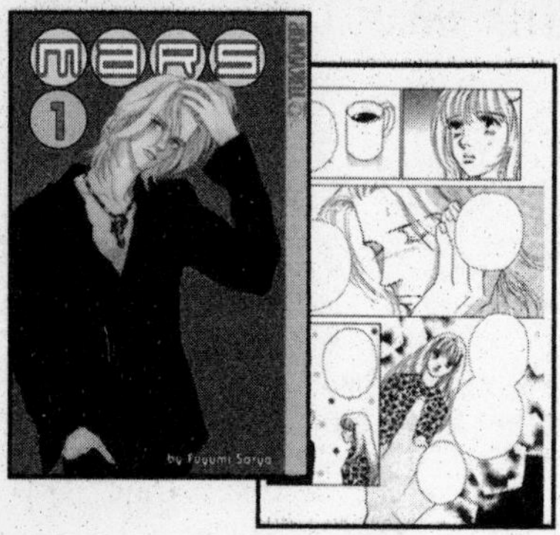
MARS
1
by Fuyumi Soryo

BY FUYUMI SORYO

MARS

I used to do the English adaptation for *MARS* and loved working on it. The art is just amazing—Fuyumi Soryo draws these stunning characters and beautiful backgrounds to boot. I remember this one spread in particular where Rei takes Kira on a ride on his motorcycle past this factory, and it's all lit up like Christmas and the most gorgeous thing you've ever seen—and it's a factory! And the story is a super-juicy soap opera that kept me on the edge of my seat just dying to get the next volume every time I'd finish one.

~Elizabeth Hurchalla, Sr. Editor

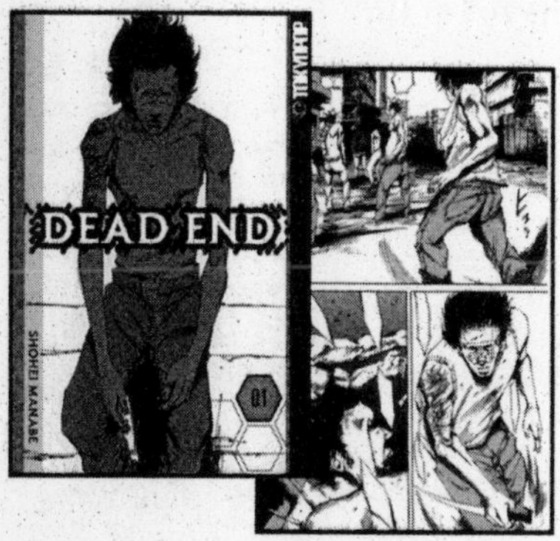
DEAD END
SHOHEI MANABE
01
TOKYOPOP

BY SHOHEI MANABE

DEAD END

Everyone I've met who has read *Dead End* admits to becoming immediately immersed and obsessed with Shohei Manabe's unforgettable manga. If David Lynch, Clive Barker and David Cronenberg had a love child that was forced to create a manga in the bowels of a torture chamber, then *Dead End* would be the fruit of its labor. The unpredictable story follows a grungy young man as he pieces together shattered fragments of his past. Think you know where it's going? Well, think again!

~Troy Lewter, Editor

© Rivkah and TOKYOPOP Inc.

STEADY BEAT
BY RIVKAH

"Love, Jessica"... That's what Leah finds on the back of a love letter to her sister. But who is Jessica? When more letters arrive, along with flowers and other gifts, Leah goes undercover to find out her sister's secret. But what she doesn't expect is to discover a love of her own—and in a very surprising place!

Winner of the Manga Academy's Create Your Own Manga competition!

T
TEEN
AGE 13+

© MIN-WOO HYUNG

JUSTICE N MERCY
BY MIN-WOO HYUNG

Min-Woo Hyung is one of today's most talented young Korean artists, and this stunning art book shows us why. With special printing techniques and high-quality paper, TOKYOPOP presents never-before-seen artwork based on his popular *Priest* series, as well as images from past and upcoming projects *Doomslave*, *Hitman* and *Sal*.

A spectacular art book from the creator of *Priest!*

T
TEEN
AGE 13+

© 2003 Liu GOTO © SOTSU AGENCY • SUNRISE • MBS

MOBILE SUIT GUNDAM SEED NOVEL
ORIGINAL STORY BY HAJIME YATATE AND YOSHIYUKI TOMINO
WRITTEN BY LIU GOTO

A shy young student named Kira Yamato is thrown in the midst of battle when genetically enhanced Coordinators steal five new Earth Force secret weapons. Wanting only to protect his Natural friends, Kira embraces his Coordinator abilities and pilots the mobile suit Strike. The hopes and fears of a new generation clash with the greatest weapons developed by mankind: Gundam!

The novelization of the super-popular television series!

T
TEEN
AGE 13+

3 9075 03813196 4

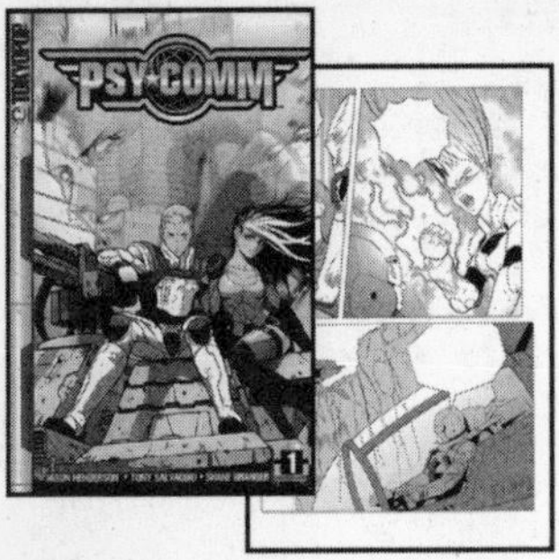
PSY-COMM

© Granger/Henderson/Salvaggio and TOKYOPOP Inc.

PSY-COMM

BY JASON HENDERSON, TONY SALVAGGIO AND SHANE GRANGER

In the not-too-distant future, war is entertainment—it is scheduled, televised and rated. It's the new opiate of the masses and its stars are the elite Psychic Commandos—Psy-Comms. Mark Leit, possibly the greatest Psy-Comm of all time, will have to face a tragedy from his past...and abandon everything his life has stood for.

War: The Ultimate Reality Show!

T
TEEN
AGE 13+

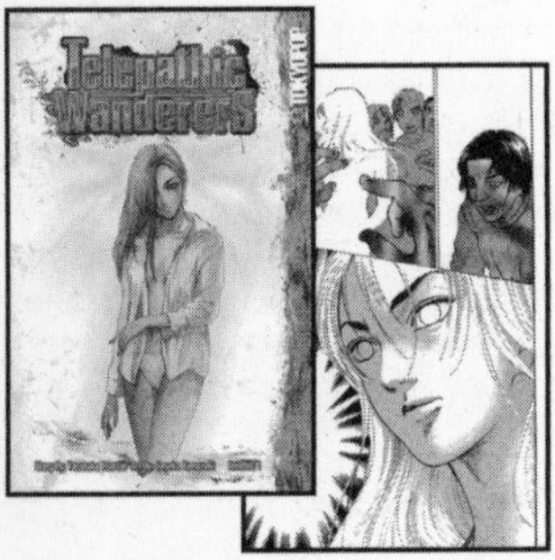
Telepathic Wanderers

© Yasutaka Tsutsui, Sayaka Yamazaki

TELEPATHIC WANDERERS

BY SAYAKA YAMAZAKI AND YASUTAKA TSUTSUI

When Nanase, a beautiful young telepath, returns to her hometown, her life soon becomes more than unsettling. Using her telepathic powers, Nanase stumbles across others who possess similar abilities. On a train she meets Tsuneo, a man with psychic powers who predicts a dire future for the passengers! Will Nanase find her way to safety in time?

A sophisticated and sexy thriller from the guru of Japanese science fiction.

OT
OLDER TEEN
AGE 16+

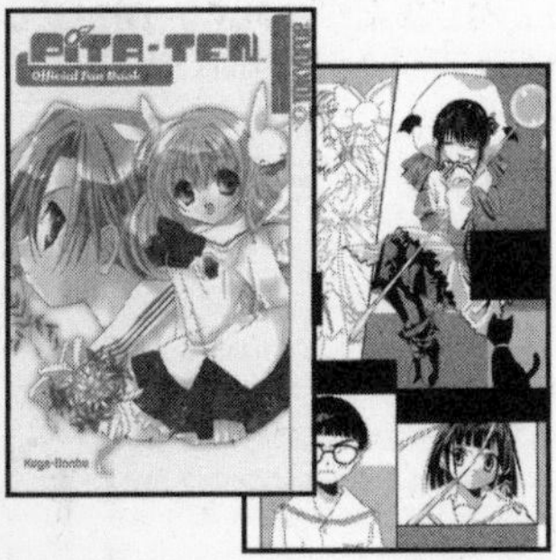
PITA-TEN
Official Fan Book

© Koge-Donbo

PITA-TEN OFFICIAL FAN BOOK

BY KOGE-DONBO

Koge-Donbo's lovable characters—Kotarou, Misha and Shia—are all here, illustrated in a unique, fresh style by the some of the biggest fans of the bestselling manga! Different manga-ka from Japan have added their personal touch to the romantic series. And, of course, there's a cool, original tale from Koge-Donbo, too!

Pita-Ten **as you've never seen it before!**

T
TEEN
AGE 13+

STOP!

This is the back of the book.
You wouldn't want to spoil a great ending!

This book is printed "manga-style," in the authentic Japanese right-to-left format. Since none of the artwork has been flipped or altered, readers get to experience the story just as the creator intended. You've been asking for it, so TOKYOPOP® delivered: authentic, hot-off-the-press, and far more fun!

DIRECTIONS

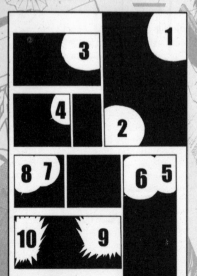

If this is your first time reading manga-style, here's a quick guide to help you understand how it works.

It's easy... just start in the top right panel and follow the numbers. Have fun, and look for more 100% authentic manga from TOKYOPOP®!